MULTICULTURAL STATES

The political debates and arguments which surround questions of ethnicity, race and cultural difference have caused a crisis in the idea of the nation as a community. For the critics and advocates of national identity and cultural difference, multiculturalism has often been a specifically national debate. *Multicultural States* challenges the national frames of reference of these debates by investigating contemporary theories, policies and practices of cultural pluralism across eight countries with historical links in British colonialism: the USA, Canada, Australia, New Zealand, India, South Africa, Ireland and Britain.

Written as history, theory, autobiography and political polemic, *Multicultural States* combines general theoretical discussions of the principles of cultural pluralism, nationalism, and minority identities with informative studies of specific local histories and political conflicts.

Seeking to identify common problems and precepts in representing cultural differences in the postcolonial era, the contributors discuss such issues as political versus cultural constructions of nationhood in the USA and Australia; communalism and colonialism in India; Irish sectarianism and identity politics; ethnic nationalism in post-apartheid South Africa; British multiculturalism as a 'heritage' industry; multicultural law and education in Canada and New Zealand; refugees, migrancy and identity in a global cultural economy.

Contributors: Ien Ang, David Attwell, David Bennett, Homi K. Bhabha, Gargi Bhattacharyya, Abena P. A. Busia, Dipesh Chakrabarty, Terry Eagleton, John Frow, Henry A. Giroux, Ihab Hassan, Smaro Kamboureli, Maria Koundoura, Beryl Langer, Susan Mathieson, Anne Maxwell, Meaghan Morris, Jon Stratton.

Editor: David Bennett teaches English and Cultural Studies at the University of Melbourne.

MULTICULTURAL STATES

Rethinking difference and identity

Edited by David Bennett

London and New York

First published 1998
by Routledge
11 New Fetter Lane, London EC4P 4EE

Simultaneously published in the USA and Canada
by Routledge
29 West 35th Street, New York, NY 10001

Typeset in Joanna and Bembo
by M Rules

Printed and bound in Great Britain by
Clays Ltd, St Ives PLC

British Library Cataloguing in Publication Data
A catalogue record for this book is available from the British Library

Library of Congress Cataloguing in Publication Data
Multicultural states: rethinking difference and identity/edited by David Bennett.
p.   cm.
Includes bibliographical references and index.
1. Pluralism (Social sciences)—Case studies.
2. Multiculturalism.
3. Ethnicity—Political aspects.
I. Bennett, David
HM276.M724   1998
306—dc21   98–17304

ISBN 0–415–12158–2 (hbk)
ISBN 0–415–12159–0 (pbk)

CONTENTS

v

CONTENTS

CONTENTS

ACKNOWLEDGEMENTS

Writing under the title *We Are All Multiculturalists Now*, the US educationalist Nathan Glazer reflects on his discovery that 'almost every book in the Harvard University libraries listed as containing the word "multiculturalism" in its title in the 1970s and 1980s is Canadian or Australian'. Glazer comments that 'it makes sense that the word should come to us from our neighbour to the north', but he expresses bemusement at the discovery that Australia 'has also been a pioneer in the use of the term'. The press-syndication of North American cultural controversies has long accustomed Australians, New Zealanders, Britons, South Africans and other consumers of the anglophone media to receiving filtered news of America's 'culture wars'; but in a media economy in which globalisation is often a mollifying euphemism for Americanisation, the exchange has been unequal. News travels fast, but only in certain directions. This book was conceived as a comparative reader in debates about theories and politics of multiculturalism in eight ex-British-colonial countries, and one of its aims is to question the national frames of reference within which these debates are still largely conducted. Most of the chapters were specifically commissioned for this book, and its publication would not have been possible without the generous patience, and impatience, with which the contributors waited on one another's and the editor's contributions to be completed. No less generous with their patience and support have been Rebecca Barden and Christopher Cudmore of Routledge, who accepted the proposal of this book for their cultural studies list. Three of the chapters are republications of essays that appeared before the volume was organised, and I gratefully acknowledge the permission of the following to reprint their work: Homi K. Bhabha, for 'Culture's In Between', *Artforum*, vol. 32, no. 1, pp. 167–8, 211–14; John Frow, for 'Economies of Value', adapted from his book *Cultural Studies and Cultural Value*, Oxford, Oxford University Press, 1995; Jon Stratton and Ien Ang, for 'Multicultural Imagined Communities', a revised version of their essay of the same title in T. O'Regan (ed.), *Critical Multiculturalism*, a special issue of *Continuum: The Australian Journal of Media and Culture*, vol. 8, no. 2, 1994, pp. 124–58; and Ihab Hassan, for 'Counterpoints', *Third Text*, vol. 41 (winter 1997–8). Thanks are due to Eleanor Hogan for copy-editing assistance, and, above all, to Gina McColl for her indispensable, unflagging support and invaluable editorial advice over the long haul of this book's preparation. Initial editorial research was supported by an Australian Research Council grant, and publication of this work was assisted by a publications grant from the University of Melbourne.

David Bennett

NOTES ON CONTRIBUTORS

Ien Ang is Professor of Cultural Studies at the University of Western Sydney, Nepean, Australia. Her books include *Watching Dallas* (1985), *Desperately Seeking the Audience* (1991) and *Living Room Wars: Rethinking Media Audiences for a Postmodern World* (1996).

David Attwell is Professor of English at the University of Natal in Pietermaritzburg, South Africa. He is the author of *J.M. Coetzee: South Africa and the Politics of Writing* (1993) and the editor of Coetzee's *Doubling the Point: Essays and Interviews* (1992). He has also published on anglophone African criticism and theory, and is currently working on the cultural history of early black South African literature.

David Bennett teaches English and Cultural Studies at the University of Melbourne. He has written widely on postmodernist and postcolonial issues and is the editor of *The Thousand Mile Stare* (1988), *Rhetorics of History: Modernity and Postmodernity* (1990) and *Cultural Studies: Pluralism and Theory* (1993).

Homi K. Bhabha is Chester D. Tripp Professor in the Humanities at the University of Chicago. He is the editor of *Nation and Narration* (1990) and the author of *The Location of Culture* (1994).

Gargi Bhattacharyya teaches Cultural Studies in the School of Social Sciences, University of Birmingham.

Abena P. A. Busia is an Associate Professor of English and Women's Studies at Rutgers University, and a poet. She has published articles on Black literature and colonial discourse and is co-editor, with Stanlie M. James, of *Theorizing Black Feminisms* (1993). She is also the author of a volume of poems, *Testimonies of Exile* (1990).

Dipesh Chakrabarty is Professor in History and South Asian Studies at the University of Chicago where he is also a member of the Committee for the

History of Culture. He is a founding member of the Subaltern Studies editorial collective, the author of *Rethinking Working-Class History: Bengal 1890–1940* (1989) and co-editor, with Shahid Amin, of *Subaltern Studies*, vol. 9 (1996). A new book, *The Unworking of History*, is forthcoming.

Terry Eagleton is Warton Professor of English Literature at the University of Oxford. He is the author of numerous books on literary and cultural theory, a novel, *Saints and Scholars*, plays, *St Oscar, and Other Plays*, and the filmscript of *Wittgenstein*, on which he collaborated with the director Derek Jarman. His recent books include *Heathcliff and the Great Hunger: Studies in Irish Culture* (1995) and *The Illusions of Postmodernism* (1996). *The Eagleton Reader*, edited by Stephen Regan, was published in 1998.

John Frow is Professor of English at the University of Queensland. He is the author of *Marxism and Literary History* (1986), *Cultural Studies and Cultural Value* (1995), and *Time and Commodity Culture: Essays on Cultural Theory and Postmodernity* (1997), and co-editor, with Meaghan Morris, of *Australian Cultural Studies: A Reader* (1993).

Henry A. Giroux is the Waterbury Chair Professor of Education at Penn State University. He is the author of numerous articles and books, including *Border Crossings* (1992), *Disturbing Pleasures* (1994), *Fugitive Cultures: Race, Violence, and Youth* (1996), *Pedagogy and the Politics of Hope* (1997) and *Channel Surfing: Race Talk and the Destruction of Today's Youth* (1997).

Ihab Hassan is Vilas Research Professor of English and Comparative Literature at the University of Wisconsin in Milwaukee. He is the author of many books, including *Out of Egypt* (1986), *The Postmodern Turn* (1987), *Rumours of Change* (1995) and *Between the Eagle and the Sun: Traces of Japan* (1996).

Smaro Kamboureli is Associate Professor of Canadian Literature at the University of Victoria, British Columbia. Her publications include *On the Edge of Genre: The Contemporary Canadian Long Poem*, *A Mazing Space: Writing Canadian Women Writing*, co-edited with Shirley Neuman, and the long poem *In the Second Person*. She is the editor of *Making a Difference: Canadian Multicultural Literature* (1996), and has just completed a study of constructions of ethnicity in Canada, *Scandalous Bodies: Readings of the Multicultural*.

Maria Koundoura is Assistant Professor of Literature and Cultural Criticism at Emerson College, Boston. She has written on culture, nationalism, and post-colonialism both in the United States and Australia. She is currently working on a book entitled *Re-imagining the Levant*.

Beryl Langer teaches sociology at LaTrobe University in Australia. In addition to her research on Salvadoran refugee settlement, she is working on the relation between local and global culture in Canadian crime fiction, and the commodification of childhood.

Susan Mathieson holds degrees in English and postcolonial studies from the University of Natal, Pietermaritzburg. She works as a researcher in the parliamentary office of the ANC in Cape Town.

Anne Maxwell teaches English and Cultural Studies at the University of Melbourne. She has published widely on postcolonial theory and colonial literary and cultural practices in the Pacific and in New Zealand. Her book *Colonial Exhibitions and Photography: Representations of the 'Native' and the Making of European Identities* will be published by Cassell in 1998/9.

Meaghan Morris is an Australian Research Council Senior Fellow at the University of Technology, Sydney. Her books include *The Pirate's Fiancée: Feminism, Reading, Postmodernism* (1988) and *Ecstasy and Economics* (1992). She is co-editor, with John Frow, of *Australian Cultural Studies: A Reader* (1993), and co-editor of the journal *UTS Review*.

Jon Stratton is an Associate Professor in the School of Communication and Cultural Studies at Curtin University of Technology, Western Australia. He has published widely in the area of cultural studies. His books include *Writing Sites: A Genealogy of the Postmodern World* (1990) and *The Desirable Body: Cultural Fetishism and the Erotics of Consumption* (1996).

1

INTRODUCTION

David Bennett

'Multiculturalism' is fast following 'postmodernism' from the isolation ward of scare quotes into the graveyard of unusable, because overused, jargon. But if the word no longer emits an audible buzz in many of the circles in which it confidently moved and mixed a decade ago, the crises of cultural identity and authority, national self-confidence and democratic conscience, to which its promiscuous uses attested, show no signs of resolution. Indeed, as many of the policies instituted in its name since the 1970s – anti-discrimination and immigration legislation, 'affirmative-action' programmes in employment, education and cultural funding, policies of ethnic 'reconciliation' and indigenous 'restitution' – are now being reconsidered in the face of disillusion and 'compassion fatigue' across the political spectrum, the issues of social justice and cultural 'survival' debated under the rubric of 'multiculturalism' have taken on fresh political urgency.

While the scare quotes seem all but obligatory in the late 1990s, however, they represent more than the signs of embattlement, or the stigmata of multiculturalism's guilt by association with 'political correctness', its presumed accomplice in the indiscretion of 'politicising' culture. Just as 'feminism' and 'postmodernism' were pluralised in the 1980s, as the obligation to take up positions on or within them multiplied the sites in which their meanings have been debated, so 'multiculturalism' has been pluralised in the 1990s. Victorian ethnographers constructed taxonomies of 'race', with more or less subtle discriminations of difference and degrees of 'mongrelity'; cultural analysts now construct taxonomies of 'multiculturalism', distinguishing such species and hybrids as 'conservative or corporate multiculturalism, liberal multiculturalism and left-liberal multiculturalism', 'critical' or 'radical', 'polycentric' and 'insurgent' multiculturalisms.[1] Scaremongering aside, then, the quotation marks are a sign of contestation within the multicultural imaginary, not just from its margins. In the disparate domains in which the term has circulated during the past three decades – from political party manifestos to fashion advertising, from law, education, arts and healthcare administration to the rhetoric of ethnic group leaders and the academic discipline of cultural studies – 'multiculturalism' has served variously as code for assimilationism and cultural separatism; campus marxism and ethnic nationalism; transnational corporate

1

marketing strategies and minority competition for state resources; radical democracy and cosmetic adjustments to the liberal-democratic status quo.

Multiculturalism in its various guises clearly signals a crisis in the definition of 'nation', but the self-conscious pluralising of the term has often been perceived as a local, intra- rather than international affair, perhaps not least in the USA, where many of the varietal names, if not the agendas they designate, first emerged.[2] Like contemporary ethno-nationalisms, however, multiculturalism is in many ways an epiphenomenon of globalisation, and since its coinage by a Canadian Royal Commission in 1965, the word itself has had a diasporic career, entering and inflecting numerous national debates about the politics of cultural difference, the 'limits of tolerance', and the future of the nation-state. This volume of essays is an attempt to cross, in the dual sense of traverse and contest, the national boundaries of some of these debates, participating in the decentring project that is one of the meanings of 'multiculturalism'. 'Culture' itself is a diacritical rather than a substantive concept – whether used in the sense that made Goering reach for his revolver or in the 'anthropologised' sense assumed to be its currency in contemporary cultural studies. In Fredric Jameson's words, culture 'is not a "substance" or a phenomenon in its own right, it is an objective mirage that arises out of the relationship between at least two groups. . . . [N]o group "has" a culture all by itself: culture is the nimbus perceived by one group when it comes into contact with and observes another one.'[3] *Multicultural States* approaches 'multiculturalism' in the same way, as no less relational, no more essential a concept than culture, articulating its 'mirages' across a range of national and institutional sites, with a view to identifying shared principles and problems in the ways that culturally diverse and divided societies are being represented today. The 'states' at issue in its title are in part territorially defined. Contributors to this book contrast and interconnect current debates around policies and practices of cultural pluralism in eight national contexts with historical links in British colonialism: the USA, Canada, South Africa, India, Australia, New Zealand, Ireland, and the no less dis-United Kingdom itself. All of them are *de facto* multicultural states, some of them *de jure* multiculturalist or biculturalist. The essays in this collection also emanate from the less territorially determinate 'states' that Homi Bhabha here calls 'culture's in between'. Many of the contributors are themselves 'transnationals', several of them 'doubly migrated' (to use Maria Koundoura's self-description); and while some of the essays reflect explicitly on personal experiences of migration, all are written from 'in-between' positions of negotiation and translation – between academic and public 'cultures', local, national and international constituencies of various kinds.

The sense that such a multinational collection would be timely arose partly from a suspicion that the 'centre–periphery' model of cultural relations, now in disrepute in postcolonial and postmodern cultural studies, still characterises the unequal awareness of multiculturalist debates, both public and academic, in such self-nominated 'centres' as the USA and such ascribed 'peripheries' as Australia and New Zealand. In the logic of the panopticon, those on the 'peripheries'

assume they know what the concerns of the 'centre' are, while the 'centre' itself
has no real need to observe the 'peripheries' (except when there are rumbles of
a break-out). Contributors to this book help to dispel this impression of the state
of multiculturalist debates, by showing how mutually informed and diverse the
perspectives on these debates can be in the different national as well as institutional sites it addresses.

The interplay of local and globalising perspectives in this book has both geopolitical and rhetorical aspects. Chapters that focus on the distinctive socio-historical
conditions in which cultural pluralism has emerged on the political agendas of
particular countries demonstrate both their national specificity and their implication in global processes and globalising discourses – processes of imperialism and
colonialism, the politics of anti- and post-colonial nationalisms, the 'grand narratives' of enlightenment and political liberalism. Other chapters that argue their
cases in 'universalist', abstract-theoretical terms also reveal the partiality and
locality of their perspectives when read in this context. The gesture of weariness
with which this Introduction began by treating the term 'multiculturalism', for
example, can seem a rhetorical necessity, an expression of privilege, or a betrayal,
depending on both where and who you are. Whether you are in Australia, say,
where 'multiculturalism' has figured as part of the rhetoric of government for
more than two decades before coming under virulent, public attack from a new
brand of white populist in the late 1990s. Or in the USA, where multiculturalism
is typically addressed as an oppositional, minority-driven demand for 'recognition'
and social advancement for racialised groups, and where the political intensity of
the disputes over its usage in education and the 'culture wars' has made it all but
unusable by its erstwhile proponents. Or in Canada, where multiculturalism is a
contested letter of the law. Or in Britain, where it became an all but dead letter
during the decades of Thatcherite Conservatism. Or in South Africa, where constitutional processes for resolving inter-ethnic conflicts have been cast in a rhetoric
of confession and 'restorative justice' rather than inter-cultural 'tolerance'. Or in
New Zealand, where state-administered biculturalism has been defended as a stag-
ing-post to multiculturalism. Or in India, where 'multiculturalism' has no grip on
the national imaginary and 'secularism' is the charged name for 'managing'
ethno-religious conflicts. How you interpret gestures of weariness toward 'multiculturalism' in these or any other national settings also depends on 'who' you
are, and whether you are marked or self-identified as 'belonging' or 'not belonging' where you happen to be at any moment. That any interest in using or
ignoring, ironising or retiring the term will always be contingent and related,
though not reducible, to one's caste, colour, class, sexual or ethnic identifications
should go without saying.

The approaches to 'multicultural states' taken in this collection, then, reflect
many differences of position apart from those of national locale, but the ambivalence expressed in most of these essays toward any usage of 'multiculturalism'
assumes a different complexion depending on whether the term is regarded as
alien or integral to discourses of national identity, and whether it is interpreted as

naming what have been called 'top-down' (state-sponsored) or 'bottom-up' (minority-led, oppositional) strategies for reinventing the nation.

The local–global interplay also has a rhetorical dimension. As readers will quickly discover, the book is as multivocal as it is multinational, and its voices range from the philosophical-theoretical to the autobiographical and anecdotal, from the historical to the polemical to the belle-lettristic. The voices of 'theory' are concentrated, but not confined, in Part I, 'The Limits of Pluralism', where contributors examine the limitations of liberal-pluralist models of multicultural society, the problems of value relativism they raise, and the positions from which cultural difference can be theorised as other than mere diversity or 'happy pluralism'. The voices of historiography are concentrated but not confined in Part II, 'Multiculturalism and the Nation: Histories, Policies, Practices'; essays in this section investigate the specific conditions of emergence (or non-emergence) of multiculturalist and biculturalist politics in different national contexts; the techniques of government and education that produce politically 'representable' 'cultural' and 'ethnic' identities; the kinds of agency ascribed to such identities; and the various faces of nationalism and the nation that are being lost or saved in the 'multicultural wars'. The voices of autobiography are concentrated but not confined in Part III, 'Positionings', where contributors reflect on their own positioning by and toward discourses of multiculturalism in the various civic, political, intellectual and national contexts in which they negotiate their 'hyphenated' identifications – as feminist-republican-Australian, for example, or lesbian-Black-British, or Ghanaian-African-British-American, or migrant-national-cosmopolitan.

THE LIMITS OF PLURALISM

Since multiculturalism emerged as a discourse of government in several British Commonwealth countries during the 1970s, opposition to it from the left has often been expressed as a rejection of its 'culturalism' and a commitment to more 'fundamental' categories of social analysis – class, race, gender – whose manifestly political dimensions multiculturalism is seen as obscuring, either more or less programmatically. In the globalised economy of fin-de-siècle cultural consumerism, 'culture' is deemed a matter of choice as much as of inheritance, and thus as a potentially less oppressive, and hence less 'politicising', category of identification than colour or ethnicity, class or gender (the latter, however, being seen as more subject to 'bending' than race or ethnicity). The charge of 'culturalism' takes various forms, well represented in the chapters of this book. One of the most common is that state-managed multiculturalisms reify and exoticise alterity; addressing ethnic and racial difference as a question of 'identity' rather than of history and politics, they translate alterity as cultural diversity, treating difference (a relation) as an intrinsic property of 'cultures' and as a value (a socially 'enriching' one), to be 'represented' as such.

Liberal pluralism conceives of egalitarianism in terms of representation: the more inclusive (of non-whites, women, gays, minorities of various kinds) the membership of public institutions is, the more 'representative' such institutions will be, the more justly will they 'reflect' the constitutive interest-groups of society.[4] Similarly in the institutions of education: the more inclusive the 'canon', the more 'representative' it will be of the cultures that are assumed to define social identities. This has been called the 'additive' model of representation, which treats minorities as 'add-ons' to the pressure-group spectrum.[5] What is left out of this model is the specific cultures of institutions themselves, and their historical roles in reproducing social inequalities variously marked as racial, ethnic, sexual or cultural differences. The logic of this 'additive' model of representation is a pseudo-dialectic of consensus and dissent. A given community is defined by its consensus on questions of value and interest: it is this consensus, rather than any overarching structures of power, privilege and inequality, that defines a group as a 'community'. Hence, those who dissent from a given consensus are compelled to constitute themselves as another distinctive 'community' – and this is the 'fragmentative', proliferative logic of identity politics, in which 'communities' break down into progressively smaller groups of solidarity and values, raising the spectre of national disintegration or 'multinationalism' invoked by anti-multiculturalists.[6] But the consensus-effect, which mystifies social determinations as 'collective decisions',[7] is always produced by a process of exclusion, operating variously as persuasion, silencing, domination. Thus the next stage in the dialectic of 'difference' is the recognition that, if all communal identities are in a sense 'fictions' founded on exclusions which are oppressive for some or many, then the 'individual identities' that form the atomic particles of these communities are themselves strategic fictions masking a chaos of subatomic particles. The recognition of differences *between* communities, or group identities, and between individuals who are members of such communities, must give way to recognition of differences *within* individuals, or the ways in which consciousness does not coincide with identity.[8] This premise of 'postmodern' identity politics, which gives the lie to the notion of 'community' as consensus, is characterised by Barbara Herrnstein Smith thus: 'each of us is a member of many shifting communities, each of which establishes, for each of its members, multiple social identities'.[9] It seems there cannot even be a consensus of one: no judgement of value or interest can have even what Herrnstein Smith calls 'local universality', and the chances of any individual forming an alliance or a coalition with herself look slight.

As the essays in this book testify, identity politics is as protean a concept as any other in multiculturalist debates, changing its connotations and designations as easily as 'ethnicity', 'race' or 'culture', from one milieu of debate to another. Signalling essentialism, separatism, withdrawal from the liberal-democratic polity on one hand, it can signify complicity with the 'culturalism' and identity-consumerism thought to be promoted by liberal-pluralist and corporate, 'Benetton-style' multiculturalisms on the other. Multicultural 'representation' as it was translated into educational and political practice in Britain during the 1970s and 1980s, for example, was seen by anti-racists as mobilising identity politics while endorsing the claims to tolerance and inclusiveness of the liberal traditions of Anglo national culture and the British state. 'Official' multiculturalism, it was argued, isolated racial and ethnic conflicts from other political antagonisms (between the sexes, labour and capital, first and third worlds, overdeveloped and under-resourced societies), while serving to distract public attention from the radical social restructuring involved in the monetarist 'stripping' of the welfare state and the ongoing exploitation of cheap labour markets worldwide.[10] As a doctrine of tolerance of 'ethnic' difference, it preached a change of consciousness, leaving social structures and institutions largely unchanged. The liberal imperative to 'tolerate' cultural difference, predicated though it is on a doctrine of equal rights, is inherently hierarchical, the structural privilege and prerogative of the 'majority'; for in what sense can a minoritised culture be asked to 'tolerate' the majority or 'national' culture that assigns it the marginal status of a minority? Such are some of the charges levelled against multiculturalism for its 'culturalism', or its tendency to translate racial, ethnic and sexual difference as cultural diversity, inequality as multiplicity.

'Culturalism', however, has not been without its progressive moments. The interpretation of racial differences as 'cultural', for example, was one of the strategies by which nineteenth-century humanist ethnographers, holding loyally to the Enlightenment ethos of human equality and sameness, attempted to combat 'racial science' by explaining the social differences uncovered by colonialism as historical and not biological ones – unequal stages of 'development' in a single narrative of human 'civilisation'. The doctrine of cultural relativism to which this Eurocentric view of civilisation gave way in modern anthropology was no less humanist in its credentials: by pluralising the concept of culture, it sought to resist imperialist world-views and colonialist practices, viewing cultures as relatively autonomous and incomparable, rather than as more or less civilised or barbaric than one another. One of the legacies of this 'anthropological culturalism', however, is what Etienne Balibar has called 'neo-racism', or 'racism without races', which holds that racial divisions have no biological or scientific foundation but that populations will continue to behave as if they did, and that this racist conduct needs to be 'managed' (by immigration policies, for example) in ways that respect the 'tolerance thresholds' of social groups, allowing them to maintain 'cultural distances'.[11] 'Racial science' thus gives way to a theory of 'race relations' in multi-ethnic societies, which naturalises not racial identity but racist behaviour, by pointing to the 'normality' of xenophobia and social aggression where cultures 'clash'. Anti-racism, stigmatised as 'abstract' for its failure to be 'realistic' about universal 'human' weaknesses and needs, is accused of testing tolerance thresholds to the limit, denying 'natural' expression of pride in cultural differences, compromising meritocratic principles with 'artificial', 'reverse discrimination' policies, and thus provoking, by reaction, the very racist behaviour it seeks to eliminate.

If 'neo-racism' is one of the perverse legacies of the 'anthropologising' of cultural differences, another is the 'abstract' cultural relativism from whose Olympian perspective the diversity-management policies of state-multiculturalism have appeared all too often compromised. Pointing to the repressions of difference and fictions of 'community' on which state-administered multiculturalism must rely for interpellating representable 'ethnic' and 'cultural' identities, this critique views multiculturalism as a purely pragmatic strategy of diversity-containment, a token showing of 'the many faces of the nation'. For the radical relativist, identity is always hybrid, multiple, porous and mutable, and any consensus, such as 'official' multiculturalism requires, on which identities may 'count' in the competition for public recognition and resources constitutes an arbitrary 'fixing' and oppressive homogenising of identities. As Meaghan Morris points out in her essay for this collection, however: 'In response to those appalled by the idea of managing differences', the pragmatist discourse of managerial multiculturalism 'points to the extreme violence of those contemporary nationalisms that treat differences as unmanageable, challenges its critics to name alternatives actually available to government, and invites concrete proposals for improving the management process'.[12]

If 'liberal multiculturalism' is the label commonly given to this diversity-management model of cultural difference (known in the European Union as 'harmonisation'), liberalism is also the name of a powerful tradition of opposition to state-multiculturalism – a tradition re-examined from a range of critical perspectives in the essays in Part I of this book. The liberal critique of multiculturalism has found some of its most articulate legal and philosophical exponents in the USA, the nation-state that established the precedent for a constitutionally ratified bill of rights and principle of nondiscrimination, which American liberals have often invoked to challenge the 'reverse discrimination' measures of multiculturalist agendas. Liberalism's opposition to state-managed multiculturalism follows from its insistence on the need for constitutional limits to governmental power in order to protect what J. S. Mill called the 'negative liberty' of individuals, or their freedom to exercise unimpeded what are variously cast as 'natural', 'unalienable' or 'human' rights to free opinion, expression, association and so on. The notion of negative liberty, with its in-built distinction between 'public' and 'private' life-spheres, presupposes the neutrality of the liberal state on questions of what constitutes the 'good life'; and in so far as the 'cultural' and 'ethnic' identifications of citizens can be regarded as pertaining to such 'ethical choices', it presupposes the constitutional 'blindness' of the state to ethnic and cultural differences among its citizenry. ('Let us agree', suggests a liberal authority on American multiculturalist education policies, 'that ethnic and racial affiliation should be as voluntary as religious affiliation, and of as little concern to the state and public authority.'[13]) In the view of so-called 'rights-liberals', such 'difference-blindness' is as crucial to the protection of minority-group interests as it is to individual liberty. Thus Ronald Dworkin has argued that the liberal society's 'procedural' commitment to equality of treatment for all citizens is incompatible with a 'substantive' commitment to any particular conception of the 'good life', since in a democratic polity the latter would be likely to reflect majority views at the expense of dissident minorities.[14] For such 'Kantian' liberals, decisions about the good life are the prerogative of autonomous individuals exercising self-expressive and self-determining choices.[15]

To paraphrase Herbert Marcuse on 'Repressive Tolerance', however, in patriarchal, class and multi-ethnic society, constitutional equality is perfectly compatible with institutionalised inequality,[16] and it is to give a substantive 'content' to egalitarian principles, by articulating civil and political rights with social justice for disadvantaged groups, that 'multiculturalists' have sought to correct the 'vision' of democratic governments and institutions and to cure their 'difference-blindness'. In this view, the unprecedented challenge for democracy in multicultural societies is that of translating political into 'cultural democracy'[17] without reverting to pre-anthropological or 'aesthetic' conceptions of 'culture', reducing cultural difference to mere diversity in 'lifestyles' or 'forms of expression' (language, dress, the arts and so on). Modern political democracy, emerging as it did with the commodity forms of the market economy, produced the individualist concept of the citizen as a purely formal, culturally 'empty', exchangeable identity – unmarked by regional, ethnic or cultural differences. The recognition that this 'emptiness' is in practice filled by the naturalised or 'invisible' properties of the socially dominant (or 'national') group is what underlies the revisionist critique of 'rights-liberalism' undertaken by communitarians like the influential Canadian philosopher, Charles Taylor. Taylor views what he calls the '"difference-blind" liberalism' of US philosophers like John Rawls and Ronald Dworkin from across the border of a Canada divided by constitutional and political debates over Quebecois cultural separatism. The communitarian case against the claims of 'difference-blind liberalism' 'to offer a neutral ground on which peoples of all cultures can meet and coexist'[18] is that the notional separation of 'private' from 'public' spheres (religion from politics, ethnicity from citizenship) is itself culturally specific: in Taylor's phrase, 'an organic outgrowth of Christianity' and foreign, he assumes, to Islamic society. Since the liberal polity is in this sense always already culturally particular, for communitarians like Taylor there can be no question of a liberal society's withholding value-judgements on matters of cultural difference. Taylor none the less proposes meeting multiculturalists part-way with what he terms a 'politics of equal respect' for different cultures, which makes a 'presumption' of equal worth as a 'starting hypothesis' for dialogue with the cultural Other – a presumption which, if confirmed by dialogue, must result in a 'fusion of horizons' for the judging and the judged and hence a revision of the criteria of cultural value with which the 'dialogue' was begun.[19] Taylor's reservation of this 'presumption' of equal worth for what he characterises as 'cultures that have animated whole societies over some considerable stretch of time', and his exclusion from it of ephemeral or 'partial cultural milieux within a society',[20] is the starting-point for Homi Bhabha's critique of communitarian and liberal views of the multicultural polity in Chapters 2 and 3 of this book.

As Bhabha points out in 'Culture's in between', 'multiculturalists' must do more than mount philosophical critiques of liberalism: they must grapple with the 'irrationality' of xenophobia, racism and sexism as social practices that constitute 'discriminated' minority identities. But as Bhabha himself goes on to illustrate in his essay and the interview that follows it in this book, it is liberalism that still claims the high ground in many national debates about multiculturalism, and any valorisation of minority identities must engage with its terms. Bhabha writes primarily in the context of the 'margins-inwards', minority-driven politics of American multiculturalisms, and in contrast to contributors like Dipesh Chakrabarty and Beryl Langer, who stress the roles of government in constituting 'representable' minority identities in India and Australia, Bhabha focuses on the self-formation of minority identities as a form of collective agency – forged from acts of collective 'memorisation' – that 'does not conform to the individualist norm where the "autonomy" or sovereignty of the self is an ultimate and untouchable value'. Asking how non-national or 'minority' cultural communities are defined, and how their agency differs from that of groups speaking in the name of the nation, Bhabha rejects the binary terms – part/whole, outside/inside, difference/assimilation, traditional/modern – in which most debates about multiculturalism are cast. To valorise the 'partial culture' of minorities, Bhabha argues, entails more than affirming its intrinsic validity by recovering its 'root' or 'authentic' forms; it must be relocated somewhere other than in its native 'home' or contained place within the 'host' culture. Addressing minority identity as a collective performance of historical reconstruction, Bhabha figures this 'relocation' as temporal rather than territorial. The minoritised indigenous or migrant culture is defined by post-imperial, Western national culture as 'behind' or belated in time, still to catch up and conform itself with the modernity of national culture. Bhabha's case, however, is that this 'partial culture' of minorities is 'temporally disjunctive': neither simply contemporaneous with the modernity of the dominant culture nor simply 'out of date', lagging behind that modernity. It is temporally 'in-between'; and the weakness of liberalism is its inability to recognise this. Liberalism assumes a common time and shared terrain (Charles Taylor's 'level playing field'), and seeks an equalisation of cultures within them. But the 'minority' demand, in Bhabha's view, is a demand not for equality but for recognition of difference, a demand that opens up a difference within 'national' culture itself. The disturbing assertion of minority identity is both a present act and an 'untimely' one, in so far as it looks back to a history that it insists on reinserting in the present – the history of uneven and unequal social development for different groups which is a structural feature of the nation's own arrival at liberal modernity. It is this potential power of minority culture to disrupt linear histories and cultural totalities (in Deleuze and Guattari's phrase, the power of 'the minoritarian' 'to trigger uncontrollable movements and deterritorializations of the mean or majority'[21]) that most interests Bhabha, rather than any programme of social reconstruction or self-advancement that minorities might undertake toward equalising their opportunities of access to the 'representational' power of the nation.

Whether this conception of minority agency can function as a politics in any programmatic sense, and whether the 'discourse of minorities' is necessarily counterhegemonic, are questions taken up in the interview that forms Chapter 3 of this book, where Bhabha elaborates on his view of minority culture as a less 'will-full', less 'intentional' kind of agency than liberal or communitarian paradigms of multiculturalism presume.

In 'Five types of identity and difference', Terry Eagleton approaches liberalism as 'a form of structural irony' whose end – individual self-realisation – is seemingly at odds with its means, the '"artificial" equalising, homogenising and identifying' that are necessary to ensure equality of opportunity in the pursuit of self-differentiation. The principal target of Eagleton's polemic, however, is not liberalism but 'postmodern libertarianism', or the doctrine of radical difference as both epistemological premise and political telos, which rejects the abstract Enlightenment ideal of human equality as essentialist and invariably oppressive, even 'terroristic', in its political administration. Eagleton's concern is to demonstrate the covert universalism of 'postmodern libertarians' who want 'to claim that *all* individuals must count equally as far as the chance to realise their difference goes' but without having recourse to a doctrine of universal rights and thus universal commensurability. Treating this position as an orthodoxy of 'today's cultural left', Eagleton opposes to it an 'incommensurabilist' view of equality itself, as an instrumental rather than ontological concept, predicated on difference, not sameness. Paraphrasing Bakunin's dictum, 'From each according to his faculties, to each according to his needs', Eagleton interprets liberal egalitarianism as the belief that 'everyone . . . must have an equal chance of becoming unequal', or that treating different individuals equally means treating them differently – a 'deeply paradoxical' notion that undermines the antinomies of sameness and difference, identity and non-identity, universal and individual, which have structured much of the theoretical debate about liberal and libertarian models of multicultural society. In Eagleton's typology of political regimes, socialism subsumes rather than cancels 'bourgeois democracy', whose 'equalising, homogenising political mechanisms' he regards as a desirable, because historically necessary, stage in the trajectory toward socialism's overcoming of the identity/difference antinomy. For all their ideological differences, Eagleton's vision of socialism as anticipating new forms of 'reciprocity' and 'mutual belonging' emerging from the 'fullest flourishing of individual freedom' for which liberal democracy undertakes to provide is not entirely remote from Bhabha's vision of 'hybrid agencies' forging non-hierarchical 'communities' of difference.

John Frow's 'Economies of value' is an extended examination of the positions from which what Bhabha calls liberalism's 'Ideal Observer', or Frow himself calls the 'knowledge class', 'tolerantly' surveys the plurality of value systems characteristic of 'postmodern', multicultural society. Charged with the task of mediating between potentially irreconcilable 'regimes of value', Frow's 'knowledge class' – cultural critics, teachers, public intellectuals – have an implicit commitment to liberal principles of tolerance and understanding of cultural difference; but if they aspire to kinds of knowledge and analysis free from sectional interest, these must be reinterpreted, Frow argues, as the defining practices of a specific 'class' of intellectuals with an investment in protecting the social value of its expertise. One 'enlightened' response to the recognition of incommensurable cultural value systems is for the critic to renounce the discourse of value and instead engage in analysis of 'the social relations of value', including the institutional frameworks within which value judgements are generated and valuing-subjects accredited. The flaw in this 'objectivist' approach is that it cannot comprehend its own position and institutional interests within the ambit of analysis. Frow's critique of the cognitive and sociological relativism characteristic of contemporary cultural studies offers another perspective on the crisis of ethical authority in liberalism to which Bhabha points when suggesting that liberal discourses on multiculturalism reveal 'the fragility of their principles of "tolerance" when they attempt to withstand the pressure of revision'.[22] In Frow's analysis, the (phantom?) figure of the cultural relativist – for whom all 'cultures' are somehow equal yet incommensurable – is an avatar of the 'bourgeois subject' of political democracy and legal contract, the citizen endowed with equal rights and formal equality before the law. But since the formal equalities on which this figure is predicated are, in Frow's words, 'always systematically interwoven with, and work to conceal, structural inequalities in the economic sphere and the actual control of the legal and political spheres by the dominant class', this figure of the 'equal' citizen, ethically sensitive to the equal rights of all others, is not a straightforward gain for progressive politics; but nor can we afford to jettison its fictions 'out of nostalgia for a social order, past or future, free of these fictions'. Like Eagleton, Frow remains ambivalent about the ideological legacy of liberalism, but he situates this ambivalence institutionally, as part of the pedagogical role of 'cultural intellectuals' whose job is to mediate between apparently irreconcilable regimes of value, seeking to neutralise the inevitable partiality of their own judgements, while protecting and reproducing the 'cultural capital' on which their interests as a 'knowledge class' are based. (The role of the teacher-intellectual as both an exemplary figure of self-criticism and a possessor of cultural capital will be taken up by Henry A. Giroux and Ihab Hassan, explicitly and implicitly, in later chapters of this book.)

It was the forerunners of Frow's 'knowledge class', the teachers of 'English studies', whom nineteenth-century liberals like J. S. Mill and Matthew Arnold charged with the crucial educational mission of forming individuals into citizens capable of self-representation and self-government, and thus worthy of representation by the state. In 'Multiculturalism or multinationalism?', Maria Koundoura examines the nineteenth-century origins of the idea of state-management and promotion of 'culture' as a 'solution' to economic, sectional or class-political conflict. For Mill and Arnold, education as 'cultivation' was the prerequisite of political representation; in Arnold's view, the cultured or cultural self eclipses the economic and sectional self, and since, in Koundoura's words, 'the state should represent the citizen's "best self" . . . and the "men of culture" are representatives of this self, the state should represent culture'. It is this character-forming and nation-building conception of culture study (implemented in British education as English literary studies) that Koundoura sees persisting in the idea of multiculturalist education as a 'democratising' project. With its agenda of representing and teaching cultural difference, it offers 'cultural awareness' both as an answer to sectional conflict and as the ethical qualification for citizenship. Koundoura finds traces of the hegemonic mission of 'English studies' in theories of multicultural education as a practice of 'border crossing' or 'border pedagogy', which undertake to displace the divisive 'identities' of nation, race or ethnicity with an image of universal 'borderhood', where the notion of 'border' functions as a representative metaphor, or 'universal cultural symbol', which hides those very acts of nation (immigration policies, domestic and foreign economic policies) that inscribe specific geopolitical borders. Influential American proponents of multiculturalism who present the culturally liminal as universally 'representative' are thus in danger of participating, despite themselves, in the Arnoldian culturalist project of forging unity out of difference, by subordinating political representation to 'cultural' awareness, in the act, if not the name, of nation-building. Asking how multiculturalist pedagogy can 'avoid operating at the level of aesthetic representation − or the token showing of the many faces of the nation', Koundoura proposes a theory of 'multinationalism' which, in stressing geopolitical rather than metaphoric or 'cultural' borders, would resist the liberal tendency to represent inequality as cultural diversity to a citizenry qualified, by virtue of its 'cultural awareness', for 'equal' rights to self-representation and self-government.

MULTICULTURALISM AND THE NATION: HISTORIES, POLICIES, PRACTICES

The common complaint that multiculturalism 'aestheticises' politics (the 'progressive' counterpart of the 'conservative' complaint that it politicises culture) always underestimates the role of 'culture' in producing politically 'representable' citizens − whether for the modern nation-state or for those policies designed to redress the injustices of racism, colonialism and sexism perpetrated in its name. Pursuing the critique of the 'limits of pluralism' begun in Part I, the essays in Part II of this collection examine specific histories and policies of nation-building in which 'cultural' difference has been produced as a principle of political mobilisation. By what collusions and collisions between colonialism, nationalism and political liberalism have today's 'politics of identity' been shaped in different national contexts? How do techniques of government, education and the law fashion the identities and interests they undertake to represent? From what policies of nation-formation do specifically 'cultural' differences emerge, and what is the nexus in multicultural agendas between representation and democratisation? These are among the questions addressed in these essays, which illustrate how 'cultural' identity has been variously defined as a relationship with place, time or history, language, education and the law.

The irony of so-called 'fundamentalist' movements, Jürgen Habermas has suggested, 'lies in the way traditionalism misunderstands itself. . . . As a reaction to the overwhelming push for modernization, it is itself a thoroughly modern movement of renewal.'[23] That contemporary ethnic separatisms are not an aberrant return of modernity's repressed, or a stubborn relic of pre-Enlightenment thinking, but rather a structural feature of modern European governing practices is perhaps nowhere more obvious than in post-Independence India and post-apartheid South Africa. As Susan Mathieson and David Attwell remind us in their discussion of Zulu nationalism in Chapter 8, the apartheid doctrine of 'separate development' was an attempt to impose on a polyglot society an enlightened European conception of the nation-state based on a principle of territorial and cultural integrity; and while the West's ostracism of Botha's South Africa could be represented as a demand that it submit, 'belatedly', to a global historical logic of enlightenment and modernisation, the identitarian agendas of some multiculturalists in Western democracies during the 1980s and early 1990s could seem from the ANC's viewpoint to be merely apartheid-thinking by another name. Similarly, in 'Modernity and ethnicity in India', Dipesh Chakrabarty argues that the tendency of the Indian left to view the recent rise of ethno-religious nationalisms and upper–lower-caste conflicts in India as a 'return' to precolonial, premodern, 'tribal' mind-sets depends on a false dichotomising of the histories of ethnocentrism and political liberalism, defensive nationalism and Enlightenment rationalism. To represent 'instances of racial or ethnic hatred as though they were aberrations in the history of modern nation-states', Chakrabarty suggests, may be one way of rescuing 'the story of modern liberalism from any necessary association with imperialism' – or of separating the democratic pluralism that the British practised at home from the imperialism (legitimated by doctrines of European racial superiority) that they pursued abroad. But if the construction of such oppositions is strategic, their deconstruction can be no less so. To stress, as Chakrabarty does, that ethnic separatism and the founding principles of modern liberal democracies belong to the same history is to resist the Orientalist assumption that ethno-religious and caste conflicts in India today are somehow *sui generis* to the subcontinent's history, to be understood in uniquely 'Indian' or 'Hindu' terms, and in need of a distinctive nomenclature of their own: (Indian) 'secularism', for example, not (European) 'liberalism'; (indigenous) 'communalism' or 'casteism', not (white) 'racism'. (Chakrabarty prefers to use the term 'racism', which 'has the advantage of not making India look "peculiar"'.) The modern methods of governance that the British introduced to India, notably the techniques of statistical measurement of 'communities' for the purposes of administrative 'fairness' and (in measured doses) proportional political representation, served to reinscribe and rigidify boundaries between social groups that in everyday lived practice could be 'fuzzy' and across which individuals might negotiate their multiple group affiliations. In making political representation 'communal', or proportional to the size and number of differentiated communities, the British constructed discrete categories of identity with which groups had to identify in order to participate in public life – teaching Indians that 'communities' could be enumerated, that their political leverage depended on numbers, and that their 'progress' or 'backwardness' could be measured relative to national norms and even 'universal' standards of 'civilisation'. But as Chakrabarty acknowledges, if the divisive reinscription of ethno-religious boundaries was one of the legacies of 'enlightened' British political administration in India – a legacy of which ethno-nationalisms like 'Hindutva' are in part an expression – so, too, was the ethos of secularism with which Nehru sought to separate the 'everyday religiousness' of Indian social life from government decision-making, a separation of 'private' from 'public' commitments, religious belief from political principle, as 'artificial' in India as it is in Iran or, some would claim, in Northern Ireland. In the face of these contradictory legacies of colonialism and liberalism, Chakrabarty advocates an 'ironic embrace' of the 'civilising narratives' and political institutions of modernity, acknowledging that his critique of liberal principles of 'representative' government has undisguisably liberal credentials.

As in India, so in South Africa, ethnic separatisms and cultural purisms are no less a legacy of 'enlightened' European political thinking than the democratic plu-ralism with which they are often in conflict. However, as Mathieson and Attwell illustrate in 'Between ethnicity and nationhood: Shaka Day and the struggle over Zuluness in post-apartheid South Africa', the demographic divisions or sectional-ising of populations that undergird contemporary ethnic conflicts were not merely imposed by colonial-settler governments on a multilingual society; they were remobilisations of indigenous differences and traditional hostilities, and groups within the colonised population struck compromises with colonial administrative interests in order to protect their power-bases and ensure their own survival. Ethnic nationalism in South Africa, as elsewhere, has functioned variously, and simultaneously, as a focus for an emancipatory politics of national self-governance; as a medium for shoring up traditional sites of power and privilege (feudal, monarchical, patriarchal, bureaucratic) within indigenous populations and pro-tecting them from the eroding influences of modernisation; and, no less importantly, as a medium for making modernity palatable for dislocated popula-tions by securing a sense of belonging and collective self-determination in a volatilely changing society. These contradictory political modalities of ethnic nationalism have posed acute dilemmas for the ANC's programme of democratic pluralism and economic development in South Africa. Should ethnic nationalisms be 'respected' in the name of acknowledging differential traditions and 'identities' and of resisting what Mathieson and Attwell call cultural 'dilution' and 'homogenisation'? Or would this be to capitulate to the segregationist and feder-alist vision of colonial South Africa, betraying the emancipatory, Enlightenment ideals under whose banner anti-colonial struggles for national self-governance were mounted? The means and ends of ANC policies are potentially incommen-surable: the immediate objective of 'reconciliation' between ethnic groups is in conflict with the longer-term objective of democratisation or 'national recon-struction'.

The irreducibly double aspects of nationalism are a central theme of Terry Eagleton's 'Postcolonialism: The case of Ireland', an essay cast as polemic against 'the customary culturalism of postcolonial theory' which Eagleton associates with 'left postmodernists' in the Irish republic, who 'dogmatically' oppose 'nationalism (homogenising, essentialist, spiritualist, chauvinist)' with 'radical pluralism, hybridity or multiculturalism'. Identifying this binaristic thinking as a stubborn, though disavowed, feature of much postcolonial theory, Eagleton matches 'postcolonialists' in their own performance of ambivalence, finding Irish nationalism at once xenophobic and cosmopolitan, repressive and liberal, ethnically purist and ecumenical, atavistic and modernist. As in his 'Five types of identity and difference', however, Eagleton's political sympathies are for the most part with neither nationalism nor cosmopolitan pluralism, neither traditionalism nor 'postmodern identity politics', but with a still incomplete project of political modernisation which, as far as much of Ireland's population is concerned, has yet to deliver on its promises of equality and self-realisation, and which he sees as the precondition for the experience of 'flexible identities, the ceaseless transgression of frontiers and categories' that nationalism is reputed to police.

The dilemma that Mathieson and Attwell represent the ANC as facing today can be seen as a conflict between what Jon Stratton and Ien Ang figure as 'ideological' and 'cultural' constructions of the nation in 'Multicultural imagined communities: Cultural difference and national identity in the USA and Australia'. As ex-British-colonial settler societies, America and Australia were both 'nations by design', but in addressing the 'modern' problem of how to meld nation with state in the unitary nation-state, they staked their claims to postcolonial nationhood on different grounds. Jefferson's Declaration of Independence founded the American nation on an Enlightenment doctrine of universal ethical and political principles (the 'self-evident' truths of human 'equality' and 'unalienable Rights' to 'Life, Liberty and the pursuit of Happiness'), principles which transcended ethnic and racial differences and hence any links with specifically British cultural traditions. Australian national identity, by contrast, was founded on a principle of racial particularity and cultural homogeneity, which enabled Australia to retain its ties with the imperial mother-culture while seeking administrative autonomy from Britain. Ironically, in Stratton and Ang's analysis, it was precisely the officially and 'consensually' racialist foundation of the Australian nation, in contrast to the universalist 'ideological' foundation of American national identity, that made multiculturalism possible as a 'top-down' or state-administered policy in Australia, rather than the minority-led, oppositional politics that it has been in the USA. The assimilationist doctrine of 'Americanisation' (reputedly discredited since World War II, yet still resilient) presupposed that the 'ideological' could be made 'cultural', and thus the state twinned with the nation, by gaining the consent of an ethnically diverse citizenry to live by the enlightened, universal principles on which the state's claim to legitimacy and postcolonial sovereignty was founded. In the assimilationist vision, the so-called 'hyphenated American' (Asian-, African-, Hispanic-American) represents the coupling of an ethnically particular identity with an ideologically universal one; for American nationalists, patriotism depends on the subordination of the former to the latter identity, and the telos of American nation-building is the 'smelting' (Emerson) or 'melting' of the particular into the universal, a process represented both as a movement from marginality to inclusion and as an emancipatory individualising of the members of racial and ethnic groups in the 'difference-blind' eyes of the state. If the glue of the American nation is not shared ethnic origins or cultural traditions, but shared moral and political principles, then its potential solvent is the programmatic promotion of cultural difference and value-relativism known to classical liberals like Arthur Schlesinger, Jr as 'multiculturalism'.[24] Meanwhile, what Stratton and Ang term 'the colour-blind universalism of American principles' (formalised in 1870 with the extension of citizenship rights to 'persons of African descent') entails blindness to the very 'colour line' that has structured the practice of those principles since the consolidation of racial slavery in the late seventeenth century, and to which the separatist impulses of today's racially based multiculturalisms in the USA are a continuing reaction. (Black Americans, as Nathan Glazer puts it, are the 'storm troops' of American multiculturalism: historically excluded from the assimilationist project, they have made it an unattractive ideal for all.[25])

If American national unity is predicated on the ideal invisibility of racial and ethnic differences, Australian national identity was predicated from the outset on their visibility. The Australian Commonwealth's first major legislative act, the 1901 Immigration Restriction Bill, announced racial homogeneity as the cornerstone of a nation-building policy that privileged British racial stock and the Western European culture presumed to be organically tied to such stock. As Australia adopted more flexible immigration policies under a perceived pressure to 'populate or perish' in the post-World War II years, however, it began recruiting northern and, later, southern white European immigrants who were deemed capable (as non-Europeans and non-whites were not) of assimilating to the British-Australian 'way of life'. This doctrine of cultural assimilationism opened up a gap between race and culture that would later make it possible for non-European races, too, to be assimilated to an increasingly distinctive 'Australian way of life', now distanced from its British origins by European immigration. As Stratton and Ang illustrate, however, the new anti-colonial cultural nationalism enabled by this assertive policy of assimilationism had the effect of diluting the cultural 'content' of 'the Australian way of life': no longer predicated on the continuity of folk traditions transplanted from Britain, it could become synonymous in nationalist discourse with little more than certain material standards of living – the normative expectations of a suburban middle-class lifestyle. The 'official' multiculturalism that emerged as Australian government policy in the 1970s was both a pragmatic response to the failure of assimilationism (Southern European immigrants had conspicuously failed to adopt British-Australian lifestyle habits) and also part of a narrative of national development and 'enrichment', in which cultural diversity was represented as, above all, 'productive' – of everything from employment, exports and entertainment to the survival of the nation as such. While 'culture' thus remains central to the self-definition of the Australian nation, its 'content' has been redefined as plural and heterogeneous, not unitary, and the perceived role of the state is no longer to protect the cultural and ethnic homogeneity of the nation, but to regulate its economic well-being. It was as a threat to the 'productivity' of the nation and the traditional distribution of its 'common wealth' that indigenous peoples' land rights, minority-targeted economic support and 'open-door' immigration policies came under renewed attack from white populist critics of multiculturalism in 1997.[26] But governments have typically countered multiculturalism's opponents with economic arguments in kind, defending 'cultural diversity' as indispensable to the economic 'health' of the nation and its good diplomatic relations with its Asian trading partners.

While state-sponsored multiculturalism has been able to figure as a nation-building policy in Australia in a way historically implausible in America, then, it remains in danger of foundering on the same disillusionments with the material promise of the 'national way of life' as defeated what Schlesinger terms 'the historic American goals of assimilation and integration'.[27] 'Official' Australian multiculturalism may demand that the stigmatised, essentialist concept of 'race' be exchanged for the more 'flexible' ones of 'ethnicity' and 'culture'; but in both countries, 'race' remains a marker of exclusion from the 'common wealth' of the nation – with the difference that in Australia 'race' now challenges the multicultural national imaginary, whereas in America 'multiculturalism' is the name of the racial challenge to nation.

'Race' is also one symbolic marker of the refusal to make what Beryl Langer identifies as the 'history–ethnicity exchange' effectively demanded by state-multiculturalism. In 'Globalisation and the myth of ethnic community: Salvadoran refugees in multicultural states', Langer reminds us that multiculturalism as policy and ideology was negotiated in countries such as Australia and Canada in the context of post-World War II immigration from nations that, politically fractured in themselves, had been on different sides of the war; thus, 'if countries of immigration were to be reconstituted in terms of harmonious narratives of cultural diversity, immigrants had to put these contested histories and potentially disruptive imaginaries of "nation" behind them and embrace the convenient fiction of "ethnicity"'. For racialised groups like black Americans and Australian Aborigines, to accept this 'history–ethnicity exchange' would mean 'putting behind them' the histories of transportation, slavery, legal segregation; colonisation, dispossession, genocide. For Salvadoran refugees migrating to multiculturalist Canada or Australia, it means exchanging citizenship in a nation historically divided by region, racial ancestry, class and political ideology for identification with an 'ethnic community' ('Latin American') deemed culturally homogeneous by virtue of a common language and religion, shared folkloric practices and tastes in music and food. The history–ethnicity exchange can have its political advantages none the less. For countries of immigration, Langer points out, the presumption of 'ethnic community' can be 'a useful fiction which minimises conflict in the public sphere by delegitimising its expression', while enabling such countries 'to avoid endless entanglement in disputes beyond their borders'. 'Ethnicisation' can also be embraced, not merely imposed – as a welcome respite for refugees from 'historical exhaustion', or a shelter for those with personal histories to hide, and as an instrument for political leverage and lobbying in the country of adopted citizenship.

Constructing 'ethnic difference' is an interactive, multilateral process: a matter of negotiation and contestation no less within and between minoritised groups than between the 'ethnicised' minority and the 'national' majority. It is also a process in which transnational networks and agencies can be as influential as the politics of nation-state-building. Langer's analysis of the various ways in which Salvadoran 'ethnic community' is interpellated and deployed in multiculturalist discourse illustrates how processes of globalisation can both diminish and reproduce 'ethnic' and 'cultural' differences. The homogenising effects of globalised consumer culture – or what Langer styles the 'shared experience of "Coca-Colonisation"' – may draw countries of emigration and immigration increasingly within the same cultural economy; but no less a part of global culture are the international aid, welfare, human-rights, religious and environmentalist organisations that have helped to globalise the discourses of 'multiculturalism' and 'indigeneity', interpellating oppressed national minorities as representable 'ethnic' and 'indigenous' subjects, and forging networks of affiliation between groups and individuals with no prior history of solidarity. Such counterhegemonic global networks have a contradictory relation to the territorial imperative of 'culture' on which the idea of the modern nation-state was founded, and with which state-managed, liberal multiculturalisms are fundamentally at odds. While they may reinvent the 'ethnic neighbourhood' as tourist site, the ghetto as theme park, liberal multiculturalist policies demand that 'culture' be decoupled from territory by projecting a public sphere in which only 'cultural' differences can be legitimately expressed, while territorial disputes must be consigned to 'history'.

It is as a 'search for nonterritorial principles of solidarity'[28] that identity politics are often valorised and opposed to the politics of nationalism in the rhetoric of 'radical multiculturalism'. Henry A. Giroux casts his essay, 'The politics of national identity and the pedagogy of multiculturalism in the USA', as a manifesto for a 'radical multiculturalist' pedagogy, but Giroux hesitates to disavow nation-based politics, partly from scepticism about claims that they have been superseded by what Arjun Appadurai terms 'nonnational identities and aspirations';[29] partly from a refusal to concede definitions of American national identity to self-styled 'patriotic conservatives'; and partly from confidence in the power of appeals to 'progressive' national traditions to mobilise popular sentiment in support of democratising and liberating causes across, as well as within, US national borders.[30] Giroux's perspectives on multiculturalism are those of the education-centred debates of the American 'culture wars', in which political differences over the legacies of American nationalism have been articulated as differences between 'conservative', 'liberal' and 'radical' models of cultural exchange. In Giroux's implied typology of multiculturalisms, the 'conservative' variety teaches 'tolerance' of minority culture; the 'liberal' teaches inter-cultural 'empathy'; while 'radical' multiculturalism teaches all 'culture' as borderline negotiation of difference and identity, and insists that cultural study be articulated with critique of the institutions and social practices that produce cultural differences as socio-economic and political inequalities.

If nations are, in Benedict Anderson's phrase, imagined communities, to be distinguished and judged by 'the style in which they are imagined',[31] then a crucial site of intervention for Giroux's 'radical' or 'insurgent multiculturalism' must be the pedagogies of imagination deployed in the mass information and entertainment media. Giroux presents his programme for an 'insurgent multicultural curriculum' as a polemical response to 'the shock troops of the new nationalism' in the USA – mass-media demagogues and public intellectuals whose appeals to patriotism and defences of a beleaguered 'national' culture traffic in monoculturalist, racist and homophobic sentiments, stigmatising theorists of 'difference' as apologists for divisiveness, and multiculturalists as 'America-bashers'. Against the 'tough liberalism' (or left-baiting) and self-legitimating 'patriotism' (or monoculturalism) of a Richard Rorty, Giroux in effect pits a tradition of national pride in US democracy as the political legitimation of dissent, contestation and the representation of differences – a legitimation now in need of a 'postmodern' turn, however, to allow for an understanding of the 'identities' being 'represented' as subject to continuous renegotiation and reinvention. Much as Langer criticises state-multiculturalism's tendency to view difference as a 'problem' to be managed, so Giroux argues that the Rorty-esque view of cultural differences 'only as a problem' offers little defence against 'the forces of ethnic absolutism and cultural racism that are so quick to seize upon national identity as a legitimating discourse for racial violence'. The brief of an 'insurgent multicultural curriculum', then, must be to teach cultural differences neither as objects of tolerance nor as problems to be solved, but as dialogical effects of the open-ended negotiation for which the democratic polity claims to provide. Nor should such a curriculum merely 'represent' the hitherto occluded historical experiences and interests of minoritised groups; it must also make whiteness, the 'unmarked' colour of the national subject of 'tolerance', visible as an ethnic category by recovering its constitutive histories.

Giroux's 'border pedagogy' provides Anne Maxwell with an exemplary alternative to biculturalist models of history-teaching in her discussion of educational policy in New Zealand, where the Maori demand for 'reculturation' has combined with territorial claims to realise both indigenous 'ethnic' enfranchisement and constitutional change. In 'Ethnicity and education: biculturalism in New Zealand', Maxwell recounts how Maori political activism transformed an immigration-management policy of multiculturalism, adopted by the New Zealand government in the 1970s, into the state-administered biculturalism that has prevailed there since the mid-1980s. One effect of the bureaucratic administration of biculturalism in New Zealand has been the 'rationalised' reconstruction of Maori interests and political representation around pan-tribal rather than tribal identities, with what Maxwell describes as 'devastating consequences for tribal identity and equal access to compensation' for smaller tribes and for Moriori (Polynesian predecessors of the main wave of Maori settlers), whose distinctive myths of origin have been subsumed under a unitary, 'Europeanised' version of Maori oral history, which is the legitimating text or pretext of biculturalism in New Zealand. Maxwell acknowledges the indispensable tactical advantages of authorised history and uncontested identity in producing 'representable' indigenous subjects and land claims; but her essay tests the case for more relativistic and pluralistic models of history-writing and cultural study, which might respond to the democratic demands of a plurality of minority groups, including Asian and South-East Asian migrant communities formed during the 1980s and 1990s.

In Canada, by contrast with New Zealand, biculturalist policies were not implemented in the name of the historical rights and interests of indigenous peoples; their organisations are in fact explicitly exempted from the implementation of the Canadian Multiculturalism Act. In 'The technology of ethnicity: Canadian multiculturalism and the language of law', Smaro Kamboureli examines the slippages and contradictions between bi- and multiculturalist policies by focusing on the bilingual text of the Canadian Multiculturalism Act/Loi sur le multiculturalisme canadien, which presents itself as at once a law and an act of translation, while leaving it indeterminate which of its parallel (but divergent) English and French texts is a translation of the other. Shared language is a necessary, though not sufficient, condition of 'community'; hence multiculturalist law and education are necessarily processes of translation; but by designating French and English as the 'official languages of Canada', the Act/Loi assigns an 'unofficial' ('ethnic') status to other languages. The 1971 White Paper with which Pierre Trudeau attempted to foreclose any misprision of multiculturalist policy inadvertently separated language from 'culture' in its effort to dispel any misconception that the nation had a legally endorsed culture: 'although there are two official languages, there is no official culture, nor does any ethnic group take precedence over any other'. The central mandate of 'official' Canadian multiculturalism is to assist in the 'preservation and enhancement' of ethnicity; but as Kamboureli illustrates in her exploration of questions of translation, address and authorship in Canadian constitutional legal discourse, there is a cluster of anomalies or contradictions in this mandate. Is ethnicity here being represented as a supplement to an 'unmarked' dominant culture (officially not, for 'there is no official culture')? Or is multiculturalism in fact being defined as the official national culture, even while the preservation and enhancement of ethnic particularism are being declared as official policy? Or is there a separation here between state and nation, the former single-mindedly multiculturalist in its policies, the latter ethnically specific and plural? Among other things, Kamboureli concludes that 'official multiculturalism grants ethnicity subjectivity, but it does so without granting it agency'; the Canadian constitution's concern to 'preserve and enhance' ethnic identities notwithstanding, she argues, the law's simultaneous reliance on, and erasure of, translation 'reveals contestation to be what produces the discursive site of ethnic otherness'.

POSITIONINGS

The essays grouped in Part III of this book take up many of the concerns that interlink the collection as a whole and make such 'partitionings' essentially arbitrary. What they do more strikingly than most, however, is to dramatise position-taking and -making in multiculturalist discourse as a performative process, a matter of address, rhetorical genre, and discursive mediation, illustrating how identities and differences are always 'realised' performatively in specific media – whether these be the 'mass media', the media of local-government politics, of familial relationships, or the genres of the autobiographical memoir or literary essay.

Meaghan Morris's 'Lunching for the republic: Feminism, the media and identity politics in the Australian republicanism debate' demonstrates how complexly mediated is 'today's multicultural Australia': a cant expression which Morris addresses as 'a media phrase' naming a complex 'discursive field that shapes as well as celebrates contending models of national culture'. The disparate rhetorical sites and forms of address that make up this discursive field – including the TV studio debate, the public policy submission, the talk-back show, the letters page, the documentary or drama series – are as much constitutive of the imagined, 'multicultural' community of Australia as are the contending blueprints for 'national culture' that they mediate. Asking how feminists can articulate their interests in mass-mediated debates about Australian republicanism as a nation-rebuilding project, Morris presents her essay as an 'attempt to think through my own unease about the relationship of feminism to republicanism in my immediate situation as an intellectual': an unease she explains as the non-coincidence of her responses to republican politics in her 'multicultural' identifications as citizen, feminist intellectual, Aboriginal sovereignty advocate, 'white middle-class Anglo-Celtic' loyal Labor voter. The staging, and stage-managing, of a 'national' debate over whether Australia should shed the constitutional vestiges of its colonial history would seem to demand a synthetic and synthesising politics: a 'feminist republicanism', for example, or 'republican feminism'; but Morris rejects an 'additive' for a 'pluralist' politics of identity, which would enable her to articulate, without synthesising, feminism *and* republicanism *and* indigenous peoples' rights *and* environmentalism *and* so on. The 'venerable *opposition* between identity politics . . . and . . . national politics' deserves to be questioned, she suggests, when national politics is itself 'a vast, intricate mesh of distinct but connected debates', in which disparate interest groups are 'casually' linked with government and the mass media through the '"public opinion" network'. Morris focuses her questioning on how a 'national' and 'nationalising' debate can be representative and represented – of and by such 'non-national' interest groups as feminists, gay-rights or Aboriginal activists. What models of open, inclusive debate about the nation-form can be made to serve as nationally representative – representative of the nation as, precisely, an inclusive, open-ended, public debate? Rejecting the Australian Republican Movement's models of round-table (or round-the-lunch-table) opinion-exchange between free and equal individuals in the broadcasting and print media, Morris looks to the exemplary representational practices of Aboriginal activists for models of how identity politics can have 'a nationalising force' – altering 'the contents and priorities of national politics' – even while mobilising incommensurable interests. Her models are the flexible performances of identity by Aboriginal activists who at once represent their interests to 'the nation' and reshape the national imaginary by addressing it, variously, in the roles of diplomat, pedagogue, translator, dramaturge, bargainer and undiplomatic protester. Morris's open-framed, generously inclusive essay brings a fresh 'realisation' to Benedict Anderson's definition of the nation as an imagined community. Performing the participatory tactics and flexible identities she advocates, Morris at once describes and imagines a 'national debate'; mimes the plurivocal, decentred forms of this debate in her own essay; and projects her image of this debate as a model for the open-edged, multicultural republic that she would like to be its outcome.

Gargi Battacharyya's 'Riding multiculturalism' also considers how to articulate citizenship with ethnic and sexual difference, but in the very different climate of 1990s Britain, where racism has proven too violent a force to be 'fixed' by culture, and the now muted rhetoric of multiculturalism has been displaced from the anti-racist, nation-building manifestos of 1980s education policy into the heritage, leisure and lifestyle-marketing industries of the 1990s. Multiculturalism, no longer regarded in Britain as an answer to racism, has sedimented as commercial common sense. Bhattacharyya writes in and of de-industrialised Birmingham, a city that has attempted to regenerate its civic core as an 'Arcadian Centre' of ethno-tourism and cultural diversity – the 'sino-camp', samosas, steel bands of pluri-ethnic 'Brummies' unified around their common investment in 'Birmingham the product', even as they are called on to 'personate' their 'ethnic' differences. Considering how minorities within minorities, such as black lesbians in Britain, can 'ride multiculturalism' in its heritage-marketing guise, positioning themselves as 'representable' in the budgets of local authorities bound by homophobic laws, Bhattacharyya illustrates how the rhetorics of place and heritage which civic multiculturalism shares with far-right nationalists in Britain can still carry anti-racist addresses and anti-homophobic 'riders'.

Abena Busia's open letter to her late father, 'Re:locations – Rethinking Britain from Accra, New York and the Map Room of the British Museum', poses the question of address poignantly. What inheritances, memories and ghosts of memory does she address when undertaking to speak as both a theorist-teacher of cultural difference and a contradictorily 'located' national, ethnicised, gendered subject? How can autobiography be articulated with theory, or memoirs of migration with narratives of nation? For the exiles, emigrés and refugees who, in Busia's words, 'have turned the world into multicultural states', translation is less a condition of survival than a 'state of being', of being familiarly self-estranged ('we translate to keep ourselves familiar with ourselves, against all the odds'). Among the familiarly strange terms that demand translation across the disparate locations in which contributors to this book write are the categories of difference and identity that multiculturalisms undertake to interpret. Busia dramatises some of their differences in a narrative of personal relocations, registering the dislocatingly variable meanings, for her, of 'African', 'black', 'British', 'race' and 'race-consciousness' in her movement from Ghana to Britain to America and back, from girlhood to womanhood, from pupil to teacher, from the 1960s to the 1990s.

Translation is also a dominant trope in the final essay in this book, Ihab Hassan's aptly named 'Counterpoints', which is further testimony to the disparate connotations that terms like 'identity politics' and 'multiculturalism' carry in this collection. Like Terry Eagleton, but from a different location on the political spectrum, Hassan stresses the ambiguous and duplicitous faces of nationalism and colonialism in his polemic against what he sees as prevailing orthodoxies of postcolonial and multicultural theory. Self-confessedly 'allergic' to the politics that Eagleton finds repressed in much postcolonial and multicultural discourse, however, Hassan finds such politics all too oppressively dominant in them, and he registers a weary distaste for the automatism with which cultural study is translated into political analysis and interest by his colleagues in the US academy. The identity politics which for Eagleton signify 'postmodern particularism', for Hassan (professing particularism as a creed) signify 'forced affiliations', group separatism, 'the adhesive instinct', an erasure of particularity. Writing as a 'self-exile' sans pathos, who experienced versions of British and American cultural colonialism in Egypt as a cosmopolitanising of his literary imagination and intellect, Hassan 'eschews the colonial complex' and offers autobiography as a medium for questioning 'ideology' and 'theory', contrasting nomadism of the intellect with multiculturalism as 'the care and cultivation of roots', a desire for and simulation of rootedness. Hassan's own affiliations are with neither national nor minority culture but a cosmopolitan intellectual and literary tradition whose language of metaphor he interprets as a desire for open-ended translation and self-difference. Hassan's suggestion that, 'someday, we may hope for an aesthetics of multiculturalism to match its ethics and politics' returns us, uncannily, to the very questions about the political and ethical missions of 'culture study' with which the essayists in Part I of this book began.

NOTES

1 For the first set of terminological distinctions, see P. McLaren, 'White Terror and Oppositional Agency: Towards a Critical Multiculturalism', *Strategies: A Journal of Theory, Culture and Politics*, no. 7, 1993, p. 100. For an early manifesto of 'critical multiculturalism', see Chicago Cultural Studies Group, 'Critical Multiculturalism', *Critical Inquiry*, vol. 18, no. 3, Spring 1992, pp. 530–55. For usage of 'radical' and 'insurgent multiculturalism', see H. A. Giroux's essay in this book (Chapter 12); and for 'polycentric multiculturalism', see E. Shohat and R. Stam, *Unthinking Eurocentrism: Multiculturalism, Film and the Media*, London and New York, Routledge, 1994, p. 48.

2 As Shohat and Stam report: 'while postcolonial discourse usually focusses on situations outside the US, multiculturalism is often seen as the name of a specifically American debate' (ibid., p. 46).

3 F. Jameson, 'On "Cultural Studies"', *Social Text*, vol. 34, 1993, p. 33.
4 In political theory, pluralism, otherwise known as 'empirical democratic theory', offers a descriptive-explanatory account of the actuality of democratic politics as the institutionalised competition of interest groups for relative power, rather than as the free and equal exercise of personal rights and liberties held by individuals against the state. For variants of pluralist theory, see P. Q. Hirst (ed.), *The Pluralist Theory of the State: Selected Writings of G. D. H. Cole, J. N. Figgis, and H. J. Laski*, London and New York, Routledge, 1989; and D. Held, *Models of Democracy*, Stanford, CA, Stanford University Press, 1987, Ch. 6. For a pluralist model of 'liberal multicultural society', see J. Raz, 'Multiculturalism', *Dissent*, Winter 1994, pp. 67–79. Raz's essay is a focus of discussion between H. Bhabha and D. Bennett in Ch. 3 of this book.
5 A. Rattansi, 'Changing the Subject', in J. Donald and A. Rattansi (eds), *'Race', Culture and Difference*, London, Sage/Open University, 1992, p. 39.
6 See, for example, A. Schlesinger, Jr, *The Disuniting of America*, New York, Norton, 1992.
7 See J. Guillory, *Cultural Capital: The Problem of Literary Canon Formation*, Chicago and London, University of Chicago Press, 1993, p. 27.
8 In Rosi Braidotti's words, 'multiculturalism does not get us very far if it is understood only as a difference *between* cultures. It should rather be taken as a difference *within* the same culture, that is to say within every self.' R. Braidotti, *Nomadic Subjects: Embodiment and Sexual Difference in Contemporary Feminist Theory*, New York, Columbia University Press, 1994, pp. 12–13.
9 B. Herrnstein Smith, *Contingencies of Value: Alternative Perspectives for Critical Theory*, Cambridge, Mass., Harvard University Press, 1988, quoted in Guillory, *Cultural Capital*, p. 287.
10 See the introduction and the essays by A. Rattansi and P. Gilroy in Donald and Rattansi (eds), *'Race', Culture and Difference*.
11 E. Balibar, 'Is There a "Neo-Racism"?', in E. Balibar and I. Wallerstein, *Race, Nation, Class: Ambiguous Identities*, London and New York, Verso, 1991, pp. 17–28.
12 'Lunching for the Republic: Feminism, the Media and Identity Politics in the Australian Republicanism Debate', Ch. 15 of this collection.
13 N. Glazer, *We Are All Multiculturalists Now*, Cambridge, Mass., Harvard University Press, 1997, p. 159.
14 See R. Dworkin, *Taking Rights Seriously*, London, Duckworth, 1977, and *A Matter of Principle*, Cambridge, Mass., Harvard University Press, 1985.
15 See E. Kant, 'What Is Enlightenment?', in C. J. Friedrich (ed.), *The Philosophy of Kant: Immanuel Kant's Moral and Political Writings*, New York, Modern Library, 1977, pp. 132–9.
16 H. Marcuse, 'Repressive Tolerance', in R. P. Wolff, B. Moore, Jr and H. Marcuse (eds), *A Critique of Pure Tolerance*, London, Jonathan Cape, 1969, pp. 98–9.
17 'Cultural democracy' is a concept often invoked but rarely defined in debates about multiculturalism. Since political democracy is grounded in a relation between the individual and the state, and 'cultures' are by definition collective, 'cultural democracy' seems oxymoronic. It implies a principle of collective entitlements, or proportional representation based on group membership (ethnic, cultural, sexual etc.), rather than the existing political-democratic system of representation which privileges regional location with the geopolitical boundaries of constituencies. Even supposing the mathematics of such proportional 'cultural' representation could ever be agreed upon (which and how many groupings would qualify for recognition as 'cultural communities'?), the results would not be recognisably more 'democratic'. If the respective claims of 'cultural' groups to proportional representation were based on their numerical sizes, for example, how would the outcome differ significantly from the prevailing majoritarian logic of liberal democracy?
18 C. Taylor, 'The Politics of Recognition', in A. Gutman (ed.), *Multiculturalism: Examining the Politics of Recognition*, Princeton, NJ, Princeton University Press, 1994, p. 62.
19 ibid., pp. 61, 66–7.

20 ibid., p. 66.
21 G. Deleuze and Félix Guattari, *A Thousand Plateaus: Capitalism and Schizophrenia*, trans. B. Massumi, London, Athlone Press, 1988, p. 106.
22 Bhabha, 'Culture's In Between', Ch. 2 of this collection.
23 J. Habermas, 'Struggles for Recognition in the Democratic Constitutional State', in Gutman (ed.), *Multiculturalism: Examining the Politics of Recognition*, p. 132.
24 In Schlesinger's view, the multiculturalist vision of America 'as a nation composed not of individuals making their own choices but of inviolable ethnic and racial groups' amounts to a form of multinationalism incompatible with the historic mission of the American state. See A. Schlesinger, Jr, 'The Cult of Ethnicity, Good and Bad', *Time*, 8 July 1991, p. 26 (quoted by Stratton and Ang in this collection).
25 Glazer, *We Are All Multiculturalists Now*, Ch. 6, 'Where Assimilation Failed'.
26 Following the 1996 Australian general election, the One Nation Party of independent MP Pauline Hanson established itself as a controversial focus for white resentment of Aboriginal land-rights legislation and Asian immigration – a resentment represented in the first case as a concern to protect the productivity of corporate mining and farming investments, and in the second as a concern to check state expenditure on migrant welfare and protect 'ordinary' (Anglo-Celtic) Australians' jobs. Hanson's campaigners have attempted to shrug off charges of racism by maintaining that the target of their campaign is not racial minorities but state-administered multiculturalism.
27 Schlesinger, 'The Cult of Ethnicity', p. 26.
28 A. Appadurai, 'Patriotism and Its Futures', *Public Cultures*, vol. 5, no. 3, 1993, p. 417.
29 ibid., p. 418.
30 If we allow Stratton and Ang's analysis in Ch. 10 of this collection, it is the abstract universalism of 'American values' that at once marks American national uniqueness and renders American 'culture' globally exportable; in so far as the 'American way of life' is founded on 'universal' moral and political principles, it is by definition universally desirable.
31 B. Anderson, *Imagined Communities*, 2nd edn, London, Verso, 1991, p. 6.

Part I

THE LIMITS OF PLURALISM

2

CULTURE'S IN BETWEEN

Homi K. Bhabha

A recent change in the writing of cultural criticism has left the prose plainer, less adorned with the props of the argument's staging. Where once 'scare quotes' festooned the text with the frequency of garlands at an Indian wedding, there is now a certain sobriety to semiotic and poststructuralist celebrations. The 'isms' and 'alities' – those tails that wagged the dogma of critical belief – no longer wave new paradigms or problematics into being. The death of the author, or the interral of intention, are occurrences that arouse no more scandal than the sight of a hearse in a Palermo suburb. Critical practices that sought to detotalise social reality by demonstrating the micrologies of power, the diverse enunciative sites of discourse, the slippage and sliding of signifiers, are suddenly disarmed.

Having relaxed our guard, hoping perhaps that the intellectual modes we sought to foster had passed into the common discourse of criticism, we are now caught with our pants down. Deprived of our stagecraft, we are asked to face the full frontal reality of the idea of 'Culture' itself – the very concept whose mastery we thought we had dissolved in the language of signifying practices and social formations. This is not our chosen agenda, the terms of debate have been set for us, but in the midst of the culture wars and the canon manoeuvres we can hardly hide behind the aprons of aporia and protest histrionically that there is nothing outside the text. Wherever I look these days I find myself staring into the eyes of a recruiting officer – sometimes he looks like Dinesh D'Souza, sometimes like Robert Hughes – who stares at me intensely and says, 'Western Civ. needs you!' At the same time, a limp little voice within me also whispers, 'Critical theory needs you too!'

What is at issue today is not the essentialised or idealised Arnoldian notion of 'culture' as an architectonic assemblage of the Hebraic and the Hellenic. In the midst of the multicultural wars we are surprisingly closer to an insight from T. S. Eliot's *Notes Towards the Definition of Culture*, where Eliot demonstrates a certain incommensurability, a necessary impossibility, in thinking culture. Faced with the fatal notion of a self-contained European culture and the absurd notion of an uncontaminated culture in a single country, he writes, 'We are therefore pressed to maintain the ideal of a world culture, while admitting it as something we cannot *imagine*. We can only conceive it as the logical term of the relations between cultures.'[1] The fatality of thinking of 'local' cultures as uncontaminated or self-contained forces us to conceive of 'global' culture, which itself remains unimaginable. What kind of logic is this?

It seems to me significant that Eliot, at this undecidable point in his argument, turns to the problematic of colonial migration. Although written in the main about settler colonial societies, Eliot's words have an ironic resonance with the contemporary condition of third world migration:

> The migrations of modern times . . . have transplanted themselves according to some social, religious, economic or political determination, or some peculiar mixture of these. There has therefore been something in the removements analogous in nature to religious schism. The people have taken with them only a part of the total culture. . . . The culture which develops on the new soil must therefore be bafflingly alike and different from the parent culture: it will be complicated sometimes by whatever relations are established with some native race and further by immigration from other than the original source. In this way, peculiar types of culture-sympathy and culture-clash appear.[2]

This 'part' culture, this *partial* culture, is the contaminated yet connective tissue between cultures – at once the impossibility of culture's containedness and the boundary between. It is indeed something like culture's 'in-between', bafflingly both alike and different. To enlist in the defence of the 'unhomely', migratory, partial nature of culture we must revive that archaic meaning of 'list' as 'limit' or 'boundary'. Having done so, we introduce into the polarisations between liberals and liberationists the sense that the translation of cultures, whether assimilative or agonistic, is a complex act that generates borderline affects and identifications, 'peculiar types of culture-sympathy and culture-clash'. The peculiarity of cultures' partial, even metonymic presence lies in articulating those social divisions and unequal developments that disturb the self-recognition of the national culture, its anointed horizons of territory and tradition. The discourse of minorities, spoken for and against in the multicultural wars, proposes a social subject constituted through cultural hybridisation, the overdetermination of communal or group differences, the articulation of baffling alikeness and banal divergence. These borderline negotiations of cultural difference often violate liberalism's deep commitment to representing cultural diversity as plural choice. Liberal discourses on multiculturalism still experience the fragility of their principles of 'tolerance' when they attempt to withstand the pressure of revision. In addressing the multicultural demand, they encounter the limit of their enshrined notion of 'equal respect'; and they anxiously acknowledge the attenuation in the authority of the Ideal Observer, an authority that oversees the ethical rights (and insights) of the liberal perspective from the top deck of the Clapham omnibus. In contemplating late-liberal culture's engagements with the migratory, partial culture of minorities, we need to shift our sense of the terrain on which we can best understand the disputes. Here our theoretical understanding – in its most general sense – of 'culture-as-difference' will enable us to grasp the articulation of culture's borderline, unhomely space and time.

Where might this understanding be found?

Despite his susceptibility to consensus, for which he is so widely criticised, Jürgen Habermas's work suggests something of the stressed terrain of culture in the face of social differentiation. Once we give up the universalising sense of the 'self-referential subject-writ-large, encompassing all individual subjects', Habermas suggests, the risky search for consensus results in the kind of differentiation of the life-world of which loss of meaning, anomie, and psychopathologies are the most obvious symptoms.[3] As a result, 'the causes of social pathologies that once clustered around the class subject now break into widely scattered historical contingencies'.[4] The effect of this scattering – migratory difference once more – produces the conditions for an 'ever more finely woven net of linguistically generated intersubjectivity. Rationalisation of the life world means differentiation and condensation at once – a thickening of the floating web of intersubjective threads that simultaneously holds together the ever more sharply differentiated components of culture, society and person.'[5]

Multiculturalism – a portmanteau term for anything from minority discourse to postcolonial critique, from gay and lesbian studies to chicano/a fiction – has become the most charged sign for describing the scattered social contingencies that characterise contemporary *Kulturkritik*. The multicultural has itself become a 'floating signifier' whose enigma lies less in itself than in the discursive uses of it to mark social processes where differentiation and condensation seem to happen almost synchronically. To critique the terms in this widely contested, even contradictory terrain one needs to do more than demonstrate the logical inconsistencies of the liberal position when faced with racist belief. Prejudicial knowledge, racist or sexist, does not pertain to the ethical or logical 'reflectiveness' of the Cartesian subject. It is, as Bernard Williams has described it, 'a belief guarded against reflection'. It requires a 'study of irrationality in social practice . . . more detailed and substantive than the schematic considerations of philosophic theory'.[6] Multiculturalists committed to the instantiation of social and cultural differences within a democratic socius have to deal with a structure of the 'subject' constituted within the '"projective field" of political alienation'.[7] As Etienne Balibar writes, the identificatory language of discrimination works in reverse: 'the racial/cultural identity of "true nationals" remains invisible but is inferred from . . . the quasi-hallucinatory visibility of the "false nationals" – Jews, "wops", immigrants, *indios*, *natives*, blacks'.[8]

Thus constructed, prejudicial knowledge is forever uncertain and in danger, for, as Balibar concludes, 'that the "false" are *too* visible will never guarantee that the "true" are visible *enough*'.[9] This is one reason why multiculturalists who strive to constitute nondiscriminatory minority identities cannot simply do so by affirming the place they occupy, or by returning to an 'unmarked' authentic origin or pre-text: their recognition requires the negotiation of a dangerous indeterminacy, since the too visible presence of the other underwrites the authentic national subject but can never guarantee its visibility or truth. The inscription of the minority subject *somewhere between the too visible and the not visible enough* returns us to Eliot's sense of cultural difference, and the intercultural connection, as being beyond logical demonstration. And it requires that the discriminated subject, *even in the process of its reconstitution*, be located in a present moment that is temporally disjunctive and affectively ambivalent. 'Too late. Everything is anticipated, thought out, demonstrated, made the most of. My trembling hands take hold of nothing; the vein has been mined out. Too late!' Frantz Fanon, clearly, is speaking from this time lag[10] in the place of enunciation and identification, dramatising the moment of racist recognition. The discriminated subject or community occupies a contemporary moment that is historically untimely, forever belated. 'You come too late, much too late. There will always be a world − a white world − between you and us . . . it is understandable that I could have made up my mind to utter my Negro cry. Little by little, putting out pseudopodia here and there, I secreted a race'.[11]

By contrast, the liberal dialectic of recognition is at first sight right on time. The subject of recognition stands in a synchronous space (as befits the Ideal Observer), surveying the level playing field that Charles Taylor defines as the quintessential liberal territory: 'the presumption of equal respect' for cultural diversity. History has taught us, however, to be distrustful of things that run on time, like trains. It is not that liberalism does not recognise racial or sexual discrimination − it has been in the forefront of those struggles. But there is a recurrent problem with its notion of equality: liberalism contains a nondifferential concept of cultural time. At the point at which liberal discourse attempts to normalise cultural respect into the recognition of *equal cultural worth*, it does not recognise the disjunctive, 'borderline' temporalities of partial, minority cultures. The sharing of equality is genuinely intended, but only so long as we start from a historically congruent space; the recognition of difference is genuinely felt, but on terms that do not represent the historical genealogies, often postcolonial, that constitute the partial cultures of the minority.

This is how Taylor puts it:

> The logic behind some of these [multicultural] demands seems to depend upon a premise that we owe equal respect to all cultures . . . true judgements of value of different works would place all cultures more or less on the same footing. Of course, the attack could come from a more radical, neo-Nietzschean standpoint, which questions the very status of judgements of worth. . . . As a presumption, the claim is that all human cultures that have animated *whole* societies over some considerable stretch of time have something important to say to all human beings. I have worded it in this way to *exclude partial cultural milieux within a society as well as short phases of a major culture.* [my italics]

Or again:

> Merely on the human level, one could argue that it is reasonable to sup-
> pose that cultures that have provided the horizon of meaning for *large*
> *numbers* of human beings, of diverse characters and temperaments, *over a*
> *long period of time* . . . are almost certain to have something that deserves
> our admiration and respect. [my italics][12]

Obviously the dismissal of partial cultures, the emphasis on large numbers and
long periods, is out of time with the modes of recognition of minority or marginalised cultures. Basing the presumption on 'whole societies over some
considerable stretch of time' introduces a temporal criterion of cultural worth that
elides the disjunctive and displaced present through which minoritisation inter-
rupts and interrogates the homogeneous, horizontal claim of the democratic
liberal society. But this notion of cultural time functions at other levels besides that
of semantics or content. Let us see how this passage locates the observer – how it
allows Taylor to turn the presumption of equality into the judgement of worth. The partial, minority culture emphasises the internal differentiations, the 'foreign bodies', in the
midst of the nation – the interstices of its uneven and unequal development,
which give the lie to its *self-containedness.* As Nicos Poulantzas brilliantly argues, the
national state homogenises differences by mastering social time 'by means of a
single, homogeneous measure, which only reduces the multiple temporalities . . .
by encoding the distances between them'.[13] This conversion of time into distance
is observable in the way Taylor's argument produces a spatial binary between
whole and partial societies, one as the principle of the other's negation. The
double inscription of the part-in-the-whole, or the minority position as the outside of the inside, is disavowed.

Yet something of this 'part-in-the-whole', the minority as at once the internal
liminality and the 'foreign body', registers symptomatically in Taylor's discourse.
It is best described as the desire for the 'dialogic' – a term he takes from Mikhail
Bakhtin. But he deprives the 'dialogic' of its hybridising potential. The most telling
symptom of this is that despite his 'presumption of equality', Taylor always presents the multicultural or minority position as an imposition coming from the
'outside', and making its demands from there: 'The challenge is to deal with *their*
sense of marginalisation without compromising *our* basic political principles' (my
italics).[14] In fact the challenge is to deal not with 'them/us' but with the historically and temporally disjunct positions that minorities occupy ambivalently
within the nation's space. Taylor's evaluative schema, which locates the presumption of equality and the recognition of value (the before and the after of
liberal judgement) in the *longue durée* of major national and nationalising cultures,
is in fact antithetical to the Bakhtinian hybrid, which precisely undermines such
claims to cultural totalisation:

> The . . . hybrid is not only double-voiced and double-accented . . . but
> is also double-languaged; for in it there are not only (and not even so
> much) two individual consciousnesses, two voices, two accents, as there

are [doublings of] socio-linguistic consciousnesses, two epochs . . . that come together and consciously fight it out on the territory of the utterance. . . . It is the collision between differing points of view on the world that are embedded in these forms. . . . such unconscious hybrids have been at the same time profoundly productive historically: they are pregnant with potential for new world views, with new 'internal forms' for perceiving the world in words.[15]

Indeed, Bakhtin emphasises a space of enunciation where the negotiation of discursive doubleness *by which I do not mean duality or binarism* engenders a new speech act. In my own work I have developed the concept of hybridity to describe the construction of cultural authority within conditions of political antagonism or inequity. Strategies of hybridisation reveal an estranging movement in the 'authoritative', even authoritarian inscription of the cultural sign. At the point at which the precept attempts to objectify itself as a generalised knowledge or a normalising, hegemonic practice, the hybrid strategy or discourse opens up a space of negotiation where power is *unequal* but its articulation may be *equivocal*. Such negotiation is neither assimilation nor collaboration. It makes possible the emergence of an 'interstitial' agency that refuses the binary representation of social antagonism. Hybrid agencies find their voice in a dialectic that does not seek cultural supremacy or sovereignty. They deploy the partial culture from which they emerge to construct visions of community, and versions of historic memory, that give narrative form to the minority positions they occupy: the outside of the inside: the part in the whole.

In Toni Morrison's novel *Beloved*, cultural and communal knowledge comes as a kind of self-love that is also the love of the 'other'. It is an ethical love, in that the 'inwardness' of the subject is inhabited by the 'radical and an-archical reference to the "other"'.[16] This knowledge is visible in those intriguing chapters[17] where Sethe, Beloved, and Denver perform a ceremony of claiming and naming through intersecting and interstitial subjectivities: 'Beloved, she my daughter'; 'Beloved is my sister'; 'I am beloved and she is mine'. The women speak in tongues, from a fugal space 'in-between each other' which is a communal space. They explore an 'interpersonal' reality: a social reality that appears within the poetic image as if it were in parenthesis — aesthetically distanced, held back, yet historically framed. It is difficult to convey the rhythm and the improvisation of those chapters, but it is impossible not to see in them the healing of history, a community reclaimed in the making of a name. As I have written elsewhere:

Who is Beloved?

Now we understand: She is the daughter that returns to Sethe so that her mind will be homeless no more.

Who is Beloved?

Now we may say: She is the sister that returns to Denver and brings hope of her father's return, the fugitive who died in his escape.

34

Who is Beloved?

Now we know: She is the daughter made of murderous love who returns to love and hate and free herself. Her words are broken, like the lynched people with broken necks; disembodied, like the dead children who lost their ribbons. But there is no mistaking what her live words say as they rise from the dead despite their lost syntax and their fragmented presence.

'My face is coming   I have to have it   I am looking for the join I am loving my face so much   I want to join   I am loving my face so much   my dark face is close to me   I want to join'.[18]

The idea that history repeats itself, commonly taken as a statement about historical determinism, emerges frequently within liberal discourses when consensus fails, and when the consequences of cultural incommensurability make the world a difficult place. At such moments the past is seen as returning, with uncanny punctuality, to render the 'event' timeless, and the narrative of its emergence transparent.

Do we best cope with the reality of 'being contemporary' – its conflicts and crises, its losses and lacerations – by endowing history with a long memory that we then interrupt, or startle, with our own amnesia? How did we allow ourselves to forget, we say to ourselves, that the nationalist violence between Hindus and the Muslims lies just under the skin of India's secular modernity? Should we not have 'remembered' that the old Balkan tribes would form again? These questions emphasise an observation that is becoming increasingly commonplace: the rise of religious 'fundamentalism', the spread of nationalist movements, the redefinitions of claims to race and ethnicity, it is claimed, have returned us to an earlier historical moment, a resurgence or restaging of what historians have called the long nineteenth century. Underlying this claim is a deeper unease, a fear that the engine of social transformation is no longer the aspiration to a democratic common culture. We have entered an anxious age of identity, in which the attempt to memorialise lost time and to reclaim lost territories creates a culture of disparate 'interest groups' or social movements. Here affiliation may be antagonistic and ambivalent; solidarity may be only situational and strategic: commonality is often negotiated through the 'contingency' of social interests and political claims.

Narratives of historical reconstruction may reject such myths of social transformation: communal memory may seek its meaning through a sense of causality, shared with psychoanalysis, that negotiates the recurrence of the image of the past while keeping open the question of the future. The importance of such retroaction lies in its ability to reinscribe the past, reactivate it, relocate it, resignify it. More significant, it commits our understanding of the past, and our reinterpretation of the future, to an ethics of 'survival' that allows us to work through the present. And such a working through, or working out, frees us from the determinism of historical inevitability, repetition *without a difference*. It makes it possible for us to confront that difficult borderline, the interstitial experience, between what we take to be the image of the past and what is in fact involved in the passing of time and the passage of meaning.

NOTES

1 T. S. Eliot, *Notes Towards the Definition of Culture*, New York, Harcourt Brace and Company, 1949, p. 62.
2 ibid., pp. 63–4.
3 J. Habermas, 'The Normative Content of Philosophy', in his *The Philosophical Discourse of Modernity*, trans. F. Lawrence, Cambridge, Mass., MIT Press, 1987, p. 348.
4 ibid.
5 ibid., p. 346.
6 B. Williams, *Ethics and the Limits of Philosophy*, Cambridge, Mass., Harvard University Press, 1988, p. 116.
7 E. Balibar, 'Paradoxes of Universality', in D. Goldberg (ed.), *Anatomy of Racism*, Minneapolis and Oxford, University of Minnesota Press, 1990, p. 284.
8 ibid.
9 ibid., p. 285.
10 See my 'Race, Time, and the Revision of Modernity', in my *The Location of Culture*, London and New York, Routledge, 1994, pp. 236–56.
11 F. Fanon, *Black Skin, White Masks*, trans. C. Markmann, New York, Grove Weidenfeld, 1967, pp. 121–2.
12 C. Taylor, *Multiculturalism and 'The Politics of Recognition'*, Princeton, NJ, Princeton University Press, 1992, pp. 66–7.
13 N. Poulantzas, *State Power and Socialism*, trans. P. Camiller, London, New Left Books, 1978, p. 110.
14 Taylor, *Multiculturalism and 'The Politics of Recognition'*, p. 63.
15 M. Bakhtin, 'Discourse in the Novel', in his *The Dialogic Imagination: Four Essays*, ed. M. Holquist, trans. C. Emerson and M. Holquist, Austin, University of Texas Press, 1981, p. 360.
16 See E. Levinas, 'Reality and Its Shadow', in *Collected Philosophical Papers*, trans. A. Lingis, Dordrecht (the Netherlands) and Boston, Mass., Martinus Nijhoff, 1987, pp. 1–13.
17 T. Morrison, *Beloved*, New York, Plume/NAL, 1987, pp. 200–17.
18 From my essay, 'The Home and the World', *Social Text*, vol. 10, nos. 2 and 3, 1992, pp. 141–53, in which I develop this line of argument concerning Morrison's *Beloved* at greater length.

3

LIBERALISM AND MINORITY CULTURE

Reflections on 'Culture's In Between'

David Bennett and Homi K. Bhabha

DAVID BENNETT: Your writing has provided a shared reference-point and inspiration for many commentators on multiculturalism in a range of national settings, including several of your co-contributors to this book, so I appreciate this opportunity to explore further with you some of the issues raised by your meditations on the politics of minority culture. I would like to begin with a question about your linkage of the notion of cultural 'hybridity' with minority culture, specifically, and what you see as its 'unhomely' power to challenge the self-definitions of 'national culture', which you assume suppresses recognition of its own hybridity. In 'Culture's In Between', for example, you suggest that 'the discourse of minorities, spoken for and against in the multicultural wars, proposes a social subject constituted through cultural hybridisation'. Now, I take it that an ambiguity attaches to the 'of' in your first phrase – 'the discourse of minorities' – and that this ambiguity is central to the question you're addressing: the question of who speaks or uses the 'discourse of minorities' and who is spoken by this discourse. To take a seemingly perverse example: South Africa's white Afrikaner separatists have been lobbying since 1995 to be classified by the United Nations as an oppressed indigenous people – like Australia's Aborigines, North America's Inuit, Venezuela's Yanomami Indians and South Africa's own Zulus and Bushmen – which they believe will legitimise their demands for a Boer republic. Since many who identify with particular minorities have often spoken in defiance of 'hybridisation' and in defence of cultural 'preservation', 'survival' and indeed 'purity', are you referring as much to the discourse of liberals who speak *about* minorities and their 'rights' (as if from some panoptical perspective) as to the discourses used or spoken by self-identified minorities themselves?

HOMI BHABHA: Yes. I am suggesting that the current interest in the issue of the 'minority' is addressed by a range of political traditions, and critical voices, that are now participating in the debate around 'multiculturalism'. If there is the

Deleuzian and the 'subaltern' minority, there is also the notion of the minority that has become such a focus of attention for late liberalism. I am so glad that you raise the issue of liberalism in the context of this argument; in fact you raise it so insistently in our discussion, in various forms – the liberal state, liberal circles, liberalist politics of equality – that liberalism becomes not the familiar antagonist against which the politics of difference are poised, but an active agent and interlocutor in the discourse, whose role is profoundly ambiguous and ambivalent, and perhaps more interesting than usually acknowledged. Let us acknowledge that alongside the panopticism there is something more going on. Liberalism may well be regulative of difference and minorities – assimilationist and appropriative in the best and worst senses – but it is now troubled, anxious, even exhilarated (in unequal measures) about what it sees as the 'new diversity'. For instance, the highly influential liberal legal philosopher Joseph Raz has recently suggested that for multicultural political societies 'there is no room for talk of a minority problem or of a majority tolerating the minorities'; and as far as panopticism goes, there is, at least, the hint of a 'micropolitical' alternative: through liberal multiculturalism 'we should learn to think of our societies as consisting not of a majority and minorities, but of a plurality of cultural groups. . . . A political society, a state consists – if it is multicultural – of diverse communities and belongs to none of them.'[1]

Doesn't this kind of radical pluralism resonate with those very theoretical approaches that have been profoundly antithetical to liberalism? For instance, the notion of a political society that belongs to 'no one' raises the question of the liminal and ambivalent structure of modern democratic society, as Claud Lefort has suggested. To constitute political society from diverse communities without a normative sovereign order suggests a departure from the organicist models of community, and presumably opens up the notion of the social as *processual or performative*: the disjunctive 'articulation' of differential social sites and communal spaces that are not premised on homogeneity or consensus. In what way does the new 'postmodern bourgeois liberalism' (to cite Richard Rorty's self-description) fail the more radical projection of minoritisation? I can only list the differences here.

The new liberalism, as Raz says, must speak from and for the 'here and now' and must be valid for the conditions of 'communal disintegration and individual alienation' rather than seeking to claim a distinguished classical or canonical liberal lineage from Locke and Mill etc. This is interesting and innovative in itself, but does this 'presentism' (touched by pragmatism) deal adequately with the great social media of contemporary ethnic conflict – both international and *intranational* – that is, the traumatic and affective deployment of historical memory? The Hindu–Muslim conflict over the Hindu 'past' of the Ayodhya mosque; the Rodney King event in south-central LA and the return of the history and iconography of lynching; the ghost of 'balkanisation' in Sarajevo, etc., etc. It is not even *what we* remember as 'event' that seems to be crucial, as much as it is the *process of memorisation/memorialisation in the interstices of the present, even a pastiche of pastness within the contemporary*, that becomes a powerful form of communal affiliation and psychic identification.

D.B.: The problem with such 'presentism', at least if it implies a Nietzschean 'deliberate forgetting' of the past in order to act effectively in the present, is that Someone Else will always be doing the 'remembering', occupying the site and authority of memory. 'Presentism' is, after all, the familiar – paradoxically, the traditional – injunction of modernity itself, and, while 'being modern' may entail forgetting that the imperative of modernisation has a history, such forgetting also has a history: the history of forgetting that most stories of modernisation are also stories of barbarism, for example. But you were listing the differences between the 'new liberalism' and what you describe as the 'more radical project of minoritisation'.

H.B.: The subject of the 'here and now', its chronotopical/typical subject, becomes the 'individual' *self-present to itself*, the bearer of the ethical weight of liberal responsibility and tolerance, *in the last instance*. In Raz's words: 'Cultural and other groups have a life of their own. But their moral claim to respect and to prosperity rests entirely on their importance to the prosperity of individual human beings.' By contrast, the attempt amongst 'minority' activists and theorists has been to construct forms of agency that are collective and affective. This is not to say that they are against 'the individual' or opposed to rationality! The discourse of 'rights' through which they have to represent themselves, and the bureaucratic logics within which they have to intervene, require both 'individualism' and administrative rationality. However, the most radical quest has been for a 'minority' subject of agency that provides alternatives to the accounts of historical chronology and hierarchy (historicism), as well as theories of political action that are installed through intentionalism. This search is fuelled by the fact that minority or marginalised subjects have to construct their histories from disjunct and fragmented archives, and to constitute their subjectivities and collectivities through attenuated, dislocated and exclusionary practices.

The 'of' in the phrase 'discourse of minorities' – rather than the more familiar usage, 'minority discourse' – represents my attempt to disturb the expressive, or spontaneous, relation between the site of the minority (as designated subject) and the status of its reference in discourse, or its regulation in cultural and political practice. This separation of the two is not to merely repeat that all signs signify within a systemic discursive environment. My purpose is to draw attention to the enunciative histories of minoritisation, to be aware that the minority is not only a particular sector of the nation-people but also a certain kind of ethical attribution in 'theory' or cultural debate. This should introduce a caution in speaking 'for' the minority, as well as the minority speaking 'for itself'.

D.B.: I'm not sure what you have in mind when you link the radical quest for minority agency with a search for alternatives to 'theories of political action that are installed through intentionalism', but I note an ethical valorisation of minority agency in another passage of 'Culture's in between', in which you write: 'Hybrid agencies find their voice in a dialectic that does not seek cultural supremacy or sovereignty. They deploy the partial culture from which they emerge to construct visions of community, and versions of historic memory, that give narrative form to the minority positions they occupy.' This suggests a dialogical form of historical discourse in which the definitions of 'events' are continually being contested or challenged; but can contestation and challenge be dissociated from struggles for supremacy or sovereignty? And if they can't, must visions of community remain agonistic, divisive and divided – between, for example, subordinate and dominant, 'minority' and 'majority'?

H.B.: Contestation and challenge presume antagonism and negotiation of very complex sorts; they also assume negation and translation – but the issue of sovereignty and supremacy as a way of articulating conflict comes from a very hierarchical and vertical reading of the representation and practice of power. It is certainly part of an imaginary that cannot think of the articulation of antagonism outside of the binaries of subordinated/dominant, minority/majority. Does this reflect reality as we see it? Consider the Shi'ites in England and India – minorities in both cultures, but do they signify the same cultural 'difference' in both contexts? I think not. My concern is with differences within minoritisation and the possibilities of articulating affiliation or solidarity on the grounds of differences that may not be 'resolved' but have to be worked through and worked with, causing structures of ambivalence and 'supplementary' moves. In a most interesting passage on 'subalternity', Gramsci suggests that we have to look for movements and emergences outside the formal dialectical structure – well, think of the movement of 'laterality' in Levinasian ethics, where the notions of proximity and antagonism are 'doubled'. Foucauldian strategies of power-knowledge as 'strategic elaboration' are, again, inscribed in contestation, but there is no necessary supremacism there, nor a 'divided' binarism.

D.B.: Perhaps I am less optimistic than I should be that a politics of minority coalition or affiliation, or what you have elsewhere described as a 'vision of hybrid community' which creates 'agency through incommensurable (not simply multiple) positions',[2] is imaginable as anything more utopian than the historically all-too-familiar politics of otherwise conflicting interests forming temporary strategic alliances against 'third' parties.

H.B.: I don't quite understand why my notion of a minority agency seems utopian. Your description – 'conflicting interests forming temporary strategic alliances' – is a good popular front tactic that has been part of many movements for revolutionary social transformation, as well as other more social or liberal 'democratic' reforms. And that is the difficult non-utopian thought that one has to think: what structures and strategies of praxis, organisation, interpellation,

40

coalition can be held, painfully and paradoxically, 'in common' between antagonistic political philosophies in the performative and practice-bound realm.
Utopianism arises, I'm afraid, when you treat the 'historically-all-too-familiar'
with contempt, and undermine history's contingent causality as 'temporary' (as in
your phrase, 'temporary strategic alliances'). What eternal verities or immanences
do you seek, what invariant structures of political affiliation are you proposing?
Haven't all those political acts and discourses that have insisted on the *necessity* (historical or theoretical) of their ontological origins ended up as authoritarian or
totalitarian regimes? And, finally, the phrase 'strategic alliances *against* third parties'
really doesn't reflect my views at all. Because the way you present the 'contradiction', we are back with the old binary structure of thinking social antagonism:
the strategic alliance vs. third party. My interest lies more in the effects of the supplementary movement wrought through the performative process of articulation
or translation: forms of contradiction, sites of affiliation, temporalities of representation, norms of regulation that emerge with something of that Benjaminian
'shock' to transform the *prior or primary* identifications or elements (affiliative or
antagonistic) that entered into the dialogic process of exchange. Whatever it is that
claims authority on the grounds of being 'anterior' or *a priori* is alienated from
itself, made uncanny. It is not a third party that interests me, but this move or
movement of an intercessive, even excessive, thirdness.

D.B.: My aim in pointing to the sheer historical *ordinariness* of coalition politics in
which otherwise antagonistic interests co-operate against 'third' parties – and we
could here be talking as much about alliances like the Hitler–Stalin nonaggression
pact to enable the 'Fourth Partition of Poland', or the Indochinese Communist
Party's policy of co-operating with 'antifascist colonialists' in 1936, as about indi-
genist coalitions like the Amazonian Forest People's Alliance against international
bankers, developers and technocrats[3] – was certainly not to suggest that there
might be 'purer' and hence more desirable forms of political collectivity and
agency – heaven forbid! It was to press what I take to be your deliberately paradoxical image of a 'community' of 'incommensurable positions' for the meaning
you are attaching to the term 'community' in this context. If this concept is to
carry an affective value greater than that simply of 'force-field', say, then it
would seem to imply a 'second-order' or 'higher-level' solidarity, a level at
which the 'incommensurable' resolves into commonality. This is certainly the
case, for example, in Joseph Raz's blueprint for a 'liberal multicultural society',
in which a plurality of cultural groups, each seeking to perpetuate its differences,
must none the less achieve consensus on the best political, economic and educational means of maintaining and developing those 'cultural' differences. As Raz
puts it, liberal multiculturalism 'requires the existence of a common culture' – a
procedural one – despite itself, as it were.[4]

Political representation is, of course, a *productive* practice, a matter of bringing
political subjects and agencies (and, indeed, objects) into being, not merely of
naming what Donna Haraway has called 'pre-packaged referents';[5] and as you

41

suggest, coalition, affiliation, or 'articulation' if you prefer, will always displace the parties involved from their prior positions and reconfigure the political terrain in which they perform their identities and interests. But what seems to interest you most as a 'radical' possibility is the *incalculable* element in these displacements and reconfigurations. If we assume that coalition politics, like every other kind, entails calculation and hence *representation* of goals and risks, of possible and desirable outcomes, then it is unclear how the incalculable outcomes that you characterise as an 'excessive thirdness' can be objects of quest for a given political or cultural interest-group, or perhaps for any but a chaos-theorist of politics. How can such incalculables be factored into the *Realpolitik* of groups seeking to participate in a non-hierarchical 'community' of 'incommensurable' positions?

H.B.: I don't think I would use the word 'incalculable', nor do I think that 'incalculability' is the problem: the issue is neither a nullity of knowledge nor an 'excess' that marks the (all too familiar) argument about the status of the non-signifiable in the process of representation. The radical possibility that I am striving to capture is part of an older and ongoing discourse of the place and function of the 'contingent' in the dialectical tradition. The problem is definitely *not* the 'incalculable'; if you want to work around that word, it is more properly the problem of recalculation. The contingent or 'recalculative' emerges at that moment in the dialectic where determinism is faced with its double – the iterative. At that point there is a struggle between the process of negation and the force of transformation, between the necessity of erasure and the contingency of epiphany. Totalisation and teleology provide no clear measure of the 'direction' of the dialectical process. Past and present are continually inter-mediated, selfhood and otherness intensely intercalated.

What I have sketched out in theoretical form is part of the world of *Realpolitik*; it is part of the experience of groups in our times. Don't you think that one of the persistent themes of cultural and political conflict now is the 'undecidability' of what emerges as old and/or new within the contemporary moment of late modernity? The rise of fundamentalisms of all hues – Hindu, Christian, Muslim – inhabits this liminal space where the contemporary can only be designated and experienced as a kind of disjuncture in the 'present'. Is the Bosnian conflict old – Balkan blood feuds – or new – post-Soviet Union? Isn't the same question asked endlessly about Northern Ireland? This confounding of the very notion of contemporaneity as a site of stability or novelty – this is what I want to foreground in descriptions of political representation. This doesn't sound to me like either voluntarism or chaos theory. It is the task of recalculation (to re-cast your word) or, in my language, the responsibility of negotiation.

You ask, most pertinently, how can such a situation be the 'object of quest' for a political or interest group? What I have tried to describe is the process prior to the object, the conditions under which an object may arise – less about the politics of identification, more focused on conditions of emergence and address. This is not an evasion, only an explanation of my intent. I think I may also be trying to understand political 'will' in a way different from the assumptions of your question. I really can't say more at this stage, in this space, than that I think I need to do much more work on our desire to invest politics with a will-*fullness*. It is the presumption of *fullness* as the guarantee of direction and purpose (purpose-full-ness?) that I need to understand better. I have a suspicion that the language of intention/direction does not really measure up to the complex kinds of collective, communal processes – both rational and unconscious, effective and affective – that come to be represented in those diverse and diffuse activities that, for the sake of convenience and intelligibility, we call culture and politics. The concept of 'ide-ology' has been developed to do this very work, but I remain less than convinced by most of the theories of ideology that I am aware of. There remains a lot of work to be done.

D.B.: As this book testifies, the question of whether or how cultural differences should be recognised by the institutions and policies of liberal-democratic gov-ernments has been widely debated under the rubric of 'multiculturalism' in many countries, but it seems to me that the frames of reference of these debates have too often remained narrowly national. This is, at best, a paradox. How well informed by extra-national perspectives do you think public debates about mul-ticulturalism have been in the USA or the UK, the two national contexts with which you are personally most familiar? If multiculturalism puts 'national iden-tity' into crisis, does it point necessarily to post-national, and not merely transnational, forms of cultural, political and social organisation?

H.B.: Absolutely. One of the most exciting developments of new political move-ments – and their emphases on media, culture, communication, the sign (while not ignoring the phenomenal and causal forms of work, labour, class) – is the sense that the national 'ontopology' (Derrida) has been productively breached. There is a way in which location/locution/the field of representation (both political and symbolic recognition) and the concept of action, are reconfigured. It is not that the national boundary is erased or breached or ignorable; it is much more that it becomes a kind of liminal 'edge' which then reflects back on the problems inherent in the hegemonic and homogeneous claims for national com-munity, and which then, in turn, changes the whole status of what it means to be a minority *as a double articulation*: within the nation the minority is part of the inherent problem of the articulation of disparate sites and communities that the nation-form and its homogeneous empty time are meant to salve and solve; but the minority also has its outsideness, its hyphenated status and structure that relates it to a 'Mexico', an 'India', a 'diaspora' in such a way that if it is the inside-outside of the national form, it also rearticulates from its diasporic position what it means to belong to the traditional or atavistic culture. A similar but different structure would have to be worked out for sexual minorities.

D.B.: We shouldn't forget the *hegemonic* potential of the minority as an economic elite, or versions of diaspora which dramatise border-crossing and 'hybridity' as privilege rather than deprivation, the privilege of mobility associated with economic and cultural capital. I'm thinking, for example, of what was characterised as 'the astronaut phenomenon' of Hong Kong Chinese businesspeople who, with the imminent expiry of Britain's ninety-nine-year lease on its colony, moved their families to countries like Canada and Australia while themselves returning regularly to work in Hong Kong, where their earning capacity remained far greater than in their adoptive, 'residential' countries. A 1996 report by Australia's Bureau of Immigration, Multicultural and Population Research suggested that such 'astronaut families', with their 'parachute children', may represent an embryonic form of transnational citizenship which will break down distinctions between permanent and temporary migration and challenge prevailing notions of the nation-state. Perhaps such elite minorities represent the 'outside-inside', rather than what you term the 'inside-outside', of the nation-form.

Writing of a nation-state now struggling precisely to preserve not only its territorial integrity but its cultural 'hybridity' against the secessionist ambitions of certain ethnic minorities, Sue Mathieson and David Attwell in their essay for this book pose the question: 'What is identity politics . . . but apartheid thinking in another guise?' They suggest that from the perspective of the ANC, always resolutely opposed to the ethnic chauvinism of apartheid, the identitarian agendas being pursued in the name of multiculturalism in liberal democracies like the USA could seem deeply conservative. In their words: 'Apartheid's ruse was to use ethnicity as a way of deflecting claims to power at the centre; in this context, identitarian agendas could easily be, and were, co-opted under a constitutional arrangement which protected white interests'. Would you agree with their assessment that 'multiculturalism and apartheid are not such antithetical visions'?

H.B.: I agree with Mathieson and Attwell that multicultural agendas can often be deeply conservative and can lead to the politics of assimilationism or integrationism – and this is particularly the case when the claim to ethnicity or identity is made within a theory of democratic pluralism that so happily fits in with the liberal concepts of: unitary identity and the values of individualism; imagined national community as co-existing within 'homogeneous empty time'; emancipation understood in terms of a progressivist history of 'modernisation'; culture as part of an organic linkage of ethnicity/community/tradition etc. Often, the unintended effects of identity politics are collusive with such centrist, constitutional orders. However, if that is the case, why has the constitutional (constituted!) conservative centre been so shaken and threatened by the politics of 'identity'? This is a very large question but one that needs to be answered. I suspect that one of the reasons for the perceived threat – to say nothing about the paranoia that raged in the canon wars – is that the claim to identity as articulated by people of colour or the 'minority' does not conform to the individualist norm where the 'autonomy' or sovereignty of the self is an ultimate and untouchable value. The militant minority demand for 'recognition' is never so singular; it is a demand made on behalf of a people whose historical experiences have, in the main, made them live the values of 'personhood' as a collective, social experience – the 'community' becomes the site of social agency. To 'disrespect', or to 'diss' as a performative act that is so often the point of 'ethnic' tension, is a much more socially symbolic act than a personal insult, and acceleratedly goes beyond the individual to the communal body. Secondly, the pluralistic agenda assumes a political imaginary where equality or equity and emancipation are often 'future'-oriented projects (which is why the democratic ideal is so inherently utopian, as is the 'classical' Marxian project, too). But the unsettling thing about current 'minority' claims to historical being is that history is underwritten by the need to come to terms with memory and trauma: there can be no mirage about a 'level playing-field' until the soil is dug up and the whole terrain re-built. This notion of freedom as looking to the past while 'working through' the present is deeply disturbing to consensual 'centrists', however liberal, because it makes the historical present 'strange' to itself, estranged from the sources of its authority, harrowed in its very presence-ing.

D.B.: One of the more contentious terms in which the status of certain minorities has been represented ethically within the nation in recent years is that of 'victimage'. The terms 'victimology' and 'victim art', for example, have gained an ironic currency in apparently liberal circles in the USA as terms of disparagement, especially for educational and artistic projects that seek to represent the histories and experiences of 'subaltern' groups or disadvantaged minorities, or to insist on their visibility to a dominant (proverbially white, homophobic) culture. In this respect, the terms seem to have joined 'political correctness' as rhetorical allies of the conservative backlash against affirmative-action and positive-discrimination programmes in education, employment, and cultural-funding policies. When you yourself handle the phrase 'victim art' gingerly between scare quotes in a recent essay,[6] what particular reservations about the rhetoric of 'victimage' are you signalling?

H.B.: I place 'victim art' within quotes because it is such an overused term located in discourses fired by the 'culture wars'. It is often forgotten that 'victim art' – whatever that may be – is about the emergence, into the cultural public sphere, of a range of voices that were once silenced by the process of minoritisation (of various kinds). It is hardly surprising that they speak of their most vivid experiences, experiences that have informed their existential conditions: disadvantage, discrimination, AIDS. . . . Without raising the value question – which I will come to in a moment – let me ask a few pointed questions. Since when was suffering-on-stage or on-the-page seen as 'victimage' rather than the 'human condition' or 'la comédie humaine'? Has the singular imaginative and narrative force of Eliot, James and Woolf – who wrote from a rather narrow circle of philosophical belief and social experience – ever been properly served by calling them 'privilege artists'? Why is the experience of 'victimage' in rock music, blues and jazz welcomed as part of a multi-billion-dollar industry while the same 'material' in fictional or dramatic or painterly form, as part of the curricula of the museum or the academy, always results in this desultory charge? If these are merely rhetorical questions, let them pass; if they have a grain of truth, then they speak for themselves.

Let's continue: having established, at once, a certain anomalousness in the term itself, it is only obvious and fair to say that when a work does not provide a 'willing suspension of disbelief', does not achieve the alienating Brechtian Gestus, does not find its 'objective correlative', then, however 'authentic' the experience, it lapses into a kind of sentimental mimeticism. It fails because it asks to be measured against 'reality' (unspecified), and does not provide us with its own standards and modes of transvaluation; it fails to translate the inherited terms of judgement, and the received indices of identification. So the artistic failure of victimage is no different from the aesthetic failure of privilege.

So what are we talking about? What needs to be said? There is an argument that suggests that the problem with the charge of victimage is that those who make that claim (sympathetically) enact a phantasmatic scenario in which the 'other' is in a position of docile subservience, which also provides a kind of panoptic surveillance. The victim-other as 'good' object reflects back a philanthropic benevolence that feeds the narcissism of the 'good samaritan' or the victim's witness. This may be one kind of positionality in identifying the victim. But there is another, where it is precisely the victim who is seen as being in an 'unpatriotic' position of privilege: the Welfare queen who has boyfriends and babies on welfare and saps the economy; the AIDS victim whose supposed promiscuity leads to the exploitation of Medicare etc. Is this merely class-hatred, racism, homophobia? Another attempt to secure the American dream and the magic of global capital?

There is something more profound going on here. There is a 'willed' disavowal (I'm conscious of the irony) of those darker life-forms or negative 'affects' that constitute the social and sexual lives of late modernity. There is a forgetting of what is entailed by the messy and entirely necessary business of survival – not survival as a zero-degree form of bare existence, but survival as the awareness of what it means to be in the 'midst' of life and language, always belated, and yet productive of history and its conditions of action.

To survive, strictly speaking, is to continue to live after the cessation of some thing, event, or process; it demands an articulation or bridging of the moments 'before' and 'after' a discontinuity – and the courage to live through the flux of that moment of trauma, cessation, or loss. If survival is predicated on a break in continuity – in the structures that sustain the sense of identity, tradition, or historical continuum – then the notion of community or group identity becomes a crucial location for the dialogic practices of culture, including those of historical revision and the (re)invention of tradition. Our sense of community is an imagined and creative performance enacted across the double injunction of survival: cessation and continuance. Simply to forget trauma is to be amoral and amnesiac, but to remember trauma alone is to refuse to turn cessation into continuance. What I wish to counterpose with the rhetoric of 'victimage' and 'victim art', then, is this sense of survival as at once an ethic and, yes, an aesthetics of community.

NOTES

1 J. Raz, 'Multiculturalism', Dissent, Winter 1994, pp. 67–79.
2 H. K. Bhabha, 'How Newness Enters the World', in The Location of Culture, London and New York, Routledge, 1994, p. 231.
3 See Donna Haraway's discussion of this instance of 'a politics of articulation', rather than 'the politics of representation', in 'The Promises of Monsters: A Regenerative Politics of Inappropriate/d Others', in L. Grossberg, C. Nelson and P. Treichler (eds), Cultural Studies, New York and London, Routledge, 1992, pp. 309–15.
4 Raz, 'Multiculturalism', p. 77.
5 Haraway, 'The Promises of Monsters', p. 313.
6 H. Bhabha, 'Dance This Diss Around', Artforum, vol. 33, no. 8, April 1995, pp. 19–20.

4

FIVE TYPES OF IDENTITY AND DIFFERENCE

Terry Eagleton

It is hard to see what is so wrong about human inequality. Human beings are obviously unequal: some are more generous and resilient than others, more adept at playing the tin whistle or memorising the *Iliad*. The egalitarian will naturally protest that it is not *these* sorts of inequalities which are at stake, but social and political ones. But it is not absurd to imagine, as many conservatives have, that some of these 'given' inequalities should be directly translated into political terms, so that, in Platonic style, the wiser and kinder should rule the meaner and more foolish. Almost everybody but card-carrying free marketeers feels that a society in which a tiny minority is monstrously affluent while the vast majority live lives of wretched impoverishment is unjust. In other words, almost everyone feels that the kind of global social order we actually have is unjust; it is simply that most of them do not recognise the actual global order we have under this description of it, or else recognise it but imagine that it is going to improve, or is somehow unavoidable.

Such a case of glaring and extreme inequality, however, gives the egalitarian too easy a political ride. One needs instead to confront liberal capitalism at its best – to take the point, for example, of the model proposed by John Rawls in his *A Theory of Justice*, in which a just society would be, among other things, one in which the least well-off were well-off *enough*. If they were well-off enough, why should they complain, other than out of envy, that others were even better off? One would surely need to resort here to the traditional Marxist riposte, which is that the less well-off are as they are *because* a minority is much better off. 'There are rich people and poor people' is not yet a narrative; 'There are rich people because there are poor people' is the glimmerings of one. One would need, in other words, to counter the liberal case at its most humane by appealing to some theory or other of exploitation – a theory of which postmodernist thought has been busily depriving itself. And such a theory would no doubt expose the Rawlsian ideal for the illusion that, in practice, it is bound to be.

Liberals believe in equality of opportunity – that everyone is entitled to the so-called primary spiritual and material goods essential for their free individual self-development, which is to say, for carving their own unique path to happiness. Everyone, on this theory, must have an equal chance of becoming unequal. But this fails to capture our strong intuition that human equality goes further down than this – that it is an ontological affair rather than merely a matter of social arrangements, to do in some obscure sense with equality of being. But what could such equality of being possibly mean? A character in D. H. Lawrence's *Aaron's Rod* suggests that all human beings are equal in their souls, only to be brusquely informed that this is precisely where they are least equal. What does it mean to treat two individuals equally? It cannot, surely, mean treating them the *same*, since if individuals have different needs and capacities this is bound to issue in injustice. It was in this sense that Marx, in his *Critique of the Gotha Programme* and elsewhere, regarded equality as a typically bourgeois abstraction, one which overrode the sensuous particularity of individual men and women. Which is not to say, as we shall see later, that he therefore rejected the idea out of hand. Marx rejected none of the great bourgeois moral ideals out of hand, indeed, had an unflagging admiration for them. His only concern was why they could never be realised in practice. But the abstraction of equality is for him modelled on the commodity form, in which objects exchange in grand indifference to their sensuous specificity or 'use value'. To treat two individuals equally must surely mean not giving them the same sort of treatment, but paying equal attention to the specific needs and desires of each. It is not that they are equal individuals, but that they are equally individuals. To this extent, any authentic concept of equality already implicates the notion of difference. Equality, on this view, is a question of the subject rather than the object – a matter of how we conduct ourselves towards others, not a question of some equally shared property or condition of being inherent in them. This, which one might dub the 'incommensurabilist' case about equality, is an appealing line for those who, politically speaking, believe in equality but, philosophically speaking, want to deny that human beings have much of significance in common – who want, that is, to reject the idea of a common human essence. Human beings, on this view, have little or nothing in common, no spiritual bedrock of equality, which might *objectively* warrant treating them as equal; treating them equally is rather a question of distributing one's attention in equal measure to precisely what they *don't* have in common, namely their unique differences. But since these differences are themselves objective, one can still ground one's political ethic in the way human beings are, much as this style of thought dislikes speaking in those terms. To assert that what matters about people is their differences is quite as much a totalising, universalistic claim as to insist that they all share certain crucial properties in common, and that this is the reason why we should treat them equally.

It would seem, then, that an incommensurabilist case can be opposed to an essentialist one. But this would be too premature a conclusion. For it is more than idle wordplay to claim that what human beings have in common is exactly their differences, and so to reconcile these apparently antithetical views. This, more or less, would appear to be Marx's own position. Marx seems strongly to believe in a common human nature (he calls it 'species being') and is surely quite right to do so. It is just that it belongs to this species being to individuate ourselves, as it does not, or does a lot less, to non-labouring, non-world-transforming, non-linguistic and thus non-historical species like moles and badgers. The clue to our capacity for differences lies in the structures of our shared material nature, which determine us to be, within limits, self-determining. Difference, in the sense of individuation, is natural to the kind of beings we are, just as culture has its roots in (but cannot be reduced to) certain biological facts about us of which moles and badgers are both mercifully and unhappily free.

The abstract Enlightenment concept of equality was a revolutionary one in its day. Its brutal overriding of individual differences, its savage rationalist suppression of sensuous particularity, meant in political terms that everyone now had a right to equal consideration just because they were human, not just because they were the son of a minor Prussian count. It is remarkable how violently today's cultural left has repressed this emancipatory dimension of an otherwise oppressive narrative, having thrown dialectical thinking to the winds. The concept of a human essence, *pace* the anti-essentialists, figures here as an explosively radical idea. It was the *ancien régimes* which were the devotees of difference, in the sense of the custodians of traditionalist privilege, and for which – as for many postmodernists today, if for rather different reasons – the notion of universal human equality was deeply suspect and highly dangerous. For the radical Enlightenment you now had a right to respect, to a voice and a hearing, just on account of your membership of the species, not on account of your membership of the church or the aristocracy or the *literati*. Everyone's destiny now mattered equally, at least in theory – and 'in theory' is a sizeable improvement on not mattering even as that.

Equality, then, is a deeply paradoxical notion. It means that everyone must non-particularly have their particularity attended to – 'non-particularly' here meaning without privilege or exception or exclusion. Everyone must be exactly equal in respect of the incommensurable treatment they receive – which means that you must be divested of your individual properties, which then in the scholastic sense of the term become accidental, to qualify as a candidate for individual respect. A genuine concept of equality thus deconstructs the notions of identity and non-identity, sameness and difference, the individual and the universal, in contrast to those more rigidly binary theorists of postmodernism who would line up difference on one side of the ontological fence and abstract universality on the other.

The conservative case I touched on earlier holds that political differences should be translations of 'given' ones, in a stratified social order. One cannot, in my view, oppose this elitist vision merely by mobilising a radical conception of difference against a reactionary one. As long as that radical case wants to claim that *all* individuals must count equally as far as the chance to realise their difference goes, and that this is unlikely to happen under a rigidly hierarchical order, it is, like it or not, summoning to its defence some form of essence or ontology. It has to involve itself, as the liberal recognises, in some kind of discourse of human rights; and in so far as the liberal acknowledges this, he or she marks a theoretical – if not a political – advance on a radical libertarianism wary of that whole style of speaking. You cannot consistently (though many now try it on) reject elitism on political grounds while philosophically abandoning universalism, and this is one of the major embarrassments of postmodern thought. The libertarian labours here under a contradiction, desiring a society in which all men and women will be free while hostile to the very notion of their being in any sense commensurate. But the commensurability, however formally and abstractly, has just been asserted. The liberal, by contrast, recognises that in order for individual freedom to be achieved all round, a political apparatus which apparently runs counter to it must be first of all set in place. For men and women to have the chance to become or discover what they uniquely desire, an 'artificial' equalising, homogenising and identifying must be at work, ensuring that none of them is unjustly disabled in this pursuit. In this sense, the means of guaranteeing such freedom sits uncomfortably (but unavoidably so) with the end, and liberalism becomes a form of structural irony. This may be an awkward creed to live with, as some liberal self-agonising attests; but it is in an important sense more intellectually honest than that of the postmodern libertarian, for whom – as for a certain kind of radical Tory – identity, homogeneity and commensurability are simply oppressive or even, in the more baroque flourishes of the trend, 'terroristic'. Such libertarians are simply unable to say how the free release of difference would be secured for all, without distastefully involving themselves in the very discourse they regard as inimical to that goal. The libertarian is right to see that the concept of difference finally travels beyond the ideas of both equality and inequality – that (as Lawrence of all people puts it) when I am in the presence of another human being I experience neither equality nor inequality, but simply otherness. But that, as it stands, could apply to one's response to a slave. 'Otherness' cannot be allowed, in some premature utopianism, to ride roughshod over the equalising, homogenising political mechanisms which make of such respect for the other more than just an attitude of mind. To claim that 'there is no question of inequality here, and thus no question of equality either' may play either to a radical or to a conservative case.

The problem is that the libertarian cannot get as far as bourgeois democracy, whereas the liberal cannot get beyond it. For the former, the idea of some abstract equality threatens to undermine difference; for the latter, the differences which liberal society actually produces, in the form of social and economic inequalities, threaten to strike hollow the apparatus of formal equality which allows these differences to thrive. What both creeds have in common, however, is that the free play of difference is the ultimately desirable goal – as against social democracy, in which the desirable end is an equality that still permits some degree of difference, or the more brutal forms of Stalinism in which difference is sunk entirely beneath identity. One could, then, draw up a typology of political regimes in terms of the way they conceive of the relation between difference and identity. One could also argue that socialism transcends them all because it sees this process as proceeding through four distinct stages, one or more of which these other forms of politics pass over. The first stage is where we came in: the 'given' (of course, culturally conditioned) differences of human beings in, so to speak, a 'pre-political state'. This, as we have seen, is where a certain traditional-ist type of conservative abruptly ends, saddled with two stages only. For him or her, the political structure merely mimes, translates or represents these existing distinctions. For one sort of libertarian, there are similarly just two phases: what is valuable about human beings is their difference, and society must foster and emancipate this, though, unlike the conservative, in a non-elitist way. For the Stalinist or social democrat, there are also two stages in question: an original dif-ference must be politically equalled up, with various degrees of completeness. The liberal case is more intriguingly triadic: 'given' differences must be 'artificially' equalised, but in order that more important differences may then be universally realised and explored. Equality and universality are key values, but essentially instrumental ones, finally in the service of individual freedom.

The trajectory of both conservatism and libertarianism can be summarised as difference–difference; of social democracy as difference–identity (or equality); of liberalism as difference–identity–difference. Socialism, by contrast, adds a fourth stage and introduces a new term: its trajectory is difference–equality–differ-ence–reciprocity. I mean by 'reciprocity' the fact that a socialist society, having travelled through difference, aims to come out somewhere on the other side with-out, however, having left it behind. The goal is no longer either difference or identity, but an attempt to reconstruct, on the basis of the fullest possible libera-tion of difference, new forms of human solidarity. And this is one sense in which socialism, as Marxists have classically understood it, is the sublation rather than merely the cancellation of liberalism. One can trace this trajectory in Marxist thought at the economic level too: from the given difference of things, to their 'artificial' identity in commodity exchange, on to the release of sensuously par-ticular use value from this abstract equalisation, and from there – since use value is a relational notion – to new forms of social relations between individuals. We cannot, of course, know now what forms of global relationships that working in and through difference would possibly mean; but one sort of libertarian, in viewing sheer difference as the goal, is too uncomfortably close to the liberal to be of much assistance here. The difference with the liberal is that the libertarian, in a prematurely utopian gesture, wants to short-circuit the abstract equality which the liberal recognises as essential to the fullest flourishing of individual freedom. The socialist, like the liberal, wants to enter into those abstract, univer-sal forms of identity only in order to move out of them again into some richer human order which will have surpassed them. But the telos of this movement is not a stubborn resting in difference, which then becomes just the flipside of a spurious universalism, but the discovery of those new forms of mutual belong-ing. And this in turn would be inseparable from the discovery and definition of our real differences, which can only in the end be worked out in reciprocal ways, and which may well turn out to be different from what, in present conditions, we consider our differences to be.

5

ECONOMIES OF VALUE[1]

John Frow

I begin with the assumption that it is no longer either possible or useful to understand cultural production in terms of a general economy of value, and thus that we can no longer imagine ourselves into a vantage point from which conflicting judgements of value could be reconciled. What may in some sense always have been the case has become self-evidently so now: that different social groups employ criteria of value which may well be incompatible and irreconcilable. Jurij Lotman's distinction between the aesthetic of opposition that organises post-Romantic high culture and the aesthetic of repetition that organises much of folk and popular culture is perhaps the simplest way of exemplifying this incompatibility;[2] but in general the disjunctions between the organising aesthetics of European and non-European cultures, between 'men's' and 'women's' genres (in so far as this opposition can be sustained), between religious and 'aesthetic' functionalisations of a text, between literate and oral cultures, between the cultural norms of different age-classes or different sexual subcultures or different national regions, and so on, can be taken as indications of a vastly more complex network of differentiations which is not, or is no longer, reducible to a single scale.

As soon as it is conceded that there no longer exists a general economy of value, however, a series of difficult consequences comes into play.

For the category of value does not disappear with the collapse of a general economy; it continues to organise every local domain of the aesthetic and every aspect of daily life, from the ritualised discussions of movies or books or TV programmes through which relations of sociability are maintained, to the fine discriminations of taste in clothing or food or idiom that are made by every social class and every status subculture, to the organisation of school and university curricula, museum and gallery exhibitions, and the allocation of commercial and public financing to the culture industries. There is no escape from the discourse of value, and no escape from the pressure and indeed the obligation to treat the world as though it were fully relational, fully interconnected. But what becomes entirely problematical is just the possibility of relation: that is, of critical movement across the spaces between incommensurate evaluative regimes. If the use of cultural objects is something more than a matter of individual preference (and the whole vocabulary of 'preference' as it is elaborated by the rationalist individual-ism of neoclassical economics simply begs the question of why different choices are made and of whether some choices are better than others; 'preference' has the great theoretical advantage of being ineffable),[3] then it becomes a problem to account for the systemic formation of value without assuming criteria that hold good right across the cultural field.

One possible strategy for dealing with this transformed economy would be through a move that seems, in fact, to get neatly beyond the whole problem of valuation. The move involves deciding that, rather than engaging in a discourse of value, calculating the relative worth of this text against that text according to some impossibly universal criterion of value, the job of the critic is rather to analyse the social relations of value themselves: to analyse the discourses of value, the socially situated frameworks of valuation from which value judgements are generated by readers. More broadly, this would be an analysis not only of norms and procedures but of the institutional structures through which value is formed, transmitted, and regulated; of the social distribution of literacy; of the mechanisms for the training and certification of valuing subjects; of the multi-plicity of formations of value, differentiated by age, by class, by gender, by race, and so on.

Such a practice of dispassionate analysis, where normativity is passed from the subject to the object of study, has the virtue of generosity towards the very dif-ferent, often contradictory discourses of value held by different groups; rather than privileging the values of an intellectual elite, proclaiming as universal a set of norms that can be demonstrated to be historically and culturally variable – norms of 'good taste' that are invariably class- and gender-specific – it concedes in advance the validity of the discrepant norms of other social groups: a validity that is now always relative to those groups and grounded in them, as are the norms of a socially situated high culture.

Certainly this seems to me an indispensable first step in dealing with questions of value. It has the major flaw, however, of being unable to comprehend its own position, in ways that matter, within the ambit of its analysis. It is as though the understanding of value took place within some space that was free of social con-flict, free of the play of interests, free of prejudice and misunderstanding; and as though (in a counter-movement to that passage of normativity from subject to object) the principle of totalisation had been displaced from the object, the cul-tural field, to the self-effacing space of analysis itself. Methodological objectivism works as a denial of the principle that '"culture" is always relational, an inscrip-tion of communicative processes that exist, historically, between subjects in relations of power'.[4]

A further strategy closely related to this strategy of dispassionate analysis of value systems is the espousal or at least the acceptance of a kind of happy rela-tivism: a model (which we might call 'postmodern') of the world as being irreducibly plural and informed by no principle of totalisation.

Zygmunt Bauman, for example, sets up an opposition between two distinct modes of intellectual practice: on the one hand, a framework characteristic of modernity, according to which the orderly totality of the world is patterned by the uneven distribution of probabilities, and order is exerted by the manipulation of probabilities. The stochastic nature of this universe thus implies no final chaos and no separation of knowledge from practice; on the contrary, 'effectivity of control and correctness [of knowledge] are tightly related (the second explains the first, the first corroborates the second), whether in laboratory experiment or societal practice'. On the other hand, there is what he calls the postmodern world-view of 'an unlimited number of models of order, each one guaranteed by a relatively autonomous set of practices. Order does not precede practices and hence cannot serve as an outside measure of their validity. Each of the many models of order makes sense solely in terms of the practices which validate it', and is upheld by the beliefs of a 'community of meanings'. These local forms of knowledge are not subject to any meta-principle of explanation: 'there are no criteria for evaluating local practices which are situated outside traditions, outside "localities". Systems of knowledge may only be evaluated from "inside" their respective traditions.' Thus, 'if, from the modern point of view, relativism of knowledge was a problem to be struggled against and eventually overcome in theory and in practice, from the postmodern point of view relativity of knowledge (that is, its "embeddedness" in its own communally supported tradition) is a lasting feature of the world'.[5]

This 'postmodern' model continues to have the merit of generosity towards the discrepant and often disdained structures of value of different social groups; in asserting the validity and the local specificity of a plurality of practices and codes of valuation it refuses to maintain the privilege of any one culture over any other. But this generosity can easily become a kind of contempt in its own right, since it entails a certain indifference towards the otherness of other domains; no domain of value has anything to say to or about any other, and indeed there is an active prohibition on intercommunication; each domain is hermetically sealed from every other.

A more complex and more restless formulation of the problem of commensuration between heterogeneous value systems can be found in the work of Jean-François Lyotard. Following Lyotard's turn, after the major texts of the early 1970s, from an energetics to a 'generalised rhetoric',[6] it is possible to isolate two main phases in this formulation.

The first is built around the concept of language games and the problematic of incommensurability between games that Lyotard derives from it. The form that Lyotard gives to this idea of an absence of measure is the postulate that the diversity of languages (including the diversity of ends informing them) cannot be reconciled at a higher logical level. Three different reasons are given to support this thesis. The least interesting, and the most dogmatically offered, is the argument that prescriptives cannot be derived from descriptives; by implication, prescriptives are understood here as operating at a higher level of generality than statements of fact, and what is denied is a relation of logical necessity between these two levels that could be extrapolated to a systematic framework which would then, in a reverse movement, control the world of events and behaviours. The second reason that Lyotard offers has to do with the impossibility of transcending what he calls 'story' or 'opinion'[7] in order to attain a mode of understanding that could not itself be objectified as story. The logic invoked here is that of the Gödelian paradox so crucial to poststructuralist thinking:

> The idea that a supreme genre encompassing everything that's at stake could supply a supreme answer to the key questions of the various genres founders upon Russell's aporia. Either this genre is part of the set of genres, and what is at stake in it is but one among others, and therefore its answer is not supreme. Or else, it is not part of the set of genres, and it does not therefore encompass all that is at stake, since it excepts what is at stake in itself. . . . The principle of an absolute victory of one genre over the others has no sense.[8]

The third reason is ethico-political rather than logical. It is an argument that the postulate of an integrating metadiscourse represents an attempt to impose discursive homogeneity where there not only is but ought to be heterogeneity. Far from constituting a problem, the diversity of language games is a prerequisite for the openness of the social system; conversely, the achievement of a 'consensus' – and therefore of an end to discussion – would represent a form of violence (or 'terror') done to the dynamic of social argument. Two points are worth noting here: first, that Lyotard's refusal of the possibility of deriving ethics and justice from the principles of a 'universal' reason is explicitly linked to a rejection of the privilege of intellectuals;[9] and second, that the values underlying the emphasis on open-ended political/discursive systems – the values of inventiveness and of the unpredictability of moves – are those of a recognisably modernist aesthetics.

The arguments that Lyotard develops in this phase of his work seem to me to come to grief in two different ways. The first concerns the positivism that follows from the strict distinction between fact and value. This is perhaps most marked in those passages of The Post-Modern Condition that delineate the necessary separation between intellectual work ('positive knowledge') and political judgement (the purview of the 'practical subject'). The bluntest statement is this:

> The only role positive knowledge can play is to inform the practical subject about the reality within which the execution of the prescription is to be inscribed. It allows the subject to circumscribe the executable, or what it is possible to do. But the executory, what should be done, is not within the purview of positive knowledge. It is one thing for an undertaking to be possible and another for it to be just. Knowledge is no longer the subject, but in the service of the subject. . . . [It] has no final

legitimacy outside of serving the goals envisioned by the practical subject, the autonomous collectivity.[10]

The argument is taken up again in an ambivalent statement (at once scornful and
ironically detached) to the effect that it is power alone that (now? or always?)
legitimates knowledge, since power 'is not only good performativity, but also
effective verification and good verdicts. It legitimates science and the law on the
basis of their efficiency, and legitimates this efficiency on the basis of science and
law. It is self-legitimating, in the same way a system organised around performance maximisation seems to be' (47). And what is wrong with these statements,
and with their technocratic conception of knowledge, is that they directly con-
tradict Lyotard's own criticism of the 'positivism of efficiency' (54) by which
science is increasingly organised, and which is problematical for the simple but
devastating reason that scientific knowledge does not work according to a model
of a predictable input/output ratio fed through a stable system; the principle of
performativity is not conducive to the efficient production of knowledge, since the
latter depends precisely upon unpredictability.

The other area of contradiction has to do with the aporia inherent in any
absolute relativism. It is perhaps most evident in the text that directly explores the
possibility of a concept of justice 'without criteria', *Just Gaming*. The prescriptive
game of justice, says Lyotard, cannot and should not intrude in the games of narration or of description/denotation, since each is and should be autonomous of
the others. There is one crucial exception to this rule, however: the idea of justice 'intervenes inasmuch as these games are impure', that is, 'inasmuch as these
games are infiltrated by prescriptions'. This is a purely formal, regulatory intervention, however, the purpose of which is solely to maintain the specificity of
each game.[11] Its justification is that the 'justice of multiplicity' can be assured only
by 'a prescriptive of universal value', namely 'the observation of the singular justice of each game'. The obverse of this prescription is a prohibition on exceeding
the limits of the game by attempting to impose it on others.[12]

The tension between the value of singularity and the universally binding prescriptive that maintains it is, by the end of this book, drawn to its limit. As Samuel
Weber observes, 'the concept of absolute, intact singularity' remains 'tributary to
the same logic of identity that sustains any and all ideas of totality'; and 'the concern with "preserving the purity" and singularity "of each game" by reinforcing
its isolation from the others gives rise to exactly what was intended to be avoided:
"the domination of one game by another", namely, the domination of the prescriptive'.[13]

David Carroll has noted that

> the entire notion of language games (a notion which is based on the
> possibility of making clear distinctions among the various games) seems,
> if followed literally, to allow for no slippage between games and to
> exclude, as well, the possibility of games that do not fit into one

category alone . . . Lyotard argues strenuously against such slippage throughout *The Post-Modern Condition* and *Just Gaming* in order to preserve the heterogeneity of the discursive universe.[14]

The second 'phase' of Lyotard's later work (one that in part overlaps chronologically with the 'first') can be read as an attempt to overcome the insoluble problems that attach to any notion of *pure* heterogeneity, of *absolute* difference. Here, with the introduction of the concepts of the *différend* and of the genre of discourse, the question of the linkage (or 'slippage') between sentences displaces that of incommensurability – although the latter still remains the starting-point for Lyotard's thinking.

It is the greater flexibility given to Lyotard's understanding of discourse by the distinction between the regime of sentences (that is, types of speech act and the corresponding forms of modality) and the genre of discourse (the level of discourse at which sentences are linked together) that makes it possible for him to move beyond the apparent closure of the language game. At the level of the regime, sentences continue to be characterised as quite heterogeneous, both functionally (an exclamation, a question, a narrative are caught up in different games) and semantically ('for every sentence regime, there corresponds a mode of presenting a universe').[15] Translation between sentences belonging to different regimes is therefore not possible.[16] What is, however, not only possible but absolutely unavoidable is the linkage (*enchaînement*) of one sentence to another. The function of genres is to bring sentences that may belong to quite distinct regimes within the ambit of a single end, a single teleology. It does not follow from this, however, that the incommensurability between sentences is eliminated or reconciled, since 'another genre of discourse can inscribe it into another finality. Genres of discourse do nothing more than shift the differend from the level of regimens to that of ends.'[17] And this process of reinscription, of shifting 'ends', is in principle endless.

One way of describing the movement in Lyotard's thought that is sketched here would be to say that there is a passage from an ontology of the sentence to a pragmatics of the sentence – to a concern with the uses to which sentences are put. Rather than formulating a general rule about the necessary separation of language games, Lyotard describes a process which encompasses both the practical commensuration of sentences as they are tied together by a discursive *telos*, and the endless dissociation of sentences as they are put to conflicting uses (or as there is conflict over the uses to which they may be put). This is to say that commensuration is possible (and is a practical necessity) not at the level of a metadiscourse that would somehow reconcile the semantic and pragmatic tensions between sentences, but at the more limited, 'local', and always contested level of the genre. It is not that there is no metadiscourse, but that there is a plurality of them. If this conclusion ends by restating the problem of the lack of measure between distinct orders of knowledge and value (and if, as Connor notes, it continues to beg the question of the ground against which radical difference can be perceived),[18] it does so, nevertheless, no longer on the basis of an assertion of the self-contained purity of these orders, but in the recognition of the constant passage and the complex and conflictual transactions between them.

For Lyotard as for Wittgenstein, the entrenched separateness of language games is grounded in the specificity of the forms of life in which they are embedded.[19] What is at stake politically – at least for Lyotard – in this correlation is the irreducible diversity of human interests, and in particular a deep suspicion of any claim to represent a universally valid structure of interest – a claim typically made by the *particular* class of intellectuals.[20] But much hangs on the way these two orders of being are bound together (and, indeed, on the conceptual separation made between them in the first place).

The problem is that of the forms of unity and identity ascribed to social groups; it is a problem that has been particularly acute for cultural studies, with its habitual reliance on a sociological relativism. At the limit, if aesthetic texts and practices of knowledge are closely tied to shared forms of life, and if their force is purely relative to these forms, then they are deprived of all except the most limited cognitive power – since they have no hold over any other domain. There is no scope for challenging the givenness of a cultural order: if every social group, every valuing community or subculture produces only those texts that express and validate its way of life, there is no *strong* ground from which to argue for alternative forms of textuality or indeed alternative ways of life.

A more general objection to the relativisation of texts and codes of reading to communities, however, might be the organicism inherent in the notion of community itself: a concept that calls to mind the pre-industrial village rather than the abstract and highly mediated cultural spaces of the late twentieth century. The model of a plurality of valuing communities or subcultures is a model of a dispersed set of social clusters which are at once separate and self-contained; as John Guillory argues, the concept posits social identity as the basis for the solidarity of evaluation (and disagreement is therefore always *a priori* evidence of belonging to a different community: the argument is in this sense circular). Thus the concept of value cannot adequately account for differences of judgement *within* a valuing community, since it is used above all to 'exalt the difference of the community from other communities'.[21]

It is probably not, I think, any longer problematic to say that value is always *value-for*, always tied to some valuing group; what does raise a problem is the fact that in our world the boundaries of communities are always porous, since most people belong to many valuing communities simultaneously; since communities overlap; and since they are heterogeneous. Moreover, to tie texts to forms of life in this way assumes that texts enter exhaustively into their context, without residue, and without the possibility of further, unpredicted and perhaps unpredictable uses being made of them. The concept of community in cultural studies works as an *archè*, an organic and totalising origin.

Janice Radway speaks of the naturalisation of presence inherent in the

comparable concept of an empirical 'audience', and hence of the difficulty of theorising 'the dispersed, anonymous, unpredictable nature of the use of
mass-produced, mass-mediated cultural forms', where the receivers of such forms
'are never assembled fixedly on a site or even in an easily identifiable space' and
'are frequently not uniformly or even attentively disposed to systems of cultural
production, or to the messages they issue'.[22]

But rather than adopting her tactic of attempting an even more exhaustive
empirical analysis, a total ethnography, of 'the ever-shifting kaleidoscope of cultural circulation and consumption',[23] it seems to me more useful (and more
economical) to posit a mediating institutional mechanism to account for the
absence of any simple or necessary coincidence between social groups and the
structure of valuation.

The concept I want to propose is that of the *regime of value*, a semiotic institution generating evaluative regularities under certain conditions of use, and in
which particular empirical audiences or communities may be more or less fully
imbricated. Arjun Appadurai uses the concept in this sense to define the cultural
framework within which very variable investments are made in the exchange of
commodities. Adopting from Simmel the notion that economic value has no general existence but is always the particular result of 'the commensuration of two
intensities of demand', and that this commensuration takes the form of 'the
exchange of sacrifice and gain', he argues that it is thus exchange that underlies
the formation of value, and exchange occurs within specific regimes where
'desire and demand, reciprocal sacrifice and power interact to create economic
value in specific social situations'.[24] Regimes of value are mechanisms that permit
the construction and regulation of value-equivalence, and indeed permit cross-cul-
tural mediation. Thus the concept

> does not imply that every act of commodity exchange presupposes a com-
> plete cultural sharing of assumptions, but rather that the degree of value
> coherence may be highly variable from situation to situation, and from
> commodity to commodity. A regime of value, in this sense, is consistent
> with both very high and very low sharing of standards by the parties to
> a particular commodity exchange. Such regimes of value account for the
> constant transcendence of cultural boundaries by the flow of commodi-
> ties, where culture is understood as a bounded and localised system of
> meanings.
>
> (15)

The regime of value constitutes 'a broad set of agreements concerning what is
desirable, what a reasonable "exchange of sacrifices" comprises, and who is per-
mitted to exercise what kind of effective demand in what circumstances' (57); this
regulation is always political in its mediation of discrepant interests.

The concept is roughly similar to Tony Bennett's concept of the *reading formation*,
which is likewise used to bypass a sociological realism that would tie modes of

reading directly to social groups. The reading formation is a semiotic apparatus, a 'set of discursive and intertextual determinations that organise and animate the practice of reading, connecting texts and readers in specific relations to one another by constituting readers as reading subjects of particular types and texts as objects-to-be-read in particular ways'.[25] What this means is that neither texts nor readers have an existence independent of these relations; that every act of reading, and hence every act of ascribing value, is specific to the particular regime that organises it. Texts and readers are not separable elements with fixed properties but 'variable functions within a discursively ordered set of relations',[26] and apparently identical texts and readers will function quite differently within different regimes. Regimes of value are thus relatively autonomous of and have no directly expressive relation to social groups. The concept of regime thus expresses one of the fundamental theses of work in cultural studies: that no object, no text, no cultural practice has an intrinsic or necessary meaning or value or function; and that meaning, value, and function are always the effect of specific social relations and mechanisms of signification.

Judgements of value are always choices made within a particular regime. This is not to say that the regime determines which judgement will be made, but that it specifies a particular range of possible judgements, and a particular set of appropriate criteria; in setting an agenda, it also excludes certain criteria and certain judgements as inappropriate or unthinkable. Regimes therefore allow for disagreement, specifying the terms within which it can be enacted. Disagreement may also take place in the space of overlap between regimes, or between discrepant and non-intersecting regimes; but in a sense disagreement is only ever really possible where *some* agreement on the rules of engagement can be held in common.

If commensurability of criteria within a regime enables both concurrent and divergent judgements to be made, the incommensurability of criteria *between* regimes thus tends to preclude the possibility of productive exchange. Disagreement of this kind can be settled by an agreement to disagree, or by the attempt to impose one set of criteria over another. The latter has traditionally been the way of high culture and its institutions, if only because those institutions have had the power to do so; and the universalisation of high-cultural values may take the shape either of a discrediting of other criteria of value, or of an appropriation of those criteria.

The difficulties that arise from any attempt to avoid the politics of totalising judgement are often cast in terms of the philosophical dilemma of axiological (and, by implication, epistemological) relativism. At their core lies, I think, the anxiety generated by the fiction that is strategically posited by any politically informed relativism: the fiction that, in order to neutralise my own inevitable partiality, I should consider all domains of value to be *formally* equivalent. (This, it should be noted, is also the fiction put into place by any democratic electoral system: that, however passionately I may believe in the rightness of one party, I

must suspend this belief in order to recognise the formal right of any other political party to win power, and, conversely, to accept as politically legitimate the
possibility that my party will lose. This suspension of belief, for all its apparent
ordinariness in the established democracies, in fact involves a sophisticated politics of knowledge.[27]) What causes anxiety is a belief that recognition of the equal
right of other values to *formal* (but not necessarily substantive) respect implies that
all values or arguments must therefore be considered equally 'valid'; and that this
means that all arguments, by being held equal, are thus in some sense trivialised.
Arguments, on this reading, cannot be defended or adjudicated because there is
no possibility of winning an argument.

One response to this would be to elaborate a theory of what it means for an
argument or a value to be *locally* valid: that is, for it to be judged correct or incor-
rect within a specific and limited framework, where such a judgement is entirely
appropriate, but beyond which it ceases to hold any force. But Barbara Herrnstein
Smith is on stronger ground in refusing the terms of the dilemma altogether. If
the concepts of validity and objectivity, which continue to be presupposed by the
arguments against relativism, are rejected as vacuous, this by no means entails that
judgements of value cannot be evaluated and said to be better or worse (just as
Foucault's argument that judgements of truth and falsity are always generated
within a particular regime of truth does not mean that he himself will not make
such judgements within a particular regime). What is entailed is that judgements
of value and truth are relative to a social position of enunciation and to a set of
conditions of enunciation (which are not necessarily the same for each instance
of an utterance). 'Better' and 'worse' will be meaningful terms to the extent that
a framework of valuation is agreed, and that the authority of speakers is accepted,
at least provisionally, within it.

Nevertheless, neither of these responses confronts the question of how it is possible to make judgements across the boundaries of regimes. The analogy between
the strategic fictions deployed by axiological relativism and by political democracy
can perhaps serve to clarify the limits of the former, since these fictions belong
to a larger historical framework. Both the rational valuing subject and the citizen
endowed with rights and with formal equality before the law are aspects of the
bourgeois subject of legal contract, a figure that integrates the dimensions of rational economic calculation, ethical integrity, consistency of will over time, and
positional equality within and for the duration of the contractual framework.[28]
The figure of the bourgeois subject is neither a pure illusion nor a straightforward
social gain, since the formal equalities on which it is predicated are always systematically interwoven with, and work to conceal, structural inequalities in the
economic sphere and the actual control of the legal and political spheres by the
dominant class. Relativism of value and of knowledge is closely connected with –
and is perhaps even a logical extrapolation from – this structure of formal equality; and this connection, which is formally 'progressive', indicates both its political
usefulness (it is not a position from which we can ever afford to retreat, out of
nostalgia for a social order, past or future, free of these fictions), and its

limitations. In so far as cognitive relativism posits a plurality of equivalent spheres, it necessarily fails to conceive of inequalities and asymmetries between these spheres (and therefore leaves the existing distribution of power untouched); and it is likely to conceptualise valuing communities in terms of self-contained positional identities, such that difference is posited between rather than within spheres of value.

In order to move beyond the limitations of relativism (which does not mean the reinstatement of some non-positional perspective), it becomes necessary to redefine the notion of positionality itself, together with the notion of representation on which it depends. The crucial argument here, it seems to me, is the one that follows when regimes of value are detached from a directly expressive relation to a social community. To speak is then never quite the same thing as 'to express the interests of' or 'to stand for' a particular group. At the same time, the dissociation of regime from group means that it is likely that members of any group will belong to more than one regime of value. This is particularly the case with 'cultural' intellectuals, who are specifically trained in the ability to switch codes, to move readily between different practices of reading and of valuation.

Two sets of questions branch out from these difficult and intricate problems of positionality. The first is a set of practical difficulties within the cultural institutions. Given the fact (if this is conceded) of incommensurability between different regimes of value, and given the intense social interests that play around these fractures and asymmetries, how is it possible for judgements of value to be applied in the routine and everyday manner required by school and university curricula, by editorial decision-making, by decisions about arts funding and research funding, and by the exhibition of artefacts? What gets floor-space and wall-space in the museum and the gallery? What gets discussed in the arts pages of the newspapers and magazines? What do we teach our students: the canonical texts (whose authority they cannot fight against because they do not know them)? Non-canonical texts (and do not these then become precisely an alternative *canon*)?[29] Some mix of the two – and if so, then according to which criteria do we choose?[30] Is it *practically* possible, as Steven Connor proposes, to live with 'the paradoxical structure of value as immanent transcendence',[31] a system of contingent universals – and indeed, is it 'practically' possible not to?[32] These are questions not just about criteria, but about whose stories get told, and, crucially, about who gets to make these decisions, who does not, and on what grounds.

The second set of questions is separate from but directly connected to the first set. They are ethical and political questions: Who speaks? Who speaks for whom? Whose voice is listened to, whose voice is spoken over, who has no voice? Whose claim to be powerless works as a ruse of power? Under what circumstances is it right or wrong, effective or ineffective, to speak for others? And how can relations of enunciative power – which by definition are shifting and situational – adequately be described?

An essay by Linda Alcoff may serve as a point of entry to these questions of representation (in both senses of the word). In 'The Problem of Speaking for Others'[33] Alcoff casts the question of representation in terms of enunciative modality, the relation between social position and the semantics of utterance. Beginning with the 'growing recognition that where one speaks from alters the truth of what one says, and thus that one cannot assume an ability to transcend one's location', she then extends this on the one hand to the argument that 'the practice of privileged persons speaking for or on behalf of less privileged persons has actually resulted (in many cases) in increasing or reinforcing the oppression of the group spoken for' (6–7), and on the other hand (shifting from persons to discursive positions) to the thesis that 'certain contexts and locations are allied with structures of oppression, and certain others are allied with resistance to oppression. Therefore all are not politically equal, and, given that politics is connected to truth, all are not epistemically equal' (15).

Alcoff's aim is to produce something like an ethics, or an ethico-politics, of speaking. Her argument is complicated, however, by the collapse, during the course of the essay, of the solidity of the concept of position (or 'context' or 'social location'). Thus she concedes that the notion of social location cannot be used as an index of determinant origin, since speakers can never be said to be fully in control of the meanings of utterances, and certainly have little control over the uses that are made of them. To be an 'author' is not to be the source of an utterance, but rather to be credited as its source; and the import of an utterance cannot be deduced simply from its propositional content or from the enunciative position or credentials of its speaker, since the utterance will also generate an open-ended chain of effects that is not reducible to those two moments.

In order to retrieve from this concession some of the force of the concept of enunciative modality – but also to guard against the converse danger of the reduction of meaning to position – Alcoff introduces a more qualified model of the semantics of context: location 'bears on' meaning and truth rather than determining them, and it is multiple and mobile. The act of speaking from within a group is consequently 'immensely complex. To the extent that location is not a fixed essence, and to the extent that there is an uneasy, underdetermined, and contested relationship between location on the one hand and meaning and truth on the other, we cannot reduce evaluation of meaning and truth to a simple identification of the speaker's location' (16–17).

Moreover, even so far as the thesis linking a privileged right and competence to speak with symbolic oppression holds good, the appropriate response to this link is not necessarily to abdicate from speaking for others. For two reasons: first, because this 'assumes that one can retreat into one's own discrete location and make claims entirely and singularly based on that location that do not range over others'; and second, because 'even a complete retreat from speech is of course not neutral since it allows the continued dominance of current discourses and acts by omission to reinforce their dominance' (18). Whereas the act of speaking for others denies those others the right to be the subjects of their own speech, the refusal to speak on behalf of the oppressed, conversely, assumes that they are in a position to act as such fully empowered subjects.

Alcoff's argument here follows closely that of Gayatri Spivak in 'Can the Subaltern Speak?',[34] where, taking issue with Foucault and Deleuze's influential remarks on the 'fundamental . . . indignity of speaking for others',[35] she argues that any invocation of the oppressed as self-representing and 'fully in control of the knowledge of their own oppression' (274) serves to effect a double concealment: on the one hand, of the fact that these self-representing oppressed are still (since they are *invoked* to play a role) a fact of discourse, a representation; and, on the other, of the role of intellectuals in constructing this self-negating representation, their representation of themselves as transparent. There can be no simple refusal of the role of judge or of universal witness, since to do so is to denegate the institutional conditions, consequences, and responsibilities of intellectual work.

The particular circumstances under which it is appropriate or inappropriate to represent the interests of others, and to attempt to bracket off one's own interests in the process, are of course always complex and contingent; precisely because of the complexity of the category of position. What Alcoff's argument usefully does, however, is move away from a naïve realism of social positionality towards a more differentiated politics of enunciation.

The problem with tying an utterance to social position or social 'identity' is that the latter tends to act as (or to be taken as) something fully external to discourse, the place of the Real *as against* the discursive. But position and identity are discursively realised and imagined; and they are shifting and multiple. Speaking positions, and the authority (or lack of it) that accompanies them, are, however, powerful and very real discursive *effects*. By this I mean that they are the effects of discursive institutions of authorisation which selectively credit the speaker with membership of one or more speech communities and with a place on one or more hierarchies of authority and credibility. They are not effects, that is to say, of 'objective' social position, but of an imputed position; they are moments of a semiotic politics, not reflections of a political reality that takes place elsewhere.[36]

There is no point of leverage *outside* the politics of representation, only an endless and unequal negotiation of relations of power within it (and within its institutions, which are largely controlled but not owned by the knowledge class). The determinations operating on the rights of 'cultural' intellectuals to speak for others are twofold, and pull in contradictory directions. The first (an enabling condition) is the 'uneasiness' of the relation between group and speaker, the slight but significant detachment of speaking position from *representation* of a speech community (in the sense of standing for it, sharing its characteristics). I have used the concept of regime of value to theorise this partial detachment. Like the infinitesimal swerve of Lucretius's atoms, it is this gap that allows the universe of discourse to be at once rule-governed and open-ended. The second determination is their membership of a social class with real, though ambivalent, class interests in the implementation of modernity. The privileged possession of cultural capital translates into an exercise of power that can well take the form of an apparent self-negation or self-abasement.

'Culture is our specific capital', says Bourdieu, 'and, even in the most radical probing, we tend to forget the true foundation of our specific power, of the particular form of domination we exercise.'[37] In seeking to place the work of cultural intellectuals in the framework of a class formation and a set of more or less definite class interests, I have sought to make this work less transparent, and so to take seriously the ways in which it might further the knowledge class's own interests rather than those of the groups for whom intellectuals claim to speak, or any more universal interest.

The question of our relation to regimes of value is not a personal but an institutional question. A key condition of any institutional politics, however, is that intellectuals not denegate their own status as possessors of cultural capital; that they accept and struggle with the contradictions that this entails; and that their cultural politics, right across the spectrum of cultural texts, should be openly and without embarrassment presented as their politics, not someone else's.

NOTES

1 This essay draws on material first presented in my book, *Cultural Studies and Cultural Value*, Oxford, Oxford University Press, 1995.

2 J. Lotman, *The Structure of the Artistic Text*, trans. R. Vroon, Michigan Slavic Contributions No. 7, Ann Arbor, University of Michigan Press, 1977, pp. 289–93.

3 c.f. J. Fekete, 'Introductory Notes for a Postmodern Value Agenda', in J. Fekete (ed.), *Life After Postmodernism: Essays on Value and Culture*, New York, St Martin's Press, 1987, p. viii.

4 J. Clifford, 'Introduction: Partial Truths', in J. Clifford and G. Marcus (eds), *Writing Culture: The Poetics and Politics of Ethnography*, Berkeley, University of California Press, 1986, p. 15.

5 Z. Bauman, *Legislators and Interpreters: On Modernity, Postmodernity and Intellectuals*, Cambridge, Polity Press, 1987, pp. 3–4.

6 G. Bennington, *Lyotard: Writing the Event*, Manchester, Manchester University Press, 1988, p. 117: 'Once the libidinal language is recognised as essentially that (a language), and can in principle become one more *dispositif* rather than a general ground of explanation for all *dispositifs*, then a general field of "façons de parler" is opened up, which might be described in terms of a generalised rhetoric.'

7 c.f. J.-F. Lyotard and J. Thébaud, *Just Gaming*, trans. W. Godzich, Theory and History of Literature, Vol. 20, Minneapolis, University of Minnesota Press, 1985, p. 43: 'We are always within opinion, and there is no possible discourse of truth on the situation. And there is no such discourse because one is caught up in a story, and one cannot get out of this story to take up a metalinguistic position from which the whole could be dominated. We are always immanent to stories in the making, even when we are the ones telling the story to the other.'

8 J.-F. Lyotard, *The Differend: Phrases in Dispute*, trans. G. Van den Abbeele, Theory and History of Literature, Vol. 46, Minneapolis, University of Minnesota Press, 1988, p. 138.

9 Lyotard, *Just Gaming*, p. 74; cf. also the title essay in J.-F. Lyotard, *Tombeau de l'intellectuel et autres papiers*, Paris, Galilée, 1984.

10 J.-F. Lyotard, *The Post-Modern Condition: A Report on Knowledge*, trans. G. Bennington and B.

Massumi, Theory and History of Literature, Vol. 10, Minneapolis, University of Minnesota Press, 1984, p. 36. Further references are given in the text.

11 Lyotard, Just Gaming, p. 96.

12 ibid., p. 100.

13 S. Weber, 'Afterword: Literature – Just Making It', in Lyotard, Just Gaming, pp. 103–4.

14 D. Carroll, Paraesthetics: Foucault, Lyotard, Derrida, New York, Methuen, 1987, p. 162.

15 Lyotard, The Differend, p. 128; I have modified the translation by replacing the word 'phrase' with 'sentence'.

16 In Just Gaming (pp. 53–4) Lyotard makes the distinction that 'languages are translatable, otherwise they are not languages; but language games are not translatable, because if they were, they would not be language games. It is as if one wanted to translate the rules and strategies of chess into checkers.' This makes it clear, of course, that non-translatability is part of the definition of language games.

17 Lyotard, The Differend, p. 29.

18 S. Connor, Theory and Cultural Value, Oxford, Blackwell, 1992, p. 112.

19 There is a useful genealogy of the term Lebensformen as Wittgenstein found it 'in the air' in Vienna (most immediately among the neo-Kantian characterologists) in A. Janik and S. Toulmin, Wittgenstein's Vienna, New York, Simon & Schuster, 1973, p. 230 ff.

20 In a discussion of racism, Immanuel Wallerstein has made an explicit claim that the value of universality is specific to the small class of 'cadres', whereas 'by assuming a particularist stance – whether of class, of nation or of race – the working strata are expressing an instinct of self-protection against the ravages of a universalism that must be hypocritical within a system founded both on the permanence of inequality and on the process of material and social polarisation'. E. Balibar and I. Wallerstein, Race, Nation, Class: Ambiguous Identities, London and New York, Verso, 1991, p. 230. I think it is possible to accept that this argument is correct without thereby being driven to abandon all aspiration to the achievement of 'universal' values.

21 J. Guillory, Cultural Capital: The Problem of Literary Canon Formation, Chicago, University of Chicago Press, 1993, p. 278.

22 J. Radway, 'Reception Study: Ethnography and the Problems of Dispersed Audiences and Nomadic Subjects', Cultural Studies, vol. 2, no. 3, 1988, p. 361.

23 ibid.

24 A. Appadurai, 'Introduction: Commodities and the Politics of Value', in A. Appadurai (ed.), The Social Life of Things: Commodities in Cultural Perspective, Cambridge, Cambridge University Press, 1986, p. 4.

25 T. Bennett, 'Texts in History: The Determinations of Readings and Their Texts', Journal of the Midwest Modern Language Association, vol. 18, no. 1, 1985, p. 7.

26 ibid., p. 10.

27 c.f. A. Przeworski, Democracy and the Market: Political and Economic Reforms in Eastern Europe and Latin America, Cambridge, Cambridge University Press, 1991, p. 93. In making this analogy I do not want to downplay the extent to which political choice in most of the established democracies has become virtually meaningless.

28 c.f. B. Mensch, 'Freedom of Contract as Ideology', Stanford Law Review, vol. 33, April 1981, pp. 753–72; R. Unger, The Critical Legal Studies Movement, Cambridge, Mass., Harvard University Press, 1986, p. 63 ff.

29 'What should have been clear before now is that the canonising effect does not in the least require a stable corpus of works in which to be embodied. Since canonisation depends not on what one says about texts, so much as where one says it from, there is no real reason why a postmodernist world of shifting or open canons need do anything to the canonising effect of discourses within institutions, except perhaps to make them ideologically more subtle and inconspicuous.' S. Connor, 'The Modern and the Postmodern as History', Essays in Criticism, vol. 37, no. 3, 1987, p. 188; cf. J. Guillory, 'Canonical and Non-Canonical: A Critique of the Current Debate', ELH, vol. 54, no. 3,

1987, p. 519: 'The movement to open or expand the canon is, among other things, an attempt to save the bourgeois sociolect by expanding its base of textual representation'.

30 For an extended analysis of the problems that arise from such basic pedagogic questions, cf. C. Brunsdon, 'Problems With Quality', *Screen*, vol. 31, no. 1, 1990, pp. 67–90.

31 Connor, *Theory and Cultural Value*, p. 33.

32 c.f. ibid., p. 2: 'It is both the desire for an absolute grounding of political practice, and the attempt to imagine a political practice without grounding, which are hopelessly impractical and unresponsive to the practical complexity attaching to questions of value.'

33 L. Alcoff, 'The Problem of Speaking for Others', *Cultural Critique*, no. 20, 1991–2, pp. 5–32; further references will be given in the text.

34 G. C. Spivak, 'Can the Subaltern Speak?', in C. Nelson and L. Grossberg (eds), *Marxism and the Interpretation of Culture*, Urbana, University of Illinois Press, 1988, pp. 271–313.

35 'Intellectuals and Power: A Conversation Between Michel Foucault and Gilles Deleuze', in M. Foucault, *Language, Counter-Memory, Practice*, trans. D. Bouchard and S. Simon, Ithaca, NY, Cornell University Press, 1977, p. 209.

36 I elaborate some of the political aspects of the distinction between knowing and being supposed to know in 'Discipline and Discipleship', *Textual Practice*, vol. 2, no. 3, 1988, pp. 307–23.

37 P. Bourdieu, *In Other Words: Essays Towards a Reflexive Sociology*, trans. M. Adamson, Stanford, CA, Stanford University Press, 1990, p. 107.

6

MULTICULTURALISM OR MULTINATIONALISM?

Maria Koundoura

THE CRISIS OF REPRESENTATION

As the 'crisis of representability' produced by what Homi Bhabha has called the 'jargon of the minorities' – identity politics, ethnic particularism, multiculturalism – takes hold of educational institutions, their response is, in Bhabha's words, 'either to generate anxiety around the threat to . . . the "common culture", or to "capitalize" on the changes by commodifying minority cultures into new disciplines and programs'.[1] Such a response, however, is not new. In the last decades of the nineteenth century, when the crisis of representation produced by the worker's demand for the franchise shook British political and cultural institutions, the response of two of the then leading intellectual figures was to argue, similarly, for more 'discipline'. J. S. Mill, responding to the crisis of political representation seen in the Parliamentary Reform debates of 1861, wrote *Considerations on Representative Government*. Matthew Arnold, responding to the Hyde Park riots of 1866, wrote *Culture and Anarchy*.[2] Showing the class interests that informed their positions, both responded to the demand for political representation by shifting the debate to the realm of cultural representation.[3] For Mill, only the 'minority of instructed minds', the 'elite of the country', are able – because of their 'moral power' – to prevent the 'natural tendency . . . [to move] toward collective mediocrity' that the extension of the franchise would hasten.[4] For Arnold, the men of culture, pursuing 'sweetness and light', unlike the representatives of classes (the Hyde Park rioters), are the 'true apostles' of equality. Men of culture scrape away economic, sectional and class identity, 'unite classes', and leave behind only the 'best knowledge and thought of the time' and, as a result, only the disinterested and thus 'best self'.[5] On this premise, Arnold argues that the state should represent its citizen's 'best self', and since the 'men of culture' are the representatives of this self, the state should represent culture.[6]

So influential was Mill's and Arnold's programme that the Newbolt Report of 1921, the first of a series of government reports on the teaching of English in England, incorporated it in its recommendation that English literature should take precedence over every other form of knowledge for English children.[7] The report appointed the teacher of English as the mediator between the state and its citizens in arguing that his or her role was to teach the student through self-example to want to do the right thing, to be his or her 'best self' and, as such, the 'best citizen'. English studies thus became the means through which national identity could pleasurably be confirmed in the individual. 'A feeling for our own native language would be a bond of union between classes, and would beget the right kind of national pride', the report argues in its introductory remarks, making the teaching of literature represent the socialising function of the school rather than a straightforward instruction in knowledge.[8]

Such is the history of the discipline from which multiculturalism as an educational policy – with its agenda of representing and teaching cultural difference – arises. It is also the methodological legacy that it aims to dislodge. Unfortunately, the history of the implementation of multiculturalism in the discipline of English studies shows us that disciplinary reform usually means more discipline(s). The rise of minority literatures (black, chicano, gay and lesbian, and so on) within North American English departments, the increasing number of jobs offered in these specialties, or, conversely, the conservative reaction to these moves in the form of a critique of the politics ·of representation, all testify to this. Whether in the name of maintaining the 'imagined community' of the nation or in the name of broadening the national imaginary through the representation of cultural difference, both of the above reactions summon an antiquarian iconography which – psychically, at least – promises to pull 'us' (the USA) away from the abyss and back to the imagined certainties of an earlier age. The case of Mill and Arnold shows us that those certainties were the product of a tough battle in which politics lost out to aesthetics. History thus comes to haunt current methodology and turn the political aims of this methodology into the brushstrokes with which history's own picture can be enlivened.

How can the implementation of multiculturalism avoid operating at the level of aesthetic representation – or the token showing of the many faces of the nation? How can the practice of multiculturalism avoid its commodification and inclusion in the socialising function of the school that has remained unchanged in its mission of begetting 'the right kind of national pride'? Under the logic of multiculturalism, whose 'national pride' would this be – given that different individuals and groups maintain different versions of the nation in their culture(s)? These are some of the questions that will be addressed in this essay.

Without wishing to seem to be arguing against the enfranchising objectives of multiculturalism, I will examine the projects of two of multiculturalism's most influential North American proponents, Gloria Anzaldúa and Henry Louis Gates, Jr, and argue that they unwittingly maintain the very structures that they seek to dismantle: the structures of 'uniculturalism' or, more specifically, the idea of a single yet diverse nation, a nation made up of particularities which none the less compose a totality ('e pluribus unum', as the American Constitution has it). I will argue that multiculturalism's calls for a 'democratic culture', a 'common culture', a 'radical culture' – one that would include all participants in the story of the nation – run the risk of becoming another transformation of liberal democracy's crisis-management of representation.[9] The premise of my argument lies in the following question: how can identities that are formed by, and are a part of, the political structure they seek to dismantle (the contemporary liberal pluralist heritage of Mill's representative government in most Western nation-states) be transformed concretely and specifically when the very terms of that transformation are dictated by that structure's abstract and universal promise of freedom?

In my critique of multiculturalism I do not want to jettison its political agenda of mobilising the concept of different cultures to question the image of the nation. I do, however, want to begin to imagine what the nation will look like in the light of the progressive commodification of a reified concept of culture (in various touristic, 'authentic', or nostalgic forms) manipulated and produced not only within the nation-state and its institutions but also within the complex cultural and economic processes of multinational capitalism.[10] I offer a theory of multinationalism as a means of resisting the single-nation-building project that is behind the concept of multiculturalism in the USA. By arguing that in Western history the concepts of nation and culture were shaped simultaneously, and by demonstrating the structural complicity between this history and contemporary narratives of the nation under multiculturalism, I hope to disrupt the teleological alibis of progress found in these narratives. My purpose here is to question canonical method (that of multiculturalism included) and to offer a different articulation of the multicultural nation that would accommodate its multiple cultural histories without resolving them into a unitary narrative of nationhood.

RIGHTS AND REPRESENTATION

Shifting between poetry, historical narrative, autobiography, philosophical speculation, fabulation, newspaper report and bureaucratic legalese, and all the while shifting repeatedly between English, Castillian Spanish, North Mexican dialect, Tex-Mex and a sprinkling of Nahuatl, Gloria Anzaldúa characterises her book *Borderlands: La Frontera* as an 'invitation to you – from the new mestizas'.[11] This invitation challenges the reader to cross the border of secure cultural, national and sexual identity and to recognise that the symbols of such unities – language, common culture, gender – are the tools through which cultural, national and sexual identities are both gathered and dispersed. Faced with the national, sexual and cultural crosser's task of finding a way of 'keeping intact one's shifting and multiple identity and integrity', her message in *Borderlands* is one of universal 'borderhood' made up of 'the queer white, Black, Asian, Native American, Latino', and of the 'queer in Italy, Australia and the rest of the planet': 'we come from all colors', she writes, 'all classes, all races, all time periods. Our role is to link people with each other.'[12]

Despite the obvious tension between this admirable project of linkage and the disjunctive languages and modes of address of her book, it is easy to salvage Anzaldúa's text for an apparent radicalism in which the policy of letting a thousand flowers bloom and a hundred schools of thought contend is treated as a liberating stance. It is important, however, to remember the history of such stances. The memory of that history reminds us of the dangers of the not long obsolete 'melting-pot' theory and the often and easily repeated mistakes of the Second and the Third Internationals, which subordinated culture, nation, race and gender to class.[13] When Anzaldúa calls for the 'queer of the world to unite' and to act as the unifying force, differences of class, nation, ethnicity, culture and sex – even though acknowledged – are superseded by the image of the universal unity of 'borderhood': the transnational, transhistorical, trans-sexual and transcultural 'link[age] of people with each other'. In the image of identity that this narrative invokes, the specificity of the 'border' becomes the general image of difference. The 'border' thus becomes a metaphor and, as a metaphor, it loses its particular national socio-political relevance and turns into a universal cultural symbol that hides the acts of nation that construct it (acts which here include American immigration policy and national economic and cultural policies towards Mexico and Mexican Americans). Political representation, then, is subsumed under the aesthetic (the border as metaphor) and such a joyous celebration of alterity as Anzaldúa's can be easily assimilated as another manifestation of the nation's unity: Borderlands can be and has been incorporated into the canon either as an act of tokenism or as an act of radical chic.

Such involuntary complicity is also found in the texts of critics such as Henry Louis Gates, Jr, whose admirable project in 'Authority, (White) Power and the (Black) Critic: or It's All Greek to Me' is to 'work through contemporary theories of literature not to "apply" them to black texts but rather to transform them by translating them into a new rhetorical realm', the realm of 'black idiom, renaming principles of criticism where appropriate, but especially naming indigenous black principles of criticism and applying these to explicate our own texts'.[14] Aware that to 'attempt to appropriate Western critical theory uncritically is to substitute one mode of neo-colonialism for another', and issuing a caution 'not to succumb to the tragic lure of white power, the mistake of accepting the empowering language of white critical theory as "universal" or as our own language', Gates nevertheless finishes his powerful essay by urging the black American (in DuBois's words) to '"know and test the power of the cabalistic letters of the white man", to know and test the dark secrets of a black and hermetic discursive universe that awaits its disclosure through the black arts of interpretation'.[15] Thus what begins as a critique of the sovereign subject's construction of itself as universal, and as a call to particularise the self-projection of the hegemonic discourse, turns in the end of Gates's argument into a universalising of the particular: the black arts of interpretation will disclose the 'hermetic discursive universe' of theory. In the DuBois reference and the play on images of dark and light, Gates's offer of the act of renaming as a strategy of empowerment, and his recommendation of a shift into the relative system of value of black theory, are undermined as black theory's use value is shifted yet again into the system of equivalence of theory in general. His bold encouragement to name indigenous principles of criticism, to do 'black theory' and not to succumb to the lure of ('unmarked') theory, turns into the defensive justification that black theory is just as good as any other theory. The presence of the black is thus placed at the centre of interpretation as the adjectives 'dark' and 'black' are applied both to the exclusionary discursive universe of interpretation and theory in general, and to black theory and interpretation in particular.

In light of the above reading, it appears that Gates, while arguing for the right of a group victimised in its particularity to be on equal terms with others as far as their self-determination is concerned, enacts a politics of difference and specificity in the cause of sameness and universal identity. He replicates in this way the core truth of the Enlightenment: the abstract universal right of all to be free, or autonomy as the shared essence of all human subjects. Remembering Horkheimer and Adorno's critique of the Enlightenment and postcolonial criticism's unmasking of the elaborate strategies of domination involved in its institutionalisation, we cannot ignore the ideology behind the enunciation of the fiction of 'truths' such as 'liberty' and 'autonomy'.[16] By situating the 'black arts of interpretation' in the context of the Derridean 'always already' presence of difference in Western theoretical discourse, Gates turns these arts into latecomers despite his rhetorical placement of them at the origin of theory. In this culturally empowering Afrocentric move, he ignores his own warning and falls victim to 'the tragic lure of white power', and the 'originality' of the 'black arts of interpretation' is declared in the unspoken name of theory. As such, this declaration is catachrestic: wrested from its proper meaning as a declaration of independence from theory, its origin is secured from an 'other' place which, ironically in this case, is theory itself. Thus the 'black arts of interpretation', with which Gates aims to constitute a new political and aesthetic structure, are formed by and within the political and aesthetic structure that he seeks to dismantle.

Seen in this light, it is obvious how the political and aesthetic representational objectives of multiculturalism can unwittingly become part of the crisis-management of uniculturalism, and texts such as Anzaldúa's, Gates's essay, and this essay end up becoming tools through which the dominant culture can maintain the status quo. The slow labour of acknowledging this complicity, marking the ethico-political agenda that informs one's project in keeping the terms unicultural and multicultural distinct, and taking an interested stand in order to bring theoretical meticulousness to crisis, might transform this kind of project from opposition to critique. 'Opposition' would contend for the inherent value of multiculturalism. But my concern is not with its intrinsic 'goodness' or 'badness', such moralistic terms of debate being grounded in the 'natural' truth of the Enlightenment 'right' mentioned above. It is precisely in terms of this right that most debates on multiculturalism are now staged, and it is this right that I propose to question for multiculturalism.

NEGOTIATING CULTURE AND NATION: THE
HISTORY OF A TRANSFORMATION

The concept of nation and an awareness of nationhood were first legitimated in the period of the French Revolution. Lynn Hunt, in her book *Politics, Culture, and Class in the French Revolution*, argues that the political culture of the Revolution was made up of symbolic practices such as language, imagery and gestures, which did not simply reflect the realities of revolutionary changes and conflicts but rather were themselves formed into instruments of political and social change. She gives the following explanation of the French legitimation of the idea of the nation:

> Revolutionary rhetoric got its textual unity from the belief that the French were founding a new nation. The Nation and the Revolution were constantly cited as points of reference, but they came with no history. . . . The new community of American radicals was a living tradition; Americans had always inhabited a 'new world' far from what they saw as the corruption of English politics. The English radicals referred to the purer community of their Saxon and dissenting pasts. French revolutionary rhetoric had nothing similar . . . [so] they harkened to a 'mythic present', the instant of creation of the new community, the sacred moment of the new consensus.[17]

Hunt's study shows the effects of this political move: it denies history; politics become inadmissible as a way of negotiating social conflict; civil society and the state merge into one realm of a general will and rational freedom; individuals as nationalised subjects become, not a diverse and hierarchical mixture of different manners and customs, but transparent to and equal to each other; and a whole range of symbolic practices enters into the public sphere: the wearing of liberty caps, planting liberty trees, images of the Republic as Marianne, carnivals and so on.[18] Thus signifiers were found to fill empty signifieds and imbue them with meaning, a meaning that was metaleptically constructed in order to hide the politics behind 'nation as natural'.

Noticing the lack of a definition of 'the people', J. S. Mill was the first English thinker to address the French Revolution's model of popular self-determination. His linkage of the idea of nationality with government in *Considerations on Representative Government* – a publication that, after discussing different forms of government and offering representative government as the ideal, addresses the question of nationality and offers ways in which the two can blend – was instrumental in legitimising the equation, nation = state = people, and linking the idea of the nation to territory, hence defining the nation-state.

Mill's criteria of nationality are 'identity of race and descent . . . community of language and community of religion . . . geographical limits . . . [and] the strongest of all, identity of political antecedents' (308). In an effort to clarify the connection between nation and state, he offers a set of values that determine and define the people. The most important of these, and one that he finds existing 'naturally' among the English (59), is the people's 'virtue and intelligence', which, if fostered by the government, can be increased (39). Government's desire and ability 'to increase the sum of good qualities in the governed collectively and individually' are a sign of its virtue and intelligence (40).[19] Believing that 'the character of a government or set of political institutions cannot be sufficiently estimated while we confine our attention to the legitimate sphere of governmental functions' (26), Mill offers education as the means of negotiating the sensitive ideological point between the people and the official state. Education, he writes, is one of the 'foremost benefits of free government' (170), and, connecting politics and pedagogy, he continues: 'unless substantial mental cultivation is to be a mere vision', the exercise of political franchise by manual labourers 'is the road by which it must come' (170–1). Later, he reverses this prioritisation: 'if society has neglected to discharge two solemn obligations, the more important and fundamental of the two must be fulfilled first; universal teaching must precede universal enfranchisement' (175).

Education and political representation are thus clearly connected. The reason for Mill's prioritisation of education over the franchise is found in his theory of government and institutions:

> The national institutions should place all things that they are concerned with before the mind of the citizen in the light in which it is for his good that he should regard them; and it is for his good that he should think that every one is entitled to some influence, but the better and the wiser to more than others; it is important that this conviction should be professed by the state, and embodied in the national institutions. Such things constitute the *spirit* of the institutions of a country. . . . [Institutions] produce more effect by their *spirit* than by any of their direct provisions, since by it they shape the national character.
>
> (188–9)

It is clear here that Mill's emphasis on the importance of political antecedents in his definition of nationality originates from a desire to construct the political antecedents that would halt the 'national decline' and prescribe the course of the future of the nation (59). Such a project, he understands, can only be successful when popular education educates the people for no other state but 'that which it will induce them to desire, and most probably to demand' (63).[20] 'State' functions quite ambiguously here since all of its definitions are being invoked: temperament, position, and polity. This ambiguity is not accidental when one remembers that Mill's criteria of good government are the virtue and the intelligence of the people and the ability of the political institutions to form that virtue and intelligence. For Mill, the intelligent 'elite of the country', because of that superiority of mind which enables them to transcend class affiliations, are the best representatives and the only ones who can be trusted to shape the institutions that shape the state that, in turn, shapes the institutions that shape value. Culture, and the political antecedents created with it, thus define the nation (no matter that the nation's definition becomes the means through which class can either be ignored or lauded as the nation's saviour).

This is the argument at the heart of *Considerations on Representative Government*. This argument, however, which serves as a solution to the problems in England's political institutions at the time, unfortunately becomes the logic on which arguments like the following are based:

> Nobody can suppose that it is not more beneficial to a Breton, or a Basque of French Navarre, to be brought into the current of ideas and feelings of a highly civilized and cultivated people – to be a member of the French nationality, admitted on equal terms to all the prestiges of French citizenship, sharing the advantages of French protection, and the dignity and prestige of French power – than to sulk on his own rocks, the half-savage relic of past times, revolving in his own little mental orbit, without participation or interest in the general movement of the world. The same remark applies to the Welshman or the Scottish Highlander as members of the British nation. . . . Whatever really tends to the admixture of nationalities, and the blending of their attributes and peculiarities in a common union, is a benefit to the human race.
>
> (314)

Culture, as it is seen in this passage and in Mill's text as a whole, allows for the production of a normative temporality that places unequally constructed contestants against each other. The Breton nationality is made up of archaic 'relics' living in a monumental or universal time made particular in its abstractedness, and it is backward-moving or at best static, 'revolving in [its] own little mental orbit'. The French nationality's particular time, on the other hand, is made universal and concrete, world-historical and forward-moving, enjoying prestige and involved 'in the general movement of the world'. By necessity the two can never coincide, unless 'whatever really tends to the admixture of nationalities . . . [and] is a benefit to the human race' is identified. This 'whatever', which seems so vague here, is something that the rest of *Representative Government* is very clear about: it is the political institutions that define the nation. The 'more civilized' nation uses these institutions as markers of time and progress. Thus Mill writes: 'A community can only be developed out of one of these states [the state of being archaic 'relics'] into a higher by a concourse of influences, among the principal of which is the government to which they are subject' (46).

Knowing that 'any minority left out, either purposely or by the play of the machinery, gives the power not to a majority, but to a minority in some part of the scale' (148), and wanting to avoid 'anarchy', Mill proposes a scale of representation in government for the various nationalities involved. Race is the determining factor in this representation: those in a lower scale of civilisation and those in a higher scale of civilisation 'cannot live together under the same free institutions' (316). White colonies have 'the service of government in all its departments' open to them (344); all others have well-trained intermediaries to represent their interests (345, 357). In order for these representatives to be of service, both to their immediate constituency and to the central government, 'the system must be calculated to form them'. Thus we are back to the central treatment of representation (both political and aesthetic) as a formal programme that shapes the imagined community of the nation through culture.

This argument is metaleptically echoed in contemporary debates on culture, nation and difference. Henry A. Giroux, for example, follows Mill in linking education with political representation and offering education as the means of negotiating the sensitive ideological point between the people and the state. In his article 'Post-Colonial Ruptures and Democratic Possibilities: Multiculturalism as Anti-Racist Pedagogy', Giroux urges 'cultural workers and educators' to 'shape history within rather than outside of a political imaginary in which differences are both affirmed and transformed as part of a broader struggle for a radical, cultural democracy'.[21] He offers the concept of 'border pedagogy' as a model of teaching that, unlike the unicultural model, is grounded in 'the imperatives of a radical public philosophy that respects the notion of difference as part of a common struggle to extend the quality of democratic public life' (32). Teachers practising border pedagogy through self-example – by demonstrating to students through their own behaviour the role that the latter should take as critical citizens – are the instruments through which self-government and representative government are taught. Giroux writes:

> If students are going to learn how to take risks, to develop a healthy skepticism toward all master narratives, to recognize the power relations that offer them the opportunity to speak in particular ways, and to be willing to confront critically their role as critical citizens who can animate a democratic culture, they need to see such behavior demonstrated in the social practices and subject-positions that teachers live out and not merely propose.
>
> (32–3)

This pedagogical method, Giroux suggests, 'redefines not only teacher authority and student responsibility, but places the school as a major force in the struggle for social, economic, and cultural justice' (33).

For Giroux, the school is the place where students are educated to 'animate a wider and more critically engaged public culture'; it is thus a significant 'public force for linking learning and social justice to the daily institutional and cultural traditions of society and reshaping them in the process' (33). Thus the school, and the reading of literature (now in the form of narratives of difference and not 'great works'), is still the place where our 'ethical' and 'best self' is animated; it is the place where the socialising function is represented.

In Giroux's impassioned and admirable work, one can see that contemporary demands have changed but that the role of 'English studies' in its revised form as 'border pedagogy' remains the same. Now, as then, a technē of self is taught, one in which self-government and, as a consequence, representative government are pre-eminent: the students are helped to recognise 'their own historical locations and subject positions' and with this recognition they must become agents, representatives, and 'shape history within rather than outside of a political imaginary'. Culture in Giroux, as in Mill and in Arnold, is associated with history and politics, that is, with the state, a state that includes and affirms differences, as it transforms them, through its educational institutions. This association of culture and state takes place within the 'broader struggle for a radical, cultural democracy', a struggle of which it is a 'part' (35). The 'part', however, contains within it the whole; the cultural technology of border pedagogy, Giroux tells us, contains within it 'cultural democracy', which, in turn, contains another whole: the nation whose borders are mysteriously left untouched despite border pedagogy's claim that it wants to transform them.[22] Thus culture and, in particular, education remain the means of negotiating the sensitive ideological point between the people and the state in order to confirm the idea of the nation.

This version of the nation, unlike Arnold's and Mill's, is inclusive and contains as it transforms difference: it 'shape[s] history within rather than outside of a political imaginary in which differences are both affirmed and transformed'. Giroux thus differentiates border pedagogy's notion of ethics and culture from the Arnoldian notion of culture as inherently ethical, since Giroux's definition and practice of culture contains rather than excludes such social facts as gender, race, class, knowledge, power. Border pedagogy 'makes primary the language of the political and the ethical'; it places itself with 'those who care for the other in his/her otherness and [not] with those who do not'; hence, Giroux argues, its cultural technology is valuable because it is moral and ethical (24).

I do not want to be seen as arguing against ethics when I stress here that culture and value have a long history in the conservative arena: they can be quite slippery terms when one is forgetful of that history and uses them carelessly in the politics of the struggle for a 'radical democracy'. If border pedagogy's cultural technology − proffered as the alternative to the conservative arguments on culture − ignores this history, its practitioners may end up organising subjects (both human and academic) which exist only in the ideal image of their own rhetoric. At the same time, in addressing the question of culture and value and laying claim to value without addressing the nation-building history of such formulations (Mill and Arnold), those of us who are interested in multiculturalism and its practice cannot but implicate ourselves in the normative temporality set up by the discourse on culture that critics of postcoloniality expose for its racism. Remembering culture's tradition in nation-building, particularly in and through the history of the educational institution(s) of English studies, we the teachers and practitioners of border pedagogy must examine our role as midwives in the birth of the nation, whether uni- or multicultural.

In order for border pedagogy to refine its cultural technology, a technology with which I am ultimately in full sympathy, its practitioners must realise that a more complicated relationship exists between ethics, politics and pedagogy. The kind of educational training that I have outlined in Mill (and briefly in Arnold) was, at its inception, a political tool to construct model citizens of the state's vision of the nation. If we do not realise this and if we do not accept our complicity in maintaining this training's history, literary education will remain the place where moral behaviour and national identity are de facto defined as being interdependent. If its implication in the history of nationalism is not remembered, 'English', or the more generally used 'literature', will remain the privileged conservative paradigm of ethical education, a paradigm that will turn such liberal ideas as 'democratic culture', 'cultural democracy', and 'common culture' (a term still used by cultural critics despite its Leavisite heritage) into expressions of nationalist sentiment not unlike those found in their political antecedents: the nation and culture debates in Mill and Arnold, and earlier, in the French Revolution. If we do not remember this history, our multicultural critiques of the dominant culture are in danger of becoming precisely such antecedents for the continuing definition of a nation whose boundaries we want to remap.

MULTICULTURALISM AT THE ORIGIN

Australia, a country that is both postcolonial and multicultural and (along with Canada) a country where multiculturalism was first instituted as state policy, provides the USA with a strong example of the shifting definition of the history of the 'nation' from Revolutionary France to nineteenth-century England and of the problematic 'forgetful' remapping described above. In 1987 the Committee to Review Australian Studies at Tertiary Level reported on ways to 'enhance citizenship, patriotism and nationalism; secure a productive culture; increase international awareness; bring intellectual enrichment and lead to cultural broadening'. However, in this report, the aim of 'understanding and studying the cultures from which all and not only Anglo-Celtic Australians come' was cited under the goal of 'increasing international awareness' and not under 'enhancing citizenship, patriotism and nationalism'.[23] It would seem that 'foreigners' are granted international status and not citizenship, even though legally they have citizenship as either naturalised Australians like myself (a Greek-Australian now doubly migrated in the USA) or second- or third-generation 'migrants'. When the report cites multiculturalism under the rubric of 'broadening cultural concerns', it is only to point out that Australia was always a multicultural society, not merely since the 1970s when multiculturalism was adopted as official policy. Aborigines, we are told, were multicultural since they had such 'disparate' ways of life and so many distinct languages. Non-Aborigines were disparate too: there were Germans, Chinese, and Pacific Islanders; the 'British component' was made up of 'Scotch, Irish, Welsh and Cornish communities'. And this section of the report concludes: 'One benefit from recent multi-cultural policies has been to restore to all Australians an appreciation of our diverse heritage whose recognition is one further guarantee that Australian studies will be culturally broadening'.[24] The subtext here is that, since we have always been multicultural, there is no need to worry about producing proper policies that reflect the true multicultural nature of Australia. Instead, we will institute the symbolic practices of the rhetoric of multiculturalism: the teaching of 'community' languages and literatures (but only as an extra-curricular activity) and the promotion of public imagery and gestures such as multicultural festivals and media representations of the always-already multicultural Australia.

The difference between this scenario of national origins and that of the French Revolution is that whereas in the French Revolution there was a willingness to break from the past because there was no revolutionary tradition on which to build, Australia, like the USA, was living a long tradition of dissension precisely because it inhabited a 'new world'. This has been and is the myth of the 'New World', with all its gestures of Adamic innocence, utopian freedom and new beginnings. History, however, in the form of the Wakefield project, again proves this to be a cultural-nationalist myth. It was on the Wakefield project of colonisation (of which Mill was a strong advocate) that white English colonies were founded: transportation expenses were paid for out of the economic surplus generated in the colonies by the transported labour whose cheapness was what encouraged capitalists to emigrate and export their old-world capital to the 'new world'.[25]

The Wakefield project tradition, now in the form of post-World War II accumulation and expansion, was also responsible for the policies that generated the later Southern and Middle European immigration streams: some of the components, in other words, of multicultural Australia. The Australian economy's need to produce and absorb labour power and capital surpluses that would spill either outwards as capital exports or inwards as immigrant imports generated the huge immigration streams of the 1950s, 1960s and 1970s. Multiculturalism as state policy in Australia was implemented as a means of negotiating this multinational flow of people into the socio-economic structure of a single nation under capitalism. In naming and treating as cultural the economic conditions that necessitated this flow, multiculturalism erases the history of capitalism's need to import and exploit cheap labour. Multiculturalism thus becomes another of the crisis-managements of capitalism, since to raise the spectre of economics in the minds of white Anglo-Australians always succeeds in rousing them against this cheap labour on which they rely. Meanwhile, raising the same spectre in the minds of the various immigrant groups that make up multicultural Australia invariably ends in factional fights (the 250,000 Greeks in Melbourne receive as much public money as the 50,000 Turks since, in the eyes of multicultural Australia, all ethnicities are equal). In the early 1980s, with the influx of Vietnamese boat people to Australia, first- and second-generation 'new Australians', fearing a loss of their low-paying blue-collar jobs, joined forces with the dominant Anglo-Celtic majority in brutalising and discriminating against the so-called 'Asian scare'. This is not a history on which multiculturalism in the USA should model itself. Nor is it a history that the champions of multiculturalism can ignore – especially in the context of the scare tactics that are constantly used to discourage a more benevolent immigration policy in the USA. One need only remember Ross Perot's invocations of the great 'sucking sound' coming from the south (Mexico) in the NAFTA debates and their effectiveness in generating anti-Mexican feeling among the US working class, who felt that their jobs would be threatened when all big business moved to Mexico because of its lower standard wages. The biggest success story of these tactics came in November 1994 in California with the passing of Proposition 187, which withdrew education and health-care entitlements from illegal immigrants and their children.

MULTINATIONALISM: NEGOTIATING NATIONALISM AND GLOBALITY

It is clear that contemporary critiques of culture whose project is to transform the contents of Western history and historicism by demonstrating the politics and histories of race, gender and class at work in them leave untouched the rational abstractions in and through which these historical contents are legitimated: namely, totalities like 'culture', 'nation', or 'we the people'. By reading the multicultural projects of Giroux's border pedagogy or Australian education policy against the traditions from which they emerge (Mill's and Arnold's liberal democratic culture, and the tradition of the Wakefield project, respectively), we can begin to unmask the effects of the history founded in these traditions. We can see, for example, that in Mill's reading of nationality the dominant culture's history is made universal and concrete, while the history of the various 'ethnic enclaves' is made universal and abstract – and *as* universal and abstract, it provides a reassuringly 'concrete' counter-collectivity to the abstract collectivity promised by the political institutions of the more 'advanced' dominant culture. These political institutions, ironically, rest their claim to superiority on the abstractedness of other very concrete cultures. Thus multiculturalism is lauded in Australia because its 'citizens' need it to enhance 'international awareness'; the ethnic enclaves, meanwhile, are 'trapped' by Australia's multicultural policies into celebrating and preserving the ethnos or culture of origin through festivals and the like, and thus into moving further and further away from the realities and transformations of not only the nation of origin but also Australia itself. On the border between the international and the national, Australia's multicultural people occupy the no man's land of the 'not quite yet' citizen; forever 'new' Australians, they serve to continually reinforce the borders of the constitution of the Australian nation through their many cultures. Their histories are seen as fragments of a whole that is never quite articulated but always alluded to: the ideal Australian nation which always informs questions of culture and nation as either historical or natural but never political.

Should the debate shift from multiculturalism to multinationalism? Multinationalism, with its emphasis on nation rather than culture, would deal with individual groups as wholes and not as fragments of the whole. In this way, particular cultures would not be forgotten under the rubric of the general culture, or, if they have been, the memory of past forgetfulness could not easily be erased; the history of decolonisation, the 'ethnic' troubles of the former Soviet Union and the current struggles for 'nationhood' in its former republics, the 'racial' tensions in England and the USA, the 'minority' infighting in Australia, all testify to this.[26]

In the politics of multiculturalism such tensions are used by its opponents as another reason why 'we' need a strong policy of assimilation, and by its proponents as another reason why 'we' need a better implementation of multiculturalism. Both positions are part of the logic of the new nation-building of planetary capitalism. The former wants to return to an originary, mythical moment of authentic unity, while the latter, in an effort to make sense of the fragmentation surrounding it, falls unwittingly into the crisis-management of capitalism: in an effort to produce narratives in a fractured semiotic field, it ends up making everything 'ethnic'. This is where it is important to remember that there is a difference between internal colonisation (the patterns of exploitation and domination of minority groups in countries such as the USA or Australia) and the operations of international colonisation.[27] To forget this difference is to make use of a particular ethnocultural agenda, one which, as we saw in the examples of Australia and Mill, either secures a 'we' against a 'them' and stabilises the idea of the nation, or ends up bringing the world home and reading it as different from, and hence inadequate to, the nation's already existing political institutions – institutions which, since Mill, emphasise totality because they are based on the idea of the good of the many.

Because of its construction of history as sequence, the idea of the singular nation and its political institutions, whether they be liberal or socialist, cannot hold in today's reality of the collapse of the Soviet bloc and the not-quite-complete triumph of capitalism. This is not to say that nationalism is dead: the many examples of its survival would make an obituary absurdly premature. It is, however, to say that we must negotiate between nationalism and globality and that we must not allow the ethnocentric politics of multiculturalism to stand in for a study of the world.[28] This is why I offer multinationalism as a means of negotiating between globality and nationality in the age of multinational capital, where the imperial influence of the single integrated market dominated by the USA demands a struggle for a different kind of national project, a different articulation of nation, state and people. This articulation would make clear that the idea of totality found in multiculturalism's construction of the USA – a totality that is the world, in fact, since such a version of the nation has representatives of all nations in its culture – has a national political agenda that cannot be ignored in the context of the USA's role in the 'New World Order' and its nation-mending project.

Negotiating between the national and the global, the practice of multinationalism offers a new methodological direction for literary studies, one that does not fall into the nation-and-culture trap by seeing history (the history of its own discourse included) as a sequence of ameliorative efforts. Under multinationalism, 'History' would be a simultaneity of histories. This simultaneity would vacillate between cultures, languages, nations and identities in such a way that national or cultural priority could not be portrayed easily. In contrast with multiculturalism's aesthetic location of differences in the realm of culture, any locating of the space occupied by a representation of culture and nation under multinationalism would map the politics of the 'geographer critic's' place and all that those politics entail.

I conclude this introduction of the concept of multinationalism with some final clarifications. Although located in the era of multinational capital and its operations, multinationalism is different from multinational capital in that it does not unquestioningly participate in the evolution of capitalist forms of organisation and their alibi of 'cultural' supremacy (whether that alibi be modernisation in economic policy or in the latest theory formation).[29] Because socio-economic space is figured differently under multinational capitalism (the multinational corporation has the power to command space and use geographical differentials in a way that the family firm and industrial capitalism of the nineteenth century could not), it is easy to make the mistake of universalising the very specific effects of multinational or late capitalism and of reading them as global.[30] In the field of literary studies this could lead to either the construction of a canon of 'Third World' or 'Minority' literature with certain Western-imposed trademarks ('national allegory', 'magical realism', 'authentic narrative') or the turning of the 'orient' into a career by the indigenous elite of the countries or cultures involved – in other words, the playing-out of identity politics at either the local or the world level.[31] The study of literature, with its history of confirming individual identity through the teaching of national identity, can function as a prime example of the kind of political practice that brings the world home and sanctions a 'kind of global ignorance'. These are some of the dangers of participating unquestioningly or (like Fredric Jameson) resignedly in the malaise of multinational capitalism.

Multinationalism is also different from nation-based paradigms of minority politics. Focusing on the black nationalist movement, Michael Omi and Howard Winant trace the nationalist tradition found in the various minority communities in the USA back to its historical and theoretical origins in the dynamics of colonialism. After looking at Pan-Africanism, cultural nationalism, and internal colonialism, they conclude that because the USA was created from a colony, 'the US political scene allows radical nationalism little space'.[32] However, contrasting nation-based paradigms with ethnicity and race paradigms, they suggest that 'it is the very inability of the nation-based account to specify precisely what exactly is "national" about racial oppression in the United States which leads it to lend a certain "primacy" and integrity to racial phenomena'.[33] Thus, although they argue that 'the nation-based account fails to demonstrate the existence of racial minority or colonised "nations" internal to the US and structurally separated from the majority society', they nevertheless suggest that nation-based approaches 'may unite the micro- and macro-levels of racially shaped experience, or permit comparisons among different groups'.[34] Omi and Winant's account holds true if the USA is read as 'naturally' a nation. I have already shown such a conception of nation to be problematic, however, in that it presumes the idea of the unity of the people in order to define the nation. Such popular unity is a construct and the metaleptic product of state efforts to construct nationhood. The example of colonised places shows us that the nation is made up of three elements: the people, the nation and the state, the latter being the representation of the idea of the unity of the people to the people, in other words, the embodiment of the nation, which, in colonised places, was in the hands of the coloniser. In these terms, decolonisation is the mobilisation of the people under the rubric of the idea of the nation in order to take over the state. In the USA such a scenario cannot be envisioned, since that particular myth of decolonisation and nationhood has already been acted out once: this is what America is, the American founding myth tells us; history cannot repeat itself. Critics of national separatism will tell us that history has already repeated itself as farce: look at Malcolm X and the Black separatist movement. This is where Omi and Winant's failure to see any evidence of internal colonisation in the USA is apparent: they accept the dominant history of the nation and read any effort at the reinscription of the narrative of the nation as a *part* of that history and not a *whole* different story. Following in the tradition of Mill, in other words, they accept the value-coding of nation as natural and proceed to create a space for it within the discourse of ethnicisation and racialisation, constructing the latter as national in the process and turning the part–whole relationship inside out.

I am not proposing a part–whole relationship in offering multinationalism as a means of negotiating a politics for the various cultures of a nation. In mapping the origin of culture, and the discourse of ethnicisation and racialisation that emerged from it, a multinational critique locates that moment in the history of a nation and situates the history of that nation in a dialectical relationship with the poetics of displacement and the situation of being between countries, cultures, languages and identities that such a critique entails. In this dialectic, the private and the public, the part and the whole, cannot be one, and the 'moral' imperative of culture, found in such diverse positions as Mill's, Arnold's and Giroux's, can finally be seen as the 'ethical' mistake that it is. The recognition of this mistake allows the critic to spot the strategic exclusion of rational abstractions that provide the grounding of the name 'culture' and, as a result, stop the still current narrative of culture as moral. Acts of nation are what are at issue in this narrative, and they should be recognised as such.

NOTES

1 'Interview: Homi Bhabha', *Stanford Humanities Review*, vol. 3. no. 1, 1993, p. 4.
2 J. S. Mill, *Considerations on Representative Government*, New York, Henry Holt & Company,

1882; M. Arnold, *Culture and Anarchy*, New York, the Book League of America, 1929. See C. Gallagher, *The Industrial Reformation of English Fiction: Social Discourse and Narrative Form 1832–1867*, Chicago, University of Chicago Press, 1985, for a good account of Mill and Arnold in the context of this crisis.

3 Although it might appear that, in arguing for the extension of the franchise, Mill located the answer to the problem of representation in politics, his reversal of this proposal near the end of *Representative Government*, where he prioritises education before universal suffrage, clearly aligns his programme with Arnold's aesthetic solution to the problem. While they come at the issue from different political perspectives, both Mill and Arnold see culture as the measuring stick of a nation: it determines its place in the history of progress of the human race. Both regard culture as belonging to the realm of nature and reason – either because of its inherent ethical qualities (Arnold) or because it *creates* ethical qualities (Mill). Nation, on the other hand, is aligned with history and politics: class affiliations, political interests and (since it responds to the ephemerality of these interests) temporality.

4 Mill, *Representative Government*, pp. 161, 158, 165 and 160.

5 Arnold, *Culture and Anarchy*, p. 67.

6 When one remembers Arnold's mid-nineteenth-century context, his 'classless' and 'disinterested' culture can be seen as reinforcing and demonstrating the class affiliations of the Victorian men of letters and their rising power in the state. See P. Anderson's *English Questions*, London, Verso, 1992, p. 47, and T. Eagleton's excellent mapping out of these affiliations in *The Function of Criticism*, London, Verso, 1984, pp. 60–7.

7 *The Teaching of English in England*, London, HMSO, 1921, particularly pp. 6 and 12.

8 See G. Bhattacharyya, 'Cultural Education in Britain: From the Newbolt Report to the National Curriculum', *Oxford Literary Review*, vol. 13, no. 1, 1991, pp. 2–11, for a detailed account of the history of the Newbolt Report and of its legacy in current education policy in England.

9 This is the problem with Henry A. Giroux's otherwise admirable concept of 'border pedagogy' in 'Post-Colonial Ruptures and Democratic Possibilities: Multiculturalism as Anti-Racist Pedagogy', *Cultural Critique*, vol. 21, 1992, pp. 5–39. The problem with the fight for a 'common culture', of course, is that it has to eradicate from its 'commonness' any difference that does not fit its category of differences-in-common.

10 A. Appadurai, in 'Disjuncture and Difference in the Global Cultural Economy', *Public Culture*, vol. 2, no. 2, 1990, pp. 1–24, offers a picture of how culture operates in multinational capitalism. Although sketchy, it provides the groundwork for imagining a global social theory of postmodernity in the age of multinational capitalism. The problem with Appadurai's acceptance of the imperial dominance of the single integrated market orchestrated by the USA, and his offering of the concept of 'imagined worlds' mediated by different 'landscapes' (ethnic, media, financial, technological, ideological) as a means of negotiating citizenship in today's postcolonial, postmodern world, is that his account offers no means of negotiating for different kinds of national projects or for a revolutionary restructuring of one's own nation-state.

11 G. Anzaldúa, *Borderlands: La Frontera: The New Mestiza*, San Francisco, spinsters/aunt lute, 1987, Preface.

12 ibid., p. 84.

13 For a concise history of Marxism's negotiation of the question of identity, see E. Laclau, 'Universalism, Particularism, and the Question of Identity', *October*, vol. 61, 1992, pp. 83–90.

14 H. Louis Gates, Jr, 'Authority, (White) Power and the (Black) Critic: or It's All Greek to Me', *Cultural Critique*, no. 7, 1987, p. 31.

15 ibid., p. 33.

16 M. Horkheimer and T. W. Adorno, *Dialectic of Enlightenment*, trans. J. Cumming, New York, Seabury Press, 1972.

17 L. Hunt, *Politics, Culture and Class in the French Revolution*, Berkeley, University of California Press, 1984, p. 27.

18 ibid., pp. 7–21.

19 Mill, at this point, embarks on a world-wide search for nations whose government does just that and a search for virtue and intelligence in those nations' people. He comes up with a geopolitical map of the world with the following legend: a nation's 'size' is its place in the scale of civilisation. In this map, less civilised nations should see that it is in their interest to be subsumed and become part of more civilised nations. This is emblematic of a basic problem in Mill: his championship of liberalism at home and his acceptance of colonialism abroad.

20 The populace has to be trained in this mode of thinking and Mill offers concrete ways of doing it: the most important one is national education, a national education that reads like an education on nationalist sentiment (307). Prefiguring the Newbolt Report, he writes: 'The only thing which can justify reckoning one person's opinion as equivalent to more than one is individual mental superiority, and what is wanted is some approximate means of ascertaining that. If there existed such a thing as a really national education or a trustworthy system of general examination, education might be tested directly. In the absence of these, the nature of a person's occupation is some test' (182).

21 Giroux, 'Post-Colonial Ruptures and Democratic Possibilities', p. 35.

22 Giroux's is not the only omission here. Even in critiques of the rise of English studies, where the term 'English' is problematised and shown to have a history of exclusion, the value-coding of 'English' remains unquestioned and a space for it is created within the discourse of 'Englishness'. See, for example, Brian Doyle's otherwise excellent critique, 'The Invention of English', in R. Colls and P. Dodd (eds), *Englishness: Politics and Culture 1889–1920*, London, Croom Helm, 1987. There is, of course, a double contradiction at work when one talks about English studies in the USA (especially in the context of multiculturalism). While I am not equating the history of border pedagogy with that of English studies, I am pointing to their cognate functions in government.

23 *Windows Onto Worlds: Studying Australia at Tertiary Level*, The Report of the Committee to Review Australian Studies at Tertiary Level, Canberra, June 1987, p. 12.

24 ibid., p. 27.

25 See E. Gibbon Wakefield, *A View of the Art of Colonization, with Present Reference to the British Empire; In Letters between a Statesman and a Colonist*, London, John Parker, West Strand, 1849. Wakefield dedicated the book to John Hutt, Esq., the governor of Western Australia. One of his central theses is the following: 'With a sufficient price for *waste* land [my emphasis], capitalists would obtain labour by means of paying for the emigration of poor people' (372). Mill, in Book II of *Principles of Political Economy*, London, 1848, gave enthusiastic support to this project and encouraged its publication. Thus one sees that there is a history behind the 'benevolent' acceptance of immigrants in Australia, a history that ties its colonial past with its multicultural present, the Liberal policies of Mill with the later policies of multicultural Australia.

26 Of course, I am not arguing here that the projects of multiculturalism and postcolonialism are identical; that would be to read the very local multicultural debates within the USA or Australia as global and universal, not parochial and particular.

27 M. Omi and H. Winant in *Racial Formation in the United States: From the 1960s to the 1980s*, New York, Routledge & Kegan Paul, 1986, identify the three major stages that the ethnicity paradigm has gone through in the United States as the following: 'a pre-1930s stage in which the ethnic group view was an insurgent approach, challenging the biologistic . . . view of race which was dominant at the time; a 1930s to 1965 stage during which the paradigm operated as the progressional/liberal "common sense" approach to race, and during which two recurrent themes – assimilationism and cultural pluralism – were defined; and a post-1965 phase, in which the paradigm has

taken on the defense of conservative (or "neoconservative") egalitarianism against what is perceived as the radical assault of "group rights"' (14).

28 Gayatri Spivak, discussing the question of cultural studies on a global scale, has argued in a similar vein: 'I am not speaking against the tendency to conflate ethnos of origin and the historical space left behind with the astonishing constructions of multicultural and multiracial identity for the United States. What I am suggesting is that if, as academics in the humanities, we take this as the founding principle for a study of globality, then we are off base. In the most practical terms, we are allowing a parochial decanonization debate to stand in for a study of the world.' See Outside in the Teaching Machine, London, Routledge, 1993, pp. 279–80.

29 Multinational capitalism exemplifies what Lash and Urry call 'disorganized capitalism', whose characteristics they identify as: a de-concentration of rapidly increasing corporate power away from national markets; an increasing internationalisation of capital; a decline in effectiveness of national collective bargaining; the industrialisation of the third world and the competitive de-industrialisation of core countries which turn to specialisation in services; the decline, but not collapse, of class-based politics and institutions; the dispersal of capitalist relations across many sectors and regions; the dispersal and diversification of the territorial–spatial division of labour; the decline of industrial cities and the de-concentration from city centres into peripheral or semi-rural areas resulting in acute inner city problems; and the cultural–ideological configurations of 'postmodernism'. See S. Lash and J. Urry, The End of Organized Capitalism, Cambridge, Polity Press, 1987.

30 Fredric Jameson, in his essay 'Third World Literature in the Era of Multinational Capitalism', Social Text, no. 15, 1986, p. 69, performs such a mistake when he asserts that all first-world texts are libidinal while 'all third-world texts are necessarily allegorical' and should be read as 'national allegories'. See Social Text, no. 17, 1987, for Aijaz Ahmad's response to this essay, and Jameson's riposte, in which he exemplifies precisely what Ahmad is criticising in his work.

31 Both Aijaz Ahmad in his controversial book In Theory: Classes, Nations, Literatures, London, Verso, 1992 and Gayatri Spivak in Outside in the Teaching Machine give meticulous and eloquent accounts of how this can and does happen. For the controversy generated by Ahmad's book, see the essays printed in Public Culture, vol. 6, no. 1, 1993.

32 Omi and Winant, Racial Formation in the United States, p. 50.

33 ibid.

34 ibid.

Part II

MULTICULTURALISM AND THE NATION

Histories, policies, practices

7

MODERNITY AND ETHNICITY IN INDIA

Dipesh Chakrabarty

Over the last few decades, some distinguished Indian intellectuals have been engaged in a critical revaluation of the intellectual and institutional legacies of the European Enlightenment in the subcontinent.[1] For a long time, this critique was seen by the Indian left as a quaint form of intellectual Gandhism – sentimental, perhaps even noble-minded in its rejection of materialist values, but in the end unpractical and unthreatening. The left did not take much notice of it. Things changed, however, in the 1980s. There was poststructuralist and deconstructionist philosophy, now available in English translation, which increasingly called into question Enlightenment rationalism and the metanarratives of progress/emancipation that the left had never questioned. There was also the development in the United States, particularly after Said's critique of Orientalism, of a whole field of study that devoted itself to understanding the formation of colonial subjectivities through examining 'colonial discourses'.[2] Within the field of Indian history, anthropologist-historians such as Arjun Appadurai, Nicholas Dirks, Gyan Prakash and other scholars working under the intellectual leadership of Bernard Cohn in the 1980s also began to draw our attention to the way that colonially instituted practices and knowledge-systems affected the formation of new subjectivities in India and cast a lasting shadow over the emerging politics of identity in the sub-continent. And then, at the same time, there was the *Subaltern Studies* collective, Gramscian in inspiration and led by Ranajit Guha, who developed a critique of nationalism and of the political imagination for which the nation-state represented the ideal form for a political community. These heterogeneous strands are now part of what is sometimes broadly referred to as the 'critique of modernity' debate in India.

The rise of a fascistic variety of ethnic nationalism in India – often known as the 'Hindutva' (the quality of being a Hindu) movement – has now caused an understandable backlash against these critiques of 'modernity' and of the so-called 'Enlightenment rationalism'. The sense of a crisis on the part of the left in India was aggravated and deepened by the way the leaders and followers of this Hindutva movement vandalised and destroyed a sixteenth-century mosque in the North Indian city of Ayodhya on 6 December 1992, on the pretext that the mosque had been forcibly built on what was, to their minds, a temple marking the birth-place of the mythical Hindu god-king, Ram. This Hindu extremist movement, brewing since the early 1980s, with anti-Muslim hatred and a fear of a weakened 'Hindu' race/nationality as its main ingredients, and enjoying the backing of a large number of Hindus inside and outside India, has caused both concern and debate among Indian intellectuals on questions of 'secularism', 'tolerance', 'modernity' and what the European Enlightenment means for intellectuals in India. It is this debate that provides the context for what follows. I have nothing to say in support of the Hindu extremists whose actions in many instances have only bred a politics of ethnic hatred and murder. But it does seem to me that the way the 'critique of modernity' debate has been positioned by some Indian marxist and left-liberal intellectuals in their rush to fight the so-called Hindu fundamentalists forecloses the space for critical thinking instead of expanding and enriching it. Faced with the Hindu challenge, these intellectuals have gone back to some of the classical shibboleths of marxism and liberalism: the call for class struggle and a non-religious, if not altogether atheist, public sphere. They express the fear, as do some in the West, that to develop a critique of the legacies of Enlightenment thought at this moment of (Indian) history is to betray the cause of marxism and liberal principles and thus play into the hands of the 'reactionaries' (in this case, the Hindutva mob). Some subcontinental marxists, true to a long tradition of debate within the Communist Party, have begun to describe others as enemies of the left. Aijaz Ahmad, who clubs together 'Lévi-Strauss, Foucault, Derrida, Glucksmann [and] Kristeva' as 'reactionary anti-humanists', dismisses the important Indian critics, Homi Bhabha and Partha Chatterjee, in a footnote to his book In Theory, with the intriguing implication that while 'poststructuralism', whenever applied to things Indian, acquires of necessity a 'subordinate and dependent' character, 'marxism' (including, presumably, Ahmad's own) wonderfully escapes the problem.[3] In the more hyperbolic statements, it is even suggested that to develop critiques of 'Enlightenment rationalism' is to produce at best 'cultural relativism' and at worst, strident, fascist 'indigenism'. Thus the Indian marxist historian Sumit Sarkar has remarked in an article on the Hindutva movement that the 'rejection of Enlightenment rationalism' by the Indian critics of modernity is frighteningly evocative of what happened in the intellectual history of fascism in Europe.[4] The argument, which conflates 'critique' with wholesale 'rejection', is based on a simple syllogism and on some perceived historical parallels. Here is how the syllogism runs in Sarkar's argument: (1) 'Fascist ideology in Europe . . . owed something to a general turn-of-the-century move away from what were felt to be the sterile rigidities of Enlightenment rationalism'; (2) 'not dissimilar ideas have become current intellectual coin in the West, and by extension they have started to influence Indian academic life'; (3) that these 'current academic fashions' (Sarkar mentions 'postmodernism') 'can reduce the resistance of intellectuals to the ideas of Hindutva has already become evident'. Examples: 'The "critique of colonial discourse" . . . has stimulated forms of indigenism not easy to distinguish from the standard

Sangh Parivar [i.e. Hindu fundamentalist] argument . . . that Hindutva is superior to Islam and Christianity (and by extension to the creations of the modern west, like science, democracy or marxism) because of its allegedly unique roots'. Sarkar warns that 'an uncritical cult of the "popular" or "subaltern", particularly when combined with the rejection of Enlightenment rationalism . . . can lead even radical historians down strange paths' which, for Sarkar, bear 'ominous' resemblance to Mussolini's condemnation of the 'teleological' idea of progress and to Hitler's exaltation 'of the German *Volk* over "hair splitting intelligence"'.[5]

I have to admit that I have a vested interest in continuing this debate because I have been named by Sarkar as one of the 'radical' historians undergoing this 'strange' transformation.

I do not deny the political need to fight Hindutva, for the danger of an Indian 'Hindu' fascism is real, though it is sometimes exaggerated. Nor are the parallels drawn with European history always accurate (or when they are, their significance runs contrary to the direction of Sarkar's argument).[6] But we short-change ourselves intellectually when we attempt to understand the current ethnic conflicts in India through a grid that has liberalism and fascism locked into an unremitting binary opposition to each other, as though they belong to entirely different and unconnected histories. In the Western democracies there has been a long tradition of doing this, precisely by 'ethnicising' the histories of modern authoritarianisms, fascist or otherwise, that is, by treating them as problems produced by other 'peoples" cultures, those of the Germans, the Japanese and now the so-called 'Asian tigers'. In writing histories of modern European thoughts and institutions, no anti-imperial historian can ever afford to forget what W. E. B. DuBois once said:

> There was no Nazi atrocity – concentration camps, wholesale maiming and murder, defilement of women or ghastly blasphemy of childhood – which the Christian civilization of Europe had not long been practising against colored folk in all parts of the world in the name of and for the defense of a Superior Race born to rule the world.[7]

The connection that DuBois makes between this atrocity and the foundations of modern, liberal democracies in both the New and the Old Worlds will ring true to all those whose histories have been irretrievably altered by the rapacities of modern European imperialisms. That a high priest of Enlightenment rationalism such as Voltaire would think of Blacks as people who approximated the 'physical features and mental processes' of animals was a structural and not an accidental feature of Enlightenment thought.[8] One cannot simply separate out the 'decent tendencies' in Enlightenment thought from the indecent ones. Yet there is a discernible intellectual habit that makes us treat contemporary instances of racist or ethnic hatred as though they were aberrations in the history of modern nation-states, civil societies and their attendant institutions. This tendency is not surprising in male intellectuals of the West who want to rescue the story of modern liberalism from any necessary association with imperialism. The connection was contingent and historic, they in effect argue, holding forth the promise that, if only the fascists/fundamentalists could be kept at bay, we would enjoy a nice, benign modernity (which might even graduate one day, when capitalism has played itself out, to the higher historical stage of socialism). It surprises me, however, when intellectuals from a colonial formation embrace the institutions of modernity, however inevitable and powerful they might seem, without any sense of irony qualifying their welcome.

There is an Indian character in *The Satanic Verses* who says (and I imagine here the 'Indian' shaking of the head and a heavy upper-class Delhi accent): 'Battle lines are being drawn in India today, secular versus religious, the light versus the dark. Better you choose which side you are on.'[9] It is precisely this choice that I am going to refuse in this analysis. I want to explore, instead, some of the complex and unavoidable links that exist in Indian history between the phenomenon of ethnic conflict and the modern governing practices that the British introduced into India as the historical bearers of Enlightenment rationalism. This is not an argument against liberal values nor against the idea of modernity as such. But shadows fall between the abstract values of modernity and the historical process through which the institutions of modernisation come to be built. It is true that at this moment there do not seem to be any *practical* alternatives to the institutions of capitalism and the modern state in India. In all our actions we have to take into account their reality, that is, their theoretical claims as well as the specific histories through which they have developed in India. But it is nevertheless important that we create an Archimedean point, at least in theory, in order to have a longer-term perspective on our problems. Today's understanding of what is 'practical' does not have to constitute our philosophical horizon; if we let it, we submit, even inside our heads, to what already exists. The short review I shall present of the history of modern governmental practices in India is offered in the spirit of a dictum by a great thinker of the European Enlightenment (in reproducing it, I only reverse the order of his statement): 'Obey, but argue as much as you want and about what you want.'

If a pristine form of liberalism (the Indian word is 'secularism') is one danger besetting the analysis of contemporary racism in India, the other danger is that of Orientalism, sometimes indistinguishable from statements that claim that India could be understood only on 'Indian' or, better, 'Hindu' terms. The possibility that the current Hindu-versus-Muslim or upper-versus-lower-caste conflicts in India may be, in a significant sense, a variant of the modern problem of 'ethnicity' or 'race' is seldom entertained in discussions in the Western media, both Hinduism and caste being seen, not altogether unreasonably, as particular to the subcontinent. Even serious and informed scholars are not immune to the tendency. Klaus Klostermaier's knowledgeable survey of Hinduism, published from New York in 1989, warns us against understanding Hindu politics on anything but 'Hindu' terms:

Political Hinduism, I hold, cannot be understood by applying either a

Western-party democratic gauge or a Marxist-socialist pattern. Its potential has much to do with the temper of Hinduism, which was able throughout the ages to rally people around causes that were perceived to be of transcendent importance and in whose pursuit ordinary human values and considerations had to be abandoned.[10]

Even when the problems are placed in an international framework, as in some passages of V. S. Naipaul's book, *India: A Million Mutinies Now*, what one gets is a patronising pat on the back, a view of history somewhat reminiscent of what Hegel said about India in his lectures on the philosophy of history. 'Hindoo political existence', said Hegel, 'presents us with a people but no state'.[11] This, for Hegel, meant the worst kind of despotism and a necessary absence of History:

It is because the Hindoos have no History in the form of annals (*historia*) that they have no History in the form of transactions (*res gestae*); that is, no growth expanding into a veritable political condition.[12]

Naipaul's Hegelianism is neither conscious nor sophisticated. He simply reproduces the idea that an awakening to 'history' is the condition for democracy. For him, therefore, all the ethnic ferment in the Indian scene is only a sign of the youthfulness of India's historical consciousness; with time would come the maturity that nations with an older sense of their history presumably possessed:

To awaken to history is to cease to live instinctively. It was to begin to see oneself and one's group the way the outside world saw one; and it was to know a kind of rage. India was now full of this rage. There had been a general awakening. But everyone awakened first to his own group or community; every group thought itself unique in its awakening; and every group sought to separate from the rage of other groups.[13]

Within India, too, the same law of oversight rules, for 'racism' is thought of as something the white people do to us. What Indians do to one another is variously described as 'communalism', 'regionalism' and 'casteism', but never 'racism'. There are, of course, particularly 'Indian' twists to this story, and it is also true that 'racism', properly speaking, has social-Darwinist connotations and should not be conflated with 'ethnocentrism'. Yet, for me, the popular word 'racism' has the advantage of not making India look 'peculiar'. A relative of mine wanting to sell a plot of land near Calcutta was recently told by the local Communist leaders that he could indeed sell his land but not to Muslims. How is that any different, I would want to know, from an English landlady asking, on being told on the phone the name of a prospective tenant, 'Is that a Jewish Kahn or a Pakistani Khan?' (both varieties being, at least in this apocryphal story, undesirable).

In focusing on the theme of contemporary Indian ethnic intolerance, I will argue that the experiment of nation-making in India shows how modern problems of ethnicity cannot be separated from modern means of government and communication. My emphasis, in other words, will be on the way the development of a modern public-political life in India has called into being constructions of both 'Hinduism' and 'caste' that do not admit of such simple binary distinctions as Salman Rushdie's character invokes: secular/religious, liberal/fundamentalist, nationalist/communal.

But first let me try to anticipate and forestall a few misunderstandings. It is not my intention to deny the traditions of violence that existed in India before British rule. There are recorded instances of Hindu–Muslim tensions during the pre-colonial period. Historians and anthropologists are in agreement that the Brahmanical claim to ritual supremacy was seldom accepted without challenge and contestation by other social groups, including those whom we know as the 'untouchables'. The eminent Indian historian Romila Thapar, citing examples from the period between the seventh and the twelfth centuries of 'Hindu' sects destroying Buddhist and Jaina monasteries and sometimes killing the monks, has usefully reminded us in a recent article that the 'popular belief that the "Hindus" never indulged in religious persecution' is simply untrue.[14] This ancient history is something that I neither discuss nor deny in this essay, for my point is different. Something has fundamentally changed about both Hinduism and caste since British rule and particularly since the beginning of the twentieth century. If I may put it simply by using the example of caste, the change may be crudely described as follows. We know from anthropologists and historians of the so-called caste-system that there were no strong systemic rules guiding everybody's caste-identity; this could be a matter of negotiation between individuals and groups. Marriage-rules or rules of commensality could change within one's own lifetime or over generations, depending on factors such as social, economic and geographical mobility. In other words, caste-society operated as a non-standardised system; rules guiding caste-transactions would have required on the part of the participant a sensitivity to the context. Just as the British sought to give India a standardised legal system, they also attempted to fix and officialise collective identities (such as caste and religion) in the very process of creating a quasi-modern public sphere in India. The concept and the institutions that make up the public sphere – free press, voluntary associations, avenues for free debate and enquiry in the public interest – are modern Europe's intellectual and practical gifts to the people they considered less fortunate than themselves and at whose doors they arrived as raging, mad imperialists. My point is that modern problems of Hinduism and caste are inseparable from the history of this modern public life in India, which the British instituted and the nationalists preserved in what they thought were the best interests of the country.

MODERN GOVERNMENTAL PRACTICES IN INDIA:
A BRIEF HISTORY

British rule in India lasted from 1757 to 1947, a little short of two hundred years. The most fundamental and far-reaching innovation that the British introduced to Indian society, in my view, was the modern state – not a nation-state, for that was what the nationalist movement created, but a modern state nevertheless. One symptom of its modernity was that its techniques of government were very closely tied to techniques of measurement. From surveys of land and crop output to prospecting for minerals, from measuring Indian brains (on behalf of the false science of phrenology) to measuring Indian bodies, diets and life-spans (thus laying the foundations of physical anthropology and modern medicine in India), the British had the length and breadth of India, her history, culture and society, mapped, classified and quantified in detail that was nothing but precise even when it was wrongheaded. The most dramatic examples of this governmental concern with measurement were the decennial Indian censuses, the first of which was published in 1872. Since the British did not go to India in search of pure knowledge, all these studies were produced in the cause and in the process of governing India, and it is this pervasive marriage between government and measurement that I take as something that belongs to the deep structure of the imagination that is invested in modern political orders.[15] Without numbers, it would be impossible to practise bureaucratic or instrumental rationality.

This is not to say that pre-modern government had no use for numbers. The Mughals had statistics of produce, land and revenue, among other things. William the Conqueror had Domesday (1086). Historians of demography talk about ancient censuses in such distant and disparate places as ancient China or ancient Rome (the word 'census' itself being of Roman origin) and in the Inca society of Peru. But much of this information was haphazardly collected and seldom updated with any regularity.

Systematic collection of detailed and classified statistics for the purpose of ruling seems to be intimately tied to modern ideas of government. The history of the very discipline of 'statistics' carries this tale. The word 'statistic', etymologically speaking, has the idea of statecraft built into it. *The Shorter Oxford Dictionary* tells us that, 'in early use', statistics was 'that branch of political science dealing with the collection, classification, and discussion of facts bearing on the condition of a state or community'. Gottfried Achenwall, who, as Ian Hacking informs us, was responsible for coining the word 'statistics', intended it to imply a 'collection of "remarkable facts about the state"'.[16] While the census itself is an old idea, the first modern census, according to some scholars, was taken in the United States in 1790, and the first British census in 1801. The Indian censuses were not to appear until late in the nineteenth century, but the East India Company caused quite a few regional censuses to be taken before that period.

Measurement is central to our modern ideas about fairness and justice and how we administer them – in short, to the very idea of good government. Foucault has emphasised in several places, especially in his essay on 'governmentality', how this idea has been critically dependent on 'the emergence of the problem of population' in the eighteenth century, and is therefore connected to the development of the other important 'science' of the same period, that of economics.[17] Benthamite attempts at using law for social engineering – the idea, for instance, that punishment should be in proportion to the crime committed, or the utilitarian aim of devising a society that would maximise the pleasure of the maximum possible number of people – all speak a language borrowed from mathematics and the natural sciences (unsurprisingly, given the connection between Enlightenment rationalism and scientific paradigms). The 1790 American census had to do with the idea of proportionality in the sphere of political representation. Ideas of 'correspondence', 'proportionality' and so on mark Rousseau's thoughts on 'equality'. Without them, and without the numbers they produced, the equal-opportunity legislations of our own period would be unworkable. And, to move from the institutional to the personal, a gesture toward measurement is inherent in the question that we have now made into a universal litmus test of conjugal happiness: 'Does he share the domestic chores *equally*?' A generalised accounting mind-set is what seems to inhabit modernity.

The British, as the representatives and the inheritors of European Enlightenment, brought these ideas to India. It is, in fact, one of the ironies of British history that they became political liberals at home at the same time as they became imperialists abroad. British policy in India was forever haunted by this contradiction. While the British would never take the step, until 1947, of granting India full self-government, they were often concerned about being 'fair' to the different competing sections that, in their view, made up Indian society. And these sections had been defined by the British, quite early on, in religious and caste terms. A count made of the population of Bombay in 1780, for instance, divided the population into 'socio-religious communities'.[18] In the eighteenth century, British amateur historians often portrayed India as a society weakened by its internal divisions into various religions and castes, an understanding shared later by Indian nationalists themselves. Understandably, then, categories of caste and religion dominated the censuses that the British undertook in India. At every census, people were asked to state their religion and caste and, as the American historian Kenneth Jones has pointed out, this was in marked contrast to what the British did at home. Religion, says Jones, was never an important category in the British censuses for the period from 1801 to 1931. Only once, in 1851, were the British asked about their religious affiliations, and answering the question was optional.[19] Counting Hindus, Muslims, Sikhs and Untouchables became a critical political exercise, particularly in the twentieth century as the British began to include Indian representatives in the legislative bodies in very measured doses. What made the census operations critical was that the British, in trying to be fair referees, made the process of political representation 'communal': seats in the legislative assemblies were earmarked for different communities according to ideas of proportionality. Nationalists like Nehru and Gandhi abhorred this process and the

ideology that governed it, namely, 'communalism', a word that still leads a stigmatised existence in India and functions as a surrogate for 'racism'.[20] They
pointed out, with some justice, that it was invidious to treat 'untouchables' as a
'community' separate from the 'Hindus'. A language-based definition of political
communities would have seemed more 'natural' to them, but post-independence
Indian history has shown that language is no surer a guide to ethnic identity and
inter-ethnic peace than is religion. Heads have been regularly broken in the subcontinent over linguistic issues since the 1950s, the liberation war of Bangladesh
in 1971 being only a dramatic example of the process. Political leaders of the
Muslims and the Untouchables, on the other hand, felt much happier going along
with the British-devised arrangements until the final decade before Independence
and the partition of the country. Of particular importance in the Indian story is
the category 'scheduled caste', which the British coined in 1936 (and the
Government of India has retained) and which was so called because it referred to
a schedule of particularly disadvantaged castes that was drawn up for 'the purpose
of giving effect to the provisions of special electoral representation in the
Government of India Act, 1935'.[21] It represents a pioneering attempt at affirmative action.

Historians and political scientists studying modern India have recently made
several attempts to understand what happened to ethnic identities through this
process of a quasi-modern, albeit colonial, state's instituting through modern
means of measurement a structure of political representation tied to notions of
proportionality. What, in other words, did the census do to identities? Historians
and anthropologists of colonial India have reported a social process akin to what
Ian Hacking, in his essay 'Making Up People', calls 'dynamic nominalism': people
came to fit the categories that the colonial authorities had fashioned for them.
Hacking explains dynamic nominalism thus:

> You will recall that a traditional nominalist says that stars (or algae or jus-
> tice) have nothing in common except our names ('stars', 'algae',
> 'justice'). The traditional realist in contrast finds it amazing that the
> world could so kindly sort itself into our categories. He protests that
> there are definite sorts of objects in it . . . which we have painstakingly
> come to recognise and classify correctly. The robust realist does not have
> to argue very hard that people also come sorted. . . . A different kind of
> nominalism — I call it dynamic nominalism — attracts my realist self,
> spurred on by theories about the making of the homosexual and the het-
> erosexual as kinds of persons or by my observations about official
> statistics. The claim of dynamic nominalism is not that there was a kind
> of person who came increasingly to be recognized by bureaucrats or by
> students of human nature but rather that a kind of person came into
> being at the same time as the kind itself was being invented. In some
> cases, that is, our classifications and our classes conspire to emerge hand
> in hand, each egging the other on.[22]

The Indian political scientist Sudipta Kaviraj has pursued a similar argument with regard to the history of 'communities' in pre-British and British India. 'Communities' in pre-British India, says Kaviraj, had 'fuzzy' boundaries; in British India they became 'enumerated'. By 'fuzzy', Kaviraj means vague boundaries which do not admit of discrete, either/or divisions. Census or official enumerations, however, give us discrete kinds of identities, even if particular identities change, as indeed they often do, over time. For the purpose of affirmative action, a 'scheduled caste' person is a 'scheduled caste' person is a 'scheduled caste' person. The distinction that Kaviraj draws is parallel to one that Hacking draws in his attempt to find a path somewhere between the epistemological obstinacies of the nominalist and realist positions:

> It will be foolhardy . . . to have an opinion about one of the stable human dichotomies, male and female. But very roughly, the robust realist will agree that there may be what really are physiological borderline cases, once called 'hermaphrodites'. The existence of vague boundaries is normal: most of us are neither tall nor short, fat nor thin. Sexual physiology [i.e., the categorial structure of sexual physiology] is unusually abrupt in its divisions.[23]

The kernel of Kaviraj's argument is that the post-Enlightenment governing practices that the British introduced into India, and which entailed counting collective identities in an all-or-nothing manner, enabled people to see and organise themselves in light of these categories. I shall quote here at some length Kaviraj's own gloss on these terms, since all my knowledge of Indian history as well as my lived experience of India compel me to agree with him. Kaviraj writes:

> Communities were fuzzy in two senses. Rarely, if ever, would people belong to a community which would claim to represent or exhaust all the layers of their complex selfhood. Individuals on suitable occasions could describe themselves as *vaisnavas*, Bengalis or more likely *Rarhis*, *Kayasthas*, villagers and so on; and clearly although all these could on appropriate occasions be called their *samaj* [society/community] . . . their boundaries would not coincide. . . . [Their identity] would be fuzzy in a second sense as well. To say their community is fuzzy is not to say it is imprecise. On the appropriate occasion, every individual would use his cognitive apparatus to classify any single person he interacts with and place him quite exactly, and decide if he could eat with him, go on a journey, or arrange a marriage into his family. It was therefore practically precise, and adequate to the scale of social action. But it would not occur to an individual to ask how many of them there were in the world, and what if they decided to act in concert . . .[24]

I would like to modify Kaviraj's incisive analysis in one respect, however. The movement from 'fuzzy' to 'enumerated' communities did not represent a complete change of consciousness. In their everyday lives, in negotiating the spheres of friendship and kinship, say, Indians, like human beings everywhere, are comfortable with the indeterminacies of ethnic identities and they share none of the tenacity with which social scientists and governments hang on to the labels that inform their sense of both analysis and action. Yet the very existence of administrative categories of ethnicity – whether one is looking at the international level or at developments within a country – suggests a modern, public career for ethnic tags, a 'national' identity being the highest form. It is, of course, within this sphere that the identity of being Indian or Hindu or Muslim or scheduled caste takes on a new political meaning. This meaning resides alongside, and is interlaced with, the more 'fuzzy' sense of community.

The late nineteenth-century censuses and other similar institutions, then, reconstituted the meaning of 'community' or 'ethnicity' and gave Indians three important political messages, all of which are entirely commensurable with liberal political philosophy as we know it. These messages were: (1) that communities could be enumerated, and that in numbers lay one's political clout; (2) that the social and economic progress of a community was a measurable entity, measured in the case of Indian censuses by their share in public life (education, professions, employment etc.); and (3) that this enabled governments and communities to devise objective tests for the relative 'backwardness' or otherwise of a community.

Indians were quick to learn the art of participation in this public sphere. They learnt, as we all do when we want to take advantage of equal-opportunity legislation, that modern governments have rather limited intelligence; their principles of distributive justice require simple, homogeneous, sharply delineated identities, the kinds that passports bear. While identities can proliferate and have a tendency to do so under the pressure of the politics of democratic representation, the sense of multiple identities that propels individuals in their everydayness is too complex for the rules that govern the logic of representation in modern public life, where identities, however numerous and internally differentiated they may be, must each remain distinct and discrete in the competitive race for goods and services that the state and civil society may offer. It is this pressure, which is essentially the pressure that modern political orders produce, that led many Indian leaders to profess simplistic, homogeneous ethnic identities in 'public life', disregarding all the heterogeneity and diversity of Indian social practices. These were categories by which few leaders actually lived in their private capacity.

When we look back now at India in the 1870s and 1880s, it becomes clear that the era of modern, competitive, governmentally defined ethnic identities familiar to us in liberal democracies had already arrived. The peculiarity of colonial Indian history lay in the fact that these identities were based on religious categories because of a certain degree of reification of these categories by the British. (But even if the British had picked language as a mark of distinction in this multi-lingual country, the result would have been the same.) By the 1890s, Hindu and

Muslim leaders were quoting census figures at each other to prove whether or nor they had received their legitimate share of benefits (such as employment and education) from British rule. The rise of modern caste consciousness shows a similar concern for the measurement of 'progress' in public life. The famous anti-Brahman 'manifesto', produced in Madras in 1916 by the non-Brahman caste who formed a new political party, owed its rhetorical force to the statistics the government had collected to demonstrate a Brahman 'monopoly' of the civil service.[25]

Demography was pressed into the service of such ethnic jealousies between Hindus and Muslims or between castes by several authors who used the censuses to make their points. One example of this process, discussed by Kenneth Jones, is a set of articles published by a Bengali author, U. N. Mukherji, in 1909 (a time in Indian history when the Muslims were being given reserved seats in the legislature by the British). In these articles, entitled 'A Dying Race', Mukherji used the census data from 1872 to 1901 to demonstrate, to the satisfaction of many Hindus, 'that within a given number of years all Hindus would disappear from British India'. In doing this, writes Jones, Mukherji 'was actually following the lead of M. J. C. O'Donnell, Census Commissioner of Bengal for 1891, who had calculated "the number of years it would take the Hindus to altogether disappear from Bengal if Muhammadan increase went on at the rate it was doing"'.[26]

Let us put aside for the moment what to our ears may sound 'racist' in these remarks. My point is that the social assumptions on which the classification and organisation of census figures rested were fundamentally modern: they showed India to be a collection of 'communities' whose 'progress' or 'backwardness' could be measured by the application of some supposedly 'universal' indices. That is exactly how the modern world of nation-states is structured: it is a united but internally hierarchised world where some countries are described as measurably – or should I say, immeasurably? – more 'advanced' than others. This structure of relationships has the nature of what scientists call fractals or self-similar patterns: it is capable of reproducing itself at many different levels, between nations, between modern ethnic groups, between perceived races and so on. It is what constitutes the liberal idea of competitive pluralism. As an idea, so the French historian Lucien Febvre once reminded us, it has been with us since the second half of the eighteenth century.[27] It was packed into the idea of 'civilisation', a word the French started to use in the 1760s and which soon found its way into the English language to provide the noblest justification for England's work in India. The word 'civilisation' has long since fallen out of favour; we preferred to talk about 'progress' in the nineteenth century and 'development' in the twentieth, but the idea of a united world with an internally articulated hierarchy, measurable by some universally agreed indices, has remained with us. How strongly the Indian middle classes internalised this idea is suggested by the following quotation from a Bengali book of morals that was published in Calcutta about 140 years ago for consumption by children. I quote from the eighth edition of the book, printed in 1858. Notice how the world is seen as both one and hierarchical, the observable differences in standards of living between countries being – to make a conscious gesture toward the idea of measurement – proportional to their 'total national efforts':

> Countries where people are averse to labour . . . are uncivilised. The Aboriginals of America and Australia as well as the Negroes are still in this state. They live in great hardship without adequate food and clothes, and they do not save anything for bad times. . . . The Germans, the Swiss, the French, the Dutch and the English are the most industrious nations/races [jati] of the world. That is why they enjoy the best circumstances among all nations.[28]

This language would appear offensive today but there is a homology between what this children's primer said and the sensibility that makes of the modern industrialised nations a model for the rest of the world to follow. We all partake of this sensibility and I am no exception. All I am saying is that this sensibility, our common sense on these matters, is undergirded by the mechanisms of the modern state and the universal requirements of governmentality, the same mechanisms that influence our constructions of competitive blocks of ethnicity in the public sphere. Hindus, Muslims, the scheduled and lower castes of India, both during and after British rule, have in a sense done no more than apply this sensibility to their public, political lives.

ETHNICITY AND/OR THE NATION: AN IRONIC PERSPECTIVE

But, of course, they have done more than that. If India were simply a place where ethnicity was contained within the liberal structure of competitive pluralism, it would not have made news and I would not be discussing it today. Ethnic strife in India has spilled blood in large amounts at different points in history from the 1890s onward. In the 1990s, problems in Assam, Punjab and Kashmir have been particularly glaring. What, then, is the difference between the recent experience of ethnicity in Western liberal democracies and the contemporary Indian experience?

The difference came to me forcefully in 1989, when I was resident in Melbourne and received a (form) letter from the Australian Prime Minister encouraging me (and others) to become an Australian citizen. In that letter the Prime Minister went to some trouble to spell out what it meant to be an Australian. He said: it was not the colour of your skin, or your religion or the language you spoke that made you more Australian than others; being an Australian meant believing in freedom of speech, of association, in everyone having 'a fair go', etc. This letter prompted me to subject myself to some imaginary tortures – of the Geoffrey Robertson kind.[29] For example, I asked myself, if this were all there was to being an Australian then what would be my proper patriotic response if Australia ever went to war with a nation that professed the same liberal values but was much better equipped to protect them and hence, by definition, to protect my 'Australianness' as well? (Of course, a Margaret Thatcher would argue that a liberal democratic country never starts a war, so the question would not arise!) A little reflection made it clear that the Prime Minister was speaking in a historical context that afforded him one rare luxury: he did not feel any pressure to spell out what made Australians different from others. The letter, by implication, was relegating 'cultural difference' to the sphere of the personal. If pressed, a liberal would no doubt tell me – as the British Muslims who burned The Satanic Verses at Bradford were often reminded – that 'ethnicity' could find a place in public life so long as its expressions were in conformity with the 'core values' of the nation (as defined by the state). Ethnicity functions here under the aegis of equal-opportunity principles, in the form of a pressure group – in my case, an Indian Association which demands such things as time-slots on Australian public radio or funding for community schools as part of liberal-pluralist multiculturalism. As Talal Asad has shown in his discussion of the Rushdie affair, there are hidden demographic assumptions behind this position, particularly that of a continuous dominance of a European-derived, if not an English-speaking, majority.[30] Of course, one would also have to take into account particular Australian institutions – the welfare state, a relatively prosperous economy, the structure of the Australian Labor Party, the official policy of multiculturalism, etc. – that have historically played a role in managing ethnic conflict in public life. But that Australia would be able to retain this multicultural tolerance of ethnicity in public life if the cultural dominance of its Anglo-Celtic or, at least, European majority were ever seriously threatened is far from certain.

Modern ethnic consciousnesses in India have been fashioned under circumstances in which the politics of cultural difference have been of pre-eminent value. The question of Indian unity has never been settled beyond all doubt and disputation, nor has there been any one, culturally homogeneous and dominant, majority ethnic group that could at once dominate and effectively claim to represent all Indians (at least until Independence – one might argue that the Hindu extremist party, the BJP, has been trying to develop one, precisely by denying the heterogeneity that characterises Hinduism). The British cobbled a political India together for reasons of administrative convenience. The nationality question was muddled from the beginning. In the public sphere that the British created, there was no single, universally agreed-upon 'Indian' ethnicity. The struggle to produce a sense of cultural unity against the British made mainstream Indian nationalism culturally Hindu. The Muslim search for Pakistan emphasised Islam. The lower castes' struggle for social justice produced anti-Brahmanism. After Independence, in the 1950s and the 1960s, there were the 'tribal' communities of the Nagas and the Mizos on the north-eastern frontier of the country who had to be bludgeoned into becoming Indians. The last fifteen or twenty years have seen an explosive combination of democracy and demography. Indian population has almost trebled since Independence. The growth and diversity of the middle class may be judged from the fact that while at Independence there was consensus that the number of important languages was fourteen, there are now daily newspapers published in more than seventy-eight different languages.[31] This middle class has tasted consumerism, which has increased the sense of competition in urban life. The secessionist aspirations in Kashmir, Punjab and parts of Assam have gained in strength in recent years. Caste, and particularly the Indian policy of positive discrimination in favour of the lower castes, has become an extremely contentious issue in public life. And the latest attempts by the extremist Hindu political parties to convert Hinduism into a strong, monolithic and militant religion have given many Indian Muslims understandable nightmares.

Fundamentally, India, like the former Soviet Union, remains in part an imperial structure held together by strong tendencies towards centralism. Unlike the Soviet Union, however, those centralist tendencies exist within, and must work through, a democratic political structure which also gives the state more popular legitimacy than the Stalinist states ever enjoyed. Indians have an investment in electoral democracy, as was proven in the unpopularity of Mrs Gandhi's two-year emergency of 1975–77. Yet the ideological scene has changed.

This centralising tendency was once most powerfully expressed in the ideology of Jawaharlal Nehru and it represented some kind of consensus among the political elite. This ideology, called in India by the name of secularism, drew heavily on the Western liberal heritage to argue for a separation between religion and the ideas that governed public life. In India, where a religious idiom and imagination had always been very strongly present, this ideology never described the actual culture of political practice. But so long as the national leadership lay in the hands of a tiny elite reared in and respectful of the British traditions of politics, the everyday religiousness of Indian political culture could be kept separate from the decision-making boards of the government. The custodian nature of this elite was reflected in the unity of the Congress Party, in which Nehru always remained a Bonapartist figure.

The combination of demography, democracy and political growth in India has now ensured that the political elite is no longer tiny. There are no Bonapartist figures in India today. Nehruvian secularism, a close cousin of Western liberalism represented now by marxists and the left-liberals in India, is on the defensive (remember Salman Rushdie's character talking about the battle lines?).

Why this has happened will require a different analysis. But it should be clear from the above that the problem of competitive and official constructions of ethnicity is a feature inherent in the modern civil society. In the best of times, one expects to find lawful, bureaucratic means of resolving these tensions. Even then, the mobilisation of ethnic sentiments would always risk spilling over into racism in public places, as the experience of the Australian Muslims during the Gulf War would confirm. There are, however, other times in history when bureaucratic solutions lose their appeal. The difference here is not due to a total opposition between fascism and liberalism as political philosophies. The difference here is in historical contexts. Imagine the conflict between the Bengali-Muslim sense of ethnicity and Pakistani nationalism in what was, before 1971, East Pakistan. Clearly, a model of pluralism which recommended that all signs of cultural difference be matters of private belief became untenable in that situation. Kashmir today, for many, would represent a similar situation. The point is, as I have argued, that the very structure of modern governmentality carries with it the seeds of ethnic bloodbath. Whether the seeds will ever germinate is a matter of the particular moment of history one inhabits. This is not a counsel of despair, but it is a plea for our political analysis to be informed by a larger sense of irony.

Advocating the cultivation of a sense of irony about the civilising narratives of modernity does not imply political passivity. The relationship between philosophical positions and political action is seldom straightforward. For, (1) there is no alternative to action – we are condemned to act politically in this world whether we want to or not – and (2) the subject who acts, and is mobilised to act in the face of events, is more than an intellectual-philosophical subject. Action involves emotions, memories, tastes, feelings, will and values – and these things have histories over which we have much less control than we have over our consciously thought-out philosophical positions. Whatever my theoretical understanding today of the problematic histories of practices named 'sati', 'female infanticide', 'human sacrifice' and 'thagi' – to name four names by which British colonial discourse condemned 'Indian' (yet another name) civilisation – I have been irreversibly conditioned by the histories of my childhood, education, socialisation (all of them influenced by British and nationalist critiques of Indian society) to be revolted by the practices that these names seek to describe (always inaccurately). How, in what mode of action, this revulsion will express itself depends on particular situations and the opportunities I read them as presenting.

What, then, is the relationship between this critique and political or state policies that might be put in place to combat racism under conditions of modernisation? Firstly, this critique is about the limits of policy-making under present institutional arrangements. I have argued that, given the connection between governmentality and measurement, both the modern nation-state and the civil society necessarily set up certain competitive structures of identity through the very distributive processes over which they preside. The question 'Distribution among whom?' always takes identities for granted. Identities here are not seen as porous. In fact, identities are not measurable or enumerable except on the assumption that their boundaries are abrupt and not vague. In the language of distributive justice, identities represent, at any one point in time, some kind of narrative consensus whereby everybody or every group knows who they are and this knowledge is shared by the institution that administers well-being. In other words, the existing models of modern political and economic institutions handle the question of cultural 'difference' in identity precisely by fixing and freezing such differences into divisions that are not permeable (a Hindu cannot be a Muslim) so that they are amenable to measurement and enumeration. Even if we moved from the idea of allocative justice to that of procedural justice in the sphere of distribution, as John Rawls did in his classic book, *A Theory of Justice* (1971), we would still have no way of handling differences in identities. Rawls's search for 'justice as fairness', as readers of that text will remember, led him to posit an 'original position' (a perspectival position, really, as he himself explains) in which individuals met without any conception of their social or class locations – that is to say, as humans from whom all differences had been abstracted away.[32]

Even leftist intellectuals who try to modify Rawls's arguments in order to infuse a more self-consciously political life into his theory find it difficult not to universalise a distinction that is historically very particular, that is, the distinction between 'public' and 'private'. Chantal Mouffe's attempt to move away from the Rawlsian position of holding on to the idea of an original rational agreement and to ground 'democracy' in a permanent state of disputation (since there cannot any longer be a 'single idea of a substantial common good') is instructive in this regard. Pluralism here is seen as possible on condition that the political is defined around a minimum shared agreement; that 'the principles of the liberal-democratic regime qua political association: equality and liberty' be defined as the 'common political good'. As Mouffe clarifies:

> a liberal-democratic regime, if it must be agnostic in terms of morality and religion, cannot be agnostic concerning political values since by definition it asserts the principles that constitute its specificity qua political association, i.e., the political principles of equality and liberty.[33]

Where, then, will be the place for 'morality and religion' in this (post)modern, socialist idea of liberal-democratic politics that accepts disputation as a foundation for democracy? Or, indeed, for anything else that is not part of this minimum shared political good? Mouffe is clear on this: these ideas will exist as 'private' belief, the sphere of 'privacy' being implicitly defined in such a way as to be incapable, by its very definition, of endangering the institutions that embody 'the political principles of equality and liberty'.[34]

What else can an Indian intellectual do but experience a sense of irony at what European political theory offers us? On the one hand, there are the actually existing institutions that administer our lives both in India and outside. The very administration of (ethnic) identities by the actually existing civil-political institutions needs, as I have shown, the same fixed, discrete categories that racists of all colours use. The only difference is in their idioms – bureaucracies use a certain impersonal language while racist mobilisation in public life involves an explicit use of emotions as well; but this difference is superficial and depends on the historical context. Governments, in moments of crisis, will use both. On the other hand, critics of these institutions, whether arguing from the purely liberal position of a Rawls or the postmodernist socialist position of a Mouffe, cannot but resurrect the model of a human being who holds onto a cultural distinction between the public and the private, as a condition for tolerance and pluralism. But is this human being universal? Is this human being 'universal' even in the West? Does 'political emancipation' (I borrow the expression from the young Marx's essay, 'On the Jewish Question') require us to universalise the experience and skills of a particular group in modern European history? Do we all *have to* become humans who are able to objectify their relationship to the supernatural into stateable 'beliefs' and able to hold these 'beliefs' as 'private'?

The politics of being human are different between cultures and within cultures. We are not impervious to one another but that does not mean that the differences are not real. Some people in India possess the modern sense of privacy as it has developed in the history of the middle classes in the West. Many do not. The importance of kinship in Indian society suggests other paths of social change. If we swallowed a theory – hook, line and sinker – that made tolerance and pluralism contingent on the idea of 'private belief', we would only move further away from our social realities than Rawls does from his own by his theoretical manoeuvres. The writing of Indian history, then, has to subscribe to two struggles. One is the struggle to document and interpret for contemporary needs the different practices of toleration and pluralism that already exist in Indian society, practices that are not critically dependent on the universalisation of the public/private distinction. The other would be to help develop critiques of the already existing institutions and their theoretical assumptions, for the struggle against the murderous and self-proclaimed 'Hindus' of today must, in the long run, also be a struggle for new kinds of political and economic institutions for the management of public life – institutions that do not require for their everyday operation the fiction of cultural identities with fixed, enumerable and abrupt boundaries. Nobody has the blueprints for such institutions though we know that two of the finest products of Indo-British cultural encounter of the nineteenth century, Gandhi and Tagore, experimented with both facets of this struggle at different moments of their lives. If cultural and other kinds of differences are to be taken, contested and negotiated seriously, and we want to live in a world where particular developments in the cultural histories of European middle classes do not have to function as models to which all politics of being human must aspire, then we also need institutions that can handle the fuzzy logic with which identities are built. The existing institutions in charge of producing and administering prosperity cannot do that.

NOTES

An earlier and shorter version of this essay was read at a seminar organised by the University of Western Sydney, Nepean, in May 1993 and was published in the proceedings of that seminar. I am grateful to the participants in that seminar for their criticisms. Thanks also to Fiona Nicoll, David Bennett, Meaghan Morris and Stephen Henningham for their comments. All responsibilities are, of course, mine.

1 Ashis Nandy's work has been pioneering in this respect but one can also mention Veena Das, Bhikhu Parekh, T. N. Madan and others. See, for example, A. Nandy's *The Intimate Enemy: Loss and Recovery of Self under Colonialism*, Delhi, Oxford University Press, 1983, and *Traditions, Tyranny and Utopias: Essays in the Politics of Awareness*, Delhi, Manohar,

1987; V. Das and A. Nandy, 'Violence, Victimhood and the Language of Silence', in V. Das (ed.), *The Word and the World*, Delhi, Manohar, 1986, pp. 177–95; B. Parekh, *Gandhi's Political Philosophy: A Critical Examination*, Notre Dame, IN, University of Notre Dame Press, 1989.

2 See essays by L. Mani, V. Dhareshwar and M. John in J. Clifford and V. Dhareshwar (eds), *Travelling Theories, Travelling Theorists*, Santa Cruz, California Group for the Critical Study of Colonial Discourse and the Centre for Cultural Studies, USSC, 1989.

3 A. Ahmad, *In Theory: Classes, Nations, Literatures*, London, Verso, 1992, pp. 192–3, 330 n. 22.

4 See T. Brass, 'A-way with Their Wor(l)ds: Rural Labourers through the Postmodern Prism', *Economic and Political Weekly [EPW]*, 5 June 1993; K. Balagopal, 'Why Did December 6, 1992 Happen?', *EPW*, 24 April 1993; Sumit Sarkar, 'The Fascism of the Sangh Parivar', *EPW*, 20 January 1993.

5 Sarkar, 'Fascism of the Sangh Parivar', pp. 164–5.

6 See the excellent discussion in A. Vanaik, 'Situating Threat of Hindu Nationalism: Problems with Fascist Paradigm' and Partha Chatterjee, 'Secularism and Toleration', in *EPW*, 9 July 1994, pp. 1729–48, 1768–77.

7 W. E. B. DuBois, *The World and Africa: An Enquiry into the Part Which Africa Has Played in World History*, New York, International Publishers, 1965, p. 23, cited in R. W. Bologh, *Love of Greatness: Max Weber and Masculine Thinking – A Feminist Enquiry*, London, Unwin Hyman, 1990, p. 38.

8 See the discussion in P. H. Boulle, 'In Defense of Slavery: Eighteenth-Century Opposition to Abolition and the Origins of a Racist Ideology in France', in F. Krantz (ed.), *History From Below: Studies in Popular Protest and Popular Ideology*, Oxford and New York, Oxford University Press, 1988, pp. 219–46.

9 Cited in T. Asad, 'Ethnography, Literature, and Politics: Some Readings and Uses of Salman Rushdie's *The Satanic Verses*', *Cultural Anthropology*, vol. 5, no. 3, August 1990, p. 243.

10 K. K. Klostermaier, *A Survey of Hinduism*, New York, 1989, State University of New York Press, p. 412.

11 G. W. F. Hegel, *The Philosophy of History*, trans. J. Sibree, New York, Dover Publications, 1956, p. 161. See also the discussion in R. Inden, *Imagining India*, Oxford, Blackwell, 1990, pp. 69–74.

12 Hegel, *History*, p. 163.

13 V. S. Naipaul, *India: A Million Mutinies Now*, London, Heinemann, 1990, p. 420.

14 R. Thapar, 'Imagined Religious Communities? Ancient History and the Modern Search for a Hindu Identity', *Modern Asian Studies*, vol. 23, no. 2, 1989, p. 219.

15 Our eyes have been opened to these aspects of 'modernity' by, among others, the path-breaking works of Michel Foucault. My particular observations on India owe a lot to the pioneering researches of Bernard Cohn and to the illuminating work of Richard Smith, Arjun Appadurai and Carol Breckenridge, Nicholas Dirks, Rashmi Pant, N. G. Barrier, Gyan Prakash and others.

16 I. Hacking, *The Taming of Chance*, Cambridge, Cambridge University Press, 1991, p. 24.

17 See M. Foucault, 'Governmentality', in G. Burchell, C. Gordon and P. Miller (eds), *The Foucault Effect: Studies in Governmentality*, London, Harvester Wheatsheaf, 1991, pp. 87–104.

18 T. H. Hollingsworth, *Historical Demography*, London, Hodder & Stoughton, 1969, p. 78.

19 See K. W. Jones, 'Religious Identity and the Indian Census', in N. G. Barrier (ed.), *Census in British India: New Perspectives*, Delhi, Manohar, 1984, p. 74.

20 Chapter 7 of G. Pandey's book, *The Construction of Communalism in Colonial India*, Delhi, Oxford University Press, 1990, contains a fine analysis and history of this word.

21 M. Galanter, *Competing Equalities: Law and the Backward Classes in India*, Delhi, Oxford University Press, 1984, p. 130.

22 I. Hacking, 'Making Up People', in T. Heller, M. Sosna, and D. E. Wellbery (eds),

Reconstructing Individualism: Autonomy, Individuality, and the Self in Western Thought, Stanford, CA, Stanford University Press, 1986, pp. 227–8.

23 ibid., p. 227.

24 S. Kaviraj, 'On the Construction of Colonial Power: Structure, Discourse, Hegemony', unpublished paper presented to a conference on 'Imperial Hegemony', Berlin, 1–3 June, 1989.

25 See E. F. Irschick, *Politics and Social Conflict in South India: The Non-Brahmin Movement and Tamil Separatism, 1916–1929*, Berkeley, University of California Press, 1969, App. 1.

26 Jones, 'Religious Identity', p. 91.

27 L. Febvre, 'Civilisation: Evolution of a Word and a Group of Ideas', in P. Burke (ed.), *A New Kind of History: From the Writings of Febvre*, London, Routledge & Kegan Paul, 1973, pp. 219–57.

28 R. Bandyopadhyay, *Neetibodh*, Calcutta, 1858, pp. 12–13.

29 The barrister Geoffrey Robertson was presenter of a series of British television programmes cast as mock trials and entitled 'Hypotheticals', in which topical issues were debated by interested parties and 'expert witnesses'.

30 T. Asad, 'Multiculturalism and British Identity in the Wake of the Rushdie Affair', in his *Genealogies of Religion: Discipline and Reasons of Power in Christianity and Islam*, Baltimore, MD, Johns Hopkins University Press, 1993, pp. 239–68.

31 Personal communication from Professor A. D. Gupta, formerly Director of the National Library in Calcutta.

32 See J. Rawls, *A Theory of Justice*, London, Oxford University Press, 1976, pp. 137–8. Rawls, as is well known, has modified and presented reinterpretations of his original theory in subsequent publications. A good overview of the debate around Rawls is available in C. Kukathas and P. Petit, *Rawls: 'A Theory of Justice' and Its Critics*, Cambridge, Cambridge University Press, 1990.

33 C. Mouffe, 'Rawls: Political Philosophy Without Politics', in D. Rasmussen (ed.), *Universalism Vs. Communitarianism: Contemporary Debates in Ethics*, Cambridge, Mass., MIT Press, 1990, p. 223.

34 ibid., p. 222.

8

BETWEEN ETHNICITY AND NATIONHOOD

Shaka Day and the struggle over Zuluness in post-apartheid South Africa

Susan Mathieson and David Attwell

KwaXimba lies beyond Cato Ridge, off the N3 highway between Johannesburg and Durban, a route familiar to the migrant workers of rural Natal. Crossing an empty plateau, a minor road curves down steep ridges before opening out on to the Valley of a Thousand Hills. The valley combines the picturesque with poverty: the hills range as far as the eye can see, as densely populated as any township but with mud and corrugated iron structures built haphazardly on the slopes, rather than the grids of matchbox houses one sees in the cities. The district is home to the people of Ximba, some of whom were forcibly removed to this place in 1960. Most of the people who live here, however, choose to do so because they support Chief Mlaba, whose leadership based on participatory democracy and development has attracted them to live within the boundaries of his tribal authority.

Whilst the stranger's eye is trained to see with concern the poverty, over-crowding and soil erosion of the district, our colleague Phumelele Ntombela points out the water taps, electricity cables and telephone wires connecting nearly every shack under Chief Mlaba's jurisdiction. To obtain these amenities he had to circumvent Chief Gatsha Buthelezi's KwaZulu Government which withheld development funds as punishment for Mlaba's turning his back on the Inkatha Freedom Party (IFP). In Ximba's rural development Ntombela sees an ANC-inspired, practical vision of progress for rural Natal as opposed to a regressive tribalism mobilised, as she sees it, by Inkatha. Like many African National Congress (ANC) and Communist Party (SACP) intellectuals, Ntombela has made the journey from a childhood of rural poverty to town, and then the rarer break into professional and academic life. To those trapped in the cycle of rural unemployment and migrancy, the idea of negotiating a positive relationship with progress is no doubt less tangible. Somewhere between our colleague's interpretation of the ANC's practical vision – which became formalised nationally as the Reconstruction and Development Programme – and Inkatha's projection of a defeated Zulu nation struggling to reassert itself, the residents of KwaXimba live their day-to-day lives,

111

much discussed, planned for, and described as having this or that consciousness of their situation.

But the people of Ximba define themselves not only in terms of their local geography and development needs, but also on the volatile national terrain of cultural politics during a time of dramatic transition. A particular brand of pluralism has been the rallying call of the national democratic struggle in its long history in South Africa. The vision of the ANC, in direct opposition to the ethnic chauvinism of apartheid, has always been inclusive and non-racial. South Africans who affiliated to this mainstream and now victorious tradition were frequently bemused by the apparent irrationalism of what goes under the name of identity politics elsewhere, especially but not exclusively in the United States. What is identity politics, it seemed, but apartheid thinking in another guise? Apartheid's ruse was to use ethnicity as a way of deflecting claims to power at the centre; in this context, identitarian agendas could easily be, and were co-opted under a constitutional arrangement which protected white interests. To those opposing such hegemony it seemed as though the kind of multiculturalism frequently seen in the liberal democracies was deeply conservative, concerned more with achieving access to an existing constitutional order than with fundamentally changing it. Indeed, multiculturalism and apartheid are not such antithetical visions. Apartheid was less an aberrant resurgence of pre-Enlightenment thinking (as many liberal historians and politicians had it) than a particularly acute manifestation of the Enlightenment's own ambivalence. Europe was able to disown apartheid on the basis of 'moral luck' – following the universal condemnation of racism after decolonisation – but apartheid was intimately a product of Europe: it was an attempt to reproduce and impose a European conception of the nation-state, based on the principle of territorial and cultural integrity within one country, on a polyglot society, so that South Africa was to become a constellation of mini-states each with its own language and culture. If there were obstacles in the way of this project, they could be overcome with sufficient policing.

The condescension of progressive South Africans towards multiculturalism is now being severely tested, however, in the new dispensation, in which the practice of enforcing separate identities has given way to 'rainbow' pluralism as state policy.[1] South Africa therefore now faces the tensions which are familiar in other democracies, of minority cultures' seeking to define themselves against the national mainstream. The Afrikaner Volksvront has not abandoned the dream of a white homeland, and amongst Coloured people of the Western Cape has arisen the December 1st Movement, which attempts to ground a 'coloured identity' on the memory of slavery (the date recalls the abolition of slavery at the Cape in 1838). Parliamentary committees are discussing the possibility of a Cultural Council, which will make recommendations to the legislators concerning the protection of rights in areas such as language policy and education. But, arguably, the most visible site of this reconceptualisation is that of Zulu ethnic self-consciousness. This essay will focus on this question by examining the celebrated and contested memory of Shaka, founder of the Zulu nation in the early nineteenth century, in debates that took place in the months prior to the first democratic elections of April 1994.

In September 1993, the ANC decided to celebrate Shaka Day in KwaXimba. Although the movement had been considering it for some time, this was one of its first, tentative steps in actually engaging with Zulu ethnicity, which had been so muddied by its mobilisation in the name of apartheid or separate development that it had been largely dismissed in favour of the national democratic struggle. However, with the ANC's transition during the course of 1993 from an opposition movement to a government-in-waiting, it faced the challenge of reaching out to those groups that had not identified with the national liberation movement. In Natal, its non-racialism had run aground on Zulu nationalism, and it was becoming clear that the ANC would have to accommodate Inkatha if it were to avoid a civil war. The move towards a negotiated settlement also meant an accommodation with demands for federalism, with considerable powers being devolved to regions whose administrations in some cases had been tied to apartheid's bantustans.[2] In the context of this regional compromise, Zulu ethnicity was to play a key role in the province.

If the ANC was adjusting to this new federalist politics reluctantly, it was because existing ethnic identities, far from pre-dating colonialism, had gained their present form under apartheid conditions. Ethnic identities are never what they pretend to be, but in this situation their constructedness was made ominous and problematic by the fact that they had been both encouraged and exploited in the interests of white power. For some groups, such as the Zulu loyalists, the pragmatic response to such manipulation had been partly to accede to it. From the ANC's point of view, since ethnic identity was a tool in the hands of political elites wielding or desiring illegitimate forms of power – indeed, entire groups had used ethnicity to promote their interests – on what terms could these same communities be incorporated into the new South Africa? More awkwardly, if ethnicity were acknowledged to have genuine popular appeal among sectors of the black working class, how would this affect the conceptualisation of the new nation-state? The challenge facing the ANC, then, involved having to respond positively to ethnic particularism without eviscerating its own hard-won traditions.

In deciding to celebrate Shaka Day, the ANC was showing its recognition of the increasing political significance of the symbols of Zulu nationalism whilst contesting Inkatha's assertion of a sole right to define them. For Inkatha and Chief Buthelezi, Shaka Day legitimised the KwaZulu bantustan by associating it with the founding of the Zulu Kingdom in the 1830s. KwaZulu was constructed as having pre-dated apartheid; the Anglo-Zulu wars that had been fought at the height of British imperialism provided a memory of heroic anti-colonial resistance; even Shaka himself (as we shall see) was construed as having had extraordinary foresight in protecting the nation by striking compromises with British merchants operating out of Durban Bay. In terms of this logic, both the governing National Party and the ANC became threatening outsiders, the only difference being that whereas the Nationalists had been prepared at least to recognise Zulu interests in the form of the KwaZulu homeland, the ANC sought to undermine them completely by dismantling all existing state structures. Resistance to the national democratic struggle was therefore justified in the name of the survival of the Zulu nation; the intense divisions between urban and rural Zulus, the class, gender and generational differences amongst Zulus, all these were summarily erased in a call for the unity of the Zulu people under Inkatha's banner.

Buthelezi held his own Shaka Day celebrations, as always, at Umlazi, one of Durban's townships, and at Shaka's grave in Stanger. On this occasion, in September 1993, the immediate political context was Buthelezi's refusal to participate in the Transitional Executive Council (TEC) − a structure created to oversee the passage to national elections − and the explicit advocacy by right-wing Afrikaners of a civil war which they hoped would be waged by Inkatha, to whom they pledged support. An alliance with Afrikaner extremists troubled Buthelezi less than the fear of being absorbed into the TEC, for at Umlazi he said that allowing the TEC to administer KwaZulu would be tantamount 'to allowing foreigners to rule us. . . . We must be prepared to fight for our freedom and the right to rule over ourselves.'[3] Freedom here means the freedom of the Zulus from the rest of South Africa, not the freedom of black South Africans from settler-colonialism. (Buthelezi's ability to straddle liberationist and Zulu nationalist discourses was one of the reasons for Inkatha's resilience through the years of the ANC's exile.) Later on the same day, at Stanger, he argued that 'it is not my intention to be aggressive or to start a war . . . but they are all against the Zulus'.[4] Behind such veiled threats appearing in the media, the actual texts of Buthelezi's speeches reveal a more subtle understanding of the role ethnic mobilisation might play in a project Anthony Giddens would call 're-embedding', particularly for a people whose sense of history and identity had developed in apartheid's divisive and disruptive form of modernity.[5] Zulu identity represents a continuous tradition and a source of dignity: 'It is on occasions such as this, that Zulus can stand together as one . . . that we can remember the past and plan for the future.'[6] Or again: 'We are both Zulus and South Africans. . . . If we do not achieve federalism then we face becoming a people without a face, a people which is just one among many, a people without a future. Because we are proud of our Zulu past the IFP cannot allow this to happen. As Zulus we are respected and held in high esteem by friend and foe alike.'[7]

The living embodiment of this continuity was present in the form of King Goodwill Zwelithini, heir to the royal house of Shaka.[8] 'Every Zulu knows', said the king, 'that even today before he can move his home, his ancestors have to be appeased and there is great pleading with them to relocate themselves with the relocation of the family.' Change is inevitable, but it needs to be ritualised in terms of Zulu tradition. He went on to stress the significance of the homeland: 'KwaZulu is KwaZulu, and our souls are captive in it. If KwaZulu is torn apart and we are scattered, we will lose our souls.'[9] The integrity of KwaZulu is opposed to a quasi-biblical scattering of the tribes, a newly hostile political order that resists the continued re-creation of the past. But Shaka Day is as much concerned with the promise of progress as with the past, for as the founder of the Zulu nation, Shaka is widely recognised as a modernising force in Zulu history. Shaka is also said to have had a prophetic capacity to foresee conditions that his people would face in the future – a mystic power remembered in his prediction (c. 1835) of 'great iron birds flying through the air'. King Zwelithini continued:

> King Shaka who died here in this place [Stanger] was the greatest vision-ary of his time. It was his vision which made him set aside the whole of Durban Bay as a place where Whites could feel safe as they settled in his Kingdom. The King with his deep sense of vision, started something that we must finish. There is unfinished business in Zulus seeing to it that Black and White live together to bring the great advantages of the union that King Shaka saw at the beginning of the nineteenth century. . . . I reign in circumstances which my own ancestors envisaged.[10]

The king's prophetic mode is worth some attention. Prophecy was a powerful ele-ment in precolonial oral culture, but it gained a new relevance under colonialism. As the ceaseless production of the new, modernity weakens the link between past and present, making prophetic language a source of continuity and a means of sublimating conflict and division. In the frontier wars of the Eastern Cape during the nineteenth century, the figures of the prophet and the general were sometimes indistinguishable. In the residual orality of early black South African literature, the prophetic voice can still be heard. Thus in Sol Plaatje's Mhudi, the first English-lan-guage novel in South Africa, the cyclic return of Halley's Comet is used to suggest that the 'settled system' will be superseded by an all-inclusive alliance of the African people. Written shortly after World War I, Mhudi's historical narrative of the 1830s is based implicitly on a projection of the likely turn of events with the next appearance of the comet in 1985 (Plaatjie was not far off the mark, since what he predicted had largely materialised by 1994). Such re-narrativisations humanise the present and ensure a place for Africans in the modern world.

However, one must distinguish between the psychic importance of ethnic nationalism in re-embedding dislocated subjects and its mobilisation within a spe-cific political context in the interests of a particular class or class fraction, in this case the bureaucrats who benefited from the homeland system and who now stood to lose power and financial means if these structures were dismantled. Inkatha's rhetoric therefore did not always wear such a human face. Before and after Shaka Day, while most parties were using the negotiations to try to stem the tide of violence, Inkatha repeatedly warned its opponents of the warlike capaci-ties of the Zulus, presenting an escalation of the conflict as a natural consequence – an impending storm, an alarmed snake – of their being crossed. At the Stanger rally, Buthelezi called on all Inkatha members to pay five rands each to finance armed units to 'protect' Zulu migrants in the hostels near Johannesburg; of course, such actions only polarised the townships on the Reef even further.

One might ask, why did Natal take this route of conservative Zulu nationalism when most of the rest of South Africa embraced an inclusive and arguably more radical (or at least class-conscious) nationalism? The answers to this question lie in Natal's precolonial history and in the form taken by the colonial encounter here. The Zulu Kingdom proved to be remarkably resistant and was finally broken up only in the aftermath of the defeat of King Cetshwayo by the British in 1879. Until this point, the British were unwilling to engage the Zulu Kingdom militarily as they lacked the resources to colonise Natal, but a considerable amount of ideological labour was invested, nevertheless, in ensuring that the kingdom served the purposes of the colonial administration. The first Secretary for Natal Native Affairs, Theophilus Shepstone, undertook this project assiduously, legitimating the administration by modelling it on the Shakan military system. Far from seeing Shaka as a barbaric and lawless savage, Shepstone saw in the kingdom an inexpensive, ready-to-hand mode of governance that combined the advantages of indirect rule and direct violence. Moreover, his system could be justified on grounds of its authenticity as an *African* form of administration. The value of the kingdom to the colonists was that it had already established a centralised relationship between the king and the chiefs, based on the king's extraction of surplus production for the maintenance of his army. This expropriation could be imitated by a cash-strapped colonial government, with the surplus being redirected into the coffers of the Natal administration. Colonial involvement in Zulu tradition reached its zenith when Shepstone stood in 'as Shaka' at the inauguration of King Cetshwayo. But for as long as the Zulu Kingdom remained intact, this was always an uneasy project in which the interests of the kingdom often overrode those of the colonists; thus a new set of imperatives in the latter half of the nineteenth century demanded the destruction of the kingdom. After Cetshwayo's defeat the kingdom was formally divided into several chieftaincies, with the king being sent into exile. In this later phase, Shaka's memory resurfaced ambivalently from time to time as both a bloodthirsty tyrant and a hero of nation-building, but a pattern of collaboration had already been established between the kingdom and the colonists, which facilitated the notion that Zuluness was assimilable within a colonial world-view, and it is this pattern that has been periodically revived.[11]

The Zulu Kingdom has therefore remained a contradictory symbol of both resistance and collaboration. As segregationist and later apartheid policy began to unfold in the twentieth century, and while the black petite bourgeoisie in the rest of South Africa began moving towards an alliance with an increasingly organised working class, in Natal a more conservative alliance was being forged between the *kholwa*, or christianised elite, and the remnant of the Zulu monarchy, the chiefs, and the Natal Native Administration – with an emphasis on Zulu ethnicity and nationhood. As Shula Marks has shown, the colonial administration unashamedly regarded the alliance as a bastion against the emergent working-class politics of the townships. She quotes Heaton Nicholls, Secretary of Natal Native Affairs, as saying, 'If we do not get back to communalism we will most certainly arrive very soon at communism.'[12] This view was echoed by the Rev. John Dube, a key presence in Natal politics and, initially, in South Africa as the first President of the

South African Native National Congress (the forerunner of the ANC), from which he broke away when he found it becoming too radical. Dube saw in a return to tradition a bulwark against the leaders of the Industrial and Commercial Union (ICU) with their 'misleading propaganda, their absurd promises, their international socialistic inclinations and communism'.[13]

But while the class nature of the royalist alliance has been recognised, less frequently observed is its basis in the defence of patriarchy. Marks discusses the increasing assertiveness of black women as they took advantage of the freedoms opening up to them in the break-up of older tribal structures and in their migration to the urban centres. Colonial legislation had entrenched the position of black women as legal minors; the Urban Areas Act of 1923 stated that women needed the consent of a male guardian in order to enter the cities. This was seen as a means of ensuring the success of the migrant labour system by keeping black families in the homelands, thus keeping wage costs low – families could rely on subsistence farming – and as a way of easing the pressure on the rapidly expanding towns. The alliance Dube sought with the chiefs involved calling on the Native Administration to tighten laws pertaining to women. At a meeting with the chiefs in 1937, Dube said that the magistrates were 'too lenient in dealing with their womenfolk' and asked 'that punishments might be more severe, as the leniency leads to demoralization'. The government had to take 'drastic steps to prevent the migration of women to the towns'.[14]

In sum, the history behind the currently dominant forms of Zulu nationalism is a history of local solutions, that is to say, attempts were made to re-establish the authority of certain power elites in the face of the erosion of their authority by industrialisation and segregation. This is the appropriate context in which to understand the rather different chemistry the Ximba clan sought to create between Zulu tradition and the process of modernisation. Before its banning in the early 1960s, the ANC had a strong presence in rural Natal. According to Chief Mlaba, the primary reason for the Ximba people's support for the ANC can be traced to their long history of resistance to colonialism – the Mlaba chiefs had always resisted laws that sought to control the powers of the chiefs. They had belonged to the ANC since its inception in 1912 and saw it as the legitimate organisation of resistance in KwaZulu-Natal. Mlaba's forebears were not party to any alliance of royalists, chiefs and the administration in the 1920s and 1930s; indeed, Mlaba believes they regarded Inkatha as a renegade organisation that had been created by the state to oppose the ANC.

Given its history, and Mlaba's ANC affiliations, KwaXimba was the obvious place for the ANC to launch its entry into the traditional Inkatha territory of Zulu nationalism. It renamed Shaka Day 'Heroes Day', in an attempt to redefine the event as multicultural, celebrating not only Shaka but also the Xhosa King Hintsa, the Basotho King Moshoeshoe, Mahatma Gandhi (*satyagraha* or passive resistance was conceived during Gandhi's residence in South Africa, in Natal in fact, and became a model of activism in the Defiance Campaign of the 1950s) and a host of other luminaries, including Olive Schreiner. The 'people' to whom this broad-church pantheon might appeal were all those South Africans who were struggling to overthrow apartheid. The choice of KwaXimba was more immediately strategic as well, however: it was an attempt to reach rural Natal. As the Natal Midlands ANC chairperson, Harry Gwala, proclaimed, Heroes Day would 'fire the first volley for next year's general election'.[15] The response from Inkatha's Northern Natal chiefs was immediate: 'Mlaba's meeting will surely fan the flames of violence as the Zulus will not accept traditional functions to be dragged into cheap political propaganda by political fanatics such as Zibuse Mlaba.'[16] Gwala did nothing to allay the chiefs' fears that the ANC was at the forefront of the hostile, urban influences that were eroding Zulu traditions: 'We are not going to reduce ourselves to the level of tribal chiefs who neither understand history nor geography,' he said. 'To them tribalism and ethnicity are things that are imposed by God above and are not governed by the laws of development in society.'[17] To the chiefs' objection that Shaka should not be mixed up with the heroes of other ethnic groups 'like coffee and tea', Gwala responded, 'Could it be that the apartheid ideology is so ingratiated [sic] in their bones that they cannot see beyond the confines of bantustans?'[18]

Gwala's contempt, however, belied a degree of uncertainty within the ANC about how it should approach Shaka Day. In the Natal Midlands Regional Executive there was much debate over whether the commitment to pluralism meant diluting Shaka Day as a day for all the heroes of South Africa, or whether it was legitimate to support a festival honouring the Zulu nation-builder alone.[19] Did multiculturalism mean dilution, or did it mean that the various groups ought to identify with the specific heritages that make up the nation? One view held that it was important to acknowledge the specific Shakan heritage while emphasising those aspects – nation-building, resistance to apartheid – that could most easily be reconciled with the politics of the ANC. If the ANC wished to reconcile itself to the traditionalist, rural community, it had to take Zuluness seriously and accommodate it without seeking to reduce it to a homogeneous national culture. Others felt uneasy about Shaka Day's emphasis on rebuilding the Zulu nation. The Zulu royal house and its totalitarian politics were too closely associated with Inkatha's agenda of hanging on, at all costs, to an autonomous KwaZulu homeland and could not easily be reconciled with the principle of a democratic, unitary state. Since Zulu ethnicity had evolved under specific historical circumstances, it was naïve to assume that an 'authentic' Zulu identity, free of apartheid, could be retrieved and grafted on to the ANC's pluralism. These misgivings were still unresolved when the day of the festival arrived.

In the end, the people of Ximba put their own stamp on the meaning of the event, and the rather crude projection in the media of a multi-ethnic Heroes Day gave way to a recognition of the specific, localised identity of the Ximba community itself. When asked what the festival meant, many of those who gathered said it was to show support for Chief Mlaba. The heroes mentioned in the opening praise song were neither Gandhi nor Shaka, but the heroes of the Ximba clan, both their forefathers and the recent victims of the violence. Thus, rather than a broad multi-ethnic identity, or even a Zulu identity, for the people involved the day recognised in the first instance the more local, Ximba identity. However, this local identity retained a link with the national struggle, so that there was no marked dissonance between the march by Mkhonto we Sizwe soldiers, on one hand, and the *amabutho* dancers in traditional Zulu dress, on the other. And in addition to affirming the clan, the day also affirmed the connections between Zuluness and the struggle against colonialism and apartheid, between rural and urban versions of the national struggle, connections that were understood as having been forged by Mlaba himself.

Heroes Day at KwaXimba was different enough from the township rallies of the ANC to be something of a surprise to those who had come from town to celebrate. A majority of the ten thousand who had gathered were from KwaXimba and many were in traditional Zulu dress. Mlaba's links with non-Zulu chiefs in the Congress of Traditional Leaders of South Africa (CONTRALESA) had brought chiefs and others from KwaNdebele and Transkei, both former bantustans. Buses and private cars brought ANC members from other parts of Natal, a very few of the faces white and Indian. While it was not the multicultural event anticipated in the media, it was nevertheless a Shaka Day with a difference, opening Zulu identity to heterogeneity, as traditional dancers took turns with church choirs, the men in Sunday suits and the women in long black dresses, interspersed with youthful singers in ANC colours. The programme included 'national poet' Mzwakhe Mbuli and several popular national musicians and singers. While there was the usual singing of the national anthem and stalls selling paraphernalia of the struggle – the SACP's magazine *Umsebenzi*, the women's magazine *Speak*, Mandela badges and keyrings and T-shirts – what really moved the crowd was the slaughtering of fifteen bulls and the *ngoma* dancing, which drew sections of the crowd alongside the performers. It was a celebration of Zuluness by a community that had pitted itself against a party claiming to be the authentic representative of Zulu tradition. Mlaba's own presence exemplified this refracted sense of tradition: after appearing in full ethnic regalia on the first day, he returned to a well-worn suit and open-necked shirt on the second, so that people had difficulty identifying him sitting quietly on wooden benches provided for his guests. (This unchiefly manner had once saved his life: at the height of the violence of the 1980s, security forces came to him asking for Chief Mlaba. He replied, 'He's gone into hiding', at which they departed, leaving the message, 'Tell him we'll get him.'[20])

Despite his diffidence, the festival's official centrepiece was Mlaba's speech. He argued his case not within the terms of democracy and development, but in terms of history and tradition – a tradition deeply at odds with the dominant features of Zulu history. His story began with the defeat of Mlaba's earliest remembered ancestor, Mabhoyi, at the hands of Shaka's troops when the Ximba people had been brought from Lesotho to Zululand as captives. Later, when the Zulu army was diverted, the Ximba community began making its way back to Lesotho, during which exodus they became allies of Chief Langalibalele's Hlubi people who were fleeing Shepstone's colonial army. Fortunately for the Ximba, the two communities were separated shortly before the British massacre of the Hlubi in 1873. In Mlaba's speech, Shepstone and British colonialism follow Shaka as the enemy of the Ximba people – an ironic consequence of Shepstone's adoption of 'Shakan' methods in controlling rebellious tribes. Mlaba went on to present the Ximba as having been troublemakers for the colonial authorities throughout the nineteenth century and, consequently, as falling outside of the terms of subsequent deals made with the Zulus. This maverick status culminates in the involvement of the Mlaba chiefs in the history of the ANC in the region.

All this was in response to Buthelezi's claim that the reason for Ximba disloyalty to the KwaZulu government was that they were not 'proper Zulus'. The roots of the Ximba people are in fact multi-ethnic, with Zulu, Sotho and Xhosa origins; they have become naturalised into Zulu custom, language and culture over a long period. When Susan Mathieson asked Mlaba if he thought these multi-ethnic origins explained the refusal to align with KwaZulu, he acknowledged that Inkatha's mobilisation around the idea of ethnic purity did not have much influence in a community which understood that unity lay in co-operation rather than in blood or lineage. However, the force of Zulu nationalism in rural Natal is such that political discourse has to centre on such claims, eliciting from Mlaba his counter-narrative as validation of his position, rather than the more obvious credibility that might have come from his practical achievements. However, Mlaba's position also paradoxically serves as a reminder of the historical fact that the kingdom, which in its nineteenth-century form was incorporative, implicitly defined Zuluness not in terms of lineage but in terms of allegiance. Inkosi yinkosi ngabantu is the traditional phrase: a chief is a chief of the people. Strictly, 'proper Zulus' are Zulus who define themselves as such.

Mlaba's reclaiming of Zulu history and tradition reveals the discursive limits that are imposed on the ANC, however, as it opens itself to Zulu nationalism, for the move might in fact have served to suppress certain forms of difference. The chief asserts that for his community, custom and culture are more important than party politics, a claim that is supported by the degree of enthusiasm elicited by the slaughtering of bulls and the ngoma dancing at the festival. However, custom and culture are highly patriarchal. The slaughtering of bulls, which is accomplished with bare hands, is an assertion of machismo; similarly, in ngoma dancing men perform with traditional weapons whilst women cheer from the sidelines. The violence of the confrontation between the ANC and Inkatha has a masculinist edge which is reinforced by such customs; it also enables men to project themselves as the protectors of women and children. KwaXimba's democracy might still have an effect on gender relations, however, for while power traditionally descends from the king to the chief to the male head of the household, in this instance the chief has chosen to be answerable to his community. To the extent that he has done so, he has had to acknowledge gender politics: he speaks of the right of women to call the men to address them at public meetings, and of the women's right to stand for office in the tribal authority which is no longer appointed from above. But it remains uncertain whether this fragile move towards gender equality will be unaffected by a resurgence of traditionalism in KwaXimba. When the chief was asked what aspects of custom and culture he thought were most important, his spontaneous response was to say the right to polygamy. Perhaps underlying the call to tradition is a desire to return to more patriarchal relations. Many of the older men canvassed in a research project on attitudes to AIDS in the community believed that the disease was caused by the breakdown of the lobola (bride-price) system, which had encouraged men to take responsibility for sexual activity by insisting that if a woman fell pregnant the man had to pay lobola and marry her. Younger men gave a more negative inflection to the impact of patriarchal tradition, arguing that their desire for several girlfriends arose from the popularity and status gained by older men who had several wives. The majority of women, on the other hand, saw the primary cause of AIDS as their lack of control over their own sexuality and their economic dependence on men.[21] This debate around differences of opinion within the community could be silenced under the call for a return to traditional Zulu values. However necessary a return to Zulu tradition might be in facilitating a reconciliation of generational differences or in lessening the ANC–Inkatha opposition, it has had some unfortunate implications.

Much has happened since September 1993 to give a new twist to these questions. In the 1994 elections, while enjoying an overwhelming victory nationally, the ANC lost to Inkatha in KwaZulu-Natal. Inkatha entered the elections a week before polling, ensuring that its hold over the densely populated rural areas of northern Zululand, in particular, would carry it to victory. Though it was clearly a close call, the final vote count in KwaZulu-Natal was never established; essentially, the region was conceded by the national ANC leadership against the wishes of local leaders. The feeling was that the only way to neutralise the threat of Inkatha was to make its position in the future as attractive as it had been under apartheid. Ironically, while Inkatha's victory has brought it into the national democratic process, it has also had the effect of loosening its ties to the king; indeed, Zwelithini began actively wooing the ANC central government (his overtures being, of course, kindly received) in recognition of the changed distribution of authority, while nominally trying to assert the neutrality of the royal house.

In 1994, after the elections, the ANC decided to celebrate Shaka Day not in KwaXimba but in Msinga, in the heartland of the original Zulu Kingdom, with the support and presence of King Zwelithini. To facilitate the event, Mlaba promised to visit the king's palace with an offering of bulls to be slaughtered in appeasement of the ancestors for his failure to secure the king's permission before holding a Shaka Day festival in KwaXimba. On his part, the king would apologise for allying himself with one section of his people, making it impossible for Mlaba to approach him as his subject. Nelson Mandela was invited to the Msinga festival and he responded by expressing a desire to attend both Shaka Days, Inkatha's and the ANC's. Buthelezi refused to sanction Mandela's wishes, revealing just how precarious was his embrace of the new dispensation; nevertheless, Mandela accepted Buthelezi's right to a final veto, which meant in turn that the regional ANC leadership was obliged to call off the event. The king, for his part, was left high and dry, unable to share a platform with Mandela at a nationalised festival and no longer wishing to support an exclusively Inkatha event. His attempts to establish himself as a unifying force above party divisions were in tatters: unwilling to return to his position as a captive pawn of Inkatha, and amidst the stoning of his palace by young Inkatha supporters, he made a reckless call on his people not to attend any Shaka Day celebrations at all, a call that did not prevent Inkatha from holding its rallies to a substantial audience. However, since Inkatha was commemorating the founder of the Zulu royal house against the wishes of the incumbent and without his presence, its power over the symbols of Zulu nationalism had become questionable.

While the king's support for the ANC demonstrated its success in opening itself to Zulu nationalism, the confusion around Shaka Day has revealed an impasse in ANC policy. Part of the regional ANC would like to use Zulu nationalism as a strategy to defeat Inkatha at the next elections, but Mandela, together with moderate national leaders, sees the accommodation of Zulu nationalism as implying a degree of acceptance of the power structures that have sustained it. Reconciliation as an immediate objective of the ANC government is thus to some extent in tension with the longer-term objective of creating conditions in which democracy might thrive in the region. The risks inherent in affirming Inkatha were made visible when Buthelezi, with a team of armed bodyguards, stormed a live SATV studio in Durban to confront Prince Clement Zulu who, as a spokesperson for the royal house, was questioning Buthelezi's self-appointment as the traditional Prime Minister of the Zulu Kingdom. Clearly, national reconstruction will involve much more than bringing everyone on board.

The resurgence of Zulu ethnic nationalism has posed severe challenges to the non-racialism of the national liberation movement as it has sought to implement its vision of an inclusive and unitary South Africa. But if one broadens the perspective to consider the ANC's difficulties in the light of global developments, they can be seen to represent a field of opportunity that has too rarely arisen within the life of the contemporary nation-state. As South Africa attempts to consolidate its democracy, with a new constitution finally in place after protracted negotiations at the Constitutional Assembly, it will have to try to re-invent pluralism, eschewing the indifference to difference which is the norm of established liberal democracies. It will have to recognise and even enable ethnic consciousnesses without allowing them to jeopardise the work of reconstruction after apartheid, which has barely begun. Whether South Africa achieves this feat or not, and whether its solutions will be truly unique, as many sympathetic outsiders anticipate, remains to be seen. Meanwhile, in their negotiation of their own and the country's history, the people of KwaXimba may have shown a way forward. Instead of keeping their present open only to the past, thus allowing themselves to be flooded by history's imperatives, their achievement has been the reverse: by keeping their past open to the present, they have discovered a mode of survival that serves as a lesson in transformation.

NOTES

1 South Africa's transition was influenced, of course, by global trends of the past decade, with the bipolar system giving way to a more complex picture of local ethnic struggles. The events of 1989 in Europe were decisive in persuading F. W. de Klerk's government to unban the ANC, SACP and Pan-Africanist Congress (PAC) in February 1990, because with the fall of the socialist governments that had supported these movements, the bogey of the 'communist threat' was removed. The ANC, in due course, was to realise how intractable ethnic mobilisation could be, particularly in Africa where postcolonial nations have always struggled with frontiers created arbitrarily in Europe. Increasingly, as the nation-state came within its grasp, the ANC discovered the resilience of ethnic fears and sensitivities, feelings which the nation-state in its prior form either had failed to placate or had actively promoted.

2 The term 'bantustan' was used by apartheid's apologists in reference to the partition of India in 1947. However, it quickly became pejorative in left and anti-apartheid usage, where it remained, while being abandoned by the National Party in favour of 'homelands'.

3 *Saturday News* (Durban), 5 September 1993.

4 *New Nation*, 26 September 1993.

5 A. Giddens, *The Consequences of Modernity*, Cambridge, Polity, 1990 (passim).

6 Chief Buthelezi, 'Shaka Day Speech', 25 September 1993, Stanger. Inkatha Institute Library, Durban.

7 ibid.

8 The relationship between Chief Buthelezi and King Zwelithini has always contained the seeds of ambiguity, with Buthelezi holding the politically powerful positions of leader of the KwaZulu bantustan and the IFP, while King Zwelithini as heir to the Zulu Kingdom was pushed into a purely symbolic role, acting as mouthpiece for the IFP, which, through KwaZulu, provided the financial means to sustain the royal house. With the fragmentation of bantustan structures and the ascendancy of the ANC, which has sought to accommodate tribal structures within the new dispensation, the king has been attempting to establish himself independently of the IFP. But while the king speaks of the need for the royal house to be non-aligned, distancing the monarchy from the IFP is interpreted as a move toward the ANC.

9 King Goodwill Zwelithini, 'Shaka Day Speech', 25 September 1992, Stanger. Inkatha Institute Library, Durban.

10 ibid.

11 This account is indebted largely to C. Hamilton, 'Authoring Shaka: Models, Metaphors and Historiography', PhD dissertation, Johns Hopkins University, Baltimore, Maryland, 1993.

12 S. Marks, 'Patriotism, Patriarchy and Purity: Natal and the Politics of Zulu Ethnic Consciousness', in L. Vail (ed.), *The Creation of Tribalism in Southern Africa*, London, James Currey, 1989, p. 217; see also N. Cope, 'The Zulu Petite Bourgeoisie and Zulu Nationalism in the 1920s: Origins of Inkatha', *Journal of Southern African Studies*, vol. 16, no. 3, September 1990.

13 Marks, 'Patriotism, Patriarchy and Purity', p. 222.

14 ibid., p. 227.

15 *Daily News* (Durban), 18 September 1993.

16 *Natal Mercury* (Durban), 22 September 1993.

17 *Natal Witness* (Pietermaritzburg), 24 September 1993.
18 ibid.
19 Interviews with Midlands REC representative Yunus Carrim, August 1994.
20 Interview, Chief Mlaba, *Ikhwezi*, Newsletter of the ANC Natal Midlands Region, no. 2, December 1992–January 1993.
21 International Center for Research on Women (Washington, DC), 'Women and Aids in Natal-KwaZulu. Determinants to the Adoption of HIV Protective Behavior: A Community-Based Approach', 1993. Of all South Africa's nine provinces, KwaZulu-Natal has the highest incidence of AIDS.

9

POSTCOLONIALISM

The case of Ireland

Terry Eagleton

Like many a writer about former colonies, I have my doubts about the 'post-colonial' label. For 'postcolonialism' signifies, of course, not just a body of writing about former colonies, but a whole theoretical or ideological agenda, a whole gamut of doctrines and pieties which are far from historically or politically innocent. One might note, for example – though postcolonial theorists normally do not – that among the more positive reasons for the rise of this style of thought, a resoundingly negative one was a global political defeat. I believe this, in fact, to be one ground of postmodernism in general; but it is surely clear that so-called postcolonialism gets off the ground in the wake of the crushing or exhaustion of the various revolutionary nationalisms which dealt world imperialism such a staggering series of rebuffs some twenty or so years ago. Nationalism is not a sexy term with postcolonialism, which tends on the whole to remember the British in India rather than how the Portuguese were booted out of Angola. That nationalism is at once an ideology of imperial capitalism, and from time to time its formidably effective enemy, is only one of many reasons why the term generates more confusion than it resolves. Those postmodernists who lament the violent expulsion of otherness by the drearily selfsame have clearly not been thinking about the ejection of the Americans from a few of their former cheap labour markets. The postcolonial suspicion of nationalism, which I am gratified to add is not universal to the theory, has quite definite historical conditions in the failure of third-world revolutionary nationalism, since the mid-1970s, to break the hegemony of the West. That radical impulse persisted; but it had to migrate elsewhere in transmuted guise, and postcolonialism, along with the universities, was one of the places where it took up a home.

My embarrassments with the term 'postcolonialism', shared of course by many others, are not only to do with its more flagrant limitations: the blanket nature of the term, for example, implying that you can scoop Taiwan and Tanzania under the same heading, or that everything in a so-called postcolonial society is impeccably postcolonial just as everything green is coloured green, so that postcolonial subjects must be seen to go around acting like postcolonial subjects for the gratification of Western radicals, rather than acting from time to time in a merely human way. (I use the phrase 'merely human' with all the provocation I can muster.) The Irish, of whom more in a moment, acted as colonial (and nowadays as postcolonial) subjects quite a bit, but then 'acted' is surely the word. The Irish have always needed someone to be Irish at. There is a whole political theatrics here, which would repay some careful study. Nor am I just thinking of how so much of this theory has become stuck in the tedious groove of stereotyping, than which nothing is now more stereotypical, or even of the way some postcolonial theory, absurdly and sentimentally, seems actually to support postcolonial set-ups, most of which are politically pretty hideous and would be far better off being transformed out of existence. There is nothing in the least inherently positive about marginalisation, as Nazis, UFO buffs and the international bourgeoisie might well exemplify. The comprador ruling strata of such social orders, composed in the main of corrupt, self-serving satraps of global capital, have little whatsoever that is 'other' about them from the viewpoint of Wall Street or the IMF, and even if they did this would be no reason for keeping them in power. Whatever 'postcoloniality' is about, it is by no means in the first place about culture, a notably Western academic obsession.

No, all this, of course, no question, but I am thinking also of something else – of whether it is pure middle-aged Marxist paranoia (yes, to be sure, but only that?) to discern in the very term 'postcolonialism' a certain shamefaced, strategic suppression of another term which is these days profoundly uncool, and that is imperialism. 'Postcolonialism' ineluctably suggests some kind of steady state or chronic condition, rather like myopia or rheumatism or, better (keeping that 'post' in view) a hangover, whereas the word 'imperialism' bespeaks a political and economic project, with its own peculiar historical dynamic. But to speak of imperialism is to confront the economic, and so to fall instantly foul of those designer radicals for whom, it would appear, all economic concern is 'economistic', and who have all learnt to make the vampire sign at its mere mention. Postcolonial discourse belongs for the most part (not exclusively) to a rampant left culturalism, by which I mean an implausibly excessive emphasis on what is constructed or conventional or differentially constituted about human animals, rather than on what they have in common as, in the first place, natural material creatures. Such culturalism is just as reductive as the economism or biologism or essentialism to which it is a mildly panic-stricken over-reaction. Anyway, why 'colonialism' in the first place, even if one adds a 'post' or 'neo' for good measure? For the term suggests, traditionally, a form of (intendedly permanent) settlement which is in one sense the last way to describe the relation of the transnational corporations to their client terrains. And why define a whole social order in terms of what it comes after, which – since that condition is itself cast in bleakly negative terms – then entails a sort of double displacement?

There are many names for the deconstruction of self and other, and one of them has been Ireland. One has only to glance at the bedevilled history of the country to see how marvellously the binary opposition of imperial self and colonial subject does not work. The British and Irish were – are – at once unnervingly close and out of each other's cognitive range, so that the British could never decide whether the Irish were their antithesis or mirror-image, partner or parasite, abortive offspring or sympathetic sibling. A colony is not just the 'other' of its metropolis but its *peculiar* other, part of it through antagonism – a condition well captured by the Dubliner Samuel Beckett's reply to a Frenchman's inquiry as to whether he was English: '*Au contraire.*' The Anglo-Irish Ascendancy sometimes spoke of Britain as the mother country, sometimes of Ireland as the sister nation, sometimes of a brotherly affection between the two. The logic of Anglo-Irish relations is incestuously garbled: your brother is really your father, and you are both mother and sister. The Act of Union of 1800 between Great Britain and Ireland has commonly been figured as a sexual coupling, but it is a peculiarly inbred form of congress, one in which subject-positions (siblings, strangers, partners, parents, spouses) are dizzyingly interchangeable. All this would doubtless have been different if the Irish had been black, unintelligible and ensconced in another hemisphere, savages of the desert rather than the doorstep; but the trouble with the Irish is that they are not black or white but orange and green. The British are consequently incapable of understanding what is happening in Derry today in terms of what happened in Dar es Salaam a few decades back. Ireland before its partial independence was that impossibly oxymoronic animal, a metropolitan colony, at once part of the imperial nation and peripheral to it. What other British colony had MPs at Westminster? As such, divided between colonial and metropolitan, august kingdom and primitive periphery, the juridical fiction of union and the political reality of subjugation, it figured as a kind of political monstrosity. The text of the relations between the island and the mainland was thus always to some degree indecipherable, always with some fundamental opacity or equivocation built into it, characterised by some curious slippage of the sign or skewing of narratives which stubbornly refused (every bit as much as *Finnegans Wake*) to add up to some easily readable totality. The full title of the United Kingdom today – 'The United Kingdom of Great Britain and Northern Ireland' – can suggest, in the light of Derridean supplementation, that Northern Ireland is or is not part of Great Britain. Certainly most Great Britons today do not regard the Northern Irish, including the Unionists, as their *bona fide* compatriots.

There is not, in fact, even a geopolitical name for the archipelago which includes both England and Ireland, and the whole situation is ridden with paradox, aporia, double-think, structural irony. The Northern Unionists are a majority or a minority depending upon your political persuasion. Partition of the island came about because a united Ireland was anathema to one quarter of the population, and is now anathema to one third of the state it created. What shows all the signs of a sectarian religious conflict has exceedingly little to do with religion, despite the reply of the Belfast Protestant who was asked by a journalist what he had against Catholics ('Are you daft? Why, their religion, of course!'). Donegal is geographically in the north of the island but politically in the south, and what you call the city of Derry, or indeed Northern Ireland as a whole (the six counties, the

127

North of Ireland, Ulster, enemy-occupied Ireland), depends largely on what you think of the Council of Trent. Ian Paisley is an Irishman in the eyes of John Hume but by no means in his own, whereas Yeats and Parnell were card-carrying Irishmen in their own eyes but not in those of the Gaelic League, the Gaelic Athletic Association or early Sinn Fein. Gerry Adams is for some loyalists a Briton who simply needs to be persuaded of the fact. The problem of Northern Ireland, for these devotees of the Crown, is that it contains an alien ethnic wedge known as the Irish. What both Northern communities have in common is that they owe allegiance to separate nation-states of whom they have an extravagantly low opinion. There are loyalists who detest Great Britain and want an independent North, just as there are Northern republicans whose animus against the British is outmatched only by their contempt for the Irish Republic and all its doings. There are green Marxists who support republicanism, orange Marxists for whom the industrialised North is more politically progressive than the autocratic south, and red Marxists who officially back neither party but who are for the most part pro-Union. There are ethnic nationalists, civic nationalists, ethnic nationalists thinly disguised as civic nationalists, socialist loyalists and red-neck republicans. And there are those for whom we are all Irish in the eyes of God, for whom Irishness is a spiritual condition like nirvana or schizophrenia rather than a question of birth or political citizenship.

The history of the traffic between the two nations has been one of a quite astonishingly garbled conversation, of partners speaking obdurately past one another. Whereas the writerly English tended to think in terms of law and contract, the more logocentric Irish thought largely in terms of custom, kinship, moral economy, so that the two idioms only obliquely intersected. One might claim, rather similarly, that J. M. Synge wrote in English and Irish simultaneously only to be understood by neither party, and that Finnegans Wake is the non-Irish-speaking Irish writer's way of being suitably unintelligible to the British, destroying their tongue in the act of deploying it even more dexterously than the natives. Indeed the conflict has been not just between two languages, but between two quite different conceptions of language, since the English empiricist conception of language as representational has never had much appeal to the more linguistically performative Irish. The Irish have on the whole, in the manner of subaltern peoples, tended to see language as strategic, conative, rhetorical rather than cognitive, and there is a theological dimension to this suspicion of representationalism. It may also be one reason why the only modernism worth speaking of in what were then the British Isles flourished in its most chronically backward corner. It did not take modernism, or later poststructuralism, for the Irish to be self-conscious about speech; it took the colonial attempts to throttle their native tongue, a project with which many of the natives colluded eagerly enough. And it took the Troubles to help revive the Irish language, which nowadays flourishes nowhere more robustly than in republican areas of the North. Nowhere is this ceaseless scrambling of meaning more succinctly reflected than in the present-day Irish constitution, an Irish-language document which assumes that in the event of a conflict of interpretation between its meaning in Irish and in English, the Irish sense will be deemed to assume priority. But the document is widely suspected to be itself a translation from the English, so that by some curious Derridean logic a supplement here takes precedence over the original text. If a discrepancy arose from the Irish version having mistranslated the English, a mistranslation would hold sway over the translated text. How very Irish, as they might say at Westminster. This sort of conundrum, indeed, belongs to a venerable Irish tradition to which the poet James Clarence Mangan gave the name of 'anti-plagiarism', in which you write a work subtly different from some revered artefact, then claim that the original artefact is a plagiarism from your own text, thus rudely inverting the relations between past and present, origin and effect. One thinks also of the great Tipperary novelist Laurence Sterne, whose denunciation of plagiarism in Tristram Shandy is itself apparently plagiarised. An obsession with translation, a self-devouring sport of the signifier, a compulsive intertextuality, a rash of spoofs and parodies: all of this belongs in Irish writing to the hybridised, macaronic literature of colonialism, at just the point, ironically enough, where a certain vein of nationalism is looking to a purified national language as expressive of the Irish soul.

Anti-plagiarism is among other things an impudent smack at Irish antiquarianism, putting time into reverse, whereas the Irish are, of course, generally considered to be prisoners of the past. This is at best a half-truth: for Sinn Fein as much as for Stephen Greenblatt, the past is in the service of the present. Historiography in Ireland is a civilised brand of political warfare. It has been claimed that much misunderstanding arose between the British and the Irish because of their divergent views of temporality – the Irish typically holding that an original injustice cannot simply be eradicated by the mere passage of time, the British, in a rather more linear, triumphalist perspective, giving birth to the doctrine of prescription, according to which the sheer passing of time is a kind of rationality all in itself, enough to naturalise and consecrate your original act of invasion or appropriation, or at least to thrust it into the political unconscious for a while. It is no accident that one of England's most eloquent apologists for this doctrine was the greatest of all Irish political theorists, Edmund Burke. Despite the fact that in Donegal today you can encounter road signs reading 'To the Flight of the Earls', an event which occurred in 1607, there is no conclusive evidence that the Irish have been more neurotically obsessed with their past than any other people. In one sense, a colony is unlikely to be weighed down by its history just because it does not have much of an autonomous history in the first place. Colonialism helps to stop history from happening, and certainly helped to arrest Ireland in a pre-modern mould, just as much as it is itself the very history which is happening to you.

The British treated Ireland differently when it suited them, as during the Great Famine, and as identical when that suited them too, as in the Act of Union. There is no question here of simply celebrating difference and denouncing identity in dogmatic postmodern fashion; both can act as forms of oppression, or for that matter of emancipation. The Irish have always been at once too different from the British and not different enough, and attempts to render them more identical have often merely deepened the disparity. But in case this emphasis on Ireland as deconstructing the opposition between imperial selfhood and colonial otherness yields too much comfort to a certain rather depoliticising current of postcolonial thought, let me stress too the separatist, confrontational side of the narrative, so often conveniently jettisoned by those one-sidedly concerned with postcolonial collusion, mimicry, liminality. To be a true postmodern pluralist is surely to recognise the justness of both of these stories, not simply, labour-savingly and monologically, of the latter. And of course the intellectual advantage of Ireland in this context is the historically tragic fact that we do not need to be reminded there of the realities of political conflict, as opposed to the somewhat more culturalist perspectives theorists can feel licensed to take up on postcolonial societies not currently enduring political warfare. Whatever the conflict in Northern Ireland is about, it most certainly is not in the first place about 'culture', and to assert that it is is an instantly recognisable ideological stance in Ireland today, one intimately allied with liberal Unionism in the North or some left postmodernism in the republic. What is in train in the North is an ethno-political contention, not chiefly a cultural or religious or economic one; and here the customary culturalism of postcolonial theory simply will not serve. Neither, for that matter, will its occasional dogmatic opposition of nationalism (homogenising, essentialist, spiritualist, chauvinist) to radical pluralism, hybridity or multiculturalism. Why is some postcolonial theory so hostile to nationalism? Because it is 'essentialist'? Quite apart from the fact that some versions of essentialism seem to me excellent doctrines, considerably more radical than anti-essentialism (but that is the theme of a different essay), there is also the fact that some feminism is essentialist too. But feminism is in general inscribed on the postmodern agenda, as nationalism is in general not. So one must, presumably, look further; not least because not all brands of nationalism are essentialist either, unless you essentialise the current in the manner of some postmodern theory. Why then do some postcolonial theorists, along with some people in pubs in the English Home Counties who call each other 'squire' and say 'What's your poison?' and 'Pas de problème, old bean', dislike Irish nationalism so much? Perhaps because it is sanguinary, chauvinist, patriarchal, tunnel-visioned, sectarian, nostalgic, idly idealist, morbid, masculinist, arrogantly vanguardist, suppressing social divisions in the name of some spurious spiritual essence. I suppose that might be reason enough to dislike it, unless one is a fan of Le Pen. And Irish nationalism, of late, has certainly perpetrated enough wanton slaughter of the innocents to stir one's sympathies on this subject even for the 'What's your poison?' brigade. But is this the way Irish nationalism has generally been? The answer is surely a firm yes and no. It is unfortunate that such nervous equivocation does not suit the kind of postmodernist who favours rigid, clear-cut oppositions between, say, multiplicity (always and everywhere good) and unity or consensus or identity (always and everywhere nasty), and who then proceeds to denounce the whole notion of rigid opposition as metaphysical illusion – but one really cannot please everybody. The fact is that some Irish nationalism has been repellently purist, ethnic, repressive and xenophobic, while some of it has been liberal, enlightened, civic, ecumenical and cosmopolitan. Wolfe Tone is not Arthur Griffith, nor is Daniel O'Connell (in several respects an enlightened Benthamite liberal) Patrick Pearse. And even Pearse was more progressive and liberal-minded in some ways than those who see him as Ireland's dry run for Pol Pot will concede.

Who, then, are the essentialists and homogenisers here? If some Irish nationalism has violently repressed other social questions, other Irish nationalists, from the Defenders and the left wing of Young Ireland to Michael Davitt, James Connolly, Maude Gonne, Charlotte Despard and Constance Markiewicz, placed some of those other social issues at the fore of their thought and practice. And yet, for all its simplistic reduction of nationalism to blood cults and male bonding, the postmodern critique in Ireland today has a good deal going for it. In the republic, feminism, creeping secularisation, ethnic pluralism, ethical liberalism, so-called Northside realism, the vibrant subcultures of Europe's youngest population – all of this has now advanced to the point where the whole traditional political Establishment in the country – conservative, narrowly nationalist, clientalist, Catholic, ruralist, patriarchal, philistine and spectacularly corrupt – is now feeling the skids beneath it for the first time since the founding of the so-called Free State. One needs to avoid a rush of complacent triumphalism here: the Catholic Church is still of course extraordinarily powerful, unemployment and emigration remain dismally high, an admirable liberal pluralism has so far touched only a small minority of the population, and the contract to build new roads will still go to whichever nephew of the Minister is currently the most strapped for cash. But in tension with this still deeply recalcitrant system is a rapidly modernising social order in which you can now buy contraceptives, in which divorce is likely to arrive sooner or later on the statute book, and in which there is, to be sure, no legal abortion but neither is there in the North. The Republic of Ireland is in several respects more constitutionally enlightened and democratic than the monarchical, deeply undemocratic Britain to whom some liberals and Unionists look as a paradigm of liberal modernity. In short, some of the Unionists' traditional reasons for fearing integration with the republic remain real and genuine enough, while others are likely to prove increasingly disingenuous, mere rationales for hating Celts and Catholics, as an increasingly Europeanised republic stumbles kicking and screaming into the fully paid-up modernity which seems, in the end, its destiny.

A familiar third-world tension, then, between modernity and tradition; and, so it would appear from much Irish partisanship, a straight choice between them. Do you want a thoroughly (post)modern nation, liberal, pluralist, feminist, cosmopolitan, ethically enlightened, with multiple, flexible notions of sovereignty, or do you plump for a nostalgic, patriarchal, nationalist traditionalism? If the question seems a trifle too easy to answer, let me put it another way. Do you want to forget about the North altogether, all those feckless fighting Micks and that atavistic blood-conflict, and leap, suitably streamlined and amnesiac, into the heart of multinational capitalism, erasing your cultural difference, scorning your own traditions and rewriting your national history to eradicate the embarrassing anti-imperialist bits, or do you not? It is Marxism, not (on the whole) either nationalism or postmodernism, which has constantly called attention to the two faces of modernity, as both delight and disaster, catastrophe and emancipation; and as intellectual positions in Ireland today harden often enough to the mere reflex of vested political interests, there are few enough voices around trying to state both sides of the argument. Dialectical thinking is not, by and large, much in favour either with postmodernism or with traditional nationalism, neither of which has revealed any great capacity for self-critique. Modernity in Ireland means among many other things divorce, abortion, women's rights, a secular polity, civic and rational notions of citizenship to replace all that tribal *Gemeinschaft*; it also means shutting up about the Famine so as not to annoy the Brits (not even the dead, Walter Benjamin warned, will be safe from the enemy if he is victorious), revising Irish history in order to sanitise colonialism and slander republicanism, canonising the urban businessman while castigating the countryside, and abandoning the small farmers and the working class to the mercies of a brutally neo-liberal Europe. It is also depressingly characteristic of this small, intensely combative, quarrelsome culture that even its liberal pluralists (and in some cases especially them) can be a rancorous, entrenched, sectarian bunch, as befits an erstwhile colonial, pre-industrial, spiritually authoritarian society which lacks a vigorous, mainstream liberal tradition, and where discourse has become locked into power to the point where even Arnoldian disinterestedness (that tedious bugbear of the cultural left) begins to look positively avant-garde. As for tradition, that in Ireland means patriarchy and clientalism and a morbid cult of heroism and moving statues of the Virgin out in the sticks, along with a valuing of one's cultural inheritance, a refusal to surrender without a struggle to late-capitalist homogenising, a sympathy with the dispossessed, an unfashionable refusal of historical amnesia, a suspicion of the success ethic. Nowhere is it more obvious that one can neither embrace nor reject tradition, nor embrace nor reject modernity, than in the Irish Catholic Church: a deeply reactionary, ferociously oppressive institution without which many of the common people would have been uneducated, unnursed and uncared for, and which from time to time, at grass roots if not in general at hierarchical level, placed itself in the van of anti-colonial struggle. The latter facts are not ones which paid-up postmodernists care to recall; the former are vehemently denied by religious right-wingers.

Tradition and modernity were never in fact simple antagonists in Ireland (are they ever?), which from the time of Daniel O'Connell onwards displayed a bizarre blending of the archaic and the avant-garde (another condition, no doubt, for the growth of a rich modernism in the country). What today deconstructs that sterile opposition is, in a word, the North. I mean by that that it is clear there that so-called postmodern identity politics, and the question of national autonomy, cannot finally be separated, however much they may have come to inhabit airsealed categories in the rarefied realm of theory. As long as nationalists and Unionists continue to lock one another into quasi-pathological forms of identity, all the brave postmodern talk of decentred subjects, multiple selfhoods and the rest will remain so much academicist rhetoric; and questions of selfhood can therefore only be genuinely engaged on the ground of a political transformation more deep-seated than anything J. Hillis Miller or Jean Baudrillard would be likely to countenance. The truth of postmodernism, or of a certain style of postcolonial thought, is that the Irish have to be able to share the privilege of their traditional lords and masters to be free to explore what they want to become, rather than (as in a classical nationalist paradigm) simply find the means to express already pre-formed, assured but repressed identities. The truth of nationalism, which has hardly been strong on the question of the subject, is that such transformation can only fully come about by radical and definite political change, of the kind that much postmodernism seems singularly vague about. This linkage has, I think, been part of the more constructive intervention of the Field Day group (an unholy alliance of Derry and Derrida, as its enemies have dubbed it), as opposed to its better publicised, far less constructive interventions. The best of Field Day's work has tried to couple questions of cultural identity with questions of material politics, a move increasingly against the grain of contemporary Irish opinion and likely to win you opponents in several camps. Some traditional nationalism thought, naïvely and disastrously, that a new culture could be born merely by booting out the landlords and Dublin Castle; contemporary liberal or postmodern opinion in the republic, admirably engaged on issues of subjecthood, is often callously indifferent to the structures of political oppression in the North and the need to undo them. The more hardline nationalists in the North suffer from the delusion that they know just who they are – it is simply that someone out there is stopping them from freely being it. To the extent that someone or something out there has indeed been stifling their free expression, this republican case is correct; to the extent that if someone is sitting on you then you can never really know who you are in the first place, the postmodern case has a more pointed application.

It has a more general application too. What has been afoot in the North is indeed, in part, what the middle-class liberals and postmodernists recognise it to be: a ferociously atavistic struggle inherited from the sectarian seventeenth century, a virulently metaphysical conflict grotesquely out of sorts with a postmodern world of flexible identities, the ceaseless transgression of frontiers and categories, a world with scant relation to Madonna or the Internet. And they are also, of course, quite wrong. Nationalism may be in some respects ideologically atavistic, but politically speaking it is a child of modernity and Enlightenment, barely a couple of centuries old, a drive for – among other, far less palatable things – the modernist imperatives of equality, autonomy, self-emancipation, democracy. In backward conditions, these demands are likely to be bang up-to-date. It is only those who long ago achieved a modicum of this agenda who can afford to consign those still struggling for it, and struggling for it partly because of their own political actions, to the museum of pre-history. There are societies that can afford to declare themselves assuredly 'post' all that – post, indeed, history itself – and others that are not so fortunate. For some jaded, geriatric cultures, the Enlightenment is the source of all their woes, a view they then arrogantly universalise under the title of postmodern theory; other peoples, for reasons for which they are in no sense culpable, still have to catch up with a modernity in danger of being squeezed out in their situation between pre-modern autocracy and the ambiguous attractions of the postmodern. I recently attended a literary conference which ended with a toast to the Enlightenment – a gesture which in San Francisco would no doubt have been regarded as a sick joke, but which happened to take place in Cape Town.

Tribal atavism and postmodern transnational cosmopolitanism are in various ways the flipsides of one another, rather than simple antagonists. Nothing is more up-to-date than a defensive solidarity against predatory global forces. Such solidarity can of course become rapidly morbid, and there has been a fair bit of that in traditional Ireland, as there has been in some postmodern particularism. But it also serves to remind us that we are limited bodily creatures who have to live on the spot where we are – that we are, in one sense if not in all, regional animals by virtue of our bodies, even if we become potentially universal creatures as soon as we open our mouths. If Ireland is, among other things, a mournful, melancholic culture, it is in part because its people, so traditionally dedicated to locality, were not allowed to live on the spot where they were and share at the same time in a universal autonomy and equality. The noble, doomed dream of Enlightenment was that a universal justice and reason could become instantiated in a particular place, and the hinge between them was known as the nation-state. That mediation was always formidably hard to pull off, likely as it was to bifurcate instantly into an abstract universalism on the one hand (in Ireland, the United Irishmen) and a myopic form of particularism on the other (the worst kinds of Irish cultural nationalism). We now know that the nation-state – superannuated in some ways, more powerful than ever in others – can no longer provide this mediation between local and universal – that some other, more complex, variable, uneven set of relations between those two dimensions has painfully to be negotiated, in order to replace the poor parody of that relation offered us at the moment by pathological forms of tribalism on the one hand and an anaemic, profit-driven cosmopolitanism on the other. Since getting out of Ireland was always the activity most native to the country, the Irish may just be able to teach us a few lessons on the subject.

10

MULTICULTURAL IMAGINED COMMUNITIES

Cultural difference and national identity in the USA and Australia[1]

Jon Stratton and Ien Ang

In the last few years, the question of national identity has become an intense site of concern, debate and struggle throughout the world. Emerging from this problematisation is a growing awareness of what Homi Bhabha calls 'the impossible unity of the nation as a symbolic force'.[2] The nation can assume symbolic force precisely in so far as it is represented as a unity; yet national unity is always ultimately impossible precisely because it can be represented as such only through a suppression and repression, symbolic or otherwise, of difference. It is in this context that 'multiculturalism' has become such a controversial issue. As a discourse, multiculturalism can broadly – and without, for the moment, further specification – be understood as the recognition of co-existence of a plurality of cultures within the nation. Celebrated by some and rejected by others, multiculturalism is controversial precisely because of its real and perceived (in)compatibility with national unity.

Critics of 'multiculturalism' generally consider it as a centrifugal movement: it is described with much concern by commentators as a threat to national unity. As *Time* magazine warned in 1991, the 'growing emphasis on the USA's "multicultural" heritage exalts racial and ethnic pride at the expense of social cohesion'.[3] Historian Arthur Schlesinger, Jr expresses his critique of multiculturalism this way:

> The US escaped the divisiveness of a multiethnic society by a brilliant solution: the creation of a brand new national identity. The point of America was not to preserve old cultures but to forge a new, *American* culture. . . . The growing diversity of the American population makes the quest for unifying ideals and a common culture all the more urgent. In a world savagely rent by ethnic and racial antagonisms, the US must continue as an example of how a highly differentiated society holds itself together.[4]

Here, then, multiculturalism is constructed as inherently destructive of a unified and cohesive national identity. In his book *The Disuniting of America*, Schlesinger discusses how 'the cult of ethnicity', raging across university campuses in the United States, culminates in an 'attack on the common American identity'.[5] Schlesinger is particularly scathing about Afrocentricity, a radical philosophical and educational movement that emphasises and glorifies the African roots of African-Americans and thus represents a symbolic self-Africanisation and de-Americanisation of this group of Americans. This example supports Schlesinger's view that multiculturalism inevitably contains a 'separatist impulse' which amounts to nothing other than multinationalism, leading to a 'decomposition of America'.

Schlesinger represents the mainstream stance on multiculturalism in the USA, and his political biography highlights an important shift in America's experience of itself. In the early 1960s, he was a liberal and a member of President Kennedy's personal staff. By the 1980s, however, his views – which have remained consistent – had begun to sound rather conservative. Anthony Woodiwiss argues that from the mid-1960s onwards there was an increasing disillusion with America, as the Johnsonian 'Great Society' – which was, in Woodiwiss's words, 'simply corporate liberal society writ large'[6] – failed to keep its ideological promises. This account provides an historical context for the new American debate about multiculturalism, in which the term is closely connected with the moral panic around 'identity politics' and 'political correctness'. As we will see, Schlesinger's criticism highlights the importance of a shared ideological belief as both the foundation of American national identity and the basis for a capitalist corporate liberalism which, from an American point of view, is the 'natural' economic expression of the nation-state. Multiculturalism supposedly subverts this unified vision of 'America'.

Coming from a more radical political background well to the left of Schlesinger, Lawrence Grossberg is equally critical of the supposedly divisive multiculturalist programme: identity politics, he says, leads to a 'seemingly endless fragmentation of the Left into different subordinate identities and groups'.[7] The similarity between Schlesinger's and Grossberg's positions is not surprising since, in spite of their significant political differences, both ultimately share a commitment to the Enlightenment-originated ideology privileging a shared moral universe, an ideology which permeates the American experience of society – and of national identity. Thus there is a surprising degree of agreement among US commentators of all political persuasions that multiculturalism is inimical to national unity, or, in Grossberg's case, to national radical politics.

This American rejection of multiculturalism sheds an interesting light on the very different situation in Australia. Here, as is well known, multiculturalism has virtually become a household term, and while the concept is no less controversial than in the USA, it is generally accepted in this country as integral to Australian national culture and identity. To be sure, there are great differences in the discursive formations of multiculturalism in these two national contexts, both in terms of substance and in terms of institutional status. In the USA, the discourse of multiculturalism has mostly been associated (as in Afrocentricity) with the intellectual promotion of non-Western cultures in the face of Western or Eurocentric cultural hegemony, while in Australia it is related more directly to the social position and interests of ethnic minority groups, predominantly those of Southern and Eastern European origin. It is not our intention here to elaborate on these important substantial differences in the national connotations of the term 'multiculturalism'; this would need a detailed historical comparison, which is not the purpose of this article. Rather, we want to focus our attention on a more structural difference: the fact that in the USA the politicisation of multiculturalism has been largely from the bottom up, whereas in Australia multiculturalism is a top-down political strategy implemented by government. In the USA, multiculturalist programmes have been advanced by minority groups (African-Americans, Hispanic-Americans, Native Americans, Asian-Americans and so on) who regard themselves as *excluded* from the American mainstream, and for whom the multi-culturalist idea, *pace* Schlesinger, acts as an affirmation of that exclusion; while in Australia multiculturalism is a centrepiece of official government policy, imple-mented by those in power precisely to advance the *inclusion* of ethnic minorities within Australian national culture.

Australia and the United States have two things in common: they are both products of British colonialism and they are both settler societies – that is, they are to a very large extent populated by people whose ancestors travelled to these countries from elsewhere during and after the colonial period. As we shall see, it is the combination – in varied forms – of these two conditions that frames the distinctive ways in which the problematic of national identity and national culture has been dealt with in these two nation-states, and thus the different ways in which multiculturalism is conceived in the two national contexts. To put it con-cretely, we want to suggest that the reason why multiculturalism can be a nation-wide government policy in Australia, in a way unimaginable in the USA, has to do with the fundamentally different ways in which national identity is con-structed in the two contexts. While the former Australian Prime Minister, Paul Keating, could enunciate the idea that Australia is a 'multicultural nation in Asia', thereby signalling multiculturalism as an integral and essential characteristic of contemporary Australian national identity, President Clinton would be challeng-ing fundamental aspects of American self-perception were he to make an analogous remark. Yes, the USA is a pluralist society, but America is America: it has a unified national identity; that is, while everyday US social reality is so clearly multicultural, multiculturalism is alien to the way American national identity is imagined. Below, we will elaborate on this difference and try to explain why it is the case. We will also reflect on some of the consequences of this difference for the diverse ways in which cultural heterogeneity can be negotiated in the two national contexts.

J. STRATTON AND I. ANG

SETTLER SOCIETIES AND NATIONAL IDENTITY

The term 'multiculturalism' has a short history. According to the Longer Oxford English Dictionary (which, of course, provides merely the word's English genealogy and gives us a nominalistic history only), 'multiculturalism' developed from 'multi-cultural', a term that came into general usage only in the late 1950s in Canada. The OED cites a sentence from the Montreal Times in June 1959 which describes Montreal as 'this multi-cultural, multi-lingual society'. The use of hyphens indicates the novelty of both compounds. Again according to the OED, the first use of multiculturalism was in a Canadian government report, the Preliminary Report of the Royal Commission on Bilingualism and Biculturalism, published in 1965. Just how multiculturalism is defined in this document remains obscure, and the reason for this is clear from its historical usage. From its inception, or very shortly thereafter, multiculturalism became a part of the rhetoric of the (Canadian) state: it is primarily a political term associated with government policy. Put simply (and we will return to this later in discussing the Australian adoption of multiculturalism, which owes much to the Canadian), the term is associated with an official recognition of the existence of different ethnic groups within the state's borders, and it evidences concerns about disadvantage and equity which the state recognises as its responsibility to address. This brief genealogy makes it clear that 'multiculturalism' needs to be distinguished from, say, the description of a society as 'multicultural': multiculturalism as a state policy is not necessarily present in societies that can be described as de facto multicultural (as is the case in the USA).

Viewed historically, multiculturalism could be understood as the consequence of the failure of the modern project of the nation-state, which emphasised unity and sameness – a trope of identity – over difference and diversity. This reading makes use of the same ideological assumptions as those on which the classic notion of the nation-state was based, but it reverses their value. For example, multiculturalism valorises diversity where the classic modern nation-state valorised homogeneity. When a government adopts an active policy of multiculturalism, it does so on the explicit assumption that cultural diversity is a good thing for the nation and needs to be actively promoted. Migrants are encouraged – and, to a certain extent, forced by the logic of the discourse – to preserve their cultural heritage, and the government provides support and facilities for them to do so; as a result, their place in the new society is sanctioned by their officially recognised ethnic identities. This interventionist model of dealing with cultural pluralism is to be found in Australia. Where no such government policy is present, on the other hand, migrants are left to themselves to find a place in the new society, on the assumption that they will quickly be absorbed into and by the established cultural order (or, when this doesn't happen, end up in underclass or ethnic ghettos). This describes the laissez-faire approach of the United States. There are, of course, many historically specific and contingent reasons for these very different philosophies, but here we want to connect them with the construction of national identity in the two contexts.

Discussions of multiculturalism have generally taken the entity of the nation-state for granted. But in order to understand the global historical significance of multiculturalism, we must recognise that policies of multiculturalism both develop out of, and highlight, the particular assumptions of the nation-state, the most important of which is the fantasmatic moment of 'national unity'. The political world of modernity was and is composed of individual states. The reification of the state reached its philosophical apogee in Hegel's work. Nevertheless, the state is not identical with the people living in the state. It is a structure of government and, whilst the structure itself might involve representation, the idea of the state is not, itself, representational. To put it bluntly, the modern individual cannot identify with the state. Instead s/he identifies with the nation. Where the term 'state' refers to the legal, financial, or, in short, the bureaucratic aspects of an administrative unit, the term 'nation' refers to the experience of the people within the state as unified by a common language, culture and tradition. How is this twinning of 'state' and 'nation' in the singular concept of the nation-state achieved?

Ernest Gellner argues succinctly that 'it is nationalism which engenders nations, and not the other way round'.[8] He goes on to note that 'nationalism uses the pre-existing, historically inherited proliferation of cultures or cultural wealth, though it uses them very selectively, and it most often transforms them radically'. A 'high culture' is created which is imposed on the population through a 'generalised diffusion of a school-mediated, academy-supervised idiom, codified for the requirements of reasonably precise bureaucratic and technological communication'.[9] The problem with this formulation is that it implies a natural correspondence between the (homogenised) nation and the (centralised) state. It seems to presume that, to a large extent, nationalism – the movement toward a unified nation – is an inevitable effect of the (unspecified) needs of the state.

Although Gellner's theory is useful in so far as it emphasises the centrality of cultural homogeneity as a founding ideological principle of the modern nation-state, a crucial problem with his book is that it is completely, and unselfconsciously, Eurocentric. Gellner's nation-states emerge on the particular ter-ritories where there was previously 'a complex structure of local groups, sustained by folk cultures reproduced locally and idiosyncratically by the micro-groups themselves'.[10] We have here a theorisation of the nation-state which does not recognise the specificity of European history, where the twinning of nation and state took place organically, as it were. The theory is especially problematic with regard to settler societies such as the USA and Australia, where there is no previ-ous 'complex structure of local groups' which can form the 'natural' basis for the construction of a homogeneous national culture.

In this respect, Benedict Anderson's description of the nation as an 'imagined community' is useful because it emphasises the symbolic artificiality of national identity. Anderson defines the nation as 'an imagined political community', one 'imagined as both inherently limited and sovereign'.[11] It is significant that in the title of his book the term 'political' gets left out. This is an important omission because it leaves the way clear for an account which does not problematise the political relations between nation and state. In particular, it means that the diverse local cultures whose differences are suppressed in the creation of a national imagined community are left out of Anderson's consideration, along with the requirements of a national ideology and, in the last resort, the use of force by the state to ensure its continued existence and to deny the cultural divisions which, in so many cases, have been and remain a disruptive and excessive feature in any national imagined community.

Anderson's concern is with the specificity of nations, which gives meaning to the difference between independent states. European nations have thought of themselves as essentially distinct from one another, but modern settler societies represent a very special case of imagined communities, as the construction of a distinctive 'nation' is complicated here by the fact that the settlers who have colonised the new territory migrated from another place. Thus, the experience of the colonial settler society involves the transference, through migration, of a particular national culture, generally that of the coloniser. The transference of the Mother Country's national culture is not necessarily a deliberate and self-conscious act, unlike the attempts to impose the national culture on the indigenous peoples of the colonies. Often the transference is so obvious and nat-uralised as to be unthought. The ambiguities involved in such transfers from one space to another – ambiguities compounded for people born in the new space (that is, second-, third- or later-generation migrants) – do not become crucial until the administrative unit, to use Anderson's term, is transformed into an independent state. When this happens, the problem of the national is fore-grounded. How can the settler society become a sovereign and autonomous imagined community, a nation-state, when those inhabiting and running the state have come from somewhere else and, to a certain extent, have retained a sense of 'ethnic' identity, and (since the end of the eighteenth century) of a national identity, related to that other place, the Mother Country? Here, for example, is how Richard White describes the situation in pre-Federation Australia:

> The question of Australian identity has usually been seen as a tug-of-war between Australianness and Britishness, between the impulse to be dis-tinctively Australian and the lingering sense of a British heritage. However, this attitude to the development of an Australian identity only became common towards the end of the nineteenth century, when self-conscious nationalists began to exaggerate what was distinctive about Australia.[12]

As we will see, this double-bind of sameness/difference in relation to the British parent-culture dominated the problematic of national identity in Australia until well into the 1960s. The ambivalence of what has been called 'colonial nationalism' was a central characteristic in the transformation of this settler colony into a new nation; colonial nationalism – which was characterised by a desire for autonomy and independence without severing the ties with the imperial power – 'acted as the ideological force in state-making in [this] new societ[y]'.[13] The contradictory manner in which the problem of articulating nation and state into a unitary nation-state was originally cast in Australia meant that the question of national identity was resolved in terms of the settler population's 'living and enduring connections to their European beginnings'.[14]

By contrast, the history of the USA was from the beginning characterised by the leading role of the state in defining American difference from the Old World and, as a consequence, it exemplifies a rather more explicit ideological strategy of constructing a national identity. Here, as we will demonstrate in more detail below, the state articulates the ideological foundation for its existence and derives its legitimacy from the claim that, were everybody within the state to live by the principles and values of this ideology – in other words, were its ideological foundations to become cultural – the state would have realised its promise as a nation. We want to argue that this is how the American problematic of national identity can be understood. As we shall see, this is also one reason why multiculturalism as a government policy – that is, a policy that actively promotes cultural diversity – is ideologically incompatible with American national identity.

In Australia, however, it was the adoption of the policy of multiculturalism in the early 1970s that marked a crucial moment when the state took on a more interventionist role in defining the national identity against the imperial connection with Britain. A closer look at these different historical trajectories will help us understand how in Australia, in contrast with the USA, the discourse of multiculturalism has not come to be positioned as antagonistic to the national imagined community, but, on the contrary, as one of its distinctive characteristics. With the introduction of official multiculturalism, the emphasis on a homogeneous imagined community was shifted from the level of the national to the level of the ethnic: the national is now conceived as the space within which many (ethnically defined) imagined communities live and interact.

To summarise, both the USA and Australia are, to use Anthony Smith's term, 'nations by design'.[15] As settler societies, they were faced with the problem of how to create a distinctive national identity without having recourse to a pre-existing distinctive common culture as raw material. But while the United States designed its national identity through ideological means, Australia did it through cultural means. This had fundamental consequences for the different ways in which new waves of immigrants from different parts of the world – whose settlement was seen as logistically essential for the future well-being of these countries – were assumed to fit into these new nations.

AMERICAN NATIONAL IDENTITY: IDEOLOGICAL
UNIVERSALISM

In her discussion of the creation of American identity, Heidi Tarver notes that 'it has been argued by some scholars that national identity preceded and was a significant factor in the political unification of the states under the Constitution'.[16] She goes on to demonstrate that, notwithstanding this contention, 'likeness in the pre-revolutionary period was constituted . . . in relation to the British rather than the American nation'.[17] Moreover, she notes that 'A few years after the Glorious Revolution, Cotton Mather declared: "It is no Little Blessing of God, that we are a part of the English Nation"', and that, sixty years later:

> Benjamin Franklin clearly expressed the sense of colonial/British identity when he wrote to Lord Kames: 'No one can more sincerely rejoice than I do, on the reduction of Canada; and this is not merely as I am a colonist, but as I am a Briton.'[18]

What we have here is a good illustration of the transference of British national identity to the New World, and its preservation despite political independence. It suggests a perception of nationality as arising out of a shared cultural experience and, therefore, as being more 'natural' than politically constructed divisions. It shows that, even though the Americans had fought and won a war against the British, winning their independence in the process, Britishness remained their primary point of identification. Still, as Smith remarks, by the late eighteenth century a 'vernacular ancestralism' had developed that 'looked back to the Americanised forefathers against the "wicked British stepmother" and proclaimed a unique destiny for the new "chosen people" in the New Jerusalem'.[19]

Referring to the war of independence, Tarver relates how:

> As the war progressed . . . the violence which it imposed on daily life began to reshape American perceptions of both themselves and their British opponents. For one thing, lamentations over the loss of affective ties to the mother country were replaced with vitriolic verbal attacks and bitter recriminations. American Whigs accused Britain of tyrannical and oppressive policies toward the colonies, of conspiracy, corruption and degeneracy.[20]

Disregarding Tarver's reductively causal explanation, it is clear that the American war of independence occasioned a much more fraught relation between the American settlers and the Mother Country than was ever the case between the early Australian settlers and British national culture. In Australia, there was never any fundamental political disagreement with Britain and never a strong, perceived need (until recently) to define Australian national identity in terms of political independence from Britain. By contrast, according to Tarver, in America the revolutionary war itself 'provided intense common experience and the raw material for national myth-making',[21] and 'if the war operated as a metaphor for separation from Britain, the bloodshed and suffering it inflicted on Americans also held powerful symbolic potential with respect to new visions of communitas'.[22] While this may have been the case, the complexities of the American settler experience and the settlers' struggle for independence had a fundamental effect on the way the emerging national community was to be imagined. It led to a shift away from a concern with 'natural' (British) national culture as the site for identification, and towards a messianic espousal of ideology as the basis for forging an identity for the new nation.

This is a crucial point. The choice between ideology and culture was made possible by the discursive ordering of the Enlightenment principles which underlie modernity. It came hard on the heels of the French Revolution's attempt to impose a political ideology as the basis for a new state in a situation where a unified national identity was already being forged out of pre-existing cultural components. However, as a settler society, America's situation was quite different, particularly as it needed to invent a focus for a new national identity. This need can explain why ideology itself was resorted to as the basis for an entirely new national identity. This is most clearly expressed in the rhetoric to be found in the second paragraph of the Declaration of Independence, which begins with the sentence that virtually every American still knows by heart:

> We hold these truths to be self-evident, that all men are created equal,
> that they are endowed by their Creator with certain unalienable Rights,
> that among these are Life, Liberty and the pursuit of Happiness.

It is a commonplace to note that this paragraph derives from Enlightenment philosophy and that, in particular, it owes much to the political thinking of John Locke. His political theory was being used self-consciously here as the foundation for the identifying features of a modern nation-state. In the Declaration, we find no assertion of a separate American cultural identity. Rather, what came out of the tension with the continued experience of Britishness (as testified in Benjamin Franklin's remark quoted above) was not a rejection of British culture, but a claim to create a new nation on the basis of universal ideological principles which supposedly transcended cultural and ethnic specificity. The implications of this are complex. While providing a claim to national uniqueness, it also laid the basis for a secular political universalism, paving the way for the twentieth-century American belief in the portability of 'the American way of life' (founded on ideological principles as the basis of culture) to other national sites around the world. Within the USA itself, this logic can help explain why the multiple cultures and peoples that make up the United States are always to be subsumed under the overarching ideals which make America 'the promised land'.[23]

This emphasis is repeated in mainstream American sociology, which privileges a functionalist consensus theory in which society is viewed as held together by shared moral precepts (norms, values and attitudes) rather than by shared cultural experience and practice.[24] American discussions of immigration tend to follow the assumptions of functionalist sociology, where the problem of 'social integration' is 'solved' through assimilation into what Talcott Parsons called 'the central value system'. Assimilation is defined here primarily at the level of ideology, as the acceptance of universal moral values, whereas the failure of assimilation is equated with social disintegration (that is, the fragmentation, or the lack, of shared moral values). The specifically American idea of the melting-pot is based on the concept of assimilation and it has been thought of as essential for American national identity: it is the metaphor for the construction of a unified people out of a wide variety of ethnic and racial groups. America, says Schlesinger, is 'a severing of roots, a liberation from the stifling past, an entry into a new life, an interweaving of separate ethnic strands into a new national design'.[25] What unifies Americans, in this scheme of things, is a universal dedication to a set of abstract ideals and principles. Franklin D. Roosevelt expressed this clearly when he stated in 1943 that 'Americanism is a matter of the mind and the heart; Americanism is not, and never was, a matter of race and ancestry. A good American is one who is loyal to this country and to our creed of liberty and democracy.'[26]

Two things follow from this construction of American identity. In the first place, being an American is not primarily defined in terms of specific cultural practices and symbols (such as love for baseball or hotdogs), but in more abstract, idealist terms. Thus, Mary Waters found that the Americans she interviewed, when asked about their identity as Americans, understood that identity unequivocally in terms of loyalty and patriotism; 'American' is experienced 'as a political or national category rather than as an ethnic or cultural category'.[27] This means that ethnic identity, or ethnicity – the source of cultural distinctiveness – is defined *outside* the general paradigm of a universal all-Americanness. The phenomenon of the hyphenated American – African-American, Asian-American, Italian-American, and so on – should be understood in this way: as the coupling of two separate identities, one culturally particular, the other presumed to be ideologically universal.

But the very existence of the hyphenated American points to another characteristic of American national identity: its fundamental future-orientedness, its orientation towards an idealised social destiny. Because all-American identity is situated in the realm of ideals, American nationhood is always experienced as something that will only have been fully achieved when the USA has become the perfect, lived realisation of these ideals. Schlesinger voices this sentiment clearly:

> What has held the American people together in the absence of a common ethnic origin has been precisely a common adherence to ideals of democracy and human rights that, *too often transgressed in practice*, forever goad us to narrow the gap between practice and principle.[28] (emphasis added)

But it is precisely this vision of American reality as a gap between principle and practice that makes it impossible for someone like Schlesinger, a liberal now repositioned as conservative in the new context of identity politics, to acknowledge that the transgression of these ideals may be structurally *constitutive* of the social formation of the USA rather than a practical shortcoming to be teleologically overcome in the future. For Schlesinger, the persisting (and, alarmingly for him, strengthening) cultural and ethnic differences and divisions that characterise the American social fabric can be conceptualised only negatively, as a residue of the melting process – that which fails to be successfully 'Americanised'. In this sense, the hyphenated American poses a potential danger: the danger that the particular may overwhelm the universal. Schlesinger prefers to see American history as a steady movement from exclusion to inclusion of all people living within the territory, into an ever more inclusive, idealised America. But the rise of the 'unmeltable ethnics'[29] and, more importantly, the increasingly forceful self-assertion of Blacks and other Americans of non-white, non-European ancestry (Native Americans, Chicanos, Asians) disrupts this imagined ideal history. No wonder, then, that Schlesinger sees multiculturalism – which provides the terrain for these ethnic and racial self-assertions – as the culmination of a betrayal of the American ideal.

The problem with multiculturalism, Schlesinger says, is that it gives rise to

> the conception of the US as a nation composed not of individuals making their own choices but of inviolable ethnic and racial groups. It rejects the historic American goals of assimilation and integration. And, in an excess of zeal, well-intentioned people seek to transform our system of education from a means of creating 'one people' into a means of promoting, celebrating and perpetuating separate ethnic origins and identities. The balance is shifting from *unum* to *pluribus*.[30]

However, what remains unexplained in such an account is why, if the American ideals of the melting-pot were so attractive and promising, assimilation and integration were only partially successful, and what reinforced the separatist impulse among radical multiculturalists. One answer is that the universalist myth of opportunity for all, into which the American Creed was translated for the individual, failed to materialise, leading to a sense of disillusion with official providential Americanism. This answer is implied in Woodiwiss's discussion of the post-1960s American experience of the failure of the ideology of social modernism to deliver on its promises to the American people. As Schlesinger himself concedes, 'the rising cult of ethnicity was a symptom of decreasing confidence in the American future'.[31] Another answer could point to the fact that the abstract and, basically, culturally empty nature of the lofty principles on which American identity is based (such as 'democracy', 'liberty', 'human rights') may have prevented them from becoming concrete anchors for the experience of a meaningful and distinctive common national culture. As Hugh Seton-Watson observes, 'many "ethnics" had lost their old values without gaining anything new except the materialist hedonism of the mass media'.[32] That is, in the absence of specific cultural content inscribed in the definition of what it means to be American, the assimilation of immigrants into 'the American way of life' ended up being defined by their absorption into a pervasive and homogenised 'mass culture' of consumerism.[33]

Most important, however, is the fact that the very universalist representation of America as the promised land for all, and of Americanness as a potentially universal identity, involves a radical disavowal of the fundamental historical exclusions which undergirded the foundation of the USA. But, as Pierre Bourdieu has remarked, the universal is never power-neutral, and its defenders always have a certain interest in it.[34] Thus, when Schlesinger states dismissively that 'multicultural zealots reject as hegemonic the notion of a shared commitment to common ideals',[35] he either denies the very existence of a hegemonic condition which, far from being universally accessible, structurally favours some categories over others, or he trivialises the cost of that hegemonic condition for those marginalised by it. To put it differently, the gap between Americanist principles and US social reality is not an unfortunate historical aberration to be corrected in the future, as Schlesinger would have it, but the very effect of that hegemonic universalism, which denies the structural centrality of policies of exclusion to the formation of the USA.

In US history, the key exclusionary category is that of 'race' – a category which, as Omi and Winant have argued, is a central organising principle in US social relationships at all levels of life. From the beginning, US society has been structured by a racial order which 'has linked the system of political rule to the racial classification of individuals and groups'.[36] While culture – and therefore ethnicity – was elided from the discourse of American national identity, race was not. Race, not ethnicity, has been understood by Americans as the fundamental site of difference within the USA nation-state. Omi and Winant characterise the USA state as a racial state, in which the category 'white' remains the undisputed hegemonic centre. Historically, the category 'white' (with which the European settlers identified themselves) emerged simultaneously with the category 'black', which evolved as a result of the consolidation of racial slavery towards the end of the seventeenth century.[37] This resulted in a racial logic – the establishment and maintenance of a 'colour line' – whose effects still permeate contemporary US society. Race can be understood as, in a Derridean sense, the supplement to American national identity. It both asserts the transcendental unifying possibilities of a universalist ideology – and thus the ultimate unity of the American nation in spite of race – and provides the always-already existent and irreducible site for its failure.

Since the 1960s, racially based social movements have moved from a largely integrationist stance (as in the civil rights movement), which struggled for the breaking-down of the colour barrier, to a more self-assertive black nationalist stance (as in black power), which signalled a loss of faith in the possibility of turning the USA into a 'raceless society'.[38] In other words, rather than a gradual inclusion of racial minority groups in the American melting-pot – presumably achieved by granting them 'equal rights' and 'social justice' – these groups have engendered a range of political cultures which have moved beyond these quasi-universalist principles and embraced particularist ideals of 'self-determination', a 'politics of identity' relying on the symbolic and cultural assertion of 'blackness'.

Racial self-identification represents a deliberate distancing from, rather than assimilation into, the WASP mainstream. As a consequence, the discourse of race has become a way of talking about and locating cultural difference, in a manner much more divisive than the discourse of ethnicity which, in the American context, is mainly reserved for 'whites'.[39] In this sense, the hyphenated label 'African-American' signifies a much more radical fracture in American identity than, say, 'Italian-American'. It is this separatist impulse (signified by 'multiculturalism') that Schlesinger sees as a threat to American unity. By the same token, however, we could suggest that it is precisely the persistent invocation of the colour-blind universalism of American principles – which has no room for a serious recognition of its own particularist WASP roots and the historically real exclusions brought about in its name – which might have fuelled that very separatist impulse. What we can now see is why and how, in the American context, multiculturalism is bound up with both identity politics and race. While the former operates as a critique of and response to the ideology of American universalism, the latter has become positioned as the structural signifier of difference fundamentally excessive to, and subversive of, a unified American imagined community. The connection between identity politics and multiculturalism is complex and, in some ways, distinctively American, growing out of the American privileging of ideology. The politicisation of a set of subcultural practices as an exclusive collective 'identity' suggests the ideological foundation of identity politics. In this context, universalism and particularism, assimilation and separateness, unity and disunity are constructed as mutually exclusive, oppositional ideological forces, with no in-between zone. As we will see, the policy of multiculturalism in Australia can be interpreted precisely as an attempt to create such an in-between zone.

AUSTRALIAN NATIONAL IDENTITY: RACE AND CULTURAL PARTICULARISM

Unlike the USA, Australia separated from Great Britain gradually, and over a lengthy period of time. Made up of separate colonies, the continental nation-state of Australia came into existence on 1 January 1901. This was enabled by the passing of a bill in the British House of Commons sanctioning Federation in May 1900. There was no Australian War of Independence and no establishment of a new republic, although some radical colonials did imagine such a revolutionary separation from the Mother Country following the example of America, generally considered in the nineteenth century as the most advanced 'new society'.[40]

As with the USA, what was first established in Australia was a transplantation of British culture. This culture, of course, evolved away from its British source but the primary identification remained with 'British' culture. Manning Clark has remarked that 'what the English or the European observed in the Australians was their Britishness'.[41] He goes on to quote Francis Adams, 'an English man of letters who lived in Melbourne, Sydney and Brisbane between 1884 and 1889', who wrote in 1886 that 'the first thing that struck me on walking about Sydney one afternoon . . . was the appalling strength of the British civilization'.[42] And even though comparisons with America were regularly made throughout the century, the ultimate similarity was considered to be with Britain. Australian democracy, for example, was commonly seen by the colonial bourgeoisie as inspired by British democracy, not something built on the model of American democracy, whose 'excesses' (such as mob rule and popular government) were criticised by Alexis de Tocqueville in his influential book *Democracy in America*.

In short, for most of the nineteenth century, according to Richard White, there was no strong evidence of a distinctively Australian identity: 'Australians saw themselves, and were seen by others, as part of a group of new, transplanted, predominantly Anglo-Saxon emigrant societies'.[43] It is significant that a sense of national distinctiveness grew stronger only towards the end of the century, and that this was accompanied by 'a more explicitly racial element', based on being Anglo-Saxon or, as confidence in the new society grew, 'on being the most vigorous branch of Anglo-Saxondom'.[44] The latter formed the basis for a belief in the emergence of an Australian 'national type', to which were attributed not only physical and racial characteristics, but also a moral, social and psychological identity.[45] The Australian type – sometimes spoken of as 'the Anglo-Australian race' – was believed to be a new product of the multiplying British stock, the 'race' which, in the heyday of British imperialism, saw itself as superior to all other 'races' (a view legitimated by the then immensely influential ideology of Social Darwinism) and therefore as possessing the duty and destiny to populate and 'civilise' the rest of the world. It is this racialist concern with a distinctively Australian type that undergirded the so-called White Australia Policy, which was sanctioned by the adoption of the Immigration Restriction Bill in 1901. This bill prohibited the immigration into Australia of 'non-Europeans' or 'the coloured races'. The fact that this bill was the first major legislative issue dealt with by the parliament of the newly created Commonwealth of Australia suggests the perceived importance of 'racial purity' as the symbolic cement for the imagined community of the fledgling nation.[46] In contrast to its use in the USA, then, the discourse of race was used to mark the limits of the Australian imagined community, not distinctions within it. This is a point to which we will return when discussing the Australian policy and practice of multiculturalism.

It is important to point to the historical specificity of the racism inscribed in this policy of exclusion. We want to suggest that its motivation was not primarily a negative one, in the sense of being directed against other races (although, in practice, it was mostly targeted at the Chinese and the Japanese while spanning, of course, all the 'non-white' races). Rather, the policy was implemented at a critical moment in the positive development of a distinctive national identity. If we ally Anderson's notion of the imagined community with the acknowledgment that settler societies begin their struggle for a separate identity with the raw material of the national culture brought by the settlers, then we can understand that the White Australia policy was, in the first instance, a *nationalist* policy, reflecting the new nation-state's search for a national identity in a European culture and a British-based racial homogeneity (which inevitably implies the exclusion of racial/cultural Others). In Andrew Markus's words:

> The non-Europeans of the 'near north' were seen as posing a threat to the social and political life of the community, to its higher aspirations. The perception of this threat was heightened by a consciousness of race, a consciousness that innate and immutable physical characteristics of certain human groups were associated with non-physical attributes which precluded their assimilation into the Australian nation.[47]

The Australian preoccupation with racial/cultural purity as the precondition for constructing a unified national identity is an example of how the modern idea that a nation should be homogeneous could be translated into a state policy which collapses race into culture. Arguably, it is because the nation-state used the reductive category of race (defined by physical appearance), rather than that of ethnicity (a complex of nationalised cultural characteristics), as the final arbiter of membership that it could later embrace multiculturalism based on the more culturally oriented discourse of ethnicity.

While the social reality throughout the continent was probably much more culturally diverse than was officially recognised, the *rhetoric* of racial and cultural homogeneity was constantly rehearsed in speeches and editorials surrounding the birth of the new nation. As White observes, 'It could be proclaimed that the new nation was 98 per cent British, more British than any other dominion, some said more British than Britain itself'.[48] According to the 1901 census, the largest non-British migrant groups were the Germans (1 per cent) and the Chinese (0.8 per cent). This emphasis on racial/cultural homogeneity was uniformly represented as promising to the future of the new nation-state. In 1903, the first Australian attorney-general, Alfred Deakin, who later became Prime Minister, said in the House of Representatives that the most powerful force impelling the colonies towards federation had been 'the desire that we should be one people, and remain one people, without the admixture of other races'.[49]

In other words, the White Australia policy implied the official racialisation of Australian national identity in a concerted and consensual manner which never took place in the USA. In this way, in contrast to the USA where race was historically always-already an internal national issue, in Australia the salience of race was elided in everyday life. Instead, it became primarily a policy issue which marked the conceptual limits of the imagined community – the point where nation and state met to exclude or, in the case of the Aborigines, to extinguish the racially undesirable. Markus quotes from the Melbourne *Age* in 1896 to signal the 'luck' experienced by Australians in this respect:

> The problem of Negro citizenship in the United States is given up by the philosopher as unsolvable. . . . In Australia, fortunately, we are free from this race problem. The aboriginals were of too low a stamp of intelligence and too few in number to be seriously considered. If there had been any difficulty, it would have been obviated by the gradual dying out of the native race.[50]

The fundamental difference between the American conception of national identity, based on an ideology inscribed in the foundation of the state, and the Australian conception, based on the European idea of a homogeneous national culture, should be clear by now. It should be said, however, that the construction of the external limits of US national identity was also, in practice, associated with race-based discrimination. Thus, the naturalisation statute of 1790 stated that only 'white persons' were eligible for American citizenship, an act amended in 1870 by adding 'persons of African descent', an addition necessitated by the ratification of the Fourteenth Amendment, which abolished slavery. What this amendment signalled is that, from then on, the category of race was located within the imagined community and not at its limits, as in the Australian case. As we have suggested above, this is why American discourse has included race as an always-already fracturing element within the national identity.

Furthermore, just as in Australia, Chinese immigration was restricted in the USA and Chinese residents were not eligible for citizenship for decades,[51] but while one can find many similarities in the arguments put forward by anti-Chinese lobbyists in both countries, the final decision to implement restriction in the USA seemed to have been accompanied not by a discourse of nation-building but mainly by economic and moralistic rhetoric. The many politicians who were against discrimination generally couched their arguments in terms of the universalist humanist principles of the Declaration of Independence, arguing, as Senator Sumner of Massachusetts did, that 'the greatest peril [of anti-Chinese discrimination] to this republic is from disloyalty to its great ideas'.[52] Even pro-restriction voices often referred to these principles. Markus summarises the American national stance against Chinese immigration in the following way, clearly echoing the importance of American ideology in its legitimation:

> The American nation wanted immigrants, but immigrants who believed in republican institutions, who believed in public schools to raise their children to become good citizens, who worshipped at the shrine of freedom and who could assimilate into the mainstream of American life.[53]

By contrast, Australian anti-Chinese discourse was not only much more overtly racialist, but also, especially towards the end of the nineteenth century, much more explicitly connected with the cause of nation-building. The Chinese, cate-gorised as a coloured, non-European 'race', could not belong to an Australian nation which officially defined itself as 'white'. The construction of a new, Australian national imagined community was premised on an exclusionary racial/cultural particularism, a binary oppositioning which included some and excluded others. To be sure, the category 'white' itself was a term of amassment generally referring to 'Europeans', although both categories proved to be more ambiguous and arbitrary than was first assumed. It was this racial exclusionary particularism that was to be overturned with the introduction of multiculturalism in the early 1970s – a policy that could be characterised as the establishment of an inclusionary ethnic particularism.

TOWARDS A MULTICULTURAL IMAGINED COMMUNITY

As a settler society, Australia depended, just like the USA, on sustained immigra-tion for its economic development and national security. In the post-World War II period, Australia embarked on a programme to build up its population rapidly. Recovering from the war and faced with an increasingly strong Asian 'near-north', Australia, in the words of its first Minister for Immigration, Arthur Calwell, felt it needed to 'populate or perish'. One consequence of the desire to increase immi-gration was a liberalisation of the White Australia policy. As there was an insufficient supply of immigrants from Britain, 'New Australians' were recruited first in Northern Europe (Scandinavia, the Netherlands, Germany) and later in Southern Europe (Italy, Greece, Croatia, Macedonia and so on). It is important to recognise not only the hierarchy implicit in this descending preference for dif-ferent subcategories of 'white' Europeans, but also that this liberalisation of the White Australia policy did not overturn the race-based, two-tiered structure which distinguished Europeans from non-Europeans. It did, however, introduce an element of diversity within the category 'white', which needed to be dealt with. That is, with the admission of non-British European migrants, 'whiteness' could no longer be related directly to the (British-derived) racial purity of the 'Australian type'. Racial homogeneity and cultural homogeneity could no longer be assumed to be one and the same thing. As a result, emphasis was now placed on the concept of 'the Australian way of life' as the basis of government policy to assimilate migrants and Aborigines alike.[54]

The official rhetoric of cultural assimilationism can be defined as 'the doctrine that immigrants could be culturally and socially absorbed and rapidly become indistinguishable from the existing Anglo-Australian population'.[55] Castles et al. have summed up the politics of assimilation in the Australian context like this:

> The assimilationist/White Australia package had three essential ingredi-ents, relating to the question of national identity:

151

- Australia was a culturally homogeneous society based on British values and institutions.

- This homogeneity would not be disturbed by mass European immigration.

- It could not survive any Asian migration.[56]

Castles et al. argue that assimilationism was 'a covert racism based on the proposed incompatibility of certain cultures; and it drew the limiting line at which this incompatibility began, namely, where a culture ceased to be "European"'.[57] That is, the desire to keep Australia 'white' was based on cultural considerations: white ethnics were thought to be capable of assimilation by the national culture, while coloured races were not. At this point it is useful to note the different emphases in American and Australian conceptions of assimilation. In contrast with American assimilationism, which is thought of as the melting of many different 'cultures' into a universal set of ideological principles and values (of which the 'American way of life' is the supreme embodiment), Australian assimilationism aimed at the preservation of one particular 'culture', the distinctively 'Australian way of life', by excluding all other 'cultures' which were considered incompatible and incapable of assimilation. This post-World War II assimilation policy can be interpreted as a response to the perceived need to sustain a homogeneous national culture which, as the European model showed, was the precondition of a nation-state. Thus, in contrast with American assimilationism, which tends to be concerned with the immigrants' adoption of 'American values' (themselves 'universal'), Australian assimilationism tended to be concerned with immigrants' adoption of everyday cultural practices. As Ellie Vasta notes:

> New Australians, amounting to a ninth of the whole Australian population in 1956, were settling down to understand, if not share, old Australian predilections for drinking tea, rather than coffee, beer rather than the good wine of the country. . . . Newcomers had to puzzle over the old Australian disrespect for civil order and good government, bewilderingly joined with a general observance of the peace. . . . And, new Australians had to try to understand old Australian speech.[58]

Castles et al. write that, 'in terms of dominant forms of identity and official state policy, the assimilation of the post-1945 decades . . . is the first historically significant nationalism in Australian history'.[59] That is, bearing in mind that the White Australia policy was an exclusionary and therefore restrictive nationalist policy, there was no policy for deliberately producing, or actively reproducing, an Australian national identity until the range of cultural differences allowed into the country led to an assertive policy of assimilation meant to ensure the homogeneity regarded as necessary for the maintenance of a unified imagined community. Assimilationism can therefore be understood as a cultural nationalism which had

the consequence of freeing Australia from colonial shackles and, in the end, forc-
ing it to distinguish itself from British racial/cultural identity. This was achieved
through the promotion and celebration of a distinctive 'Australian way of life', a
discursive construct which replaced the older, more British-related 'national type'.
In other words, the discourse of assimilationism destabilised the symbiotic relationship between race and culture. That the distinction between British and
Australian culture was still difficult to draw, however, is revealed in the above
quotation. After all, tea- and beer-drinking are very British cultural practices, transplanted to Australia. Australian nationalism, therefore, could not logically focus on
such cultural features to mark off the Australian imagined community from other
ones. As a result, as Castles *et al.* remark, the cultural homogeneity sought after in
the policy of assimilation

> seems to rely less on the language of kin and the ideology of folk than
> is commonly the case for nationalisms, principally because of the ambi-
> guities and tensions of the English-imperial connection and independent
> Australian nationalism. In the case of the former, the colonial link was a
> less than plausible basis for an identity that would purport to capture the
> essence of the people who lived within the boundaries of the Australian
> nation-state. And, in the case of the latter, no claims to peculiarly local
> folk primordiality were possible for the European settlers. Preeminently,
> instead, the language of nationalism, celebrating the imagined commu-
> nal 'us', was about standards of living and domestic progress. This is an
> unusually 'modern' celebration for nationalism, perhaps, but linked nev-
> ertheless with an explicit ideal of cultural assimilation.[60]

This 'modern' Australian nationalism, then, is not only un-ideological (in the
sense that it is not predicated on lofty universal ideals and principles, as is
American nationalism) but, in its desire to decolonise itself – a process which is
by no means completed even to this day – it also lacked the cultural resources to
imagine itself as 'looming out of an immemorial past', to use Benedict Anderson's
description of the nation. 'The Australian way of life' was a vague discursive construct which lacked historical and cultural density, often boiling down to not
much more than the suburban myth of 'the car, the family, the garden and a uniformly middle-class lifestyle'.[61] We want to suggest that it is this relative
underdetermination of Australian national identity by either ideology or culture
that provided the symbolic space for the Australian nation-state to develop and
implement an official policy of multiculturalism as the foundation for a reconstruction of national self-perception.

   The official end of the White Australia policy occurred some years before the
transformation of government policy in the direction of multiculturalism. As
Castles *et al.* put it, 'in the mid-1960s, the White Australia Policy was officially
abandoned by both major parties and assimilation was effectively abandoned also,
at least in name'.[62] Multiculturalism surfaced as a new government policy in 1973

when Al Grassby, the flamboyant then Minister for Immigration under the Whitlam Labor Government, issued a statement entitled *A Multi-Cultural Society for the Future*.

It has rapidly become orthodoxy to describe the advent of official multiculturalism in Australia as the effect of a failure of the earlier ethic of assimilationism. And, indeed, the fact was that many non-British European migrants − Italians, Greeks, and so on − were simply not divesting themselves of the cultural practices that they brought with them from their national 'homelands' (such as drinking coffee and wine and speaking their 'national' language), as the assimilation policy required. But this tells only half the story. We want to suggest that official multiculturalism in Australia was not just a pragmatic response to problems encountered with the absorption of migrants, but can also be analysed as the sign of a more general transformation in the thinking about the very constitution of the national culture. In a pamphlet put out by the Australian Council on Population and Ethnic Affairs in 1982 and entitled *Multiculturalism for all Australians*, we are told that:

> Multiculturalism is . . . much more than the provision of special services to minority ethnic groups. It is a way of looking at Australian society, and involves living together with an awareness of cultural diversity. We accept our differences and appreciate a variety of lifestyles rather than expect everyone to fit into a standardised pattern. Most of all, multiculturalism requires us to recognise that we each can be 'a real Australian', without necessarily being 'a typical Australian'.[63]

Given the subtitle of the pamphlet, 'Our developing nationhood', the emphasis on cultural diversity here can best be understood as a complex turning-away from the desire for a homogeneous Australian national culture. What the subtitle suggests is that Australian national identity is itself a new thing, still in development, and a consequence of the juxtaposition of different cultures and ethnicities within the territory of the nation-state.

The distinctiveness of the Australian formulation of a multicultural national identity does not reside in its recognition of cultural pluralism as such (this also happened in many other 'Western' countries, including the USA), but is located in the (politically self-conscious) shift away from an imagining of the national community in terms of a homogeneous 'way of life'. The key to this shift lies in the new emphasis on the productivity of cultural difference − located in ethnicity − rather than in the old emphasis on race as the marker of national cultural limits. In this new understanding of national identity as a process of continual reinvention through the interaction of a plurality of ethnically-defined, imagined communities, the state takes on a new role as the guarantor of historical continuity.

The theoretical underpinnings of this political shift are illuminated in the *Review of Post-Arrival Programmes and Services to Migrants* (the so-called Galbally Report), tabled in Parliament in 1978. Significantly, this report took Edward Tylor's 1871 anthropological definition of culture as its starting point. The report announces that 'we believe [culture to be] a way of life, that "complex whole which includes knowledge, belief, art, morals, law, customs, and any other capabilities and habits acquired by man [sic] as a member of Society"'.[64] The adoption of this anthropological definition of culture in the development of multiculturalism indicates the continued importance given to *cultural practices* (rather than ideological principles) for the construction of Australian national identity. The use of an anthropological – rather than a sociological – definition of culture also reinforces the holistic notion of cultures as being both integrated and bounded. What Australian multiculturalism does is locate the 'ethnic community' as the site of a particular 'culture', so that, logically, Australian national culture now consists of many 'cultures'. As we will see, this conceptualisation is at the basis of the idea of multicultural Australia as a 'unity-in-diversity'.

In other words, while it might have been a pragmatic solution to the perceived failure of assimilation, multiculturalism must also be understood as an attempt to reconstruct the definition of Australian national identity, with the (probably unintended) effect of fundamentally reworking the dynamic relation of nation and state. Multiculturalism can be seen, first of all, as a response to a crisis of identity in a settler society which, for a variety of reasons, could no longer sustain a national identity dependent on the myth of a British origin. This is not to deny that the cultural diversity that proliferated in the country as a result of post-World War II immigration created all sorts of social problems which the multiculturalist policies were designed to address. We want to suggest, however, that the comprehensive manner in which successive Australian governments (both conservative and Labor) have been concerned with cultural diversity is related to something quite different – the settler society's problems with national identity. In other words, multiculturalism here is not just a new policy for dealing with immigrants but is, in effect, a new national cultural policy. Arguably, the disarticulation of nation from state can occur more easily in a new settler society like Australia than in old nations where myths of primordial origins are much more historically entrenched and culturally sedimented. And it is on this disarticulation that multiculturalism *as a policy to redefine national culture* depends.

Multiculturalism, as government policy, has provided a new status for the state as the site where the overarching ideological principles that legitimise and vindicate the diversity of cultural practices in Australian territorial space are formulated. The state provides an ideological context for the production of the nation, but here, unlike the USA, the nation is not conceived as a cultural expression of the universal ideological principles represented by the state. Rather, the state acts as an institutional container of principles which are instrumental to the encouragement and management of cultural diversity. Thus, the very 'awareness of cultural diversity', together with related values such as tolerance, is now foregrounded as a principle on which the Australian imagined community rests. In 1989, the Australian federal government launched the National Agenda for a Multicultural

Australia. The very phrase 'multicultural Australia' suggests that 'multiculturality' has now been enshrined as a recognised essence of Australian national identity, understood as an ideal unity-in-diversity. It is in this sense that we want to describe the society constructed by multiculturalism in Australia as an *inclusive particularism*: ethnic minority cultures are now welcomed and celebrated as *enriching* Australian national culture rather than threatening it.

Along a very different historical path, then, Australia has reached a point which was taken up by the USA from its very inception: the formulation of national identity as an ideal cultural future sanctioned by the state, rather than as something emerging organically from a particular racial/cultural heritage. In contrast with the USA, however, this ideal cultural future is defined not in terms of a single set of ideological principles which all individuals should ideally make their own, but in terms of the creation of a symbolic *space* in which different cultures live harmoniously side by side, in which all Australians not only have the right, but are encouraged, 'within carefully defined limits, to express and share their individual cultural heritage, including their language and religion'.[65] This difference explains why multiculturalism can only be conceived in the USA as *subverting* the national, while the Australian national can be represented as *constituted by* multiculturalism. This results in two very different conceptions of future-orientedness. Whereas the American national identity can ultimately be conceived only as a utopian ideal (when the melting-pot will finally have Americanised everyone), a multicultural national identity, as the Australian one is now designed to be, is more pragmatically conceived as a potential reality, characterised by a managed unity-in-diversity (where different cultural communities co-exist as distinct pieces of a national mosaic – to use the Canadian metaphor – in a presumably 'appropriate' balance).

BEYOND MULTICULTURALISM?

The mainstreaming of multiculturalism in Australia – in the sense that the government-sponsored idea of Australia as a cultural mosaic has been commonly accepted – poses very peculiar challenges to critical debate. First of all, like the White Australia policy and the policy of assimilation before it, official multiculturalism – as a discourse – does not either represent or create the multifarious concrete experiences of the people living in Australia (although the particular policy measures implemented in the name of the rhetoric do, of course). It is, in the first instance, a discourse that constructs a particular account of those experiences: what it does is present to the people of Australia a public fantasy – a collective narrative fiction – of the diverse character of Australia as a nation. (In this sense, the fantasy is more hegemonic – and therefore more mythical – than in Canada, where the multicultural fantasy is more contentiously restricted to so-called English Canada.) The legitimacy of this narrative fiction is important enough, and derives from an acceptance of this account. It is precisely within the narrative space of this fiction, institutionalised, for example, in SBS television (the public 'multicultural' channel), that opportunities are created for the active public exploration of cultural difference, opportunities which were not available in times when a more assimilationist ethic predominated.

In this sense, the now common assertion that 'Australia has always been a multicultural society' is both trite and historically misleading. The point is not so much that popular cultural practices were never as homogeneous as generally thought – arguably this is a truism applicable to all modern societies – but that the ideological representation of Australian nationhood as racially and culturally homogeneous (as in the heyday of the White Australia policy) did have real effects on both the expression and the experience of racial, ethnic and cultural difference: this expression and this experience were neither acknowledged nor accepted as part of Australian life. The discourse of multiculturalism has made a real difference in this respect; it has provided a medium for dealing with identity and difference which is neither separatist nor assimilationist. That is, because Australian multiculturalism expressly incorporates ethnic difference within the space of the national, it provides a framework for a politics of negotiation over the very content of the national culture, which is no longer imagined as something fixed and historically given but as something in the process of becoming. An apparently trivial, but actually profound, example – because it relates to a cardinal cultural practice – is Australian cuisine, which is now commonly represented as an eclectic hybrid of Mediterranean, Asian and other culinary traditions, including Anglo and Celtic ones. Thus, it is now possible to think about the distinctiveness of Australian national culture not in terms of an exclusive, pre-given racial/cultural particularity, but as an open-ended and provisional formation, as permanently unfinished business. As John Docker would have it, what distinguishes Australia is its 'post-nationality', based on a 'decoupling of an Enlightenment polity from any notion of a congruent necessary single culture' and on 'an acceptance and fostering of unpredictable cultural difference'.[66] Or as Ramesh Thakur puts it, 'multiculturalism is a fluid set of identities for the individual as well as the nation'.[67]

But this might be too rosy a formulation. The problem with official multiculturalism is that it tends, precisely, to freeze the fluidity of identity by the very fact that it is concerned with synthesising unruly and unpredictable cultural identities and differences into a harmonious unity-in-diversity. So the metaphor of the mosaic, of unity-in-diversity, is based on another kind of disavowal, on a suppression of the potential incommensurability of juxtaposed cultural differences. Here we confront the limits of state multiculturalism. Against the background of the state's concern with the construction of (national) unity, multiculturalism can be seen as a policy, not to foster cultural differences but, on the contrary, to direct them into safe channels. Thus, Homi Bhabha makes the cautionary observation that policies of multiculturalism represent 'an attempt both to respond to and to control the dynamic process of the articulation of cultural difference, administering a consensus based on a norm that propagates cultural diversity'.[68] In this sense, the national community can be imagined as a 'unity in diversity' only by a *containment* of cultural difference. Seen this way, the idea(l) of unity-in-diversity is itself, ultimately, an exclusionary ideological construct. One constant source of tension is the relationship between the principle of 'tolerance' enunciated by the multicultural state and the particular ethnic/cultural practices that are to be 'tolerated'. The more 'deviant' an ethnic community is, the more tensions there are likely to be between it and the state, at which point the state has the power to put limits to 'tolerance'. In this sense, the politics of multiculturalism can be understood as coming out of the same modernist ideological assumptions as those on which the notion of the homogeneous nation-state was based. The ultimate rationale remains national unity; tolerance of diversity is just another means of guaranteeing that unity.

As we have seen, the very validation of cultural diversity embodied in official multiculturalism tends to hypostatise and even fetishise 'culture' and thus suppress the heterogeneity which exists within each 'culture', constructed as coterminous with 'ethnicity'. This is a conservative effect, underpinned by traditional anthropology, which, ironically enough, only reproduces the binary opposition (common in the USA context) of the particular and the universal. According to Docker, this is what the so-called multicultural orthodoxy does, constructing a binary relation between 'ethnic communities' and 'Australian society', as if the two were mutually exclusive, internally homogeneous entities. Such a representation not only constructs the latter as 'always devaluing, hierarchising, othering' the former,[69] but also pigeonholes 'the migrant' as permanently marginalised, forever ethnicised. It is not coincidental that 'Anglo-Celtic' Australians are not viewed as an ethnic community, while the government and the senior echelons of the public service are still largely composed of people, mostly male, from this dominant demographic group. In this image of the nation, the ethnicisation of minority cultures depends on the prior existence of a non-ethnicised Australian cultural centre (of 'Anglo-Celtic' origin and expressed as 'the Australian way of life', forged from the cultural reductions of assimilationism). This central 'Australian culture' is the ex-nominated ground on which other cultures are not only ethnicised but also enabled, quite literally, to speak to each other or, indeed, to fight one another (as happened in the clashes between Australian nationals of Greek and Macedonian origin over the government's recognition of the Former Yugoslav Republic of Macedonia). In short, official multiculturalism suppresses the continued hegemony of Anglo-Celtic Australian culture by making it invisible.

While official multiculturalism operates by fixing 'culture' in ethnic boxes, however, the proliferation of cultural difference in the practice of everyday life can never be completely contained in a static unity-in-diversity. Indeed, to reiterate Bhabha's comment with which we introduced this essay, the unity of the nation is an *impossible* one. Let us clarify this by returning, finally, to the crucial issue of race. In the Australian context, the question of race imposes itself most urgently in relation to two groups: 'Aborigines' and 'Asians'. It is significant that Aboriginal people are generally left out of debates on multiculturalism, not least because Aborigines themselves rightly do not want to be treated as 'another ethnic minority'. In this sense, the framing of the Aboriginal problematic in terms of the discourse of race – as in the debate about black–white reconciliation – serves as an important reminder of the colonial, Eurocentric, racialist exclusivism which is intrinsically bound up with the history of Australia as a settler society. Nevertheless, it is sometimes contended that to persist in viewing Aboriginal people as a racial group rather than an ethnic group is itself racist. Hence, the representation of Aboriginal culture on SBS television may be seen either as the belated recognition of Aborigines as an integral part of the mosaic of Australian multicultural society, or as the continuation of 'white' devaluation of the special status of Aboriginal people as the indigenous inhabitants of the land that provides the territory of the Australian nation-state. The politics of Aboriginality, then, signals one of the political limits of multiculturalism: its silence about the issue of race which was so formative in the historical constitution of Australia. In short, it is impossible to include Aborigines in the image of a consensual unity-in-diversity without erasing the memory of colonial dispossession, genocide and cultural loss and the continuing impact of that memory on Aboriginal lives. In this sense, the category of 'race' is the sign of a fracture inherent in Australian national identity, as it is in the USA, and one with which Australians have only just begun to come to terms.

The situation is different for 'Asians' – also excluded, as we have noted, from the Australian nation-state on racial grounds until the abolition of the White Australia policy and the adoption of a non-discriminatory immigration policy. While the Australian state now shamelessly flirts, for economic reasons, with the idea of 'enmeshment with Asia', the cultural status of Australians of Asian descent in 'multicultural Australia' is still a fragile one. While Chinese, Vietnamese, Malaysian, Singaporean and other migrants from the Asian region are now considered an integral part of Australia's ethnic mix, these groups are still collectively *racialised* whenever a wave of moral panic about Asian immigration flares up. At such moments, the old collusion of race and culture is reinstated. In other words, the 'Asian' presence in Australia provides us with a test case for examining the difficulty faced by the multiculturalist imagination in accommodating racial – rather than just ethnic – difference. In its emphasis on culture and ethnicity, race still signals the limits for the imagining of the (now ethnically diverse) national community.

In different ways, then, race is central to both the American and the Australian problematics of national identity. It was race, not ethnicity, which finally delimited access to national belonging or, in the American case, fractured the ideal homogeneity of the nation-state. If, in an important sense, race has been crucial to the American articulation of multiculturalism (represented most dramatically by the idea of Afrocentricity), in Australia multiculturalism has thrived through an eclipse of race by the more flexible concept of ethnicity. In both cases, then, the discourse of race exposes the fact that the idea of an unfractured and unified national imagined community is an impossible fiction. Whereas in the American context racial difference has become absolutised, however, in the Australian context the discourse of multiculturalism has the potential to create a symbolic space in which racial difference can be turned into ethnic/cultural difference, though without being able to make the traces of 'race' disappear completely. In this sense, we want to suggest that the category of race should be seen as the symbolic marker of unabsorbable cultural difference – difference of a kind that cannot be harmonised into multiculturalism's conservative vision of a unity-in-diversity. To seize on multiculturalism's more radical potential is to give up the ideal of national unity itself without doing away with the promise of a flexible, porous, and open-ended national culture.

NOTES

1 This essay is a revised version of a paper first presented at the Symposium on Cultural Studies in Asia, the Pacific and the USA, organised by the Program for Cultural Studies, East-West Center, Honolulu, Hawai'i, September 1993. The essay first appeared in a slightly different form in T. O'Regan (ed.), Critical Multiculturalism, a special issue of Continuum: The Australian Journal of Media and Culture, vol. 8, no. 2, 1994, pp. 124–58.
2 H. K. Bhabha, 'Introduction: Narrating the Nation', in H. K. Bhabha (ed.), Nation and Narration, London, Routledge, 1990, p. 1.
3 'Whose America?', Time, 8 July 1991, p. 20 (cover story).
4 A. Schlesinger, Jr, 'The Cult of Ethnicity, Good and Bad', Time, 8 July 1991, p. 26.
5 A. Schlesinger, Jr, The Disuniting of America, New York, Norton, 1992, 119.
6 A. Woodiwiss, Postmodernity USA, London, Sage, 1993, p. 61.
7 L. Grossberg, We Gotta Get Out of This Place, New York, Routledge, 1992, p. 368.
8 E. Gellner, Nations and Nationalism, Oxford, Blackwell, 1983, p. 55.
9 ibid., p. 57.
10 ibid.
11 B. Anderson, Imagined Communities, 2nd edn, London, Verso, 1991, p. 6.
12 R. White, Inventing Australia, Sydney, Allen & Unwin, 1985, p. 47.
13 J . Eddy and D. Schreuder (eds), The Rise of Colonial Nationalism, Sydney, Allen & Unwin, 1988, p. 2.
14 ibid., p. 7.
15 A. Smith, National Identity, Harmondsworth, Mx, Penguin, 1991, p. 40.
16 H. Tarver, 'The Creation of American National Identity: 1774–1796', Berkeley Journal of Sociology, vol. 37, no. 1, 1992, p. 63.
17 ibid., p. 64.
18 ibid.
19 ibid., pp. 149–50.
20 ibid., p. 69.
21 ibid., p. 64.
22 ibid., p. 70.
23 For a cultural history of this term, see J. Stratton, 'The Beast of the Apocalypse: The Postcolonial Experience of the United States', New Formations, vol. 21, 1993, pp. 35–63.
24 Given what has already been said about the political context, it is not surprising that American functionalism should derive from a French idealist tradition located in Comte and Durkheim's post-Revolutionary reworking of the Enlightenment tradition as characterised by, for example, Rousseau.
25 Schlesinger, Disuniting of America, p. 23.
26 ibid., p. 37.

27 M. C. Waters, *Ethnic Options*, Berkeley, University of California Press, 1990, p. 57.

28 Schlesinger, *Disuniting of America*, p. 118.

29 M. Novak, *The Rise of the Unmeltable Ethnics: Politics and Culture in the Seventies*, New York, Macmillan, 1973. See also N. Glazer and D. P. Moynihan, *Beyond the Melting Pot: The Negroes, Puerto Ricans, Jews, Italians and Irish of New York City*, Cambridge, Mass., MIT Press, 1963.

30 Schlesinger, 'The Cult of Ethnicity', p. 26.

31 Schlesinger, *Disuniting of America*, p. 41.

32 H. Seton-Watson, *Nations and States*, London, Methuen, 1977, p. 219.

33 See S. Ewen and E. Ewen, *Channels of Desire: Mass Images and the Shaping of American Consciousness*, New York, McGraw-Hill, 1982.

34 P. Bourdieu, *In Other Words: Essays Towards a Reflexive Sociology*, trans. M. Adamson, Cambridge, Polity Press, 1990, p. 31.

35 Schlesinger, *Disuniting of America*, p. 117.

36 M. Omi and H. Winant, *Racial Formation in the United States: From the 1960s to the 1980s*, New York, Routledge & Kegan Paul, 1986, p. 72.

37 ibid., p. 64.

38 See Omi and Winant, *Racial Formation*.

39 See Waters, *Ethnic Options*.

40 White, *Inventing Australia*, pp. 52–3.

41 M. Clark, *A Short History of Australia*, London, Heinemann, 1964, p. 184.

42 ibid.

43 White, *Inventing Australia*, p. 47.

44 ibid.

45 ibid., p. 64.

46 See A. Markus, *Fear and Hatred: Purifying Australia and California 1850–1901*, Sydney, Hale & Iremonger, 1979.

47 ibid., p. 256.

48 White, *Inventing Australia*, p. 112.

49 Quoted in Markus, *Fear and Hatred*, p. xxi.

50 ibid., p. 259.

51 This statutory discrimination at both federal and state levels lasted until 1952 when the naturalisation laws were changed. See R. Daniels, *Asian America: Chinese and Japanese in the United States since 1850*, Seattle and London, University of Washington Press, 1988, pp. 43–4.

52 Quoted in ibid., p. 43.

53 Markus, *Fear and Hatred*, p. xix.

54 White, *Inventing Australia*, pp. 159–60.

55 S. Castles *et al.*, *Mistaken Identity: Multiculturalism and the Demise of Nationalism in Australia*, 2nd edn, Sydney, Pluto Press, 1990, pp. 184–5.

56 ibid., p. 46.

57 ibid., p. 45.

58 Quoted in ibid., p. 113.

59 ibid., p. 110.

60 ibid., p. 114.

61 White, *Inventing Australia*, p. 166.

62 Castles *et al.*, *Mistaken Identity*, p. 51.

63 Australian Council on Population and Ethnic Affairs, *Multiculturalism for All Australians: Our Developing Nationhood*, Canberra, Australian Government Publishing Service, May 1982, p. 17.

64 Quoted in Castles *et al.*, *Mistaken Identity*, p. 69.

65 ibid., p. 190. The qualification, 'within carefully defined limits', signals some of the tensions and limits of the multicultural model of national identity itself.

66 J. Docker, 'Postnationalism', *Arena Magazine*, no. 9, 1994, p. 41.
67 R. Thakur, 'From the Mosaic to the Melting Pot: Cross-National Reflections on Multiculturalism', in C. Kukathas (ed.), *Multicultural Citizens*, Sydney, Centre for Independent Studies, 1993, p.132.
68 H. K. Bhabha, 'The Third Space: Interview with Homi Bhabha', in J. Rutherford (ed.), *Identity: Community, Culture, Difference*, London, Lawrence & Wishart, 1990, p. 208.
69 Docker, 'Postnationalism', p. 41.

11

GLOBALISATION AND THE MYTH OF ETHNIC COMMUNITY

Salvadoran refugees in multicultural states[1]

Beryl Langer

This paper raises questions about the limits of multiculturalism by reflecting on the settlement experiences of Salvadoran refugees who arrived in Australia and Canada in the 1980s. The situation of small groups of Salvadorans in the 'Anglo' outposts of American empire might be seen as of marginal importance, for the end of the Cold War has defused the discourses of 'communist insurgency' and 'people's struggle' through which El Salvador was produced as an 'issue' by the Western media. The global 'slaughterscape'[2] has also deflected attention from Central America's 'desplazados', generating new groups of refugees with claims to dwindling reserves of compassion and material aid. In the context of critical reflection on multiculturalism in Australia and English Canada, however, the Salvadoran case presents a paradigmatic challenge to the foundational concept of 'ethnic community', for refugees from civil conflicts construct the boundaries of 'imagined community' in terms of social and political divisions not easily papered over by 'ethnicity'. The Salvadoran case also calls into question assumptions of cultural integrity and stability embedded in the idea of multicultural formations in which 'ethnic' and 'dominant' cultures are clearly specifiable and incommensurably 'different'. As citizens of a country with access to the products of global culture for those who can afford them, and a long history of economic migration to the United States, Salvadoran refugees are bearers of culture(s) whose 'difference' from whatever might be specified as 'Australian' or 'Canadian' is rarely as clear-cut as romantic notions of Central American alterity might lead us to expect. This is not an argument for denying diversity, for global culture is inflected through disparate social formations and narratives of nation, and is in any case more contradictory in its effects than the glossy fantasies of a world united by Benetton or Coca-Cola might suggest. It is, however, an argument for rethinking multiculturalism in terms which do not presume the existence of ontologically given cultural communities, and for taking account of what Appadurai has called

163

the 'complex, overlapping, disjunctive order' of the 'new global cultural economy'.[3]

FROM HISTORY TO ETHNICITY

The concept of 'ethnic community' sits uncomfortably with the troubled national histories which form the background conditions of migration. Within the specialist literature, the question of why people migrate is generally answered in terms of a 'push–pull' thesis – either the conditions in their homeland 'push' them out or/and the promise of a better life somewhere else operates as a 'pull'.[4] Behind these pseudo-theoretical banalities lie epic tales of human cruelty and courage, with people 'pushed' not just by economic scarcity but by pogroms, wars, military coups and revolutions, and 'pulled' not just by 'higher living standards' but by the prospect of living where dead bodies are not part of the streetscape and torture is not included in the disciplinary apparatus of the state. Even at its least dramatic, immigration is not from harmonious social formations bound together by 'organic' cultural traditions but from nation-states in which the divisions of class, religion, race/ethnicity and region make social harmony a precarious hegemonic achievement. In constructing national groups as 'ethnic communities', multiculturalism proceeds on the dubious assumption that these divisions are rendered irrelevant by the experience of migration. The Salvadoran case is one in which the assumption that ties of language, cuisine and collective memory bind people together when they become strangers in a strange land is particularly difficult to sustain, for Salvadorans living in 'multicultural' countries like Australia and Canada are survivors of a history which fractures collective memory into competing accounts of nation, and continuously subverts the idea of unified community.

The history that has relocated descendants of Central American Indians and their Spanish conquerors in such unlikely places as Melbourne and Winnipeg is a 500-year epic of dispossession, revolt, and reprisal – a textbook case of class struggle under conditions of 'reactionary despotism'.[5] The politics of this epic involve a complex succession of military juntas, thwarted attempts at democratic reform leading to the emergence of guerrilla forces, twelve years of civil war, and precarious attempts to build a democratic public sphere following the signing of a peace accord in December 1991. The economics are depressingly simple and familiar: expropriation of arable land for export agriculture by a small class of wealthy landowners; immiseration of the landless poor; and multinational exploitation of industrial workers. My own view of this history is implicit in the manner of its telling, but 'expropriation', 'reactionary despotism' and 'immiseration' are not the only available narrative constructions, and while their 'truth' might be self-evident within discourses of social justice and human rights, their 'ideological bias' is equally so when viewed through other discursive frames. The twelve-year civil war which produced a million '*desplazados*' is either 'a struggle for peace with social justice by people who suffered hundreds of years of economic and military oppression' or 'a struggle against communist insurgency in which human rights violations were the regrettable but necessary price of freedom' – competing versions of a history which offers more than one way of constituting its agents. Add to this complexities of class, race, region and religion, and the unity evoked by the term 'Salvadoran refugee' is replaced by a range of subject-positions whose incorporation into a cohesive 'ethnic community' is an unlikely prospect. The divisions that brought their country to twelve years of civil war do not miraculously disappear on relocation in the immigrant working class or underclass of an English-speaking country, and relations between Salvadorans in exile continue to be mediated through the social and cultural structures which produced them as 'refugees'.

Contested histories which produce different subject-positions have no place within the discourse of multiculturalism, which constructs immigrants not as bearers of history but as bearers of something called 'ethnic culture' – or culture divorced from history. For Salvadorans, the journey to 'countries of immigration' like Australia and Canada is a journey from history to ethnicity, stepping out of the continuing drama of civil war and negotiated peace in Central America into the cast of an 'ethnic group' in which divisions of class and politics are glossed by unities of culture and language.[6] This exchange is fundamental to multicul-turalism, which gives immigrants the right to retain their language, music, food, religion and folkloric practices, but not the racial, religious or class conflicts in which they were embedded as part of a 'whole way of life'.[7] As ideology and state policy, multiculturalism was negotiated in the context of post-war migration from nations which had been on different sides, and whose internal divisions were a further source of potential conflict. If countries of immigration were to be reconstituted in terms of harmonious narratives of cultural diversity, immigrants had to put these contested histories and potentially disruptive imaginaries of 'nation' behind them and embrace the convenient fiction of 'ethnicity'.

As a strategy for the management of mass migration, this multicultural 'exchange' has been relatively successful. The construction of a public sphere in which only 'cultural' difference can be enunciated and all 'cultures' are deemed equally worthy of respect effectively excludes longstanding territorial disputes or communal conflict from the universe of multicultural discourse – however deeply felt the grievances of the groups involved. The idea that the conflicts of the 'old world' have no place in the 'new' is thus an article of multicultural faith, how-ever undeniable the evidence that many of these conflicts have not 'in fact' been left behind. Migrants are expected to leave their history at the door, and while the reality of life in the schoolyard and factory might give the lie to the fiction that 'we are one but we are many', it is arguably a useful fiction which minimises con-flict in the public sphere by delegitimising its expression. It should be clearly understood, however, that while 'cultural' diversity may define the limits of enunciable 'difference' if countries of immigration are to avoid endless entanglement in disputes beyond their borders, differences of 'culture' may be a minor priority for those within the fictive bounds of 'ethnic community'. For many Salvadorans, at least, multiculturalism's reconstruction of the political as cultural obliterates the 'difference' that gives life meaning – a form of 'misrecognition'[8] no less profound than the assimilationist demand that they give up their custom- ary food, music and mother tongue.

Exchanging politics and history for a hyphenated version of citizenship that recognises 'cultural difference' is undoubtedly an advance on assimilation, but it can be an awkward exchange for refugees from an ongoing civil war – particu- larly given global communications which allow immediate access to events in the homeland. It is hard to embrace the fiction that the struggles of the 'old' world have no place in the 'new' when they circulate within the 'melodoxy'[9] of west- ern concern about 'human rights' and 'trouble spots'. During the 'November crisis' of 1989, for example, El Salvador was the focus of intense media coverage which brought the civil war directly into the living rooms of refugees in Melbourne: footage of the 19-year-old leader of an FMLN combat group which held pyjama-clad Green Berets hostage in the San Salvador Sheraton; reports of aerial bombing of San Salvador's working-class suburbs; the brutal murder of six Jesuit priests at the University of Central America. Salvadorans in Melbourne were 'in' this history, organising all-night vigils to pray for peace, maintaining a permanent presence outside the United States Consulate to protest US support for the Salvadoran military, holding masses for the murdered Jesuits, raising money to help those made homeless by the bombing. The intensity of this engagement suggests that the rhetoric of 'ethnic community' has little purchase on a bloody history which is not only inscribed in biography but returned as spectacle by the global media.

The history–ethnicity exchange is not universally unacceptable to Salvadoran refugees. Many welcome the prospect of leaving 'la violencia' behind – particularly those who simply found themselves 'caught in the crossfire' and held no brief for either side. The shelter of 'ethnicity' has obvious advantages for those whose role in history does not bear close scrutiny on human rights grounds, but it can equally be a welcome respite from 'historical exhaustion' – that point at which people who have seen too many deaths and too few changes simply tire of the struggle and decide to get on with their own lives as best they can. 'Ethnicity', in other words, can be embraced as much as imposed. Many who suffered at the hands of the regime, however, do not wish to extricate themselves from history. They see continuing political work as the only conceivable response to what they have been through, and life in Australia or Canada as no more than a narrative detour in a story that begins and ends in El Salvador – a profoundly political story which has nothing to do with 'ethnicity'. They may be physically located in the 'antipodes' or the 'frozen north', but their hearts and minds are in Central America – a disjunctive 'reality' maintained by constructing communal life in the diaspora as an extension of the Salvadoran 'struggle'.

The history–ethnicity exchange implicit in multiculturalism rests on a fictive separation of culture from politics which is in practice unsustainable. In the

Salvadoran case, cultural expression is itself highly politicised, and what emerges in the multicultural public sphere is a form of cultural politics in which the folk-loric is used as a strategy for staying 'in history'. For example, Salvadoran musicians participating in a 'Latin American' concert organised by one of Melbourne's local councils sang songs which signified 'Latin American music' to Australians in the audience but 'support for the FMLN' to Salvadorans. After the concert, the council received complaints from people who said they had come to hear 'music, not politics'. Similarly, a priest's attempts to be culturally inclusive put him at odds with conservative Salvadoran congregants when a youth group's performance of 'Salvadoran music' in the church included songs from the Nicaraguan workers' mass favoured by Base Christian Communities. Communal life in the diaspora thus takes on a contested quality, as those who use it to stay 'in history' compete with those who favour a depoliticised form of 'ethnicity' for the right to represent 'the Salvadoran community' in the public domain.

CONSTRUCTING THE FICTION OF COMMUNITY

Being Salvadoran is not a matter of ethnicity but of citizenship, and within Salvadoran citizenship 'difference' is marked in terms of class, politics, region, and whether or not one's forebears were Indian or Hispanic. 'Salvadoran ethnicity' is constructed in the diaspora, where things previously taken for granted as part of everyday life – food, music, dancing, national days, religious anniversaries, ways of speaking Spanish – come to be seen as signifiers of 'being Salvadoran', adding folkloric specificity to the cluster of standard 'problems' shared with other new immigrants and refugees. Constructing ethnicity is an interactive process, with Salvadorans themselves singling out aspects of national culture which are in turn incorporated into the construction of Salvadorans as a distinctive sub-category by others. The point is not to question the authenticity of this 'ethnic identity', but to challenge the assumption that the people who share it constitute some kind of ontologically given community. Rather than being a recognition of 'difference', construction of 'Salvadorans' as a unified social category within the broader universe of 'ethnic alterity' renders them all 'the same', and takes no account of the historically constituted boundaries of imagined community drawn by Salvadorans themselves. Nostalgia for what has been lost in exile does not erase history, and the endless indignity and sadness common to the refugee experience do not in themselves create a 'community' of suffering that transcends the divisions of class and politics that defined them as actors in their homeland. As long as multicul-turalism incorporates the rhetoric of 'community' into its conceptualisation of 'diversity', in other words, it does not escape the problem of suppressing 'difference' but merely shifts it to another level of social organisation, replacing Anglo-assimilationist narratives of 'nation' with multicultural narratives of communal homogeneity no less implicated in the 'non-recognition of difference'.

Salvadorans can define their 'community' in a number of ways, depending on whether they construct the boundaries in terms of language, region, nation, locality, politics or religion. As Spanish speakers from Latin America they are administratively located as part of a clientele for state services in the 'community language' of Spanish, and generally referred to as part of either the 'Hispanic' or 'Latin American' Community. Language is a necessary condition for community formation and Salvadorans are more likely to establish relationships with other Spanish speakers – at least those from similar class and political backgrounds – than with speakers of Turkish, Vietnamese or English. It is not, however, a sufficient condition. The assumption of community among Spanish speakers ignores nuances of (post)colonial inflection, the dynamics of first world–third world relations between Spain and its former colonies, and national differences within Central and South America. What looks, from Australia or Canada, like Latin American unity is experienced as diversity within the region, where distinctions made between people from neighbouring countries are no less pronounced than in other parts of the world. These distinctions might become less acute when people formerly categorised as 'them' become 'us' with respect to language, but they do not disappear.

Contrary to expectations implicit in the idea of Spanish as a 'community' language, speaking Spanish is no guarantee of shared 'habitus', in Bourdieu's sense of the term – the highly nuanced taken-for-granted understandings and practices that mark the boundaries between 'us' and 'them' in terms of how we speak, eat, dress, shop and so on. Like English, Spanish is not the language of a single country or 'ethnic group' but of a former empire, and relations between Spanish speakers are structured accordingly. 'Speaking Spanish' may provide the conditions for mutual recognition and respect within the bounds of 'community language', but it can equally make people aware of class and national difference, and being patronised is no more acceptable for its happening in your 'mother tongue'. Spanish speakers from 'other' countries whose manner, tone or overt comment has been 'read' as condescending or insulting make frequent appearances in Salvadoran narratives of perceived prejudice and discrimination – hardly surprising given their role in mediating traumatic first encounters with the Anglophone state. Patronising preconceptions about people from the 'third world' are not the preserve of English speakers, and there is no guarantee that recent arrivals from El Salvador whose relation to the state is mediated in their 'mother tongue' necessarily feel that they have been accorded the 'recognition'[10] as equals that provision of services in 'community languages' ostensibly provides.

That the Australian or Canadian state should provide services in Spanish is not at issue here, for such services are a precondition for the equality of access on which social justice depends. Nor is the competence and goodwill of 'Hispanic' translators and social workers, who do their best for their Salvadoran clients in chronically under-funded circumstances. What is at issue is the assumption that language necessarily provides the basis for 'community' – an assumption which elides the complex histories of conquest and postcolonial struggle in the different countries from which Spanish speakers have come, and disadvantages smaller, more recently arrived national groups like the Salvadorans. Their instrumental needs may be met within structures established by earlier waves of Spanish-speaking immigrants, but not their existential need for 'recognition' and 'dignity'.[11] As a group, however, they are too small and too divided to successfully mount alternative funding claims within the framework of multiculturalism – which in any case constructs Spanish speakers in terms of an idea of language community which implicitly denies their difference. Their predicament highlights the inherent contradiction of multiculturalism as a rational bureaucratic strategy for the management of non-rational forms of association, for the fact that government money can only be directed to groups whose size and stability of 'leadership' ensure that it will be 'properly used' and 'accounted for' makes it virtually impossible for the small, conflict-ridden organisations which actually represent the 'imagined communities' of recently arrived refugees to receive either recognition or funding. The idea of a single 'Spanish-speaking community' may rest on an impossible separation of language and culture from class, politics and history, but the alternative of recognising the competing claims of national groups whose communal boundaries and leadership are continuously contested and renegotiated is beyond the already stretched resources of the host states. Salvadorans are therefore likely to remain within the administrative confines of Hispanic or Latin American 'community', whether its fictive boundaries coincide with their own communal 'imaginaries' or not.

The fiction of 'ethnic community' is particularly strained in the Salvadoran case because the history that divides them is both contested and current, but there is no reason to suppose that 'ethnic communities' in general are necessarily more cohesive. What looks like unity from the outside is invariably diverse and conflictual from the inside, particularly when the historical conditions under which 'communities' have been constituted are taken into account. The idea of 'Greek Community', for example, glosses over the complexities of relations between former nationals of a politically divided country whose recent history includes a civil war; 'Italian Community' screens out regional loyalties and political division between communists and fascists; 'Lebanese Community' seems particularly inappropriate for immigrants from a country literally torn apart by civil conflict; and so on. The fact that the fiction of 'community' survives at all might thus be seen as the hegemonic achievement of those who have mobilised it as a rhetorical strategy in the competition for, and distribution of, state resources. Like all hegemonic achievements it rests on the capacity of aspiring leaders to 'call out' the consent of their projected constituency, for the proposition that the things that unite them in the context of Australian or Canadian multicultural politics are more important than what divided them in their homeland(s) can be sustained only if it makes some sense in terms of the experience of everyday life. Equally, however, it operates to suppress needs and interests which cannot be articulated within the hegemonic discourse of 'community'.

To focus on the Australian case, the idea that 'ethnics' belong to 'communities' is firmly embedded in both the practices of the state and the claims of organisations and their leaders to represent 'community' interests. Given the centrality of the community/society opposition to conceptualisations of modernity, this construction of 'ethnic groups' as 'communal' is also their construction as 'pre-modern' – locked into fixed frozen traditions which through some miracle of ontological solidity have not 'melted into air'. There is at once a utopian nostalgia in this notion of a traditional world whose embodied representatives can be preserved as 'ethnics' in the multicultural museum, and a wilful ignorance about the economic and technological changes that have fundamentally altered the conditions of identity-formation throughout the globe. One practice that nicely illustrates the strained quality of this presumed opposition between what might be called 'hyphenated' and 'non-hyphenated' Australians is the school 'multicultural day', in which children are invited to attend in 'national dress'. While everyday life in their homeland may have been lived in the global uniform of jeans, T-shirts and sneakers, 'ethnic' children are expected to appear in 'traditional' costumes no more relevant to their lives than kilts to Australians of Scottish descent. For example, Salvadoran 'national dress' in Australia is constructed in terms of Spanish-colonial flounced satin dresses for girls and women and campesino calico shirts and trousers rather than Spanish-colonial garb for boys and men, none of which conforms to the way people actually dress in El Salvador, which might be best described in terms of variations on the 'global', including 'guerrilla', 'Gucci', and 'good ol' boy'. I am not suggesting that there is any harm in people dressing up in clothes that might have been worn by their forebears, or that there are no longer places where non-western clothing is the norm. Nor would I deny that multicultural policies have achieved major gains in relation to tolerance of diversity in Australian schools, where immigrant children in the 1950s were mercilessly 'othered' by ethnocentric classmates. What is problematic is the assumption that people marked as 'ethnic' are less 'modern' than those who are not. One way in which this assumption is sustained is by placing nostalgic signifiers of 'cultural difference' worn by 'ethnic' Australians in opposition not to equivalent markers of Anglo-Australian cultural history, but to markers of global postmodernity. The fact that the baseball caps and basketball shoes which constitute 'national dress' for Australian children might also be current fashion in the homelands of recent immigrants is lost in the fetishised production of 'cultural difference'.

GLOBALISATION AND ETHNIC IDENTITY

The clearly specifiable and distinctive 'ethnic' and 'dominant' cultures presumed by multicultural discourse bear little relation to actually existing national and regional cultures. These have been 'worked over' not only by the processes of imperialism which have given us Coca-Cola, Fanta and Hollywood as cultural universals, but by what Appadurai calls the global 'ideoscape' – including counter-hegemonic ideas about indigeneity, the environment, human rights, feminism and, one might add, 'multiculturalism' itself. The whole idea of fixed and coherent 'ethnic cultures' becomes an increasingly anachronistic fantasy when geographically distant 'life-worlds' are inflected through the same material and cultural products and processes. This idea is none the less central to multiculturalism and its associated research industry. The study on which this paper is based, for example, was initially framed in terms of a logic which assumes the prior distinctiveness and stability of both 'ethnicity' and 'Australian-ness' and constructs the 'ethnic community study' as one in which the task of the social researcher is to document the 'difference' and tease out its implications for settlement and intergenerational 'problems'. This logic did not survive the first months of field work, in which we encountered not a discretely bounded 'ethnic culture' but 'life-worlds' that had to a greater or lesser extent incorporated elements of global culture. Salvadorans were certainly 'different', but the difference was often more to do with life-shattering historical trauma and economic deprivation than with 'cultural alterity'.

That cultural boundaries were more permeable than the opposition between 'ethnic' and 'dominant' cultures would suggest was apparent from my first venture into the field. The woman I met bore no resemblance to the guerrilla fighters, suffering campesinas or mothers of the disappeared portrayed in the solidarity literature. Nor was there any sign of the 'colourful indigeneity' of Central American travel brochures. Dressed in jeans, sneakers and polyester sweat shirt, she invited me into a flat crammed with 'artefacts' which signified not 'Salvadoran culture' but its intersection with Los Angeles: plastic and china models of Mickey Mouse, Donald Duck, Snoopy and Garfield, rubbing shoulders with crinolined kewpie dolls and gilt-framed photographs of absent relatives. A small hessian wall-hanging with the words 'Su Pais Amigo' above a map of El Salvador was surrounded by 'California kitsch' religious posters. The blaring video soundtrack was definitely not Spanish. 'My brother loves Broozly,' the young woman said, with a 'what can you do' shrug of the shoulders. 'Broozly?' I asked, peering at the screen. 'Ah, you mean Bruce Lee.' Looking through the family album at brothers still in El Salvador and sisters with refugee status in Canada, we came upon a photograph of children at a birthday party whose location was indicated by the smiling figure of Ronald McDonald in the background. 'Is that your sister's family in Winnipeg?' I asked, alert to the possibility of a comparative piece on the co-option of Salvadoran refugees by multinational capital in Canada and Australia. 'No no,' she said. 'Those are my brother's children in San Salvador.'

Many of the assumptions about 'cultural difference' on which multiculturalism is premised need to be rethought in relation to global processes that situate countries of 'emigration' and 'immigration' within the same 'cultural economy'. I am not suggesting that an impoverished war-torn country like El Salvador has the same relation to global culture as affluent countries like Australia or Canada, and I would not wish to endorse Eurocentric discourses which overlook the fact that life for most of the world's inhabitants is still a struggle for daily bread rather than a playful engagement with hyper-real simulacra. There are, none the less, ways in which globalisation has transformed the conditions of identity-formation throughout the world, turning 'ethnic' and 'national' cultures into political projects rather than taken-for-granted 'whole ways of life'.[12]

Globalisation reduces the distance between Australia or Canada and El Salvador in a number of ways. First is the shared experience of 'Coca-Colonisation' which makes the global culture of McDonald's, Coke, baseball caps, jeans, sneakers, CNN, CBS and Hollywood as familiar to Salvadorans – particularly those from the urban middle class – as they are to Australians and Canadians. With both 'dominant' and 'ethnic' cultures so thoroughly imbricated with American products and cultural icons, the notion that they are incommensurably 'different' is simply unsustainable. 'Difference' is as much economic as cultural – a matter of class and its intersection with a rural/urban divide which situates 'campesinas' outside the reach of the global commodity form. The construction of Salvadoran 'ethnicity' within the multicultural frame is to some extent achieved by homing in on what is 'culturally specific' and screening out what is shared. For example, the 'ethnic' food served at Salvadoran functions – pupusas, tamales, pastelles – is invariably accompanied by 'global' beverages (Coca-Cola and Fanta) which are equally part of everyday life in El Salvador. Refugees from El Salvador are already 'inside' global culture, and while the extent of their participation varies with social class, it runs the full gamut from designer jeans and French perfume to the simple can of Coke. American and Mexican 'soaps' watched in Melbourne were also watched in San Salvador, and while the music of preference (at least for adults) at Salvadoran functions is Central American, El Salvadorans are familiar with American popular music in ways that are only surprising if one overlooks the scale of US regional 'influence' and the long history of El Salvadoran labour migration to Mexico and the United States, both legal and illegal. El Salvador's relations with the United States are complex, a matter not just of American multinationals and military advisers but of routine to-ing and fro-ing by individual Salvadorans in search of work, education, the dream of material betterment. Many Salvadoran refugees thus bear little resemblance to romantic fantasies of Central American alterity. Nor do the multicultural branch-plants of global capital to which they have come bear much relation to the 'Australia' or 'Canada' of either Anglo-nationalist or Anglophobic mythology.

If shared experience of Coca-Colonisation diminishes the 'difference' between recent immigrants from countries like El Salvador and their Australian 'hosts', the discourses of 'multiculturalism' and 'indigeneity' which also circulate as part of global culture have the opposite effect. What we are dealing with is a complex and contradictory phenomenon involving the circulation not just of 'homogenising' cultural and material commodities, but of ideologies and policies which 'call out' the 'ethnic' and 'indigenous' subject. Globalisation is not solely a function of multinational capital and its state and academic subsidiaries, but of human-rights agencies and religious and environmental organisations whose interventions on behalf of oppressed and dispossessed minorities are generative as much as

172

defensive, articulating and maintaining cultural boundaries that might otherwise be submerged, and constructing networks of 'solidarity' between groups with no prior history of common cause. For example, the institutional sites and cultural spaces through which Salvadoran entry to the public sphere is mediated in Melbourne – 'neighbourhood' houses, health centres, 'community' centres, human-rights and solidarity organisations, churches – operate in terms of assumptions about 'community building' and the 'empowerment' of cultural minorities and indigenous people shared by an international network of people working in welfare and aid organisations. The 'helping professionals', solidarity activists, priests and nuns who work in these sites and spaces can be seen as 'identity brokers' whose interaction with, and public construction of, Salvadorans in terms of global discourses of multiculturalism, indigeneity and human rights 'call out' Salvadoran specificity in terms that directly counter the homogenising tendencies of consumer capitalism.

While each of these discourses emphasises Salvadoran specificity, the extent to which they prioritise culture, history or politics frames it in different ways. 'Multiculturalism' constructs Salvadorans as the most recent arrivals in a wave of 'Latin American immigration' which began in the 1970s, or as adding to something called 'Hispanic community' whose cultural origins are 'Catholic' and 'Mediterranean'. The discourse of 'indigeneity' favours a construction of Salvadorans as 'dispossessed indigenes' whose shared history of European invasion makes for a 'natural' bond with Aboriginal Australians. Human-rights activists see Salvadorans as victims/survivors of state terror whose shared history of torture and trauma makes for solidarity with other political refugees from Central and South America. Radical Christians view the 'Salvadoran experience' through the discursive frame of liberation theology, while to 'left remnant groups' like the International Socialists it is part of a Marxist-Leninist history of 'armed struggle'. How Salvadoran identity is enunciated in Australia thus depends on which aspects of Salvadoran specificity are mobilised within different sites, and the extent to which these mobilisations connect with broader hegemonic and counter-hegemonic discourses.

Perhaps the best illustration of globalisation's contradictory effects is provided by the impact of international observance of the 500th anniversary of European invasion of America in 1992, and the United Nations Year of Indigenous People in 1993, on the recuperation of Salvadoran indigenous identity. Submerged in the interests of survival in the aftermath of the massacres which followed Farabundo Marti's 1932 uprising, Indian identity was reclaimed by Salvadoran popular movements in the 1970s – the FMLN bears Farabundo Marti's name. Its valorisation by international solidarity groups, particularly those within the 'progressive' wing of the Catholic Church, has further legitimised the idea of Indian origin among Salvadorans living in Melbourne, where Salvadoran participation in various activities and events is often premised on the assumption of their 'indigeneity'. In this instance, the impact of the global 'ideoscape' runs directly counter to the homogenising tendencies of consumer culture, 'calling out' and celebrating aspects of Salvadoran identity that had previously been suppressed.

GLOBALISATION AND THE HISTORY–ETHNICITY EXCHANGE

If the effects of globalisation on Salvadoran 'ethnicity' are contradictory, its impact on the conditions under which the history–ethnicity exchange is negotiated is less so. Advanced communications technology allows for constitution of the 'imagined community' of Salvadoran refugees as a global network maintained by ISD, FAX, TELEX and the Internet. The immediacy of this communication with the homeland and with international solidarity networks strengthens resistance to the multicultural exchange by reducing the imperative of the local through direct participation in a global network of political activity focused on the situation in El Salvador. This is not to minimise the existential pain of physical separation from the homeland, but rather to suggest that the situation of political refugees who actively participate in electronic solidarity networks on a daily or weekly basis is qualitatively different from that of earlier waves of European immigrants whose connection with the homeland was more attenuated, sustained by 'old news' which arrived in letters delivered weeks or even months after they were written. Global communications technology radically transforms the diaspora, sustaining political and family ties across national boundaries and reinforcing Salvadoran identity in terms of 'citizenship' rather than 'ethnicity'.

One of the founding myths of multiculturalism is that the status of hyphenated 'new world' citizenship is permanent. Australia's post-assimilationist narrative of migration is one that valorises the immigrant contribution to 'nation-building' and 'cultural diversity', and redefines citizenship in terms that confer legitimacy on the maintenance of 'ethnic identity' so long as it is combined with patriotic commitment to Australia and the severing of potentially divisive old allegiances. Immigrant success stories are constructed around the trope of 'a new life' made possible by the greater 'opportunities' offered in the 'new land' – a narrative of progress in which the putting-down of 'roots' that are permanent and irreversible is simply taken for granted. While this narrative of organically 'rooted' communities has always been subverted by a subtext of 'return migration', it becomes increasingly problematic as globalisation diminishes the distances – both physical and cultural – between countries and facilitates the maintenance of communal boundaries across national borders.

The narrative of 'transplanted communities' also ignores the extent to which history, notwithstanding exaggerated reports of its death, continues to be made. The conditions under which immigrants and refugees accept the status of 'hyphenated citizenship' are therefore subject to change. In the Salvadoran case, civil war has been replaced by precarious peace in which former combatants continue to negotiate the terms of social, political and economic reform. This reconstitutes the conditions of multicultural exchange, making return to 'history' an option rather than a fantasy, and extending the boundaries of 'imagined community' as new alliances are forged in El Salvador. While the possibility of return has come sooner rather than later for Salvadorans, their relation to the history–ethnicity exchange is no more conditional than that of other immigrants. The collapse of the Soviet Union, for example, allows for a recuperation of 'nation' by people constructed as 'ethnic' for over sixty years, and the fervent attachment of many Anglo-Australians to the idea of being 'British' suggests that five generations of residence do not necessarily turn a country into a 'homeland'.[13]

REWRITING MULTICULTURALISM

Critical engagement with multiculturalism is a precarious undertaking in Australia, for multicultural debate in this country takes place in the shadow of a history that begins with the dispossession and slaughter of Aboriginal people and proceeds through almost two centuries of racism and Anglocentrism. This history positions multiculturalism as a redemptive moment in an otherwise sorry saga – above criticism for all but Anglo-nostalgic reactionaries. There are obvious dangers in this – not least the fact that multiculturalism ceases to be a contested space in which new claims and shifting circumstances can be actively negotiated by those committed to inclusive narratives of nation. Papering over cracks in the multicultural edifice for fear of bringing the whole thing down leaves critical engagement to those who have no such qualms – right-wing populists ready to mobilise the injured dignity of 'mainstream Australians' who resent their multicultural narrative position as irredeemably boorish racists.

What must be defended is not 'multiculturalism' so much as 'diversity', which is demonstrably not always 'recognised' either within 'ethnic communities' or between them. More to the point, the historical conditions under which this 'diversity' has been constituted must be acknowledged, for, as the Salvadoran case eloquently testifies, we are dealing not just with 'cultural difference' but with the contested histories through which that difference has been inscribed. Fetishisation of 'ethnic culture' elides the conditions of its production, constructing groups divided by social, economic and political differences as 'communities', and rewriting the politics of 'misrecognition' in terms of narratives of communal homogeneity. In constructing difference as 'cultural', multiculturalism also fails to counter racism, or to acknowledge that post-war European migration has brought to Australia not only 'cultural diversity' but also racist histories whose bearers can be just as hostile to 'visible difference' as descendants of the English-speaking settlers who imagined Australia as 'White'. The consequences of this failure are all too evident in the recent emergence of racialised debate about 'Asian' migration and Aboriginal land rights – a profoundly disturbing 'return of the repressed' which highlights the urgent need for critical engagement.

The assumption that there are cohesive communities bound by fixed cultures, which are both internally coherent and distinctively different, bears little relation to the hybrid 'cultures' that intersect through migration at the end of the twentieth century. In the context of multicultural politics, 'ethnic community' might best be understood as a rhetorical device for legitimating claims to 'leadership' and infrastructural support, on the one hand, and as a bureaucratic fiction dictated by the need to rationalise the diminishing resources available for migrant welfare services, on the other. It is, however, a rhetorical device that recognises neither the heterogeneity of contested history nor the complex and contradictory conditions of identity-formation within the global cultural economy. Narratives of 'ethnic community' must therefore be rewritten in terms which guarantee citizenship without suppressing difference. Narratives of nation which rest on the idea of a distinctive and unchanging 'Anglo-Australian culture' shared by a 'community' of 'mainstream Australians' are similarly unsustainable. Australia is an irreversibly heterogeneous and continuously changing social formation, and the opposition between 'multiculturalism' and 'assimilation' no longer gets to the heart of the problem. This opposition keeps us trapped within a discourse of migration that emerged in the encounter between the first generation of post-war immigrants and the Australian state – a discourse constructed by representatives of 'cultures' that no longer exist.

NOTES

1 This paper draws on ethnographic research in which I have been jointly engaged with Martha MacIntyre since 1988, with the research assistance of Rocio Amezquita and Anthony McMahon. The project has been funded by the Australian Research Council and by LaTrobe University School of Social Sciences. The contributions of the many Salvadorans who have offered information and friendship is acknowledged in general rather than particular terms, as they may not wish to be publicly identified with the project. In writing about what I see as issues raised by the Salvadoran case, I make no claim to speak for or on behalf of Salvadorans themselves.

2 In the light of events in Somalia, Bosnia and Rwanda, 'slaughterscapes' might be a useful addition to the dimensions of global cultural flow identified by Appadurai: ethnoscapes, mediascapes, technoscapes, finanscapes, and ideoscapes. See A. Appadurai, 'Difference in the Global Cultural Economy', *Theory, Culture and Society*, vol. 7, 1990, pp. 295–310.

3 ibid., p. 296.

4 A useful critical summary of this 'theoretical' tradition can be found in S. Castles and M. Miller, *The Age of Migration: International Population Movements in the Modern World*, London, Macmillan, 1993, pp. 19–22.

5 See E. A. Baloyra-Herp, 'Reactionary Despotism in Central America', *Journal of Latin American Studies*, vol. 15, part 2, November 1983, pp. 295–319.

6 For a more detailed elaboration of this argument, see my 'From History to Ethnicity: El Salvadoran Refugees in Melbourne', *Journal of Intercultural Studies*, vol. 11, no. 2, 1990, pp. 1–13.

7 R. Williams, *Culture*, Glasgow, Fontana Paperbacks, 1981, p. 13.

8 C. Taylor, *Multiculturalism and 'The Politics of Recognition'*, Princeton, NJ, Princeton University Press, 1992, p. 25.

9 J. O'Neil, 'Techno-culture and the Specular Functions of Ethnicity: With a Methodological Note', in I. Angus (ed.), *Ethnicity in a Technological Age*, Edmonton, Canadian Institute of Ukrainian Studies, 1988, pp. 17–29.

10 Taylor, *Multiculturalism and 'The Politics of Recognition'*, p. 25.

11 ibid., pp. 37–9.

12 See, for example, essays on Malay 'identity' by J. Kahn and A. Gomes in A. Gomes (ed.), *Modernity and Identity: Asian Illustrations*, Bundoora, LaTrobe University Press, 1994.
13 On a grander scale, Quebec separatists are attempting to reverse the 'history–ethnicity' exchange for an entire people, reclaiming 'national sovereignty' lost three hundred years ago; and Israel is premised on a recuperation of 'nation' whose loss predates the modern era.

12

THE POLITICS OF NATIONAL IDENTITY AND THE PEDAGOGY OF MULTICULTURALISM IN THE USA[1]

Henry A. Giroux

Global changes have provided the conditions for the emergence of new theoretical discourses that pose a powerful challenge to modern assumptions regarding the unity of nationalism and culture, the state and the nation, and national identity and the imperatives of a common culture. The historic and spatial shifts that have, in part, produced new forms of theorising about globalisation, the politics of diaspora, immigration, identity politics, multiculturalism and postcolonialism, are as profound intellectually as they are disruptive politically. Judith Squires captures the scope of these changes, while expressing some reservations about what they have come to mean as they are rapidly absorbed into new theoretical discourses:

> The global economy is a given in our life now: transnational corporations cross borders to maximize productivity and transnational intellectuals cross academic boundaries to maximize knowledge. The academic discipline, along with the national state, is subject to powerful forces of change. And, as we might acknowledge the failings of the old model of state sovereignty and hegemonic nationalism but none the less remain deeply skeptical about the gains to be had from the free movement of international capital around the globe in pursuit of profit, so we must be attuned to the benefits of jettisoning the status of empirical area studies, the constricting patriarchal academic canons and oppressive hierarchical departmental structures, but also the pitfalls.[2]

The pitfalls to which Squires refers are the lack of specificity and the theoretical blurriness that sometimes accompany the scholarly rush to take up issues of the politics of globalisation, diaspora, multiculturalism and postcolonialism.[3] I am particularly concerned here with a position that does not differentiate among radical, liberal, and conservative forms of multiculturalism. Within the politics of

178

the nation-state, such generalisations often recycle or reproduce colonialist discourse. What must be resisted is the assumption that the politics of national identity is necessarily complicit with a reactionary discourse of nationalism and that it has been superseded by theories which locate identity politics squarely within the discourses of postnational, diasporic globalism, or what Arjun Appadurai calls the 'search for nonterritorial principles of solidarity'.[4]

This is not to suggest that diverse nationalisms can be addressed outside of their transnational links, or that the mechanisms of a dominant and oppressive politics of assimilation can be abstracted from the pain, anguish and suffering experienced by those diasporic groups who define themselves through 'nonnational identities and aspirations'.[5] What I am resisting is the claim that nationalism can be associated only with ethnic conflict, that nationalism is witnessing its death knell, or that the relationship between nationalism and national identity can be framed only within a transnational discourse. The significance of such arguments must be acknowledged, but at the same time it is important to recognise in the context of the current conservative ideological offensive in the United States that it is crucial for critical educators and others, on the one hand, to 'locate our theorising in the grounded sites of cultural and political resistance within the United States' and, on the other, to guard against the tendency to 'overgeneralize the global current of so-called nomadic, fragmented and deterritorialized subjectivity'.[6]

I want to argue that nationalism is crucial to understanding the debates over identity and multiculturalism in the United States, and that, as important as the discourse of globalisation might be, it cannot be used to overlook how national identity reasserts itself within new discourses and sites of learning. More specifically, I want to argue that rather than dismissing the politics of identity as another essentialist discourse, progressives need to address how the politics of difference and identity are being constructed around new right-wing discourses and policies. Central to the construction of a right-wing nationalism is a project of defining national identity through an appeal to a common culture that attempts to resist any notion of national identity based upon a pluralised conception of culture, with its multiple literacies, identities and histories, and that erases histories of oppression and struggle for the working class and minorities. Stuart Hall is right in arguing that the 1990s are witnessing the return in big and small societies of recharged nationalism that serves to restore national culture as the primordial source of national identity.[7] But this should not suggest that the relationship between nationalism and culture manifests itself exclusively in terms of oppression or domination or that any attempt to develop an insurgent multiculturalism through an appeal to radical democracy necessarily assumes, or leaves intact, the boundary of the nation as an unproblematic historical, political and spatial formation. At stake here is the need to acknowledge the existence of the nation-state and nationalism as primary forces in shaping collective identities while simultaneously addressing how the relationship between national identity and culture can be understood as part of a broader struggle around developing national and postnational forms of democracy.

The relationship between culture and nationalism always bears the traces of those historical, ethical and political forces that constitute the often shifting and contradictory elements of national identity. To the degree that the culture of nationalism is rigidly exclusive and defines its membership in terms of a narrowly based common culture, nationalisms tend to be xenophobic, authoritarian and expansionist; hence the most commonly cited example of a nationalism steeped in the practices of ethnic cleansing, genocide or imperialist aggression. On the other hand, nationalism moves closer toward being liberal and democratic to the degree that national identity is inclusive and respectful of diversity and difference. And yet, a civic nationalism that makes a claim to respecting cultural differences does not guarantee that the state will not engage in coercive assimilationist policies. In other words, democratic forms of nationalism cannot be defended simply through a formal appeal to abstract, democratic principles. How nationalism and the nation-state embrace democracy must be determined, in part, through the access that diverse cultural groups have to shared structures of power that organise commanding legal, economic, state and cultural institutions on the local, state and national levels.[8]

Cultural differences and national identity stand in a complex relationship with each other and point to progressive as well as totalitarian elements of nationalism that provide testimony to its problematic character and effects. On the negative side, recent history bears witness to the Second World War steeped in forms of national identity that mobilised racial hatred and supported right-wing, anti-democratic governments in Germany, Italy and Japan. Following 1945, one of the most flagrant legacies of such a poisonous nationalism is evident in the long-standing apartheid regime that, until recently, dominated South African politics, as well as in the continuing attempt on the part of Turkey to deny the Kurds any status as a national group.

Representations of national identity constructed through appeals to racial purity, militarism, anti-semitism and religious orthodoxy have once again surfaced aggressively in Western Europe and can be seen in the rise of neo-nazi youth movements in Germany, the neo-fascist political parties that have won recent elections in Germany and France, and the ethnic cleansing that has driven Serbian nationalism in the former Republic of Yugoslavia. This highly selective list merely illustrates how national identity can be fashioned around appeals to a monolithic cultural identity that affirms intolerance, bigotry and an indifference to the precepts of democratic pluralism. Needless to say, these forms of demagogic nationalism emerge from a diverse set of conditions and circumstances, the roots of which lie in a complex history of racial conflict, the unstable economic conditions that have gripped Europe, and the dismantling of the Soviet Union and its empire. As a social construction, nationalism does not rest upon a particular politics, but takes its form within rather than outside of specific, historical, social and cultural contexts.

The more positive face of nationalism has emerged in a number of countries through a legacy of democratic struggles and can be seen not only in various anti-colonialist struggles in Asia and Africa, but also in diverse attempts on the part of nation-states to mobilise popular sentiment in the interest of expanding human rights and fighting against the encroachments of undemocratic social forces. While many of these movements of national struggle are far from unproblematic, particularly during periods in which they assume state control, they do provide credibility to the emancipatory power of nationalism as a defining principle in world politics.[9] Equally important is the need to develop a politics of difference and multiculturalism that combines the most progressive elements of nationalism with a notion of border crossing, diasporic politics and postnationalism that recognises the transits, flows, and social formations being produced on a global scale. It is precisely in the interaction of the national and the global that a borderline space exists for generating new forms of transnational literacy, social relations and cultural identities that expand the meaning of democracy and citizenship beyond national borders.

MYTHIC NATIONAL IDENTITY

For many Americans, questions of national identity seem to elude the complex legacy of nationalism and take on a mythic quality. Informed by the powerful appeal to assimilation and the legitimating discourse of patriotism, national identity often operates within an ideological register untroubled by the historical and emerging legacies of totalitarianism. Rather than being viewed cautiously as a potential vehicle for undermining democracy, national identity in the United States has been defined more positively in commonsensical terms as deeply connected to the mythic march of progress and prosperity at home and the noble effort to export democracy abroad. Hence, national identity has all too often been forged within popular memory as a discourse that neatly links nation, culture and citizenship in a seamless and unproblematic unity. Invoking claims to the past, in which the politics of remembering and forgetting work powerfully to legitimate a notion of national belonging that 'constructs the nation as an ethnically homogeneous object',[10] national identity is rewritten and purged of its seamy side. Within this narrative, national identity is structured through a notion of citizenship and patriotism that subordinates ethnic, racial and cultural differences to the assimilating logic of a common culture, or, more brutally, the 'melting pot'. Behind the social imaginary that informs this idea of national identity is a narrowly defined conception of history that provides a defence of the narratives of imperial power and dominant culture and legitimates an exceedingly narrow and bigoted image of what it means to be an American.

In an era of recharged nationalist discourse in the United States, the populist invocation of national identity suggests that social criticism itself is antithetical to both the construction of national identity and the precepts of patriotism. Of course, national identity, like nationalism itself, is a social construction that is built upon a series of inclusions and exclusions regarding history, citizenship and national belonging. As the social historian Benedict Anderson has pointed out, the nation is an 'imagined political community' that can only be understood within the intersecting dynamics of history, language, ideology and power. In other words, nationalism and national identity are neither necessarily reactionary nor necessarily progressive politically; thus, they give rise to communities which, as Anderson points out, are 'to be distinguished, not by their falsity/genuineness, but by the style in which they are imagined'.[11]

The insight that national identity must be addressed according to the ways in which it is imagined signals for me the importance of pedagogical practices to current controversies around questions of identity which characterise much political debate in the United States. It is the pedagogical processes at work in framing the present debates on national identity that interest me most. More specifically, the questions I want to raise are: what forms of address, images, texts and performances are being produced and used in popular discourses to construct what it means to be an American, and what are the implications of these dominant representations for extending or undermining a substantive plural democracy?

The current debate over national identity represents not only a conservative backlash fuelled by the assumption that 'those common values and consensual freedoms that have defined the "American" way of life, circa Norman Rockwell'[12] are now under attack by racial, sexual and political minorities; the current conservatism also produces a new nationalism rooted in an imaginary construction of national identity that is dangerous to any viable notion of democracy. This is not meant to suggest that the discourse of national unity voiced through an appeal to a shared language of difference (not the assimilationist language of a common culture) should be summarily dismissed as Eurocentric, racist or patriarchal. National identity steeped in a shared vision of social justice and a respect for cultural differences is to be applauded. At the same time, the healing grace of a national identity based on a respect for 'lived cultures in the plural'[13] should not be confused with a politically reactionary notion of national identity whose primary purpose is to restrict the terms of citizenship and community to a discourse of monoculturalism and nativism. National identity in the service of a common culture recognises cultural differences only to flatten them out in the conservative discourse of assimilation and the liberal appeal to tolerance.[14] However, the linkage between national identity and nationalism is not bound by any particular politics, and nationalism is not, by definition, intrinsically oppressive. Hence, it is both important and necessary as part of a progressive politics of national identity to provide a theoretical space to address the potential of both a pedagogy and a politics that can pluralise cultural differences within democratic relations of power in the interests of developing an emancipatory politics of national identity and nationalism. This is especially important in the United States at a time when the discourses of nationalism and national identity have taken a decidedly reactionary political turn.

The appropriation of national identity as a vehicle to foster racism, nativism and political censorship is not unique to the 1990s but has a long history in the

United States. However, the conditions, contexts and content through which the discourse of national identity is being produced and linked to virulent forms of nationalism are new. For example, electronic media culture, with its new cable technologies coupled with the proliferation of radio and television talk channels, has created a public sphere that vastly expands the intrusion into daily life of mainstream discourses that restrict the possibility for real debate, exchange and diversity of opinion. These electronic media, largely driven by corporate con-glomerates, have no precedent in American life in terms of their power both to disseminate information and to shape how national identity is configured, com-prehended and experienced as part of everyday life. Secondly, popular culture has become a powerful site for defining nationalism and national identity against diversity and cultural differences, the latter rendered synonymous with disruption, intolerance and separatism. In this populist discourse there is a theoretical slippage that equates national identity with a common identity and the assertion of cultural pluralism with an assault on the very character of what it means to be an American. At issue here is a politics of forgetting that erases the ways in which disparate social identities have been produced, legitimated and marginalised within different relations of power. But there is more at stake than the erasure of social memory; there is also the emergence of a racially saturated discourse that mobilises national identity as the defining principle for a national community that is under siege. Similarly, the new nationalism in foreign policy employs the chau-vinistic bravado of the market-place with its call for the United States to be number one in the world while simultaneously stigmatising intense social criti-cism as unpatriotic and a threat to American culture and civility.

MEDIA CULTURE AND THE POPULIST CONSTRUCTION OF NATIONALIST IDENTITY

I want to examine briefly some populist examples of the new nationalism that speak from different places in the cultural apparatuses that shape public opinion. In different ways, these populist voices advocate a pedagogy and politics of national identity that serve to reproduce some reactionary elements of the new nationalism. For example, expressions of the new nationalism can be found in several social sites: in the backlash against multiculturalism in public schools and universities; in the rise of the English First movement; in the notion of the state as a 'stern parent' willing to inflict harsh measures on welfare mothers; and in educational reforms demanding a national curriculum. Ideological signposts point-ing to the new nationalism can be found in analogies invoking imagery of battle, invasion and war, which increasingly shape the debates over immigration in the United States, as in the passing of anti-immigration legislation such as California's Proposition 187 and 209. Crime is represented in the dominant, white media as a black issue, implying that race can only be understood through a reductionist correlation of culture and identity. Representations of black men appear *ad nauseam* on the covers of magazines such as *Newsweek, The New York Times Sunday Magazine* and *Time* whenever a signifier is needed to mobilise and draw upon the general public's fear of crime and urban decay. Recent Hollywood films abound with racist representations that link criminality to skin colour. Some of the most popular examples include *Pulp Fiction* (1994) and *187* (1997).[15] All of these examples underscore how nationalism is currently being shaped to defend a beleaguered notion of national identity read as white, heterosexual, middle-class and allegedly threatened by contamination from cultural, linguistic, racial and sexual differences.

The power of the new nationalism and its centrality to American political life can also be seen in its growth and popularity in a number of popular and public spaces. One example may be found in the media commentaries of the 1996 Republican presidential hopeful, Patrick Buchanan, on shows such as CNN's *Crossfire.* Buchanan represents a new version of the public intellectual speaking from critical public sites in the news media, especially the growing number of news programmes found on cable television which are largely dominated by right-wing commentary. For Buchanan, the new nationalism is to be defined through a bellicose nativism that views cultural differences as a threat to national unity. Buchanan argues that the reality of cultural difference, with its plurality of languages, experiences and histories, poses a serious threat to both national unity and what he defends as Judaeo-Christian values. According to Buchanan, calls for expanding the existing potential of political representation and self-determination are fine in so far as they enable white Americans to 'take back' their country. In this reactionary discourse, difference becomes a signifier for racial exclusivity, segregation, or, in Buchanan's language, 'self-determination'. For Buchanan, public life in the United States has deteriorated since 1965 because 'a flood tide of immigration has rolled in from the Third World, legal and illegal, as our institutions of assimilation . . . disintegrated'. Ushering in the discourse of nativism, Buchanan posed the questions: 'Who speaks for the Euro-Americans? Is it not time to take America back?'[16] Similarly, populist right-wing conservative Rush Limbaugh, who describes himself as the 'Doctor of Democracy', rails against the poor and disadvantaged minorities because they do not act like 'real' Americans who 'rely upon their own resources, skills, talents, and hard work'.[17] Limbaugh has become the populist equivalent of Beavis and Butt-Head. Combining humour, unrestrained narcissism and outright buffoonery with a virulent and mean-spirited attack on progressive causes, Limbaugh accentuates the current appeal of the talk show that is part of a broader reactionary offensive through popular media. Perhaps the only interesting thing about Limbaugh is that he exemplifies the way in which right-wing conservatives no longer limit their political agenda to the traditional channels of policy, news and information; they have now extended their influence to the more populist realms of radio and television talk shows, the world of stand-up comics and other texts of mass-entertainment culture.

Rush Limbaugh, Howard Stern, Andrew Dice Clay and other popular media figures represent a marriage of media culture and the lure of extremist political rhetoric in what appears as a legitimation of a new form of public pathology dressed up as entertainment.[18] Limbaugh echoes the increasingly popular assumption that an 'ethnic upsurge' threatens both the American model of assimilation and the unity of America as a single culture. Extending rather than challenging the ideological assumptions that buttress the old racism and Social Darwinism, Limbaugh and others echo a call for cultural unity less as an overt marker for racial superiority than as a discourse for privileging a besieged white 'minority'. Within this populist discourse, racism is couched in the critique of the welfare state but serves primarily as a signifier for cultural containment, homogeneity, and social and structural inequality. Just as Charles Murray and Richard Herrnstein warn in The Bell Curve against the effects of immigration on the gene pool of white middle-class Americans, and the religious right calls for a 'holy war' to be waged in the schools to preserve the identity of the United States as a 'Christian' nation, so right-wing populist commentators add a twist to the new nationalism and its racial coding by appealing to a nostalgic, romanticised view of history as the 'good old days' in which white men ruled, blacks knew their place in the social and political hierarchy, and women attended to domestic work. The appeal is no longer simply to racial supremacy but also to cultural uniformity parading as the politics of nationalism, national identity and patriotism. These anti-multicultural attacks organise themselves around a view of nationalism that stigmatises any disagreement by simply labelling critics as 'America-bashers'.

In the world of TV spectacles and mass entertainment, the Buchanans and Limbaughs represent the shock-troops of the new nationalism. On the academic front, a more 'refined' version of the new nationalism has been advanced. Two examples will suffice, though they are hardly inclusive. In the first instance, public intellectuals writing in conservative periodicals such as The New Republic, The New Criterion and The American Spectator have increasingly argued for the new nationalism in terms that both dismiss multiculturalism and reproduce the discourse of assimilation and common culture. Rather than analysing multiculturalism as a complex, legitimate and necessary 'on-going negotiation among minorities against assimilation',[19] the new nationalists see in the engagements of cultural difference less a productive tension than a debilitating divisiveness. John B. Judis and Michael Lind echo this sentiment in their own call for a new nationalism:

> there is a constructive and inclusive current of American nationalism that runs from Alexander Hamilton through Abraham Lincoln and Theodore Roosevelt. It emphasizes not the exclusion of foreigners, but rather the unification of Americans of different regions, races and ethnic groups around a common national identity. It stands opposed not only to nativism, but also to today's multiculturalism and economic or strategic globalism.[20]

Nationalism in this discourse becomes the marker of certainty; it both affirms monoculturalism and restores the racially coded image of 'Americanness' as a beleaguered national identity.[21] The new nationalism also pits national identity against the possibility of different groups articulating and affirming their histories, languages, cultural identities and traditions through the shifting and complex relations in which people imagine and construct national and postnational social formations. This is evident in the attack being waged by the right and the Republican Congress on affirmative action, quotas, immigration, bilingualism and multiculturalism in the public schools. But the new nationalism is not confined to right-wing conservatives and evangelical Christians.

A more moderate version of the new nationalism can be found in the writing of liberals such as Richard Rorty, a prominent liberal philosopher from the University of Virginia. While Buchanan, Limbaugh and their followers might be dismissed as simply populist demagogues, public intellectuals such as Rorty, Richard Boynton and Lewis Menand command enormous respect from the academic community and the established press. Moreover, such intellectuals travel between academic and popular public spheres with enough influence to bring professional legitimacy to the new nationalism as it is taken up in television and radio talk programmes and in the major newspapers and magazines in the United States. Hence, it is all the more important that arguments that reinforce the logic of the new nationalism and parade under the banner of a 'tough' or 'patriotic' liberalism be critically engaged, especially by individuals who find in such arguments a semblance of reason and restraint.

LIBERALISM AND THE PROBLEM OF NATIONAL IDENTITY

Writing in the Op–Ed section of *The New York Times*, Richard Rorty has argued under the headline 'The Unpatriotic Academy' that left-wing academics who support multiculturalism are 'unpatriotic'. For Rorty, the litmus test for patriotism is not to be found in social criticism that holds a country up to its professed ideals, but in a refusal on the part of 'this left . . . to rejoice in the country it inhabits. It repudiates the idea of a national identity, and the emotion of national pride.' Speaking for an unspecified group of 'patriotic' Americans, Rorty, in this instance, insists that 'We take pride in being citizens of a self-invented, self-reforming, enduring constitutional democracy'.[22] One wonders: for whom do intellectuals such as Rorty speak? Have they appointed themselves spokespersons for all Americans who dissociate themselves from the left? And does this generalisation further suggest that one gives up respect and love for one's country if one engages in criticism that can be conveniently labelled left-wing? Does a public assertion of love for one's own country, as ritualistically invoked by all manner of demagogues, amount to a certified stamp of legitimacy for one's own politics? The implications of Rorty's attacks on left social critics need to be considered in view of the ways in which the United States engaged in red-baiting during the 1920s and the McCarthy witch-hunts of the 1950s. Is he suggesting that left-wing theorists (as if they were a homogeneous group) should be policed and punished for their lack of patriotism? There is a recklessness in Rorty's charges that places him squarely in the camp of those who would punish dissenters rather than support free speech, especially if it is speech with which one disagrees. Perhaps Rorty was simply being rambunctious in his use of the term 'unpatriotic', but given the ways in which the term has been used historically in this country to squelch social criticism, such a lapse of historical self-consciousness seems unlikely. So what is the point?

Rorty seems to be caught between liberal guilt and the appeal of a rabid conservatism that equates cultural differences with a threat to national unity, a threat that has to be overcome. Having posited such an equation, Rorty then takes the extraordinary step of identifying all those academics who support some version of multiculturalism as posing a threat to the social order. For Rorty, there is no contradiction in feeling one's heart swell with patriotism and 'national hope' and feeling 'shame at the greed, the intolerance and the indifference to suffering that is widespread in the United States'.[23] In this theoretical sweep, multiculturalism is not addressed in its complexity as a range of theoretical positions that run the ideological gamut extending from calls for separatism to demands for new forms of cultural democracy. Multiculturalism, for Rorty, is simply a position that exists under some absolute sign. In this reductionistic perspective, there are no theoretical differences between multicultural positions espoused by academic leftists such as Hazel Carby, Guillermo Gomez-Peña, June Jordan and bell hooks, on the one hand, and liberals such as James Banks, Gregory Jay or Stanley Fish, on the other. But there is more at stake here than Rorty's suspect appeal to patriotism. Social criticism is not the enemy of patriotism, it is the bedrock of a shared national tradition that allows for many voices to engage in a dialogue about the dynamics of cultural and political power. In fact, national identity must be understood within a broader concern for the expansion and deepening of democratic public life itself.

I believe that Rorty's notion of national identity closes down on, rather than expands, the principles that inform a multicultural and multiracial democracy. However, Rorty is important in exemplifying the limits of the reigning political philosophy of liberalism. Rorty's gesture towards tolerance 'presupposes that its object is morally repugnant, that it really needs to be reformed, that is, altered'.[24] As David Theo Goldberg points out:

> Liberals are moved to overcome the racial differences they tolerate and have been so instrumental in fabricating by deluding them, by bleaching them out through assimilation or integration. The liberal would assume away the difference in otherness maintaining thereby the dominant of a presumed sameness, the universally imposed similarity in identity.[25]

National identity cannot be constructed around the suppression of dissent. Nor should it be used in the service of a new fundamentalism by appealing to a notion of patriotism that equates left-wing social criticism with treason, and less critical forms of discourse with a love of nationalism or national identity. It is precisely this type of binarism that has been used, all too frequently throughout the twentieth century, to develop national communities that make a virtue of intolerance and exclusion. Moreover, this kind of logic prevents individuals and social groups from understanding and critically engaging national identity not as a cultural monument but as a living set of relations that must be constantly negotiated and struggled over.

Rorty's facile equating of national identity with love of one's country, on the one hand, and with the dismissal of forms of left social criticism that advocate multiculturalism, on the other, is simply an expression of the new nationalism, one that views cultural differences and the emergence of multiple cultures as a sign of fragmentation and a departure from, rather than an advance toward, democracy. Rorty's mistake is to assume that national identity must be founded on a single culture, language and history, when in fact it cannot be. National identity is always a shifting, unsettled complex of historical struggles and experiences that are cross-fertilised, produced and translated through a variety of cultures. As such, it is always open to interpretation and struggle. As Stuart Hall points out, national identity 'is a matter of "becoming" as well of "being". . . . [It] is never complete, always in process. . . . [It] is not eternally fixed in some essentialized past [but] subject to the continuous "play" of history, culture, and power.'[26]

The discourse of multiculturalism represents, in part, the emergence of new voices that have generally been excluded from the histories that have defined our national identity. Far from being a threat to social order, multiculturalism in its various forms has challenged notions of national identity that equate cultural differences with deviance and disruption. Refusing a notion of national identity constructed on the suppression of cultural differences and social dissent, multiculturalism, especially its more critical and insurgent versions, explores how dominant views of national identity have been developed around cultural differences constructed within hierarchical relations of power that authorise who can or cannot speak as a legitimate American. Perhaps it is the reinsertion of politics and power into the discourse on difference that threatens Rorty so much that he responds by labelling it unpatriotic.

Pitting national identity against cultural difference not only appeals to an oppressive politics of common culture, but reinforces a political moralism that polices 'the boundaries of identity, encouraging uniformity and ensuring intellectual inertia'.[27] National identity based on a unified cultural community suggests a dangerous relationship between the ideas of race, intolerance and the cultural membership of nationhood. Not only does such a position downplay the politics of culture at work in nationalism but it erases an oppressive history forged in an appeal to a common culture and a reactionary notion of national identity. As Will Kymlicka points out, liberals and conservatives often overlook the fact that the American government

forcibly incorporated Indian tribes, native Hawaiians, and Puerto Ricans into the American state, and then attempted to coercively assimilate each group into the common American culture. It banned the speaking of Indian languages in school and forced Puerto Rican and Hawaiian schools to use English rather than Spanish or Hawaiian.[28]

What is problematic about Rorty's position is not simply that he regards multi-culturalism as a threat to a totalising notion of national identity. More important is his theoretical indifference to counter-narratives of difference, diaspora and cultural identity that explore how diverse groups are constructed within an insurgent multiculturalism that engages the issue both of what holds us together as a nation and of what constitutes our differences from each other. Viewing cultural differences only as a problem, Rorty reveals a disturbing lacuna in his notion of national identity; it is a view that offers little defence against the forces of ethnic absolutism and cultural racism that are so quick to seize upon national identity as a legitimating discourse for racial violence. There is an alarming defensiveness in Rorty's view of national identity, one which reinforces rather than challenges a discourse of national community rooted in claims to cultural and racist supremacy.

What educators need to consider is a pedagogy that redefines national identity not through a primordial notion of ethnicity or a monolithic conception of culture, but as part of a postmodern politics of cultural difference in which identities are constantly being negotiated and reinvented within complex and contradictory notions of national belonging. A collective dialogue over nationalism, national identity and cultural differences is not going to be established by simply labelling certain forms of social criticism as unpatriotic or national identity as a shared tradition that exists outside of the struggles over representation, democracy and social justice. If American society is to move away from its increasing defensiveness about cultural differences, it will have to advocate a view of national identity that sees bigotry and intolerance as the enemy of democracy, and cultural differences as one of its strengths. However, even where such differences are acknowledged and affirmed, it is important to recognise that they cannot be understood exclusively within the language of culture and identity, but must rather be seen as part of an ethical discourse that contributes to a viable notion of democratic public life. Among other things, this suggests a need for a pedagogy and language through which values and social responsibility can be discussed not simply as a matter of individual choice or relativism but as a social discourse and pedagogical practice grounded in public struggles. David Theo Goldberg is right in arguing that educators need a 'robustly nuanced conception of relativism underpinning the multicultural project', one that 'will enable distinctions to be drawn between more or less accurate truth claims and more or less justifiable values (in contrast to absolute claims to the truth or the good)'.[29] The issue here is not merely the importance of moral pragmatism in developing a pedagogy that addresses national identity as a site of resistance and reinvention. Equally important is the political and pedagogical imperative of developing a postmodern notion of democracy in which students and others will be attentive

189

to negotiating and constructing the social, political and cultural conditions for diverse cultural identities to flourish within an increasingly multicentric, international and transnational world.

MULTICULTURAL EDUCATION

In what follows, I want to suggest some general elements that might inform an insurgent multicultural curriculum. First, a multicultural curriculum must be informed by a new language in which issues of diversity and cultural difference become central to educating students to live in a democratic society. That is, we need a language of politics and pedagogy that is able to speak to cultural differences not as something to be tolerated but as essential to expanding the discourse and practice of democratic life. It is important to note that multiculturalism is not merely an ideological construct, it also refers to the fact that by the year 2010, people of colour will be the numerical majority in the United States. This suggests that educators need to develop a language, vision and curriculum in which multiculturalism and democracy become mutually reinforcing categories. Manning Marable has spoken eloquently to this issue and his definition of a multicultural democracy offers important insights for reworking democracy as a pedagogical and cultural practice necessary for what John Dewey once called the creation of an articulate public. Marable is worth quoting at length on this issue:

> Multicultural political democracy means that this country was not built by and for only one group – Western Europeans; that our country does not have only one language – English; or only one religion – Christianity; or only one economic philosophy – corporate capitalism. Multicultural democracy means that the leadership within our society should reflect the richness, colors and diversity expressed in the lives of all of our people. Multicultural democracy demands new types of power-sharing and the re-allocation of resources necessary to great economic and social development for those who have been systematically excluded and denied.[30]

Second, as part of an attempt to develop a multicultural and multiracial society consistent with democratic principles, educators must take account of the fact that men and women of colour are disproportionately under-represented in the cultural and public institutions of this country. Pedagogically, this suggests that a multicultural curriculum must provide students with the skills to analyse how various audio, visual and print texts fashion social identities over time, and how these representations serve to reinforce, challenge or rewrite dominant moral and political vocabularies that promote stereotypes which degrade people by depriving them of their history, culture and identity.[31] This is not to suggest that such a pedagogy should solely concentrate on how meanings produce particular stereotypes

190

and the uses to which they are put. Nor should a multicultural politics of representation focus exclusively on recovering and reconstituting the history of subordinate groups. While such approaches are essential to giving up the quest for a pure historical tradition, it is imperative that a multicultural curriculum also focus on dominant, white institutions and histories in order to interrogate them in terms both of their injustices and their contributions to humanity. Of course, more is at stake here than avoiding the romanticising of minority voices, or the inclusion of Western traditions in the curriculum. Multiculturalism in this sense is about making whiteness visible as a racial category; that is, it points to the necessity of providing white students with the cultural memories that enable them to recognise the historically and socially constructed nature of their own identities. In part, this approach to multiculturalism as a cultural politics provides white students with self-definitions by which they can recognise whether they are speaking from within or outside privileged spaces and how power works within and across differences to legitimate some voices and silence others.

Bob Suzuki has elaborated on the pedagogical importance of making whiteness visible as an ethnic category. In teaching a course on racism to college students, he discovered that for many white students their ethnic experiences and histories had been erased. By helping them to recover and interrogate their own histories, he found that the white students 'could relate more empathetically to the problems of people of color and become more open to understanding their experiences and perspectives'.[32] I would extend Suzuki's important point by arguing that, crucial as it is to get white students to listen empathetically to students of colour, it is also crucial that they come to understand that multiculturalism is equally about understanding how dominant institutions provide the context of massive black unemployment, segregated schools, racist violence and run-down housing. An insurgent multicultural curriculum must shift attention away from an exclusive focus on subordinate groups, especially since such an approach tends to highlight their deficits, to one which examines how racism in its various forms is produced historically, semiotically and institutionally in various levels of dominant, white culture. Multiculturalism means analysing not just stereotypes but also how institutions produce racism and other forms of discrimination.

Third, a multicultural curriculum must consider how to articulate a relationship between unity and difference that moves beyond simplistic binarisms. That is, rather than defining multiculturalism either against unity or simply for difference, it is crucial that educators develop a unity-in-difference position that will enable new forms of democratic representation, participation and citizenship to provide a forum for creating unity without denying the particular and the multiple. In this instance, the interrelationships of different cultures and identities become borderlands, sites of crossing, negotiation, translation and dialogue. At stake here is the production of a notion of border pedagogy in which the intersection of culture and identity produces self-definitions that enable teachers and students to authorise a sense of critical agency. Border pedagogy points to a self/other relationship in which identity is not fixed as either Other or the same; instead, it is both, and, hence, defined within multiple literacies that become a referent, critique and practice of cultural translation, a recognition that there is no possibility of fixed, final or monologically authoritative meanings transcending history, power and ideology. Within this pedagogical cartography, teachers must be given the opportunity to cross ideological and political borders as a way of clarifying their own moral vision, as a way of enabling counter-discourses and, in Roger Simon's words, as a way of getting students beyond the world they already know 'in order to provoke their inquiry into and challenge their existing views of the way things are and should be'.[33]

Border literacy calls for pedagogical conditions in which 'differences are recognized, exchanged and mixed in identities that break down but are not lost, that connect but remain diverse'.[34] A border pedagogy suggests a transnational literacy forged in the practices of imagination, narrative and performance; a literacy that insists on an open-endedness, an incompleteness, and an uncertainty about the politics of one's own location. This is not a literacy that pretends to be amorphous or merely self-reflexive, but one that engages the important question of how to deal with the fact of reflexivity, how to strategise about it in the interests of diverse theoretical and pedagogical projects dedicated to creating a multicultural and multiracial democracy within both national and postnational social formations.

Fourth, an insurgent multiculturalism must undertake to do more than merely re-present cultural differences in the curriculum; it must also educate students to the necessity of linking a justice of multiplicity to struggles over real material conditions that structure everyday life. In part, this means understanding how structural imbalances in power produce real limits to the capacity of subordinate groups to exercise a sense of agency and struggle. It also means analysing specific class, race, gender and other issues as social problems rooted in material and institutional factors that produce specific forms of inequality and oppression. This would necessitate a multicultural curriculum geared to producing a language that deals with social problems in historical and relational terms, and that uncovers how the dynamics of power work to promote domination within both the school and the wider society. But such a curriculum must be firmly committed to more than a politics of inclusive representation or the aim of simply helping students understand and celebrate cultural differences. The politics of cultural difference must be a politics of more than texts: it must also understand, negotiate and challenge differences as they are defined and sustained within oppressive networks of power. Critically negotiating the relationship between national identity and cultural differences, as Homi Bhabha has pointed out, is a negating activity that should be valued for 'making' a difference in the world rather than merely reflecting it.[35]

Finally, a multicultural curriculum must not simply be imposed on a community and school. It is imperative that, as a power-sensitive discourse, a multicultural curriculum refigures relations between the school, teachers, students and the wider community. In this case, schools must be willing to draw upon the resources of the community, including members of the community in making fundamental decisions about what is taught, who is hired, and how the school can become an integral part of the society it serves. Teachers need to be educated to be border crossers, to explore zones of cultural difference by moving in and out of the resources, histories and narratives that provide different students with a sense of identity, place and possibility.[36] This does not mean that educators should become tourists travelling to exotic lands; nor should the issue of community involvement in the schools be seen as unproblematic. Community and school relations require that diverse and often conflicting groups enter into negotiation and dialogue around issues of nationality, difference and identity, so as to be able to fashion a more ethical and democratic set of pedagogical relations between teachers and their students, thus allowing students to speak, listen and learn differently within pedagogical spaces that are challenging but safe and affirming. With this in view, a curriculum for a multicultural and multiracial society might hopefully provide the conditions for students to think and act otherwise, to imagine beyond the given, and to critically embrace their identities as a source of agency and possibility.

NOTES

1 I would like to thank David Bennett for his editorial work on this article. The arguments elaborated here were partly developed in two of my previous essays, 'National Identity and the Politics of Multiculturalism', *College Literature*, vol. 22, no. 2, June 1995, pp. 42–57, and 'The Politics of Insurgent Multiculturalism in the Era of the Los Angeles Uprising', *The Journal of the Midwest Modern Language Association*, vol. 26, no. 1, Spring 1993, pp. 12–30.

2 J. Squires, 'Editorial', *New Formations*, no. 24, Winter 1994, p. v.

3 Some major critiques that centre on the lack of specificity in some of the writing on diaspora, immigration and postcolonialism can be found in I. Grewal and C. Kaplan, 'Introduction: Transnational Feminist Practices and Questions of Postmodernity', in I. Grewal and C. Kaplan (eds), *Scattered Hegemonies*, Minneapolis, University of Minnesota Press, 1994, pp. 1–33; I. Ang, 'On Not Speaking Chinese: Postmodern Ethnicity and the Politics of Diaspora', *Social Formations*, no. 24, March 1995, pp. 1–18; C. Calhoun, 'Nationalism and Civil Society: Democracy, Diversity, and Self-Determination', in C. Calhoun (ed.), *Social Theory and the Politics of Identity*, Cambridge, Mass., Blackwell, 1994, pp. 304–35; B. Parry, 'Signs of Our Times: A Discussion of Homi Bhabha's *The Location of Culture*', *Third Text*, vol. 8, no. 28/9, Autumn/Winter 1994, pp. 5–24.

4 A. Appadurai, 'Patriotism and Its Futures', *Public Cultures*, vol. 5, no. 3, 1993, p. 417.

5 ibid., p. 418.

6 Both of these quotations are take from Squires, 'Editorial', p. vi.

7 S. Hall, 'Culture, Community, Nation', *Cultural Studies*, vol. 7, no. 3, October 1993, p. 353.

8 This issue is discussed in W. Kymlicka, 'Misunderstanding Nationalism', *Dissent*, Winter 1995, pp. 130–7.

9 The literature on nationalism and national identity is much too voluminous to survey here, but excellent examples can be found in B. Anderson, *Imagined Communities*, 2nd edn, London, Verso, 1991; P. Chatterjee, *The Nation and Its Fragments*, Princeton, NJ, Princeton University Press, 1993; H. K. Bhabha (ed.), *Nation and Narration*, New York,

Routledge, 1990; E. Said, *Culture and Imperialism*, New York, Alfred K. Knopf, 1993; A. Parker, M. Russo, D. Sommer and P. Yaeger (eds), *Nationalisms and Sexualities*, New York, Routledge, 1992; E. Balibar and I. Wallerstein, *Race, Nation, Class: Ambiguous Identities*, London, Verso, 1991. Some excellent recent sources can be found in C. Calhoun (ed.), *Social Theory and the Politics of Identity*, Cambridge, Mass., Blackwell, 1994.

10 P. Gilroy, *The Black Atlantic: Modernity and Double Consciousness*, Cambridge, Mass., Harvard University Press, 1993, p. 3.

11 Anderson, *Imagined Communities*, p. 6.

12 H. K. Bhabha, 'A Good Judge of Character: Men, Metaphors, and the Common Culture', in T. Morrison (ed.), *Race-ing Justice, Engendering Power: Essays on Anita Hill, Clarence Thomas, and the Construction of Social Reality*, New York, Pantheon, 1992, p. 233.

13 G. Graff and B. Robbins, 'Cultural Criticism', in S. Greenblatt and G. Gunn (eds), *Redrawing the Lines*, New York, MLA, 1992, p. 434.

14 For a critique of both of these positions, see Ang, 'On Not Speaking Chinese' and G. Hage, 'Locating Multiculturalism's Other: A Critique of Practical Tolerance', *New Formations*, no. 24, Winter 1994, pp. 19–34.

15 I take up the issue of Hollywood portrayal of racism and violence in H. A. Giroux, 'Racism and the Aesthetic of Hyper-real Violence: Pulp Fiction and Other Visual Tragedies', *Social Identities*, vol. 1, no. 2, 1995, pp. 333–54.

16 Pat Buchanan quoted in C. Krathammer, 'The Real Buchanan is Surfacing', *The Cincinnati Enquirer*, 3 March 1990, A4.

17 R. H. Limbaugh, III, *See, I Told You So*, New York, Pocket Books, 1993, p. 26.

18 For a brilliant analysis of this phenomenon, especially the marketing of Beavis and Butt-Head, see D. Kellner, *Media Culture: Cultural Studies, Identity, and Politics – Between the Modern and the Postmodern*, London and New York, Routledge, 1995.

19 H. K. Bhabha, 'Beyond the Pale: Art in the Age of Multicultural Translation', *Kunst and Museum Journal*, vol. 5, no. 4, 1994, vp. 15.

20 J. B. Judis and M. Lind, 'For a New Nationalism', *The New Republic*, 27 March 1995, p. 21.

21 This is paraphrased from Hall, 'Culture, Community, Nation', p. 357.

22 R. Rorty, 'The Unpatriotic Academy', *The New York Times Op–Ed*, 13 February 1994, p. E15.

23 ibid.

24 David Theo Goldberg, *Racist Culture*, Cambridge, Mass., Blackwell, 1993, p. 7.

25 ibid.

26 S. Hall, 'Cultural Identity and Diaspora', in J. Rutherford (ed.), *Identity: Community, Culture, Difference*, London, Lawrence & Wishart, 1990, p. 225.

27 J. Rutherford, 'A Place Called Home: Identity and the Cultural Politics of Difference', in J. Rutherford (ed.), *Identity: Community, Culture, Difference*, p. 17.

28 Kymlicka, 'Misunderstanding Nationalism', p. 132.

29 D. T. Goldberg, 'Introduction: Multicultural Conditions', in D. T. Goldberg (ed.), *Multiculturalism: A Critical Reader*, Cambridge, Mass., Blackwell, 1994, p. 15.

30 M. Marable, *Black America: Multicultural Democracy in the Age of Clarence Thomas and David Duke*, Westfield, NJ, Open Media, 1992, p. 13.

31 On this issue, see Marable, *Black America*.

32 B. Suzuki, 'Unity with Diversity: Easier Said Than Done', *Liberal Education*, February 1991, p. 34.

33 R. Simon, *Teaching Against the Grain*, Westport, Conn., Bergin & Garvey, 1992, p. 47.

34 I. Chambers, *Border Dialogues*, New York, Routledge, 1990, p. 114.

35 Bhabha, 'Beyond the Pale', p. 22.

36 The issue of border pedagogy and border crossings is taken up in H. A. Giroux, *Border Crossings: Cultural Workers and the Politics of Education*, London and New York, Routledge, 1992.

13

ETHNICITY AND EDUCATION

Biculturalism in New Zealand

Anne Maxwell

Recent efforts by indigenous Maori in New Zealand to reassert aspects of their traditional culture have given rise to a liberalist desire amongst Pakeha (New
Zealanders of European descent or origin) to reinvent the nation in a bicultural
image. This image is most noticeable in public forms of remembering such as
those to be found in art galleries and museums, but since 1987 it has also determined education policy, so that even official history-writing is now being
organised around the written and oral accounts of the two main signatories to the
Treaty of Waitangi – Europeans and Maori. Yet there are several problems with
this treaty model of history-writing that need to be considered if the rewriting of
the nation's history is to represent a genuine transformation of the legacy of
European colonialism. It is my aim here to draw attention to these problems and
to outline an alternative approach to history-writing that might begin to address
these problems in a practical way.

The driving force behind the Maori renaissance of the 1970s and 1980s was a
new generation of urbanised Maori intellectuals who joined with an older generation of Maori leaders to produce a radical and contemporary ethnic politics. What
distinguishes this group from previous agitators for Maori sovereignty is their artic-
ulateness. Hard-hitting books like Donna Awatere's *Maori Sovereignty* (1984) played
a crucial role in transmuting economic and social grievances into effective political forms. Awatere's edict, 'Don't marry us or have children to us, just take in the
Maori mind, reclaim us with time and nature',[1] challenged the liberal method of
reform by presenting Pakeha with an alternative to Governor Hobson's assimilationist goal of 'one people'. Awatere's advice to Pakeha came after a decade of
aggressive politicking by a new generation of Maori no longer content to take the
back seat with respect to ownership of land, access to education, and control of
political, legal, social and cultural institutions. During this period, the push for
'reculturation' and equal rights moved outwards from the universities and into the
wider Maori community, so that land marches, occupations and protests became
more frequent and insistent. Many Maori did not agree with this confrontational
method, but it was successful in bringing about constitutional changes.

The most important change was in the area of land rights. In 1975 the Third Labour Government passed an Act to restore the Treaty of Waitangi to a position of centrality. The treaty was the original contract signed between the country's first inhabitants and the representatives of the British Crown, and for more than a century this document had lain in a state of neglect. The Act required that a tribunal be set up to hear and advise the government on land claims that appeared to contravene the treaty's regulations.[2] The government did not intend the tribunal's powers to be very extensive as the treaty was a notoriously ambiguous document (the version signed by Queen Victoria's representatives did not match the version signed by the Maori chiefs), but they had not anticipated the intervention of two university scholars, Dr Ranginui Walker and Pat Hohepa, who enjoyed prominent positions in the Maori community. Under their influence, the tribunal began to offer advice based on the original spirit of the treaty and not on its literal meaning.[3] One consequence was that the tribunal's powers were extended to cover sales that occurred before the Land Wars as well as sales affecting Crown land. This much wider interpretation of the treaty was finally passed into law by the Fourth Labour Government in 1985.

Another important change occurred in the area of education. The 1980s saw an explosion of Maori Studies in universities and colleges and the growth of Maori language programmes such as the Te Kohunga Rao schools, in which all teaching is carried out in the Maori language. These changes in policy came about mainly as a result of Maori efforts to challenge the right of the English tongue to exist unselfconsciously in Aotearoa/New Zealand. These developments forced Pakeha to confront their consciences and re-examine the terms on which they could claim 'natural' occupancy of the land. But there was also the additional factor of Britain's entry into the European Common Market; this event stung many Pakeha into calling for a cultural break with their European past – a gesture that called for linguistic as well as literary independence.

The introduction of a policy of biculturalism in education and the arts represented a halt to what until then had been a mounting effort on the part of the Third Labour Government to make New Zealanders adopt a multicultural national identity in the wake of a recently expanded immigration policy. Throughout the 1970s, radical sections of the Maori community had been attempting to transform the participatory base of the new multiculturalism in the direction of biculturalism, and by the mid-1980s (partly as a result of stricter immigration laws and partly as a result of their own energies) they had succeeded. For the time being, at least, the multicultural agenda was to be put on hold as state departments and administrative bureaucracies attempted to come to terms with the prior claims of the indigenous ethnic community.[4] The first stage of this programme saw a massive centralisation of resources and the systemisation of planning authorities. In order that government bureaucracies could administer effectively, Maori elements had to be organised around pan-tribal as opposed to tribal identities.

If the period leading up to 1987 had seen a steady increase in the number of books on Maori culture being included in teaching programmes, the period after

1987 has seen state agencies drafting policy that requires all higher-year school students to read both the literary texts and the myth-based histories belonging to Maori, alongside the canonical texts belonging to the dominant Anglo-Saxon culture. Even the recent exposure in the early 1990s to global markets and the dismantling of the welfare state at a time of deep economic crisis have not halted this requisitioning of indigenous culture. This is perhaps surprising given that the application of bicultural principles to the study of literature and history in schools and some universities has met with much criticism. While criticisms in the area of literature have been mainly confined to old-fashioned humanists and the New Right,[5] criticisms in the area of history have come mainly from indigenous peoples themselves and from theoretically informed scholars who have sought to transform New Zealand's dominant culture radically by challenging its prevailing structures of identity.

For many sections of the Maori community, the policy-makers' decision to adhere to the homogenised version of Maori history developed by nineteenth-century anthropologists has meant that the accounts of tribal origins that have served to distinguish small tribes have been consistently overlooked, with devastating consequences for tribal identity and equal access to compensation. Te Aku Graham has pointed out that both bicultural education policy and land claims are predicated upon the European preoccupation with *waka* (canoe) traditions.[6] European experts on Maori culture, such as Elsdon Best, took the discontinuous or fragmented body of oral accounts that constituted Maori history and reshaped them into a mythical version of history in which the various tribes can trace their ancestors back to the twelve canoes that arrived in Aotearoa from the legendary homeland of Hawaiiki. The state's upholding of these *waka* narratives of identity has meant that small tribes like Ngati Hako, whose ancestor arrived on the back of a whale, have been forced to bury their historical traditions and tribal identities and adopt those of the larger, more powerful tribes if they are to compete for resources. It is the policy-makers' reliance on a European model of authentic tradition that has provoked Graham into pronouncing that the oral histories that form the mainstay of bicultural policy are no longer relevant to the indigenous community. Indeed, Graham maintains that far from fostering *Maoritanga*, they are damaging tribal identity and consciousness. Graham's contention that contemporary bicultural policy is harmful to Maori is tantamount to saying that bicultural histories conform to an epistemological prototype that is essentially European even though their inventors claim to have drawn equally on Maori and Pakeha traditions. In other words, bicultural histories are merely another version of liberalism. Her claim that biculturalism has become an essentially Pakeha institution seems reasonable enough given that the model of history being pushed by policy-makers is largely the product of a small number of Pakeha academics who have held to a romantic model of indigenous identity.

Not all Maori, however, are ready to abandon the bicultural model of history. While it is true that some have clearly benefited from a system that privileges the genealogies that can be traced back to *wakas*, others believe that it is not the concept itself that is intrinsically flawed, only its common interpretation. Ranginui Walker, for instance, has implied that there are in fact two interpretations of biculturalism – the Pakeha version, which means 'learning a few phrases of Maori language and how to behave on the Marae' (the public space in front of the meeting house), and the Maori version, which entails Pakehas 'sharing what they have monopolised for so long, power, privilege and occupational security'.[7] His point would seem to be that if many Maori have supported biculturalism, it is because it appears to be compatible with the principles of sovereignty enshrined in the treaty. In contrast to this, Graham's point is that unless the bicultural model of history-writing begins to take cognisance of the heterogeneity of Maori society in general and the rich variety of its historical narratives in particular, New Zealanders will be faced with shades of the treaty debates all over again. For then, as now, the parties who engineered the agreement did not represent the full range of representative communities to be found in New Zealand society.[8]

In addition to small tribes, there are at least two further categories of indigenous New Zealanders who have failed to benefit from the historical model being implemented by educationalists: Maori women and descendants of Moriori (the Polynesians who arrived before the first wave of Maori). For women, the stakes have less to do with compensation and more to do with regaining access to representation in a social system in which patriarchalism has become more entrenched as a result of traditional tribal life having to adapt to colonialism. Ngahuia Te Awekotuku has observed that the women who helped bring about the present Maori Renaissance have not been accorded due attention either by Pakeha historians or by Maori leaders. For this to happen, she warns, Maori women's different experiences must form part of the historical accounts that are being used to implement biculturalism.[9] But her urgings do not stop there. It is also her belief that if women are to play a greater role in the political process, historical revisionism in New Zealand will need to explode the myth of dominant heterosexism imposed on Maori society in the nineteenth century by the missionaries. This myth is not only responsible for repressing the fluidity of sexual positionings that individuals could enjoy within traditional Maori society, it is also responsible for women being denied the opportunity to assume honorary positions of authority, along with the right to speak on the area of the Marae in which political decisions of the tribe are made. For the narratives of biculturalism to be more responsive to women's experience it will be necessary not only to include the myths that celebrate powerful women, but to show that women's authority depends on Maori society's accepting a fuller range of sexual identities.[10]

The Moriori are thought to have settled the Chatham Islands well before the main wave of Maori migration to New Zealand, which occurred some time in the late sixteenth or early seventeenth centuries. In the 1870s, members of Wharekauri Rununga – the Maori tribe that settled in Taranaki – were involved in a series of skirmishes with settlers which resulted in their leader, Rua, having to flee to the Chathams. No sooner had Rua and his followers arrived there than they set about conquering local Moriori tribes, plundering their land and converting them to slaves. These events have been well documented by nineteenth and early twentieth-century historians, yet they have been systematically overlooked by the more recent treaty historians, whose whole attention has been taken up with rewriting history in accordance with the spirit of the treaty. Even the impressive history of the Moriori produced by Michael King in 1990[11] has not induced the treaty historians to expand the rewriting of New Zealand's history to accommodate this section of the indigenous community. For this to happen, Moriori would need to be included in the treaty. The series of claims that descendants of Chatham Island Moriori launched in April 1994 with the Waitangi Tribunal against Wharekauri Rununga are designed to achieve precisely that. Compensation and recognition of Moriori status along with mana (authority) are being sought. If the claims are upheld by the tribunal, then policy-makers will surely be forced to replace the present model of indigenous history with a model that is more heterogeneous.[12]

The attacks on the bicultural model of history-writing have not been confined to indigenous minorities; they have also issued from those members of the academic community concerned about the lack of representational channels (and educational resources) available to other ethnic minorities. This particular criticism is not without justification. The inappropriateness of the bicultural model of national identity to the Polynesian community (the second largest as well as the fastest growing non-Pakeha ethnic group) alone suggests that the development of a multicultural educational programme is still, for many sections of the community, a more desirable goal than biculturalism.[13] The difficulty crystallises if we ask which of the two histories currently available on the proposed school syllabus should a Cook Island, Samoan, or Tongan New Zealander regard as encompassing their own experience? Obviously, it makes no sense for New Zealand's considerable population of Polynesian and Melanesian immigrants to think of themselves as Pakeha, but does it make any more sense for them to think of themselves as Maori, particularly when some radical Maori have claimed that they are tauiwi (foreigners)?[14]

In response to this criticism, the champions of biculturalism have argued that the present historical model does not necessarily represent the end-phase of the democratic process, and that while there are certainly those who have used it to pursue the goal of Maori autonomy, there are many more who have used it to pursue a goal of ethnic relations that will eventually guarantee the equal participation of minorities in general in the political, economic and cultural process.[15] Here, biculturalism is seen as the central platform from which a future multicultural society will be launched. The argument goes like this: in order to develop a model of ethnic relations that can answer to the democratic demands of a whole range of minority groups, it will first be necessary to develop representational structures that will empower the largest minority group. This is what the Race Relations Conciliator had in mind when, in 1982, he declared that 'A New Zealand national identity must be based on a firm foundation of bi-culturalism through which multi-culturalism can emerge'.[16] But even for this to happen, the current model of history-writing will need to undergo considerable transformation before it can begin to yield up the heterogeneity of viewpoints which is a prerequisite of multiculturalism. The dissident voices from within the Maori community and land-rights challenges mounted by Moriori suggest that the liberalist model of biculturalism, based on a centralised or rationalist structure of representation, is already under threat. Recent comments by the tribunal chairman, in which he is critical of the emphasis that has been placed on land rights at the expense of social justice, can only add to this trend, as can the National Government's recently signed deal with Tainui, New Zealand's largest hapu or collection of subtribes, to settle all outstanding grievances for a lump-sum payment close to one billion dollars.[17] Finally, a new wave of Asian immigration in the 1990s from countries such as Japan, Taiwan, Korea, Hong Kong, Singapore and Malaysia is adding to the impetus for change. Unlike the political refugees from Vietnam who arrived a decade earlier, these immigrants tend to be wealthy and Western-educated, suggesting they will not stay quiet about their linguistic, cultural or political interests for very long.

The bicultural model of history-writing has also sustained heavy criticism from a number of eminent anthropologists belonging to the American academy. In March 1990, an article by Allon Hanson, bearing the controversial title 'Maori Myths Invented', appeared in the New Zealand Herald.[18] This asserted that crucial elements of Maori history and faith – specifically, the Great Fleet migration and the cult of the god Io – had no basis in fact but were the inventions either of Maori storytellers or of the Pakeha anthropologists who first tabulated Maori belief. There was nothing unusual about Hanson's claims: they conformed to a postmodernist anthropological practice called 'postcultural self-fashioning', which insists that there are no pure ethnicities. But what was unusual was his assumption that the bicultural model of history-writing would simply disappear under the weight of such revelations. What he failed to realise is that if local historians of Maori culture have not been attracted to the postcultural approach, it is not because they implicitly believe in the version of Maori myth devised by nineteenth-century anthropologists; rather, it is because they believe that in a political climate in which the appeal to indigenous history is being used to determine material outcomes, it would be unhelpful to indigenous groups if historians were to produce narratives that showed the mythical accounts of tribal origins to be mere fictions.

This was the view conveyed in the tribunal that was set up to respond to Hanson's article. Two members of the Maori Studies Department at Auckland University, Anne Salmond and Ranginui Walker, spoke against the American, arguing that 'cultural incursions by people unfamiliar at first hand with the language and customs of an indigenous people were at best irresponsible and at worst mischievous'. Walker added that 'it was politically as well as culturally insensitive to cast doubt on the authenticity of tribal memories at the very time the perceived accuracy of those memories was crucial in the negotiations being carried out for the restoration of Maori fishing rights'.[19] Others were angered by what they saw as Hanson's cultural-imperialist attitude: his belief that as a North

American scholar he was capable of a more sophisticated reading of the region's cultural history than were local scholars.

Certainly, Hanson's claim that bicultural histories were flawed because based on European versions of Maori myth should serve as a subtle reminder that the post-culturalist approach is frequently characterised by a blindness to the political uses to which history is being put in many postcolonial societies. On the other hand, Salmond's and Walker's counter-claim that 'truth' in this instance is a matter not of fact but of political expediency is itself belied by the fact that, in the treaty histories, myth is subsumed by a linguistic register that coincides with an epistemological notion of truth. It is problems such as these that have led a number of critics to conclude that a more satisfactory model of history-writing would be one that takes as a starting-point Jean-François Lyotard's notion of le différend, a term that marks that moment in a legal dispute when the claimants, finding that they have no equivalent language to that which the tribunal will admit, have their complaints dismissed. It is precisely because the concept of the différend uses the incompatibility of linguistic phrases to keep intact this notion of a basic injustice that it has been judged useful to the revisionist project.[20]

One local writer who has attempted to outline a model of history-writing using Lyotard's concept of the différend is Jonathan Lamb.[21] Lamb's concern is the crisis of history facing New Zealanders in the 1990s as they struggle to fend off a new wave of colonialism, this time in the form of the rationalist discourse of the marketplace. For Lamb, the problem is to find a historical discourse that is empowering for all New Zealanders, yet sensitive to the injustices incurred by Maori. According to him, this is a discourse in which difference would be recoverable again and again. What he finds useful about Lyotard's project is the way in which Lyotard refuses to let himself be defeated by the problem of difference that inheres in injustice; instead, he focuses all his energy on what Lamb calls 'the vigilant experience of the presence of the unpresentable' – a linguistic and aesthetic problematic that, he adds, is best conceptualised as the sublime.[22] Indeed, Lamb's own interest in the sublime is based on Lyotard's characterisation of it as the most serious engagement with injustice that we are capable of making. This is because the term describes that feeling of intense expectation which accompanies the awaiting of judgement, a feeling that has no sensuous form, but which nevertheless excites the mind sufficiently to admit of some sort of sensuous apprehension.[23]

For Lamb, the closest that New Zealand historians have come to the sublime notion of history to which Lyotard refers is the historical pageant that opened the 1990 Commonwealth Games. Here the organisers' decision to use a powerful blend of mythical and documentary modes was a sign that history was not being thought of as a 'truthful' narrative, but as a series of acute and spectacular events bristling with intensity and expectation. The comparison leads him to suggest that the most appropriate form of national history is one that turns history into 'an event of an event' as opposed to a continuous narrative of events.[24] It is because the sublime mode of historical representation disrupts the emphasis on seriality by transposing history to the realm of rhetoric that it answers to the problem posed by the différend.

Although Lamb's approach to the problem of history-writing successfully negotiates the contradictions characterising the treaty histories and the postcultural model, it is not without problems of its own, the most serious of which is its invocation of a discourse that pulls the rug from beneath epistemological certainties. Drawing on Nietzsche's concept of effective history, Lamb's sublime model of history operates in that discursive space which exists between the different linguistic registers represented, on one side, by 'fact' and, on the other, by 'fiction'. By dissolving the naturalised distinction between these two categories – a distinction that was empowering to imperialists – it shows that the narratives that compose European history are no more 'truthful', and can therefore claim no more authority, than the mythical narratives produced by Maori: both are the product of the sublime power that inheres in rhetoric.

To demonstrate his thesis, Lamb refers to a number of fictional histories from both the colonial and the postcolonial eras which operate in the rhetorical mode, arguing that these have much to teach New Zealand historians about intense expectation and the winning of belief. The texts he cites as most useful to the New Zealand revisionist project are John Hawkesworth's *Voyages*, Frederick Maning's *The Old Time Maori* and Ian Wedde's *Symme's Hole*, all of which, he says, are resistant to colonialism because they are not bound by the rules of logic that manufacture epistemological certainties; instead, they deploy 'frivolous observations founded on sophistical principles' to show that any certainty that the historian might gain from the pursuit of truth is kept in abeyance by the realisation that truth itself is underwritten by myth. While it is true (if I may still use the term) that such texts provide unique opportunities to reflect on the dynamics of power-relations in the colonial and postcolonial eras, it is equally true that they cannot provide present-day New Zealanders with the epistemological certainties needed for political struggle. In short, Lamb's model of history-writing constitutes a shift of register from the everyday to relatively abstruse European philosophical debates that offer little by way of solutions to the practical problems faced by both Maori and policy-makers. As such, it runs the risk of being seen as sublimely irrelevant, particularly by Maori for whom 'frivolous observations' and 'sophistical principles' are not of much use in a claims court.

This problem aside, Lamb's contribution to the bicultural debate is an important one, if only because he attempts to tackle the problem of theorising an historical model that is equally empowering to coloniser and colonised alike – something that will be necessary if bicultural histories are to move beyond the state-dominated, overly totalised model of New Zealand history being implemented at present. According to Frantz Fanon, the first phase of decolonisation involves mobilising the disenfranchised into a single political body that can assert itself against the coloniser.[25] It is to this phase of consciousness that I believe the treaty histories are addressed. Fanon also described the end-phase of the decolonisation process as a dissolving of the unitary ideals of the nation to allow for the

differences within. But he failed to explain how the change from unitary consciousness to inclusive consciousness was to be achieved. For example: will
empowering concepts such as the nation and identity need to be replaced by a
new set of terms which stresses the discontinuous and contradictory positionings
to be found within ethnic communities and subjects – or, as Judith Butler has
argued with respect to gender identity, will such concepts merely need to be
given new significations so that they come to be seen not as truths but as tactics?[26]

Lamb's sublime model of history-writing may indeed have much to teach the
New Zealand historian who is concerned to understand the process whereby the
first stage of decolonisation passes into the second, but there is still the problem
of how such theories are to be transposed to the classroom and to political practice. This is not the place to explain in detail how I would go about transcribing
such a model of history-writing from the realm of high theory to that of education policy and political practice. Suffice it to say that I would begin by asking:
why are so many theoretical models of history-writing consistently ignored by
Maori and policy-makers? Is it because, as some have maintained, such models are
inherently elitist, or is it because they fail to engage with the dominant relations
of power that inhere in the institutions which produce knowledge? This is to
imply that if critics of the present bicultural model want to develop a framework
of knowledge that is genuinely inclusive, and which does not run the risk of
remaining complicit with the very social order it seeks to overturn, then they will
need to do more than implement changes at the level of the canon or syllabus;
they will also need to challenge the existing structures of authority that govern
both identity and the prevailing social order.

In a similar vein, Henry A. Giroux has insisted that poststructuralist theory can
only hope to transform the public sphere of culture if, in addition to being
applied to texts, it is also brought to bear on the pedagogical practices of the classroom. According to Giroux, the analysis of the discursive conditions under which
history-writing is produced is necessary if the space of difference occupied by
insurgent groups is not to become a commodity that is absorbed into the prevailing system. Giroux's comments are designed to pave the way for a model of
history-writing that views individual and ethnic identity alike as both fragmented
and discontinuous. Such a model requires new structures of experience in which
the historian refuses the role of omniscient narrator. One purpose of such narratives would be to provide currently silenced groups with an inclusive and
polyvalenced form of self-representation; another would be to guarantee that the
dominant Anglo-Saxon culture figures as only one ethnic group alongside others,
instead of as a cultural marker against which otherness is defined.[27]

In the meantime, Maori are locked into the language of land rights, and while
land continues to be the main source of redress for Maori, histories based on a
concept of ethnic and individual identity look likely to remain in place. Nor, up
until very recently and despite efforts by American anthropologists and local academics such as Lamb to inject theory into policy debates, has the development of
a model of history-writing based on discontinuous notions of identity seemed to

be a priority amongst Pakeha historians and policy-makers, many of whom, in addition to seeing theory as elitist, have been more concerned to appease the radical elements within Maori society. I say 'up until very recently' because the events of the last few years suggest that biculturalism is no longer a priority among policy-makers. For example, in the fields of primary and secondary school education, the New English Syllabus was finally implemented in 1996 but without the compulsory Maori elements that the Labour Party had tried to introduce in 1988.

As with Maori, there are increasing numbers of Pakeha who have become disenchanted with the overly centralised, overly systematised structures of the state. Nor is this entirely the result of the massive economic and social upheavals that New Zealanders have endured in the last decade as successive governments have fought to shield an already faltering economy from the effects of global recession. It is rather attributable to the depoliticisation of the civil sphere that has been going on since the 1960s, following the success of the civil rights movement in the USA. Along with the Maori Renaissance, this saw the birth in the early 1970s of the women's liberation, peace (anti-nuclear), and environmental movements. These movements embraced a new political blueprint that was critical of the overly-regulated paradigm of the welfare state. Not only had this failed to ensure fair distribution of opportunity, power and wealth, particularly with regard to gender and ethnicity, but it had caused the realm of civil society to become colonised by bureaucracy. The new paradigm was announced by the arrival of fledgling activist organisations which came to occupy an intermediate political space between civil society and the structures of state and capital.[28] But it is not just Pakeha who have been abandoning the old style of politics based on workers' unions; the 1990s have seen a new generation of Maori leaders willing to seek radical policies from both the New Right and the left of the political spectrum. Indeed, in what has to be seen as one of the most bizarre political alliances to have been forged in the last decade, Donna Awatere herself, in 1991, joined the new break-away Labour party called ACT (Association of Consumers and Taxpayers) which at the time was headed by Sir Roger Douglas, the man who spearheaded New Zealand's free-market reforms. That this move represented disillusionment with Labour's efforts at Maori enfranchisement and a willingness to experiment with a pragmatic agenda that included substituting capitalism for socialism can be seen by the fact that during the 1996 election this party formed a strong alliance with the ruling National Party and, indeed, positioned itself economically even farther to the right. Awatere herself has recently declared that a commercial version of Marae democracy, in which assets that are returned to Maori are given to individual members of the tribe who are then free to trade them (within the tribe), will be more effective in returning power and resources to Maori than the pursuit of social welfare will be.[29]

It is not a coincidence, I believe, that the growing attacks on biculturalism have coincided with the collapse of the two-party system of government that saw New Zealand through its colonial phase and its re-entry into the global market over the last decade. The results of the 1993 general election and referendum, in which the

National Party held power by a one-seat majority, the Labour Party lost ground to the Alliance Party, and the country voted in favour of a system of mixed member proportional representation ('MMP'), were a clear indication that the days of two-party politics were over. In parliamentary democracies like New Zealand, the cultural policies implemented by state authorities will not always accurately mirror social and political trends. Nevertheless, to the extent that public policy is presided over by elected governments, it is susceptible to the mood-swings of society as a whole. If the swing towards participatory democracy which is evident at the level of national politics is anything to go by, changes in cultural policy will be only a matter of time in coming. Whether such changes will be sufficient to compel the state to resume its original policy of multiculturalism is at this stage uncertain. The first election held under 'MMP' in October 1996, which saw the New Zealand First Party (composed mainly of Maori) forming a coalition government with the ruling National Party, might suggest that support for biculturalism is likely to increase. The fact that the New Zealand First Party was opposed to Asian immigration would tend to confirm this. Conversely, since this alliance was formed at the expense of Maori voters' traditional allegiance to successive Labour governments, it could be understood as a further sign of Maori disenchantment with traditional leftist politics, if not also with the liberal model of biculturalism, and their willingness to take their chances with a more pluralist programme of culture. Equally uncertain is whether the phasing-out of biculturalism is even desirable, given that in many settler societies (such as the USA, Canada and Australia) in which multiculturalism has preceded biculturalism, indigenous peoples have tended to be treated as just one more ethnic group despite their claims to be originary or first peoples. A further problem with multiculturalism is that it arguably provides governments with even more opportunities than biculturalism does to covertly pursue a monoculturalist agenda behind the screen of a pluralist rhetoric. What is certain is that if some form of multiculturalism is to be once more placed on the nation's agenda, then the bicultural model of history-writing will need to become radically more inclusive.

NOTES

1 D. Awatere, 'In Search of Identity', in Centre for Continuing Education (ed.), In Search of Identity: University of Auckland, Winter Lecture Series, Auckland, University of Auckland, 1986, p. 79.
2 C. James, New Territory: The Transformation of New Zealand 1984–92, St Leonards, NSW, Australia, Allen & Unwin, 1992, p. 124.
3 ibid., pp. 124–8.
4 D. Pearson, 'Biculturalism and Multiculturalism in Comparative Perspective', in P. Spoonley, D. Pearson and C. Macpherson (eds), Nga Take: Ethnic Relations and Racism in Aotearoa/New Zealand, Palmerston Nth, Dunmore Press, 1991, pp. 209–10.
5 The traditionalist responses of both the New Right and the distinguished writer, C. K. Stead, probably contributed to the National Government's decision to delay the implementation of the Seventh-Form English syllabus when it was re-elected to office in

1991. Of the draft syllabus, Stead has said: 'The study of literature seems intended to serve national consciousness and moral correction (anti-sexist, anti-racist), rather than that enrichment of the imagination and opening of the sceptical intellect which was once its chief function and value. Thus the study of Patricia Grace (New Zealander, woman, Maori) becomes more important, more central, more imperatively indicated by the general thrust of the draft, than the study of Shakespeare or Dickens.' See Stead's 'English for the Sake of English', Dominion, Wellington, 22 March 1994, p. 10.

6 Te Aku Graham, 'Riding Someone Else's Waka: Academic Theory and Tribal Identity', in Suvendrini Perera (ed.), Asian and Pacific Inscriptions, Melbourne, Meridian, 1995, p. 47.

7 See R. Walker, 'The Meaning of Biculturalism', Pacific Issues, vol. 4, 1991, p. 22. See also his 'The Treaty of Waitangi as the Focus of Maori Protest', in W. Ihimaera (ed.), Te Ao Marama: Regaining Aotearoa – Maori Writers Speak Out, vol. 2, Auckland, Reed, 1993, p. 125.

8 Not only did many Maori tribes refuse to sign the treaty, but many other sections of the New Zealand community were also excluded. Among them were Maori women generally and women living in missionary and other European settlements, and Pakeha-Maori who, since the 1820s, had been employed in the local whaling industry and working as land dealers and general traders.

9 N. Te Awekotuku, 'Remembering Makereti', in her Mana Wahine Maori, Auckland, New Women's Press, 1991.

10 N. Te Awekotuku, 'Kia Mau, Kia Manawanui – We Will Never Go Away: Experiences of a Maori Lesbian Feminist', in R. Du Plessis (ed.), Feminist Voices: Women's Studies Texts for Aotearoa/New Zealand, Auckland, Oxford University Press, 1992, p. 288.

11 M. King, Moriori, London, Viking Penguin, 1990.

12 News of the Moriori appeal to the High Court to be heard by the Waitangi tribunal was first recorded in the National Business Review, 29 April 1994, p. 15. A report on the High Court's decision to allow the claim to be heard by the Waitangi tribunal appeared in the New Zealand Herald, 13 May 1994. For a detailed account of the history behind the claims, see Michael King, 'Moriori: A Pride Reborn', New Zealand Geographic, vol. 20, October–December 1993, pp. 76–84. As I write, in April 1997, there has still been no ruling in this case.

13 T. Loomis, 'The Politics of Ethnicity and Pacific Migrants', in Spoonley et al., Nga Take, pp. 43–5.

14 ibid., p. 45.

15 J. Sissons, 'Biculturalism, Bureaucracy and Tribal Democracy in Aotearoa/New Zealand', paper presented at the 'Post-colonial Formations: Nations, Culture, Policy' conference, Griffith University, Queensland, 7–10 July 1993.

16 Race Relations Conciliator, Race Against Time, Wellington, the Human Rights Commission, 1982.

17 At a recent Australian conference on the experience of native land title, the Waitangi tribunal chairman, Judge Edward Taihakurie Durie, was critical of the preponderance of land-claim settlements that 'create unequal compensation and pit tribe against tribe', and he mourned New Zealand's lack of progress on fundamental Maori needs, partly blaming the recent preoccupation with land claims (reported in the Australian, 25 February 1994, p. 11). For reports on the general Maori response to the National Government's land-settlement offer, see the Australian, 9 and 10 December 1994.

18 This article was an edited excerpt of a longer article which had earlier appeared in American Anthropologist; it is cited by J. Lamb in 'The New Zealand Sublime', Meanjin, vol. 49, no. 4, Summer 1990, p. 667.

19 ibid.

20 See J.-F. Lyotard, The Différend: Phrases in Dispute, trans. G. Van den Abbeele, Manchester, Manchester University Press, 1988, pp. 165–71.

21 Lamb's ideas are developed in two essays written while he was still resident in New Zealand: 'The New Zealand Sublime' and 'A Sublime Moment Off Poverty Bay, 9

October 1769', in G. McGregor and M. Williams (eds), *Dirty Silence: Aspects of Language and Literature in New Zealand*, Auckland, Oxford University Press, 1991, pp. 97–115.

22 Lamb, 'The New Zealand Sublime', p. 669.

23 ibid., p. 666.

24 ibid., p. 671.

25 F. Fanon, *The Wretched of the Earth*, Harmondsworth, Mx, Penguin, 1970, pp. 251–5.

26 For Butler, the concept of gender is not stable, it is rather performative because constituted through a stylised repetition of acts (bodily gestures, movements and enactments of various kinds) that are spatial rather than temporal. See J. Butler, 'Performative Acts and Gender Constitution: An Essay in Phenomenology and Feminist Theory', in S. Case (ed.), *Performing Feminisms: Feminist Critical Theory and Theatre*, Baltimore, MD, Johns Hopkins University Press, 1990, pp. 270–82. Similarly, de Certeau refers to a way of thinking (invested in a way of acting) which he calls the tactical responses of the weak. For de Certeau, small-scale acts of subversion (based on constant invention) constitute the only viable political responses available to individuals as well as to minority groups in today's highly regulated societies. See M. de Certeau, *The Practice of Everyday Life*, trans. S. F. Rendell, Berkeley, University of California Press, 1984.

27 Giroux has criticised policy that treats difference as authentic essence, arguing that the tendency to essentialise or exoticise 'otherness' is itself a form of nativistic retreat that serves to maintain traditional race, class and gender barriers. He has pointed out that for the nation to become genuinely democratised, subjectivity as well as agency will need to be rescued from the realm of essentialism. See H. A. Giroux, 'Poststructuralist Ruptures and Pedagogical Possibilities: The Turn Towards Theory', *Strategies*, vol. 7, 1993, pp. 10–30.

28 Sissons, 'Biculturalism, Bureaucracy and Tribal Democracy', pp. 3–4. For a much more detailed account of this process of depoliticisation, see A. Scott, *Ideology and the New Social Movements*, London, Unwin Hyman, 1990, pp. 13–19. According to Scott, the new social organisations sprang from the student movement of the 1960s which was anti-authoritarian and resisted incorporation into institutionalised politics; it was from this movement also that they obtained a preference for a loose organisational structure and a stress on lifestyles more than on political issues. Hence, in contrast to the workers' movement whose aim is to seize power, it was their ambition to mobilise civil society by transforming the sphere of culture.

29 D. Awatere Huata, *My Journey*, Auckland, Seaview Press, 1996, p. 102.

14

THE TECHNOLOGY OF ETHNICITY

Canadian multiculturalism and the language of law[1]

Smaro Kamboureli

In Canada, as elsewhere today, problems regarding the representation of otherness figure with a tenacity that has put considerable pressure on all those involved in practices affecting the cultural and political economy of the country. Be it the aboriginal peoples' right to self-government, or Quebec as a 'distinct society', or race, gender and ethnicity as perceived by the Canada Council, the Secretary of State, and other state and cultural agencies, otherness as a synonym for ethnic and/or racial minoritisation is riddled with the desire, indeed the imperative, to be described and re-constructed. It is certainly not accidental that at a time when we are warned daily against the dangers of cultural appropriation, we are also made witnesses to a slowly emerging new polity of the space we have come to know as Canada.

What Charles Taylor calls '"difference-blindness", "a politics of universalism, emphasizing the equal dignity of all citizens"',[2] which might have been, at least nominally, an accurate description of the Canadian status quo until recently, is currently, as Canadian liberalists would have it, under siege by what Taylor calls 'a politics of difference', a politics whereby 'everyone should be recognized for his or her unique identity'.[3] Yet the present climate of Canadian cultural politics seems to have produced an aporia – that moment and space fraught with the ambiguity engendered when difference disrupts the dialectic of 'centre' and 'margin'. The controversy, for example, over the conference 'Writing Thru Race', a controversy that took the Writers' Union of Canada and the mass media by storm a few years ago, spoke of the anxieties, cultural traumas and self-defence mechanisms that come into play when the relationships between society and culture are reformulated with the intention to redistribute power. 'Writing Thru Race: A Conference for First Nations Writers and Writers of Colour' (Vancouver, June–July 1994), organised by the Writers' Union of Canada Racial Minority Writers' Committee (chaired by Roy Miki), announced in March 1994 that enrolment of participants would be limited to First Nations writers and writers of colour. This, together with the fact that the conference was publicly funded by the Canada Council (among others), elicited what might be safely described as a hysterical response from both individual white writers and the media. The comment of Robert Fulford, a columnist for the *Globe and Mail*, that the conference was an instance of 'reinventing apartheid' sums up both the rhetoric and the ideological vestiges of universalism characteristic of most of the media coverage this event attracted. 'We have apparently moved', Fulford claimed,

> from the era of pluralism to the era of multiculturalism. The old liberal pluralism holds that each of us has rights as an individual. . . . The new multiculturalism, on the other hand, focuses on the rights of groups, and sees each of us as the member of a racially designated cluster.[4]

Miki's response to this column exposed 'the kind of pluralism Mr. Fulford yearns for really [as] the resurrected form of an earlier assimilationist ideology that was used historically to promote Anglo-European values and traditions as the Canadian norm'.[5] The public friction that surrounded this conference is not an isolated phenomenon; if anything, it exemplifies how volatile the interstitial space is that Canadian cultural politics continues to inhabit.

Indisputably, the metanarratives of Canadian state discourse – the Constitution, the Charter of Rights, the Official Languages Act – and of the Canadian literary 'canon' have fallen into relative disarray. Yet the signs that might be read as symptoms of a cultural and political malaise might also be seen as indicating a healthier course of affairs. For example, the vigorous debates about the Constitution since1987 and the ensuing 1992 referendum might have threatened, as Taylor put it, to cause 'the impending breakup of the country',[6] but they have been necessary stages in Canada's ongoing attempts to un-learn its colonial legacy by learning to understand and respect racial and cultural differences. Similarly, the changes taking place in the modes of production, reception, and institutionalisation of Canadian literature are informed by the common resolve to examine cultural practices from the point of view of power relations that had previously proven inscrutable – or, worse, invisible. Whatever the stakes might be in these cultural and political debates, there is one recurring point of great importance, namely, the increasing awareness that the political and the cultural are inextricably interrelated, that they in fact inhabit the same discursive site.

This convergence of previously exclusionary discourses and sites reflects, among other things, the new designation allotted to issues of minoritisation. The racial and pedagogical conflicts currently afflicting a number of Canadian universities, whether they come under the rubric of 'academic freedom' or proposed 'codes of ethics', are likewise determined by the same disjunctions occurring as the result of the perceived need to recast and articulate the meanings and positions of racial, ethnic and gender differences. 'The social articulation of difference, from the minority perspective', as Homi Bhabha argues, 'is a complex, ongoing negotiation that seeks to authorise cultural hybridities that emerge in moments of historical transformation.'[7] It is these kinds of negotiations that are practised today in Canada's cultural politics. Whatever the ideological allegiances of the various contesting groups, there is a consensual agreement that we must carry on with such negotiations and do so in an interdisciplinary fashion that corresponds to the diversity of concerns at hand.

Together with the increasing number of interdisciplinary conferences about multiculturalism, two recent critical volumes, *Ethnicity and Culture in Canada: The Research Landscape* and *Returning the Gaze: Essays on Racism, Feminism and Politics*,[8] mark this new entrenched awareness that the representation of otherness cannot be examined in isolation from such political and institutional realities as Canada's official policy of multiculturalism. Such interdisciplinary events are not simply instances of methodological changes; they reflect the urgent need to address the materiality of difference in ways that would broaden our terms of reference without reproducing the old polarities in the guise of benevolent hegemonies.

Within this context of political and cultural negotiations, ethnic literary discourse no longer assigns a Canadian writer to a position of relative marginality. It has recently achieved a currency that allows it to go beyond its narrowly defined image of otherness.[9] But is the circulatory power of ethnic discourse today indicative of the success of multiculturalism? Or is it the symptom of a culture in which, to use Michael Ryan's words, 'the contradictions that arise within . . . are resolved in ways that assure the continuation of a ruling group's hegemony'?[10] And for that matter, how are we to reconcile, if at all, the simultaneous rise of marginal discourses and the debate about cultural appropriation? Furthermore, to what extent does Canada's multicultural policy relate to the multicultural conditions of Canadians and ethnic literary discourse?

My discussion here will focus on the state inscription of multiculturalism and how it has been posited and employed as the context and supportive ground of ethnic discourse. E. D. Blodgett's essay, 'Ethnic Writing in Canadian Literature as Paratext', has already begun this discussion. Through his 'brief reading' of the *Report of the Royal Commission on Bilingualism and Biculturalism*, which he sees 'as a discursive origin for the discussion of ethnicity in Canada',[11] Blodgett demonstrates 'how the term "ethnic" is defined and understood in official Canadian discourse';[12] yet he also proceeds to show that the problems intrinsic to discussions of ethnicity lie not merely in the language of the Report, 'but also in the language of ethnic groups in their relation to the official languages'.[13] I wish to extend this argument by attempting to delineate what constitutes the technology of ethnicity as it is effected by the Canadian Multiculturalism Act.

Technology, as what produces and includes the apparatuses of the discourses that contain us, accounts for the ways that knowledge is both constructed and imparted. This knowledge is never homogeneous: ethnicity, a cultural synonym of otherness and incommensurability, has become a sign of differentiating practices determined from within and outside. It would not suffice, therefore, to listen only to the knowledge produced by ethnic writers themselves, not because the

ethnic subject is unrepresentable as other – that would immediately render it transcendental – but because the ethnic subject is a product of a knitting-together of
political, social and cultural forces. When it speaks of and through itself, the
ethnic subject also speaks back to what defines it and thus delimits it as ethnic.
Even when the ethnic subject seems to be entirely motivated by a discourse of
resistance to the surrounding hegemonic discourses, it never distances itself completely from them. Ethnic subjectivity is never utterly free and of itself; its
impurity is not an element intrinsic to its ethnicity. This does not mean, however,
that ethnic subjectivity becomes utterly alloyed, thus losing its signature of otherness. Rather, it suggests that the technology of ethnicity, what produces and is
produced by it, is part and parcel of the larger systems within which it operates.
Despite the ongoing attempts to come to terms with it through various definitions, ethnic subjectivity appears to be constantly in a transitional state.

Social and cultural attitudes and the ways they regraph the 'centre' and the
'margins' of Canadian society and its literary tradition keep redrawing the maps
of meaning that are meant to organise our understanding of ethnicity. In Canada,
these maps of meaning are designated by legislation in rather a firm manner that
inevitably determines the technology of ethnicity. How, then, does legal discourse
relate to ethnic literary discourse? To what extent is ethnicity effected by the letter
of the law? What are the contesting forces that characterise their relations? What
is the difference between multiculturalism as legislated by the state and multiculturalism as operating within the state? These are only some of the questions that
one ought to ask in order to understand the complexity of the representation of
ethnicity. I will attempt to deal with some of these questions by offering a textual reading of the discourse of Bill C-93, the Canadian Multiculturalism Act. My
purpose is to reverse the critical practice of taking ethnic literature to be the measure of multicultural realities, and to do so by looking at the very text that has
given that literature its official impetus and legitimation.

TRANSLATING ACTS

The Canadian Multiculturalism Act/*Loi sur le multiculturalisme canadien* is issued, as is
the convention of federal documents, in two parallel columns of English and
French texts. The Act/Loi is already more than one act even before we begin to
read it. It posits itself at once as a law and as an act of translation, but it is not
exactly clear which of the two texts is the translation of the other. In fact, the
very notion of translation – having a source text that operates as the origin and
semantic double of a text written in a different language – is suspended by the
document itself, which declares that 'the Constitution of Canada and the Official
Languages Act provide that English and French are the official languages of
Canada and neither abrogates nor derogates from any rights or privileges
acquired or enjoyed with respect to any other language'.[14] Translation is also put
under erasure not only because I have obviously cited the Bill in English alone,

but also by the fact that the two texts are not, strictly speaking, translations of each other.

The premise that in translation 'the forms must be altered if one is to preserve the content' because 'all languages differ in form'[15] is not exactly applicable here. The French version of the section cited above differs from its English equivalent by going beyond alterations made for the sake of faithfully translating meaning. We read, for instance, that the Constitution of Canada 'proclame . . . le statut du français et de l'anglais comme langues officielles du Canada'.[16] The order in which French/*français* and English/*anglais* appear in the two versions of the document asserts respectively each language's claim to official status, the result being textual and political asymmetry. The law of language introduces a cultural syntax of ago-nistic relations that exceeds the intentionality of the legal text itself; in fact it reveals contestation to be what produces the discursive site of ethnic otherness.

The relationship between the English and the French texts of the document, then, is both dialectical and diacritical. At the same time that the document as a whole affirms the official status equally shared by both English and French, thus constituting a balancing relationship, the French and the English texts establish a differential relationship to each other that deconstructs on a linguistic level the mastery purportedly claimed by both of them. As each language becomes an ana-logue of the other in its strategies of articulation, it is obvious that legitimacy of law is linked to mastery of language. As Stanley Fish has shown, the textuality of law operates in much the same way as it does in any literary enterprise.[17] The agency of language deconstructs the master narrative that law presumably con-structs. English and French in this Act, far from being each other's formal mirrors, mediate between legal discourse and its application. Since both languages are offi-cial, neither of them needs to be translated into the other, yet their simultaneous existence in the Act renders them translations, the 'other' a translation of 'itself'. The apparent contestation between them demonstrates how tenuous Bill C-93 is as a site of cultural policy.

At the same time, however, the common epithet attributed to English and French, official/*officielle*, functions both as a matter of law and as a signifier point-ing inadvertently to those languages in Canada that are not declared to be official. Although avoiding the singularity of monolingualism and ethnocentrism, the Official Languages Act, as embedded in Bill C-93, asserts its own epistemological laws, which in turn institute Canadian cultural diversity. Law, which cannot exist outside of language, legislates language and culture; it adjudicates on the very medium that allows it to operate. But how does the law of language/s relate to the laws of language itself? The rhetoric of Bill C-93 reflects the means by which it represents and legislates on ethnicity; it also shows how the ethnic subject as it is imaged by legal discourse produces a discourse that potentially alienates it from itself.

The paradox inherent in the doubleness of official discourse and its verbal strat-agems structures the immediate legal frame within which ethnicity is located. This is further complicated by yet another official discourse – the then Prime Minister

212

Pierre E. Trudeau's statements made in the White Paper on multiculturalism in October 1971. This announcement of the multicultural policy in the House of Commons functions as a supplement to the Official Languages Act and as a sub-text to Bill C-93.[18] Trudeau's brief comments at once legislate and explicate, thus attempting to foreclose any misprision of the policy, or at least of the government's intentions. As the White Paper states, 'although there are two official languages, there is no official culture, nor does any ethnic group take precedence over any other'.[19] Behind the self-contradictory, if not impossible, intention of keeping language and culture apart, there is the implication that the government is reluctant, in fact unwilling, to acknowledge an official culture. But the contradictions do not end here. What the White Paper enunciates is that, despite the presence of two official languages, there is an absence of an official culture. 'Official' here seems to operate as a synonym for 'legally endorsed'; it also functions as the blind spot in this legal discourse, for, in refusing to acknowledge the materiality of language and its interrelatedness to culture, it disregards the fact that the dominant culture in all provinces outside of Quebec is anglophone.

The simultaneously centripetal and centrifugal directions of this argument endeavour, paradoxically, to create unity out of diversity. The heteroglossia of multiculturalism – what Mikhail Bakhtin would say 'permits a multiplicity of social voices and a wide variety of their links and interrelationships' to coexist[20] – is thwarted. While the Official Languages Act sets a linguistic imperative, the mandate of this imperative is purportedly limited in its capacity to condition or occasion cultural creativity. In the meantime, multiculturalism is postulated within a textual field that has, at least theoretically, a conflicting relationship with it. Whereas translation was bracketed in regard to the two official languages, it is insinuated here as the vehicle of multicultural expression. The quandary that emerges from this intertext encountered early in the Multiculturalism Act speaks of what the Act remains silent about, namely the political agendas behind its implementation: the increasing awareness, at the time that Bill C-93 was tabled, that there was an 'ethnic vote' to be captured, as well as the desire to appease and deflect the resistance that official bilingualism introduced both in Quebec and among anglophones, especially those residing in the Western provinces.

It is against this already differential site that the main text of Bill C-93 is introduced. It is framed by eight 'preambles', subordinate clauses beginning with 'whereas', that locate the Act within the contexts of the Constitution and of such other acts as the Citizenship Act, the Canadian Human Rights Act and the International Covenant on Civil and Political Rights. These preambles establish a cause-and-effect relationship that introduces the Act as a consequence of the Constitution and, more specifically, as an Act that repeats, but also interprets through its process of repetition, what the Constitution already states with regard to the 'multicultural heritage of Canadians'.[21]

The preambles of the Act have a clearly iterative function in that they form part of a speech act that is bound to a specific site, namely, the legal discourses that precede it. The Act's interpretative challenge of the Constitution as a legal narrative of cohesiveness implies that a new set of laws is needed, given the developments of the state's and society's affairs. To borrow Ryan's words, 'no determination of meaning', including legal meaning, 'can detach itself from a context without which there could be no meaning'.[22] As a specific reading of the Constitution, Bill C-93 affirms the fact that Canada is, relatively speaking, a new state still in the process of becoming, because of its colonial and postcolonial history. There is, then, a double (and paradoxical) inscription in this legislation on ethnicity: the ethnic subject's resistance to acculturation within a state that still attempts to define itself, and the perceived potentiality of ethnicity to infiltrate the dominant culture/s.

Legislating on ethnicity signals both a recognition of the existing ethnic diversity and a desire to curtail the phenomenon of disparity, or at the very least to overlook the multiple factors that have made ethnicity such an issue of complexity in Canada. Indeed, I think it is significant that nowhere in the Act is there a reference to immigrants. We read only about 'Canadians', the 'aboriginal peoples' and 'persons belonging to ethnic, religious or linguistic minorities'. As the late Canadian historian Robert F. Harney remarked, 'leaders have generally preferred to think of those they represent as ethnic groups rather than immigrant groups since *immigrant* conjures up the thresholds of acculturation while *ethnic* implies a permanent quality of otherness'.[23] An immigrant is an outsider whose difference is defined by her or his origins, whereas the ethnic subject's difference (however visible or pronounced the traces of that difference might be) is defined by the surrounding culture. This (un)naming act, although nowhere thematised in Bill C-93, reinforces the legal ground that absorbs ethnicity into a formal and situational policy. In this context, the intertextuality structuring the Bill is at once a snag catching at the Constitution's sovereignty as a master narrative and a strategy of delay in articulating the conditions that determine ethnicity. It becomes clear, then, why the Act constitutes the technology that produces ethnicity. Whereas the ethnic subject remains undifferentiated in the Act and therefore essentialised, ethnicity becomes manifest as a practice of legal discourse. It is the law that embodies the materiality of cultural difference. The technology of ethnicity is effected by what the Act articulates and that articulation inheres in the tropes of its own representation.

NATIONAL ADDRESS

From this elaborate intertextuality of multiculturalism there emerges what Bhabha calls 'the nation as a form of narrative – textual strategies, metaphoric displacements, sub-texts and figurative stratagems'.[24] Such a nation-narrative, however, does not operate rhetorically alone, as the rhetorical figures of Bhabha's statement might suggest; its rhetoric of articulation performs a political act as well. The intent of Bill C-93's narrational devices is concomitant with the interpretation it offers of ethnicity. This is made clear in the central mandate of official multiculturalism, which is to assist in the 'preservation and enhancement' of ethnicity.[25] But this laudable (as it would seem) double intent begs the question of apostrophe. To whom does Bill C-93 address itself? What are the referents of multiculturalism? Is multiculturalism postulated as the supplement to a dominant culture that is persistently occulted by the discourse of the Act? Or is it unwittingly posited as the Canadian culture *par excellence*, since we have been told that there is no official culture? And what is the ethos of this apostrophe?

The indeterminacy that characterises the apostrophised subject in the Act echoes the instability of postmodern subjectivity. Furthermore, it points to the instantiation of the crisis characterising the technology of ethnicity, occurring, as it does, precisely at the point where law and culture meet. Bill C-93 apostrophises 'all Canadians, whether by birth or by choice'.[26] But if all Canadians are indeed the subject of apostrophe here, and if Bill C-93 makes the subject of its discourse multiculturalism, in that it 'reflects the cultural and racial diversity of Canadian society',[27] ethnicity is put under erasure. Or, more precisely, although a condition of difference that becomes an instrument of marginalisation in Canada, ethnicity is rendered by official multiculturalism as something residual to it. For whereas the Act recognises 'the diversity of Canadians as regards to race, *national or ethnic origin*, colour and religion' (my emphasis), it addresses no specific group of Canadians as ethnic. In this context, ethnicity loses its differential marker and becomes instead a condition of commonality: what all Canadians have in common is ethnic difference.

Ethnicity thus abandons its function as a nation-narrative whose particular origins might unsettle the larger cultural narrative within which it is embedded; it becomes an all-embracing concept characterising Canada. Seen in this way, it operates in a similar fashion to that in which, Bhabha argues, a national culture does: it is

> neither unified nor unitary in relation to itself, nor must it be seen simply as 'other' in relation to what is outside or beyond it. The . . . problem of outside/inside must always itself be a process of hybridity, incorporating new 'people' in relation to the body politic, generating other sites of meaning and, inevitably, in the political process, producing unmanned sites of political antagonism and unpredictable forces for political representation.[28]

The fact that the 'Canadians' referred to in the Bill are the same ones regarded as 'ethnic' attests to the diversity that 'Canadian' has come to signify. But if this kind of diversity has come to be the national signature of Canada, it becomes apparent that biculturalism and multiculturalism can coexist only as contradictory institutions whose viability depends on cancelling each other out.[29]

It would seem, then, that the legal discourse of the Act endorses and appropriates *ethnos* (nation) with no minority or marginal overtones attached to it. This strategy, however, creates more aporias than it resolves. Canada is conceptualised as a nation-narrative whose mark of difference consists not so much of the hybridity that Bhabha talks about, as of yet another kind of commonality: all Canadians are members of the same *ethnos*, Canada. Such a deconstructive reading of Canada, though, shows the extent to which the Act suspends temporality by operating synchronically: it dehistoricises the social and political conditions that have occasioned it, and it deprivileges the origins of individual Canadians by crediting only their here and now. Traditionally, of course, historical specificity does not enter the formal expressions of legal discourse because they operate within a general economy of language. But the abeyance of the Act's historicity is misleading, for it does not broach the contesting forces that frame ethnicity. The result is that Bill C-93 functions as a speech act of legal positivism. Although, as Chief Justice Antonio Lamer of the Supreme Court of Canada remarks, 'legal positivism [which] says that what is right is what the law says is right'[30] was put to an end in Canada in 1982 by the Charter of Rights and Freedoms, the Act (tabled in 1987) still operates upon that premise. The overdetermination intrinsic to the textuality of legal discourse accounts, at least partly, for the reasons why the Act reproduces what it attempts to remedy. It is a text mimicking its *raison d'être*, but only partially mimicked by those it attempts to legislate for. The positivism behind the all-inclusiveness of the signifier 'Canadians', rather than being a sign of egalitarianism, appropriates difference. By not employing a diachronic approach, as is suggested by its appropriation of *ethnos*, Bill C-93 puts in abeyance the ethnic signature of Canadians who originated in places other than Canada.

The homogeneity which is attributed rhetorically to 'all Canadians' is, interestingly enough, deconstructed by an exclusionary clause in the Act. The definition of 'federal institution' in the 'Interpretation' section of Bill C-93 which lists those institutions in charge of implementing the multicultural policy does not include

> (c) any institution of the Council or Government of the Northwest Territories or the Yukon Territory, or

> (d) any Indian band, band council or other body established to perform a governmental function in relation to an Indian band or other group of aboriginal people.

It remains textually ambiguous whether these institutions and councils are excluded because the aboriginal peoples are not deemed part of the Act's pan-Canadianism, or because they deserve 'distinct' treatment, given their aboriginal claims and rights. This exclusionary strategy, together with the Act's universalising rhetoric, which is reinforced by the recurrence of such phrases as 'all members of Canadian society', evinces the contradictions inherent in Bill C-93. Official multiculturalism addresses all Canadians irrespective of their different national origins, but in doing so it places the ethnic subject in a 'fictional' position.[31] The marginality of the groups that Bill C-93 seeks to protect is nullified by

216

its rhetoric of normalisation. The 'norm', as François Ewald argues, 'is related to power, but it is characterised less by the use of force or violence than by an implicit logic that allows power to reflect upon its own strategies and clearly define its objects'.[32] Defining the ethnic subject by normalising it, then, stresses those elements of its subjecthood that conform to 'Canadianness' rather than those about which it begs to differ.

Furthermore, this pan-Canadianness is symptomatic of one of the most important points in Bill C-93, the construction of ethnicity through a collective subjecthood, and the institutionalisation of otherness. Although in many clauses of the Act we find 'individuals and communities' brought together, the emphasis is largely placed upon 'communities', 'organisations' and 'institutions' that represent the 'diverse cultures of Canadian society'.[33] In the section of the Act regarding the 'Implementation of the Multiculturalism Policy of Canada', the Minister responsible is expected to 'encourage and assist individuals, organizations and institutions to project the multicultural reality of Canada in their activities in Canada and abroad'.[34] Yet, if we are to read into this clause the sub-text of the White Paper mentioned above, it becomes obvious that the individuality of a person is measured and acknowledged primarily through that person's ties with a specific community. 'The royal commission', Trudeau said in the White Paper,

> was guided by the belief that adherence to one's ethnic group is influenced not so much by one's origin or mother tongue as by one's sense of belonging to the group, and by what the commission calls the group's 'collective will to exist'. The government shares this belief.[35]

This statement clearly reflects the state's desire to forge a collective image of ethnicity, an image intended to construct a state that is at once centralised and decentred in that it seems to exist within the spaces linking the communities of the various 'ethnic' groups.

In the preamble to Bill C-93, as we have seen, the origins and mother tongues of the two 'heritage' groups were taken to be the parameters informing, in fact necessitating, bilingualism. Origin with regard to French and English was taken to be a natural law, its 'naturalness' being affirmed and protected by the law of the state. With the advent of official multiculturalism, however, the importance of mother tongue and ethnic origin is suspended, the implication being that they are not the determining factors of ethnic subjectivity. But if this is the case, what contributes to the cohesiveness so necessary for the construction of a community? And, moreover, what constitutes the Canadianness of subjects who share a common language and origin that is other than English and French? The Act remains silent on this matter.

Nevertheless, the points about which the Act is specific help clarify some of these paradoxes. In section 5 we read that in the implementation of this policy, the Minister 'may . . . assist ethno-cultural minority communities to conduct activities with a view to overcoming any discriminatory barrier and, in particular, discrimination based on race or national or ethnic origin'.[36] In confirming that the principal imperative of multiculturalism is to preserve and enhance the cultures of minority groups, this statement rebuts what various legislators and politicians have taken pains over the years to deny, namely, that there is a dominant culture.[37] Ironically, however, the benefits of this acknowledgment are curtailed by the Act's decree of 'preservation' and 'enhancement'. Preserving ethnicity is a suspect enterprise, for how could one preserve something as indeterminate and diverse as the ethnic subject? Preservation, in this context, suggests treating ethnicity as a museum case, if not as an object of anthropological and sociological enquiry. It depicts the ethnic subject as a stable entity whose characteristics are already fossilised, or are seen as exotica – what 'ethnic' has really come to signify in common parlance. By the same token, the beautifying, if not evolutionary or assimilatory, overtones of the intention to 'enhance' ethnicity are equally troubling. Enhancing ethnicity suggests its commodification through an agency over which the ethnic subject might have little control. Although the double intent of preserving and enhancing ethnicity acknowledges the presence of nation-narratives not indigenous to Canada, it does so in a contained fashion; it privileges the group identity of a community at the expense of its individual members, thereby not taking into account the identity politics inherent in such a situation.[38] The result might very well be what has been termed 'third solitude' or 'other solitudes'.[39] The difference of ethnic otherness is recognised not as a sign, with the sign's intrinsic potential for modified meaning, but as a symbol whose meaning is to be preserved and therefore fixed. Paradoxically, the law behaves like the dominant society within which it wishes to protest the equality of the ethnic subject. This ironic reversal is, I think, a symptom of Canadian society's and literature's pathology about origins and identity.

AUTHORING ACTS

So far I have tried to show that official multiculturalism grants ethnicity subjectivity, but it does so without granting it agency. But who or what gives agency to the Act itself? Who authors it? Despite its many contexts and intertexts, the Act appears at first to be an orphaned text. As a legislative bill, it bears the marks of a negotiating and bargaining process that is not assigned the responsibility accompanying the singularity of authorial signature. This is yet another reason why we cannot begin to interpret it as a textual entity that has fully disclosed itself to its readers. In Joseph Vining's words, 'that is not the situation in law'.[40] Vining observes that:

> When a practitioner asks, 'What is the law here? How is this case to be analyzed?' no hand thrusts out a text and says, 'Here, this is what we are now going to read and construe'. Interpretation in law is, from the beginning, of the law.[41]

This is indeed the case here – both literally and figuratively.

The particular intertexts of Bill C-93 that I have mentioned, and others that I do not have space to examine here,[42] indicate that the author/authority argument about a legal text is potentially far more complex than that of its literary equivalent. To quote Vining again: 'the most signal feature of legal discourse . . . [is] that writers of legal texts do not speak for themselves'.[43] Who does Bill C-93 speak for, then? At the end of its 'preamble' section, the Act is attributed to a single, and singular, figure: 'NOW, THEREFORE, Her Majesty, by and with the advice and consent of the Senate and House of Commons of Canada, enacts as follows'.[44] The reference to Elizabeth II, Queen of Canada, is a matter of both rhetorical and constitutional significance. It constitutes the one and only specific act of naming, a speech act that directly invites the readers to construe Bill C-93 as what it really is: a recasting, however radical, of Canada's colonial legacy.

This instance of nomination can be seen, then, as a sign that functions as a figure both of litotes and of catachresis. Through the trope of prosopopoeia, Her Majesty discloses the de-facement of the state: how the state operates as an institutional machine, and the degree to which it loses face, so to speak, by deferring to Elizabeth II. Yet the power of Her Majesty is pre-empted in that the state is itself personified by the senators and members of Parliament without whose 'advice and consent' she cannot enact. The contradictory and ambivalent relationship of advice and consent encapsulates the historical and ideological complicity that is at the heart of this Act. Through the regal decorum surrounding her, the queen is at once spoken about and speaking. She authors the Act, but her authority is only nominal. Nevertheless, as I have already hinted, it is her name that enunciates the complicitous relations Bill C-93 addresses: the figure of Her Majesty 'stands for' the colonial and postcolonial condition of Canada.

Although hardly an original disclosure, the dénouement of this reading is important, for it underscores the extent to which Bill C-93 impinges upon the ambiguities entrenched in the concept of ethnicity. If the Canadian Multiculturalism Act is to be taken as a formal and formative instance in Canadian cultural politics, it can also be seen as an instance potentially extending, if not perpetuating, the colonial features it contains. 'The rhetoric of law', according to Brook Thomas, 'helps to maintain order at the price of disguising or denying the conflicts produced by the existing order, thereby helping to legitimate that order.'[45] Reading Bill C-93 closely as a text has allowed me, I trust, to show that acknowledgment of ethnic difference – or what Taylor terms 'the politics of recognition' – does not eliminate the problems of the representation of otherness. If anything, it reinforces the epistemological structure of representation, which is to say, the degree to which representation is a matter of the relations between power and knowledge.

NOTES

1 This essay was researched and written with the help of a grant from the Social Sciences and Humanities Research Council of Canada. An earlier version of the essay appeared in *Open Letter*, vol. 8, nos. 5–6, Winter–Spring 1993, pp. 202–17.

2 C. Taylor in Amy Gutmann (ed.), *Multiculturalism and 'The Politics of Recognition'*, Princeton, NJ, Princeton University Press, 1992, p. 37.

3 ibid., p. 38.

4 R. Fulford, 'George Orwell, Call Your Office', *Globe and Mail*, 30 March 1994, p. A10.

5 R. Miki, 'Why We're Holding the Vancouver Conference', Commentary, *Globe and Mail*, 7 April 1994, p. A17.

6 Taylor, in *Multiculturalism and 'The Politics of Recognition'*, p. 52.

7 H. Bhabha, *The Location of Culture*, London and New York, Routledge, 1994, p. 2.

8 J. Berry and J. Laponce (eds), *Ethnicity and Culture in Canada: The Research Landscape*, Toronto, Toronto University Press, 1994; and H. Bannerji (ed.), *Returning the Gaze: Essays on Racism, Feminism and Politics*, Toronto, Sister Vision Press, 1993.

9 Writers like Joy Kogawa, Sky Lee, Neil Bissoondath, Nino Ricci, Rohinton Mistry, Evelyn Lau and Thomas King have received nominations, and some of them prestigious awards, that only until a few years ago would have gone almost automatically to mainstream Anglo-Saxon authors. Even a cursory look at the catalogues of the many small presses in Canada that specialise in issues of race, ethnicity and sexual preference would testify to the demand for 'minority' writing. On some of the complex aspects characterising the success of certain ethnic writing, see my essay 'Of Black Angels and Melancholy Lovers: Ethnicity and Writing in Canada', in S. Gunew and A. Yeatman (eds), *The Politics of Difference*, Sydney, Allen & Unwin, 1993, pp. 143–56.

10 M. Ryan, *Politics and Culture: Working Hypotheses for a Post-Revolutionary Society*, Baltimore, MD, Johns Hopkins University Press, 1989, p. 11.

11 E. D. Blodgett, 'Ethnic Writing in Canadian Literature as Paratext', *Signature*, no. 3, Summer 1990, p. 15.

12 ibid., p. 13.

13 ibid., p. 15.

14 Canadian Multiculturalism Act, p. 835. The Act was passed by the Parliament of Canada and assented to on 21 July 1988.

15 E. Nida and C. Taber, *The Theory and Practice of Translation*, Leiden, Netherlands, E. J. Brill, 1974, p. 5.

16 Canadian Multiculturalism Act, p. 835.

17 See, especially, his essay 'Fish v. Fiss', in S. Fish, *Doing What Comes Naturally: Change, Rhetoric, and the Practice of Theory in Literary and Legal Studies*, Durham, NC, Duke University Press, 1989, p. 135.

18 This speech was the government's response to Book IV of the *Report of the Royal Commission on Bilingualism and Biculturalism*. 'Trudeau's pronouncement', as Robert F. Harney notes, was 'his first and last parliamentary utterance on the issue.' As Harney, among others, also points out, between the White Paper and Bill C-93, 'brought to the House of Commons late in 1987, there has been no enabling legislation of any kind about multiculturalism or ethnic group rights'; however, 'since 1973, there has been a multiculturalism directorate within the Department of the Secretary of State' that administers 'grants to scholars, ·the arts, and ethnocommunity organizations'. R. Harney, '"So Great a Heritage of Ours": Immigration and the Survival of the Canadian Polity', *Daedalus*, vol. 117, no. 4, Fall 1988, p. 72.

19 White Paper (Announcement of Implementation of Policy of Multiculturalism within Bilingual Framework), House of Commons, 8 October 1971, p. 8545.

20 M. Bakhtin, *The Dialogic Imagination: Four Essays*, ed. M. Holquist, trans. C. Emerson and M. Holquist, Austin, University of Texas Press, 1981, p. 263.

21 Canadian Multiculturalism Act, p. 835.
22 Ryan, *Politics and Culture*, p. 180.
23 Harney, '"So Great a Heritage of Ours"', p. 68.
24 H. Bhabha, 'Introduction: Narrating the Nation', in H. Bhabha (ed.), *Nation and Narration*, London and New York, Routledge, 1990, p. 2.
25 Canadian Multiculturalism Act, p. 835.
26 ibid.
27 ibid., p. 837.
28 Bhabha, 'Introduction: Narrating the Nation', p. 4.
29 This contestatory relationship of bilingualism and multiculturalism has been addressed in other contexts as well. See, for example, E. Kallen, 'Multiculturalism: Ideology, Policy and Reality', *Journal of Canadian Studies*, vol. 17, no. 1, Spring 1982, pp. 51–63. See also Y. Abu-Laban and D. Stasiulis, 'Ethnic Pluralism under Siege: Popular and Partisan Opposition to Multiculturalism', *Canadian Public Policy – Analyse de Politiques*, vol. 18, no. 4, 1992, pp. 365–86.
30 A. Lamer, 'How the Charter Changes Justice', *Globe and Mail*, 17 April 1992, p. A17.
31 I am indebted for this formulation to François Ewald's discussion of the 'average man' as 'fiction', in his 'Norms, Discipline, and the Law', *Representations*, no. 30, Spring 1990, p. 145.
32 ibid., p. 139.
33 Canadian Multiculturalism Act, p. 838.
34 ibid., p. 839.
35 White Paper, p. 8545.
36 Canadian Multiculturalism Act, p. 840.
37 Under the 'Our definition of "culture"' section in the blue pages of the *Report of the Royal Commission on Bilingualism and Biculturalism*, called 'The Key Words of the Terms of Reference', we read, however, that 'clearly the two cultures designated in our terms of reference are those associated with the English and the French languages in Canada. But as there are the two dominant languages, there are two principal cultures, and their influence extends, in greatly varying degrees, to the whole country' (vol. 1, p. xxxi). For an elaboration of the commissioners' definition of culture, see also pp. xxxi–xxxviii.
38 Here I am referring to, among other things, the problems resulting from the unspoken expectation that ethnic writers are spokespersons for their communities, and that their writing ought in some ways to reflect those communities' ethos and politics. Thus Michael Ondaatje's *Running in the Family*, for example, was criticised by Arun Mukherjee for its complicity with the colonising culture of Sri Lanka and for failing to directly thematise the author's position of racial and cultural otherness. See A. Mukherjee, *Towards an Aesthetic of Opposition: Essays on Literature, Criticism and Cultural Imperialism*, Stratford, Ontario, Williams-Wallace Press, 1988. Mukherjee (in the same book) and Caribbean-Canadian writer Marlene Nourbese Philip also criticise harshly Neil Bissoondath for his alleged racism toward Black Caribbeans. See M. Philip, *Frontiers: Essays and Writings on Racism and Culture*, Stratford, Ontario, Mercury Press, 1992. See also Bissoondath's own response to official multiculturalism, 'A Question of Belonging', *Globe and Mail*, 28 January 1993, p. A17.
39 See R. Viero, 'Ethnic Groups in Quebec: Participation or Solitude', in '*Multiculturalism: Canadian Reality': A Report of the Canadian Conference on Multiculturalism*, Ottawa, Minister of State, 1978, p. 35; and L. Hutcheon and M. Richmond's anthology, *Other Solitudes: Canadian Multicultural Fictions*, Toronto, Oxford University Press, 1990.
40 J. Vining, 'Generalisation in Interpretive Theory', *Representations*, no. 30, Spring 1990, p. 1.
41 ibid., p. 2.
42 I have in mind such legal documents as the Green Paper on Immigration and

Population tabled in the House of Commons on 3 February 1975, other immigration policies, and publications of the Government of Canada. See, for example, *Highlights from the Green Paper on Immigration and Policy*, and any of the reports issued on the Canadian Conferences on Multiculturalism sponsored by the federal government before and after Bill C-93 was passed.

43 Vining, 'Generalisation in Interpretive Theory', p. 6.
44 Canadian Multiculturalism Act, p. 836.
45 B. Thomas, *Cross-examinations of Law and Literature: Couper, Hawthorne, Stowe, and Melville*, Cambridge, London and New York, Cambridge University Press, 1987, p. 4.

Part III

POSITIONINGS

15

LUNCHING FOR THE REPUBLIC

Feminism, the media and identity politics in the Australian republicanism debate

Meaghan Morris

Feminism is rarely represented as missing from public debates in 'today's multi-cultural Australia'. This is a media phrase for a discursive field that shapes as well as celebrates contending models of national culture. Within this field, the fact that models do contend – in such genres as the report, the public submission, the interview, the guest column or personality spot, the letters page and the talk show, the documentary or drama series, the critical review, the current affairs pro-gramme and the formal TV debate – is valued as marking the difference of 'today' from the bad old days of monocultural national identity. So feminists who use these genres are often confronted by images of feminism's role in national life that are cheerfully incommensurate. Australian feminism is simultaneously super-seded (by post-feminist concerns, for example), bureaucratically entrenched and repressive (according to its men's movement critics), dispersed or diversified (by feminisms of difference) and too rigidly a white/Anglo-Celtic/middle-class/baby-boomer/heterosexual movement – while still having 'a long way to go' in securing for women anything like equal empowerment in public institutions, equal representation in Parliament or really equal pay. Feminism is much con-tested. That is why it is a force in public life.

So when a republican movement re-emerged in the early 1990s, with claims to political credibility and rising community support, there was something dis-concerting about the speed with which it produced a 'woman' problem: by 1993, 'Where are the women?' was a question assumed to make sense of feminist as well as female positioning in relation to constitutional change. It made sense by denying our involvement; if women were not in there, shaping the future form of a multicultural Australia, then we must be out of it doing something else. Yet this question was most often posed in the media by women (in fact, feminist his-torians) who were trying to articulate a feminist 'republican' problem: what was wrong with the republican imaginary on offer in Australia? Why had feminists said so little in such a momentous debate? 'What', one asked, 'do women want?'[1]

These questions were also posed at a time when feminists enjoyed a relatively privileged relationship to the Australian Federal government. Between late 1992 and early 1996, under the leadership of the then Labor Prime Minister, Paul Keating, ideals of social justice and projects for cultural reform acquired a level of respectability that they had not been accorded in mainstream politics since the early 1970s. When I first began work on this essay in 1994, I was puzzled by the reluctance of many feminist academics working with cultural theory to seize this opportunity with enthusiasm. Now that the conservative Liberal–National Party coalition is in government again (after a sweeping election victory in 1996), I am still puzzled. If it is clear that what a majority of women 'wanted' in 1996 had little to do with either the feminism or the multiculturalism of middle-class academics, this is nothing new; my concern is less to understand a putative gap between 'feminists' and 'women' than it is to explore the distance, as I see it, between the politicised rhetoric of the feminist criticism I practise as an academic, and that critical feminism's capacity to act politically when the circumstances for doing so are at their most propitious.

After all, republicanism has always existed as an often radical tradition throughout Australia's short history as a constitutional monarchy, and women have always been involved. The launch in 1991 of a carefully diverse and respectable Australian Republican Movement (ARM) was supported or welcomed by a number of prominent women, including writer and activist Faith Bandler (a South Sea Islander descendant), fashion designer Jenny Kee, social policy analyst Mary Kalantzis, novelist Blanche d'Alpuget, politician Franca Arena and news-reader Mary Kostakidis. It soon became clear, however, that ethnic diversity and age differentiation were more important than gender to those arguing only for a severance of our formal ties with Britain (the 'minimalist' approach). In real-political terms, this is not hard to understand. Republicanism can be derived from multiculturalism in Australia, where the fear of cultural difference as socially divisive is commonly if not exclusively, or even correctly, linked with an 'elderly' Anglocentric perspective.

In this logic, a republic would give expression to changes already effected by the past twenty years of 'official' multiculturalism in immigration and social policy; since millions of Australians have no links at all with Britain, it is sensible to replace a monarch 12,000 miles away with an Australian as head of state. When the republican goal was endorsed by the federal Labor government of the time, this diversity-management argument, typical of domestic multiculturalism since the 1970s, was combined with the 'outward-looking' rhetoric of diversity-promotion ('Australia is a multicultural nation in the Asian-Pacific region') used to justify deregulatory economic reform in the 1980s. Since more than two-thirds of Australian trade now occurs within the region and closer political and military ties are forming with nearby countries (particularly Indonesia), while immigration and cultural policy are increasingly 'Asia-minded',[2] it is practical to establish an independent identity.

If republicanism cannot be derived from feminism in quite this intensely pragmatic way, the need to bargain for recognition does not usually discourage feminists from participating in any aspect of Australian politics. Second-wave feminism and multiculturalism are about the same age in this country; while the overlaps and tensions between them are not simple, new or static, both movements, in various ways, have been deeply involved with government. On this occasion, a special invitation to get involved was extended even to those intellectuals critical of the pragmatism of political life under Labor. 'A republic needs vision, after all', declared the Prime Minister's speechwriter, Don Watson, in a national newspaper in July 1993: 'whatever shape the federal republic of Australia takes, there will be something unstructured, if not deconstructed, about it. I imagine it as aleatory, impressionistic, figurative, eclectic, bebop.'[3]

Alas, Watson's own dazzling sketch for 'the first post-modern republic' included only one individuated woman, a reporter from the *New York Times* who says of the republic: 'But it's not important, is it?' For many mainstream republicans, the social category 'women' connotes a plodding resistance, even a fink monarchist streak, in our society. While support for republicanism fluctuates, opinion polls suggest that women are always less inspired than men by the campaign; one released in October 1993 had only 41 per cent of women supporting a republic, compared with 56 per cent of men, while another in June 1995 had the figures rising to 45 per cent of women, and 59 per cent of men.[4] Australian women are often said to be generally more conservative than men in our approach to drastic change, and there is always uncertainty, too, about the meaning of the royalty cults and scandals beloved of women's magazines, their reach and form of appeal across boundaries of age, class and ethnicity. The present monarch is, after all, a woman, and some speculate that her physical remoteness and her Englishness may be less important than her gender and her family problems to women for whom the national political process itself is both remote and overbearingly male-dominated.

In what follows, I attempt to think through my own unease about the relationship of feminism to republicanism in my immediate situation as an intellectual. The question 'Where are the women?' became a personal one for me when I tried to participate in an academic conference on republicanism, and found that I simply had nothing to say about my nominated topic, 'Feminism and Republicanism' – except that where I was in the republicanism debate was not easily accessible from my work as a feminist cultural critic. I take it, however, that the work we do as intellectuals does not necessarily or even responsibly always engage the 'totality' of our persons. I do not think that the difference between my response as a citizen to republicanism (which is positive) and my non-response as a feminist intellectual constitutes a contradiction or a split. There may be many good reasons why feminism and republicanism cannot easily or directly be articulated.[5] Clearly, a feminist does not aspire to be a 'virtuous property-owning warrior-citizen'[6] on classic civic republican lines, and Helen Irving has analysed the problems resulting from the persistence of a soldierly masculinism in the ARM campaign.[7] What is not so clear to me is how *feminism* can be held to provide a general platform from which all issues of moment must always be addressed.

BEING AND BECOMING REPUBLICAN

First, let me be explicit about my attitude to republicanism. I think it is important. Whatever my doubts, I am not part of that intellectual community which is reaffirming itself routinely around a position of exteriority and a posture of scepticism in relation to this debate. I find deeply depressing Chilla Bulbeck's claim that 'for women like me, white Anglo-descended, middle class by training if not birth, whether we are a republic or a monarchy hardly matters'.[8] After twenty-five years of feminism, I wonder, is that all we have to say? Are white middle-class Anglo women now so passive that they cannot want to make a difference to ensure that a change will matter? When did this happen? Or, to put it another way: how did white middle-class Anglo womanhood come to signify such *indifference* for its self-styled representative ('women like me') intellectuals?

For there is a gap between the 'women' and the 'me' in Bulbeck's formulation of a likeness. Worrying that only her gender divides her historically from 'white nationalism' in Australia, she goes on to say: 'I see that the national icons like the bushworker or the lifesaver are male, not that they are white.' Yet Bulbeck knows perfectly well that these icons are white. She claims not to 'see', but it is she who *writes* 'that they are white'; in fact, to emphasise their whiteness, not their maleness, is the function of the sentence. So this 'I' who does not see whiteness is a projection of some kind, fuzzily distinct from the writer of the text; perhaps a memory of an earlier self, or a mark of a part of her present self still capable of blindness, but also a sign of identification with all those *other* women who – *unlike* Bulbeck in her writerly role – do *not* see the whiteness of our national icons.

Well, I am socially like the women of Bulbeck's description, give or take the 'Anglo'. I am also a feminist intellectual who has heard and read so much about race and ethnicity in recent years that I see whiteness almost before I see maleness, now, when I look at our old national icons. But I am not indifferent to republicanism. When Paul Keating made a speech in Parliament in 1992 about Britain selling out Australia in World War II, my heart stopped. I was profoundly moved – and in a way that the relentlessly knowing, negative postures of traditional 'feminist critique' can do little to modify and, these days (speaking personally), nothing to match. But this was not an emotive response to bushworker and lifesaver icons, nor even an anti-British feeling stirred by events before I was born. I was moved by a memory from my childhood in the 1950s and 1960s. I heard my father's voice telling stories about the guns of Singapore, about Winston Churchill saying that 'Australia is expendable' and the great Labor leader John Curtin defying Churchill to bring our troops 'home' to the Pacific; and I recalled the political feeling of those stories. I remembered that other time when – back before the Vietnam War, the radicalisms of the late 1960s, and then the long, dreary years of conservative recoil – people dreamt of an Australia with its own foreign policy, thus more room for experiment at home, and of an Asian-Pacific, not a White, Australia.

In other words, I was moved by the *recurrence* of a rhetoric of independence that I had never expected to hear in this country again. At some stage, probably around 1975 when the Whitlam Labor government was dismissed by the Governor-General, Sir John Kerr (using his 'reserve powers' as the queen's representative in Australia), I must have begun to assume that independence as a goal was for other people – people in Nicaragua, for example. The year 1975 had a bitter effect on many Australians, including those of us who had, just three years earlier, helped to elect the first federal Labor government since 1949 with the first vote of our lives. The big-spending, high-wage Whitlam government was dramatically progressive on most issues dear to the 'new social movements' of the time. It also made a serious mess of the economy, and alarmed US agencies by allowing wild talk about rescinding US military installations in Australia.[9] When Whitlam was sacked in an atmosphere of crisis and intrigue, including tales of CIA activity against him, two convictions took hold in popular political wisdom: any future Labor government must put economic management at the top of its agenda; no future Australian government could risk offending the United States in defence or foreign policy.

Labor's years back in power under R. J. Hawke (1983–91) did little to shake these convictions. So to hear the old rhetoric used again by Keating was extraordinary – as though *anything* might be possible. It was heart-stopping in the same way as the ending of the *terra nullius* doctrine[10] by the High Court's *Mabo* decision, and the destruction of the Berlin Wall; and the revival of that rhetoric was connected to these events. It recurred in a new national context, an unfamiliar world; it signified change, not nostalgia. Keating's attack on Britain's treatment of its former colony came in a speech for a time when settler Australians have to renegotiate our own colonising history, just as the country's strategic value to the United States has suddenly declined; a time when 'nationhood' is in question, and 'independence', for the first time, a necessity.

Change can be quite shocking for white middle-class Cold War babies; for all the talk of revolutions, those of us who grew up in Australia did so under a political settlement of immense and dazing stability and in an ideological climate of seemingly endless fatalism. I sometimes think that the widespread tendency in feminism to know in advance that any event is just more of the same old story, more of the *same* patriarchy, the *same* racism, the *same* form of class exploitation ('nostalgia for something really old in something really different, which always [comes] down to the same old thing'[11]) is in Australia as much a legacy of the Menzies era (1949–66) as it is a defence against the disappointments of experience. A bitter refusal to acknowledge our political successes, always insisting that nothing has changed, too easily becomes that old familiar feeling that nothing ever *can* change.

Yet for all that, I can, like Chilla Bulbeck, project another 'I' that sees things somewhat differently. When I survey what Elaine Thompson calls a 'shopping list' of constitutional reforms,[12] I have a good idea what I would like. For the centenary of Federation in 2001, I would like a republican constitution including or accompanying some form of recognition of Aboriginal sovereignty; an Australian head of state, appointed not elected, with a strong ethical aura (as in Ireland) but purely ceremonial powers; an adversarial lower house elected preferentially from single-member constituencies, as at present, but with affirmative-action pressures applied to party preselection; and an upper house for 'states and minorities' elected, as at present, by proportional preferential voting, but with a strictly limited role of reviewing legislation – no rejecting of the budget, no blocking of supply (as in 1975) and absolutely no way for unrepresentative minor parties to paralyse government. While it is possible to justify these choices from a feminist position, what I'd really like them to bring me is an endless Labor government – a deeply undemocratic as well as an impractical wish.

Here is the emotionally fuzzy core of my republican/feminist problem. If my enthusiasm for a republic is not yet significantly feminist, this is in part because it is not really republican. I can accept that Barry Hindess may be right to suggest that the republican ideal is itself anachronistic in the world today,[13] and that sceptics who argue that the monarchy has a very low impact here (the 'de facto republic' position) have a point. For me, the republican ideal is even vaguer and more remote than the British monarchy. With many other people, I became a republican overnight; it is a vehement, instant thing, with shallow roots in my education and none in my experience. My enthusiasm rests, in fact, on a deep and abiding hostility to the Liberal Party; 'republicanism' is the new name for my oldest, most stable political identifications, all of which were formed and continue to make sense in our present political system. Anything that threatens the legitimation stories of the Liberal Party, as republicanism may, brings me joy.

Given the Liberal Party's mix of economic libertarianism with social conservatism, such joy is not indefensible. But it is not a solid basis for contributing to republican debate. Constitutional reform is usually unachievable in Australia without bipartisan support: many republicans believe that their goal can more easily be achieved under an unenthusiastic conservative government than with the advocacy of a divisive Labor leader like Keating,[14] and the 'moderate' Liberal minority that supports republicanism is more progressive on feminist issues. Old hatreds have their own conservative force: if mine distances me, once again, from those forms of feminism that foster a belief that nothing national or party-political really matters to women's lives, it is also sustained by memories and allegiances which decreasing numbers of Australians share, and which were shaped by that 'stable' society whose basic organisation is now so rapidly changing. So I have found media debate about the technical difficulties of becoming a republic more sobering than off-putting, and I am not sure that it is altogether a bad thing if an ebbing of wild enthusiasm has followed from that discussion. Perhaps there is something to be said for a society organised around an absent power symbol, as well as with a history of relative indifference to aggressive patriotic display.

Feminist *cultural* critique, however, is not well equipped to consider or assess what that 'something to be said' might be, let alone to orient debate towards a non-militant form of republicanism. In the many disciplines that intersect now on the broad terrain of culture, we say that the academic project of feminism has moved into affirmative mode; the demonstration of a uniform oppression has long since made way for the study of women's diverse practices as well as of our differences, conflicts and complicities as historical agents in a colonial class society. Yet most feminist input to public debate still comes from historians and political or social scientists with a confident grasp of national institutions, adversarial processes and political structures of feeling little attended to in feminist cultural theory. For all the sophistication we have brought to bear in thinking identity and difference, feminist cultural critics have had relatively little to say about the non-canonical identities and allegiances (generational, regional, state-based, party-political) that a national movement can mobilise along with, or sometimes instead of, those of class, race, ethnicity, gender and sexuality.

In this context, the problem with cultural theory is less the 'academic' inflection it has given the project of feminist criticism than the narrow model of political culture as primarily psychic, interpersonal and utopian that a preference for psychoanalysis and philosophy over more formal historical and social knowledges can impose: a model that is especially constricting in a country where a mere proposal to teach the Constitution in schools could be denounced, in 1994, as a plot to indoctrinate children. People of my age had a colonial school education; many of us know little about those aspects of the Australian political system that cannot be derived from personal experience. This may be one reason why feminist cultural critics of my generation have moved more slowly than historians to extend the affirmative work we do in our disciplines towards a positive feminist account, or a positive *version*, of Australian culture and history capable of influencing the process of national reshaping that is already underway. By 'positive' I do not mean 'patriotic'. I mean an account that would be able to sustain what Ann Curthoys and Stephen Muecke call 'a provisional reconstructive practice towards nationhood which investigates its rhetorical tactics'.[15]

Curthoys and Muecke emphasise the discontinuities, as well as the continuities, between earlier radical nationalisms in Australia and what they call 'the newer post-nationalism, a sense of nation informed by intense and cross-cutting multiplicities':

> If the earlier nationalisms were predicated on unity (of race), *exclusion* (of Others), and on white exploitation of the land, then the post-national varieties can be predicated on *difference* (both internally and externally), *inclusion* (a multiculturalism not confined to the European) and a *re-legitimation* of Aboriginal sovereignty over the land.[16]

'Post-nationalism' may not be the right term for these developments in a society where racism persists, as Curthoys and Muecke say, 'with strength',[17] and where the appeal of notions of unity remains strong; in 1996, the Coalition's slogan 'for all of us' (implying that Labor had governed only for minorities) proved to have a widespread appeal. Even in the Labor approach that Curthoys and Muecke describe, it is unclear how, or in whose interests, a re-legitimation of Aboriginal sovereignty as endorsed by white settler institutions would combine with a multiculturalism administering 'difference' on Anglo-Celtic terms. Keating transposed Australia's national military myth from Gallipoli in Turkey, 1915 (a losing battle fought by 'Anglos' against 'others' in a European war), to the Kokoda Track in Papua, 1942 (a multi-racial victory against Japan in the Pacific); any discourse organised by a theme of Men at War and an allegory of national economic self-interest remains nationalist in the most traditional way.

In calling for a *reconstructive* practice 'towards' nationhood, however, Curthoys and Muecke want to stress the open and unachieved status of Australian republicanism and the opportunities that the radically changing context of national politics provides for new forms of mobilisation. Their point is not simply that the massive scale of these changes has left practitioners of a hermeneutics of suspicion, muttering uselessly on the sidelines of most fields of contestation, open to the charge of indulging a purist and publicly funded politics of self-marginalisation. More strongly, Curthoys and Muecke argue for a re-constructive mode of participation that could operate critically by promoting 'post-modern, post-colonial and feminist' elements already circulating in national politics and the republicanism debate. This would mean working from particular examples of 'what Australians have already achieved' – such as the political gains of feminism, and the 'immense discursive and narrative power' exercised *culturally* now by Aboriginal Australians – in order to make the struggles for those achievements 'exemplary' of what nationhood might be.[18]

This strategy exploits the vagueness of the republican ideal by asking what *new* ideals this new name at our disposal might be used to mobilise: it makes a republican 'virtue' of experiment. This has a direct resonance with media formulations of the republican project: 'post-nationalism' and, more oddly, 'non-nationalism' have been used in headlines to invoke some unspecified, but highly desirable, aim.[19] For Curthoys and Muecke, it also has practical consequences for the kind of history that an Australian republic would require. While national in scale and import, it could not, they stress, be nationalist: it would have to be grounded in an effort to grasp 'the nature of the colonial relationships between indigenous and incoming peoples', and, as Curthoys points out in another context, it would have to assume that our only shared past as Australians is 'an *international* past, a myriad of individual regional and national histories that have been brought together in this place'.[20]

It should be easier and more exciting for feminists to develop a republican politics on the basis of these imperatives to work *towards* postcolonialism and to *produce* multiculturalism than to be carried away with old bipolar party enthusiasms. Yet the claims of feminist indifference suggest that matters are not so simple, and that the emotional structures of *labourism* still provide a more effective framework for responding to national issues. I think Peter Beilharz identifies something crucial about our unresponsiveness when he argues that we are living through the decline of the model of 'industrial citizenship' which labourism put in place in the 1950s. What we need now, he says, is a reinvention of citizenship in the context of a 'republicanism beyond labourism'.[21] But if this is easier said than done, more readily defined than desired, part of the problem may be that in Australia what Kobena Mercer calls the 'not so "new"' social movements, with their '"race, class, gender" mantra', have not only developed in conflict with labourism but also created positive programmes by a practical engagement with it.[22]

A certain aphasia can follow from the decline of industrial citizenship. The struggle against the privileging of the white male worker as industrial citizen has shaped feelings and investments, as well as habits of debate, over a long period of time. Without that figure and its derivatives, like the 'white middle-class woman', so powerfully *there*, as a centralising instance making sense of our talk about margins, the value of familiar gestures suddenly becomes uncertain. Perhaps the demand for a distinctively feminist version of republicanism is one such gesture. There may be a diffuse expectation in the 'margins' of republicanism that the centralising *role* played by industrial citizenship can and will be reinvented from the same old sources of social power (which do continue to exist), and that our choices are therefore limited to adopting a studied indifference or to making alternative proposals in a strictly minority spirit.

Perhaps this expectation of a reinvented symbolic centre is mistaken. I find it encouraging that an aura of buffoonery rapidly enveloped the efforts of Malcolm Turnbull and Thomas Keneally, prominent advocates of republicanism, to masquerade as emblematic citizens. What interests me is less their embodiment of an explicitly masculine patriotism than the way they also implicitly articulate a *class* model of intellectual sociality – how they present themselves as prompters of a 'popular' debate. Of course, Turnbull and Keneally present themselves to us not as professional intellectuals but as media personalities. Turnbull is the upper-middle-class lawyer/merchant banker as post-industrial citizen (with a family connection to Angela Lansbury). Keneally is the Irish-Australian novelist (author of *Schindler's List*) as organic representative of the petty-bourgeoisie. So they do not voice the interests of 'a' class transcending the media world in any simple sense. Rather, their performances predicate the national-popular as an audience for whom their own personae are central, and a popular debate as mimetic of their chat. In other words, they assume that public leadership is a function of what our pundits call (in eloquent self-hatred) 'the chattering classes'.

NOT LUNCHING WITH THOMAS KENEALLY

One of the most remarkable things about the ARM literature is its emphasis on lunching. Both *Our Republic*, Tom Keneally's book of reminiscences, and *The Coming Republic*, a much more useful collection of essays orchestrated by Donald Horne, are structured by lunch allegories in which personalities – real celebrities in Keneally's case, imaginary social stereotypes in Horne's – gather around a lavish supply of food and wine to discuss an Australian republic.[23] *Our Republic* is embarrassing in this respect, with its chapter 'A Sunday with Neville' offering lifestyle details about 'Jill' and 'Neville' (Wran, former Premier of New South Wales), complete with bottles of Chardonnay; so giddy is the social whirl that, by the end of the book, Keneally has almost lost track of any issues extrinsic to his social calendar and his amazing job-opportunity at U.C. Irvine. There is a parochialism to this that may explain the book's failure to stir much fervour in the recessionary year of its publication, 1993. I am embarrassed by it, however, because the lunch-burble is all too familiar – in form, if not in setting or stellar quality – from my own professional life. *Our Republic* had an awful fascination as a book that set out to celebrate the white male nationalist heritage (convicts, soldiers, the Irish), only to turn into a book about transnational chattering-class networking.

'Lunch' is an old-fashioned way for culturati to network; younger chatterers prefer, on the whole, to keep working the modem. But it has a role in ARM discourse that is more fundamental than its value as an index of shifting subcultural behaviours. 'Lunch' is a democratised version of the literary conceit of the bourgeois dinner – that set piece of so many novels, plays and films in which the conflicts and desires of entire social formations are fought out in exquisite detail in a unified space and time. (*The Coming Republic* in fact makes use of this antecedent in a comic and deliberate way.) In the context of republican discourse, a lunch scene stages the ideal of 'free and rational debate' that characterises classical republican thinking and limits its claims to realism. Admittedly, the ideal Australian literary lunch is a boisterous occasion at which people get a little irrational and maybe speak a little too freely. None the less, the use of this conceit to package ARM polemics suggests an elision of basic questions about the nature of public debate in a media society.

As a utopian allegory of the social, lunch has its problems. It is basically monocultural in a liberal pluralist mode, questioning neither the forms of European bourgeois sociality nor the resonance of the hospitality trope so often used to assert the dominance of an Anglo-Celtic 'home' culture over more tenuously 'invited' immigrant cultures (thus erasing our own history as the unwelcome guests of indigenous Australia). In this respect, a lunching model of national debate has much the same problems as the 'better cuisine' rationale for multiculturalism; the role of exotic elements in both cases is to flavour the mixture, not to alter the basics. As Ghassan Hage has pointed out, new forms of racism can inhabit this state-promulgated tolerance.[24] Like a badly-behaved guest at an otherwise convivial lunch, the intolerably different legal citizen of Australia can still be told to 'go home'.

To be fair, neither *Our Republic* nor *The Coming Republic* invokes hospitality in this way. Both books aim to start discussion among a broad readership used to debating multiculturalism on all sorts of grounds, precisely because it exists as a working set of arrangements with supporters as well as critics across all of the great divides – indigenous and non-indigenous, black Australia and white Australia, Anglo-Celtic and non-Anglo-Celtic, European and non-European NESB (non-English-speaking background) – used to map Australian society. The special difficulty that emerges with Keneally's slide from populism to networking is that neither the literary model of lunching nor the culinary model of multiculturalism can tell us how a conversation about changing the form of the nation can be extended to involve large numbers of diverse people on a national basis. This is really another version of the question, 'Where are the women?' – the question of the conditions for democracy today. Neither lunch nor multiculturalism is intrinsically a democratic institution. Multiculturalism is, first and foremost, a management policy, while any lunch that acts as a media talking-point is an event for social elites, who may or may not impersonate for the occasion particular social identities on behalf of different constituencies.

Now, I have no problem with the idea that the opinion industry works on a loop around which interest groups, most but not all of whom are also social elites, send each other messages and images about 'what's going on'.[25] A lucid grasp of this process and its uses and potentials is increasingly important to the mingling of marginal with mainstream politics, as the battle for the Native Title Act showed in 1993. On that occasion, the media were used by the major participants – the Aboriginal delegates, the various factions of the Labor Cabinet, the Senate minor parties, the state premiers, the mining and farming lobbies – not only to pressure and outwit each other in public but to involve a national audience in what became a deeply stirring emotional drama with a cliff-hanger structure, a classic 'underdog' or 'battler' theme that slowly distributed maximal sympathy, for a while, to the Aboriginal position, and a (not undisputed) happy ending by Christmas.[26] At the same time, they all used the media pedagogically to inform, or misinform, each other and the audience about the significance of each new development. I learned more about Australian law and history, both indigenous and colonial, during those months of watching TV than in all my years of formal education.

By an even subtler and more impersonal pedagogy, exercised by the medium of television itself, I also acquired a greater respect for the politics of bargaining and negotiation to which all of these elites, including the miners' and farmers' representatives, were committed by virtue of taking part. The losers in this battle were the Liberal and National Parties who flatly opposed the bill. In doing so, they claimed to represent majority opinion. Perhaps, at the outset, they did: racist scare campaigns, backed by some mining interests, tried to persuade non-Aboriginal Australians that our homes were at risk as a result of the government's decision to respond to the Mabo judgment with national Native Title legislation. But by shutting themselves out of the formal arena of struggle over 'what's going on', and with no other site of authority (unlike the bill's Aboriginal critics) from which to enter the discussion, the Coalition parties relegated that opinion to the limbo of the minor and un-newsworthy – in media terms, to the past.

Of course, the media 'past' is always temporary and open to revision: opinions marginalised during those crucial months of 1993 were actively 'present' in mainstream media again by 1996 (with, however, a reduced ability to reverse the effects of the *Mabo* judgment).[27] Whatever long-term effects such battles of opinion may have, it is clear that they do not operate in the 'talking tableau' mode of a literary lunch. In order to facilitate a free and rational debate, the Enlightened fine-dining tradition stages a conflict of *ideas* in a voluntarily constituted, benignly convergent setting in which all participants are equal; as Gary Shapiro points out in his discussion of Kant's aesthetics, 'the temporary community and good cheer tend to obscure real differences of power . . . which are likely to influence the outcome of any discussion of matters of taste'.[28] Media *opinion* battles, in contrast, do not abstract ideas from social struggles. They activate differences, and at least some of the power imbalances, within as well as between social groups as these diverge and converge on particular issues, by staging their conflict as part of a multifaceted, open-ended and expansive saga of national life that only ever provisionally achieves its moments of resolution. In Australia's fairly small and cohesive media system, it is now the willingness and the *capacity* to take part in this process, and not the content of one's opinions, that define what can count, at any given time, as a 'mainstream' position.

So the idea of a debate prompted by professional chatterers about the future of the nation is not necessarily ludicrous. The problem is that its exponents want to deny the specialisation of interests that gives people networking power in the first place as mediators on the loop. This denial may take nationalist and populist forms, but it thrives on a belief derived from literary culture, and from the genteel white middle-class notion of a 'general' reading public, that the distinct taste cultures constellated by particular media shows add up to a coherent national public that is *represented*, as well as amused, by media personality discourse. Lurking not too far from the surface here is a class fantasy that cultural workers may play the same symbolically central role in future that industrial workers did in the past. However, the media sphere, while vitally important, is not *central* to our society (it is not the only public sphere and it interacts erratically with others), and it is used by many political movements and social forces, very few of which are only class-defined, struggling to further their own interests in and through that sphere.

Not all intellectuals are chatterers, and not all chattering in the media can usefully be described as intellectual. I do not think that national debates are impossible today, or that intellectuals cannot take part in diverse and variable ways. I do question whether republicanism can take the form of a single, mass festival of opinion and ideas, a kind of mega-lunch, to which feminists should, as it were, bring a plate. If we let go of the idea of a long lunch-party about constitutional change, we can consider feminism's role in a more optimistic spirit. Feminists are highly skilled at using the opinion industry to further our social aims. We will have an impact in, for example, lobbying parties and public committees to allocate places to women; in formulating and promoting ideas for the 'popular conventions' that are likely, in what must be a *mediated* re-enactment of the process that achieved Federation a century ago, to organise more formal debates in future; in working for or against a Bill of Rights;[29] and in shaping the symbolism that an Australian republic will need to adopt. *The Coming Republic*, with its cover image of a red-headed white bloke in worker's shorts rolling up the Union Jack, shows how much is to be done in this respect.

But the feminism engaging with republicanism in these ways will not be a singular force that massively represents 'women'. As we never tire of pointing out in other contexts, feminism is a mixed discourse and a hybrid political space. Since feminist practices are connected as well as defined by all the involvements that women have as social agents, large numbers of women are only likely to engage with republicanism in a conjunctive mode of 'feminism *and* . . . *and*', where our interests as women will combine with our interests in the labour movement, and/or in the rights of indigenous people, and/or in the needs of differing old and new settler groups, of lesbians and/or working mothers, as intellectuals, and so on. This is to say that the formulation 'feminism and republicanism', however handy it may be, is quite misleading. Only in a history of 'isms' do these terms confront each other in a dual relationship. In practice, feminist inflections of republicanism are most visible and audible when at least three terms are in play. This does not mean that the concept of feminism is meaningless, or that white women who identify only as feminists (let alone Anglo-descended women, a goodly chunk of the population) should be invisible or inaudible. It simply means accepting that 'the women' may never arrive in one spectacular contingent to seize the floor of republican debate.

POSTMODERN REPUBLICAN NON-NATIONALISM

If we approach the modalities of women's involvement in this orthodox feminist way, other questions can arise about the broad conditions in which the activist's problem of organising differences is projected as a nation-*building* issue. What does it mean for women to be invited to an 'aleatory, impressionistic, figurative, eclectic' *unification* movement, and to bring our differences with us? What ideals are being mobilised by this particular republican movement? Before imagining republican futures, feminists need to examine more closely the political cultures that actually dominate the present. For when multiculturalism can be projected, with whatever degree of hypocrisy, as a model for reconstructing national identity,[30] forms of analysis used in the past to affirm a politics of heterogeneity and multiplicity against binary models of political opposition, and to articulate embodied social identities against an abstract form of citizenship, may no longer serve as well as they once did.

Republicanism certainly aims to produce what Homi Bhabha calls the 'problematic unity of the nation'.[31] Even the sparest forms of minimalism would transform a federal constitution preoccupied with difference as the protection of 'states' rights' into one investing national identity in the figure of a head of state; with the monarchy goes an externally oriented way of uniting Australia. For this reason, fears that a republic will stir divisive and violent passions largely inactive here today are not only expressed by 'elderly' Anglophiles. A progressive judge, Michael Kirby, defends the monarchy as a tempering force against nationalism ('I can live quite peacefully with the sombre fact that our head of government attracts only a 19 gun salute'[32]), while migrants from parts of Asia and Europe have spoken as 'Australians for Constitutional Monarchy' on the grounds that they came here to get away from nationalist conflicts. Writing as an anti-monarchist, Barry Hindess warns that 'the very idea of a modern republic' presents 'a misleading and potentially destructive image of a political community endowed with a distinctive common culture'.[33]

Voiced as fears, as experiences or as wagers on a logic of history, these arguments are unanswerable. They invoke powerful precedents from our international past that no-one can say with certainty will or will not apply to Australia in future. Another argument points to the genocide and the racist exclusivism that constitute a national past for Anglo-Celtic Australians. What makes this precedent uncertain is that our twentieth-century efforts to destroy Aboriginal culture,[34] and our exclusion of 'Asians' with the White Australia Policy, were both entangled in a history whereby immigrants from different nations – mainly but not only English, Irish, Scottish and Welsh – united under the monarchy to become assiduously British in Australia. It follows emotionally, if not logically, that to get rid of the British monarchy is to end, not to initiate, a phase of virulent nationalism. Yet this is why Hage can convincingly argue that the 'we' of republican discourse implies an Anglo-Celtic identity: despite the thematic centrality accorded to multiculturalism, the 'we' refers 'to an old Anglo-Celtic history and deals with a present Anglo-Celtic problem'.[35]

Arguments from historical precedent usefully contest the unity of existing national narratives. They also tend to reiterate old histories, either minimising the conditions in which what Hage calls 'republican nationalism' is currently taking shape, or maximising, as Hindess does, the distance between 'now' and 'then'; to paraphrase Michael Naas, they begin with a politics of which they proceed to give us examples, instead of beginning with examples out of which to invent a politics.[36] Like Curthoys and Muecke, I prefer to wager on the second course by asking what its proponents actually mean by republican 'non-nationalism'. The old nationalism was a protectionist as well as a racist settlement that thrived on Australia's cultural and physical isolation. What sort of unity is being projected for a free-trading nation at the mercy of world economic forces that no government can control? for a multicultural society officially unable to legitimate its norms with reference to a common culture? for a technologically constituted public sphere not only open to global information flows and regional political pressures but providing, thanks to a satellite launched in 1986, the first simultaneously national image-space in Australian history?

It is striking just how minimal most mainstream manifestos are when it comes to republican ideals. Rather than endowing Australians with a 'common culture' in any positive sense, they focus on ways of managing differences, on a shareable code rather than a 'community', in what they assume can only ever be a problematic national *process*. They offer plans for, not definitions of, republican government, how-to guides that declare no self-evident truths. What makes them mainstream in Australian terms – compared to, say, ideas for a corporation-based democracy or for Swiss and Californian remodellings of the electoral system – is an emphasis on formally effective, not morally redemptive, conciliation procedures that provide continuity and stability while securing the conditions for change to keep on being negotiated. Donald Horne, for example, wants a civic *instead* of a national identity, defined by a commitment to act in a certain way – legally, constitutionally, democratically, respecting equality under the law – and, in a major modification of non-Aboriginal tradition, to 'custodianship of the land we share'.[37]

Don Watson agrees that a postmodern republic 'exalts the nation less than the way of life', valuing tolerance, difference, worldliness and

> humanist and even some romantic traditions, but not schmaltz, false sentiment and fascism. I have this sense that the pragmatism and dogmatic gradualism which delayed the moment for so long might end up serving us brilliantly.[38]

This is about as close as republican non-nationalism comes to a unifying profession of faith. It has its Anglo-Celtic resonances, including the sweetly ironic approach to romanticism ('even some') and the stern attitude to schmaltz. As Jon Stratton and Ien Ang point out, the 'way of life' is an old notion vaguely investing cohesion in mundane practices, not identities or ideals.[39] The real political bite, however, is in the '*dogmatic gradualism*'. This phrase invokes with wonderful exactness a traditional labourist faith, shareable now with Horne's more classically liberal civics, in a pragmatism that stubbornly holds the line against revolutionaries, extremists, vanguardists and disruptively visionary radicals of left *and* right, while slowly, unsensationally securing the popular consent, and the practical means, that enable deep and lasting social change.

Perhaps what makes this dogma postmodern in Watson's invocation is that it has floated free of its anchorage in the dialectical struggles that over a century formed the Australian Labor Party – capital vs. labour, Catholicism[40] vs. communism – to become more diffusely available as a participatory culture, not a partisan ethos. In modern times, the gradualism had an aim, something less final than a goal, called 'civilising capitalism',[41] and its mode of solidarity was exclusionary: non-unionists out of the shop, married women out of the workforce, cheap imports and 'cheap labour' out of Australia (and Aborigines out of the picture altogether). In Watson's version of postmodern times, the aim is to create, in a self-reflexive process of civilising *pragmatism* ('with . . . even some romantic traditions'), an open and inclusionary national, not white male working-class, movement beyond 'tyrannies of all kinds', one among them 'the market fetish and greed of the 80s'– something much less absolute than capitalism. Pragmatism won its battle for a free-trade ethos in the 1980s. By 1994, Labor's unifying themes were affirmative action for women (ideally, preselection to 35 per cent of winnable seats in Parliament by 2001),[42] reconciliation between indigenous people and settlers ('Mabo'), and a republicanism based on multiculturalism. This dispersal of the singular adversary allows the shift from exclusion to inclusion to work smoothly; now racism, sexism, homophobia are all 'kinds' of tyranny, but capitalism is the horizon of the world.

I prefer to call this political culture 'corporatist' rather than Anglo-Celtic.[43] Regardless of the circumstances in which it became so diffusely available, the discourse of pragmatism and gradualism is not now ethnically bounded; during Labor's time in government (1983–96), its resources were mobilised as effectively against the 'extreme' free-market 'radicalism' of the Anglo-identified Liberal Party as they were by diverse minority groups, feminists among them, demanding to negotiate the terms of their own inclusion in the national process. In response to those appalled by the idea of managing differences, this discourse (which is, I think, agnostic about 'difference' philosophically construed, setting aside incommensurables as exceeding negotiation) points to the extreme violence of those contemporary nationalisms that treat differences as unmanageable, challenges its critics to name alternatives actually available to government, and invites concrete proposals for improving the management process: that many a différend is activated at every moment of this process is not denied but frankly accepted as part of the way things work.

As with any form of corporatism, an exclusionary bottom line divides, in this instance, those who can and do contribute ('players' and their constituencies, including the 'disadvantaged') from those who could but do not (such as the middle class 'loony' Left). The penalty for the latter's lack of pragmatism is an increased disempowerment – ridicule, irrelevance – that they are deemed to have brought upon themselves. To be excluded on this basis is, however, a provisional affair. Since one aim of the process is to shut down violent expressions of social conflict, no single group is ontologically invested at an official level with outsider status. Behaviours and attitudes, not identities, are scapegoated, including popular behaviours and attitudes (often but not only displayed by recalcitrant Anglo-Celtics) that threaten violently to scapegoat the imagined identities of others. The premise of this action is not that social conflicts are thereby solved or prejudice eradicated, but that these must never appear to acquire legitimacy or to engage majority opinion.

This is the political culture that shaped the re-emergence of a republican debate in Australia. In its managerial vesting of cohesion in party politics and in civil society, feminism and critical multiculturalism have a problem to confront that is not dispatched by invoking scary precedents or recycling critiques of ethnic or militarist nationalism. While any corporatism has tyrannical potentials, the policing of modes and thresholds of conflict in Australia is partly enabled by that 'public opinion' network that links, sometimes over lunch, government to the 'business community', the media, the professions, the lobby groups, the think

240

tanks, the culture industries and, under Labor, to the unions and those 'great and innovative social organisations' (as Kalantzis and Cope describe them) 'with more educative than legislative force: the Australia Council, the Office of Multicultural Affairs, the Human Rights Commission and so on'.[44] Along with practitioners of all forms of identity politics, feminists are firmly embedded in this network. We have helped to create it, and we continue, in our most severely critical as well as co-operative gestures, to refine and expand its capacities.

Any assessment of Australia's tyranny potential would have to consider the view that this resiliently casual network of like-minded souls represents a more immediate threat to liberty and cultural diversity than the prospect of an upsurge of flag-waving patriotism. But neither of these precedent-based scenarios, invoking Stalinism (or 'McCarthyism') and fascism respectively, attends to the actual conflicts currently shaping the future. These are not *nationalist* conflicts in any ordinary sense. They arise, every day, from the complex political tensions involved in, on the one hand, the cultural transfiguration of what were until quite recently 'local' or 'minor' interests (feminism, Aboriginal self-determination, anti-racism, gay rights) as symbolically but not always substantively major national issues, and, on the other hand, the economic *internationalism* – sometimes expressing a 'Pacific Rim' chauvinism, always accepting transnational capitalism as the limit of national policy – that accompanies and has in many ways enabled (most obviously, in the form of immigration) the displacement of the old racist nationalism by multiculturalism.[45]

A list of such tensions could be very long: it would have to include the appalling gap between the cultural prestige accorded to Aboriginality and the living conditions and prospects of many Aboriginal people; the discrepancy between the high feminist profile of the new labour movement and the effects on women workers of the enterprise-bargaining schemes supported by that movement; the harsh contrast between the cosmopolitan richness of urban cultural life and the social wasting of immigrant suburbs by long-term unemployment; the inconsistency of Australian human rights policies and practices at home and in the region. One way to frame such a list, however, is to note that a missing term in Watson's vision of tyrannies transcended by postmodern republicanism, and in Labor's historic compromise between identity politics and capitalism, is *colonialism*. Old as well as new colonial processes, 'internal', regional and global in scale, continue to impact, obliquely and directly, on the very communities whose symbolic incorporation in the nation is sought, in different ways, on both sides of politics. Yet the overlaps and discontinuities between the national imperialisms that created modern Australia, and the *corporation*-based colonialisms reshaping our society today, rarely figure in republican debate.

The conflicts resulting, however, are the everyday stuff of Australian politics in ways that becoming a republic is in itself unlikely to inflect towards catastrophe or redemption. These conflicts block the tendency of even the most gradualist of feminisms to identify with either the state or the networks of influence with which we are involved. They reinforce and help to create those 'unnegotiable' differences that good management tries to set aside, even as they ensure that the nation 'can no longer be conceived as a closed container for all that we are . . . or any sort of limit for the directions of feminist thinking':[46] they *regionalise*, within and beyond the borders of the nation, feminist frameworks of thought and action. I believe they also undermine this version of corporatism's chances of ever unifying the people in a swell of singularly national subjectivity. This political culture works with varying degrees of limited difference (*more* limited by the Liberals than by Labor) and with controlled (Labor) or *laissez-faire* (Liberal) heterogeneity; within those limits, its *models* of citizenship can be embodied as diversely as you please.

To ignore this in our polemics is to miss the complexity of the unprecedented outpouring of public support for the athlete Cathy Freeman, rebuked by an Australian team official for carrying the Aboriginal flag as well as the 'white flag' at the 1994 Commonwealth Games. Widely read as affirming multiculturalism, this media-saturated moment of massive solidarity and proto-republican sentiment in fact confirmed a limit: no *migrant* athlete feeling unrepresented by the 'Anglo-Celtic' flag would be so celebrated for making a comparable gesture. At the same time, the perception that Aboriginal athletes are entitled to differ in their relationship to Australian nationality is not a given of 'history' but the product of decades of political and cultural struggle; the iconic power for many different groups of the figure of a black woman victoriously waving two flags cannot be reduced to an Anglo-Celtic ruse. At the very least, Freeman's gesture and its reception gave notice that the very idea of the nation is being redefined not only by the Australian Republican Movement.

THE VERY IDEA OF A NATIONAL DEBATE

It seems to me that if a *popular* national debate was underway by the mid-1990s, then Mabo, rather than the monarchy, was its focus. Mabo is so central to the conflict of powers and values in Australia that it could sink the republic. Some people claim that, no matter which party holds government, a republic is inevitable some time soon. It is not, of course: it has to be accepted at a referendum by a majority of electors *and* a majority of the six states.[47] The result can depend on those states (Western Australia and Queensland) in which significant areas of land may be reclaimed under Mabo, and where white panic is most likely to fuse with an intense anti-centralism historically shared with smaller states such as Tasmania. The state-based identities and passions that republicanism aims to temper will be crucial to the outcome here; Australians usually vote 'no' to any proposal enhancing the powers of central government, even when we say we agree with the *content* of a proposal.[48] Land management has been a matter for state, not federal, governments. Mabo changes that: by recognising the rights of some Aboriginal groups, it has had, as a republic would, a nationalising force. At the same time, Mabo fragments white images of a uniform Aboriginality; in reporting the politics of Mabo, the media have had to recognise differences and conflicts in *Aboriginal* opinion.

Popular debates, in which people in all walks of life talk and argue on an everyday basis about a complex shared concern, are quite rare. Something of the qualitative difference in this respect between 'the republic' and 'Mabo' – media signifiers both – can be grasped if we try to imagine using a lunch allegory to canvass the politics of Mabo. If the idea seems incongruous it is not because 'lunch' connotes consumption and urban banter (as though no Aboriginal people ever indulge in either) but because the social circulation of Mabo cannot be contained in that way. The republican lunch is a self-referring class figure in a media-centred discourse. There is nothing wrong with that, especially if we take it as shaping conditions in which a gesture such as Freeman's can, as Donald Horne puts it, suddenly be rendered 'legendary' by a wave of enchantment that *surpasses* media discourse;[49] to make frameworks for interpreting such moments is one of the things that lobbyists do. Mabo, however, is the name of a vast, intricate mesh of distinct but connected debates: technical matters of land tenure; ongoing national political struggles over economic, social, and ethical priorities as well as federal/state relations; philosophical questions about the value of governmental acts of redress; and profoundly emotional conflicts over ways of being attached to one's own land and culture – each of which touches on something fundamental to Australian life.

Moreover, while Mabo as an instance of 'the immense narrative and discursive power' achieved by Aboriginal people had its brilliantly adroit media stars, it was not a product of personality politics. Nor was Mabo staged for 'the people' universalised as media consumers. In this respect, recent Aboriginal constructions of the public sphere can offer 'examples' of a politics capable of going beyond (in Peter Beilharz's phrase) the labourism of the past and the elite networking of the present. While Aboriginal people do not 'speak from the hyperluxury of the first world with the reflective thoughts of a well-paid, well-fed, detached scholar',[50] those of us who do speak from such positions have a great deal to learn from how Aborigines are dealing politically with first world institutions as *specific* intellectuals, while working from the base in Aboriginal institutions and politics that defines their organic relationship to their people. The national authority of a Marcia Langton or a Noel Pearson is not media-derived, though it has been media-disseminated; it preceded and exceeds the intense promotion of their personal roles in the Native Title negotiations. Such authority is community-based, and it *also* derives from their use, for Aboriginal purposes, of specific professional and symbolic skills.

These skills have included using the media to criticise 'the white "take-me-to-your-leader" syndrome'[51] that animates so much coverage of Aboriginal activists, and to circulate Aboriginal models of authority and action in other cultural contexts. During the 1980s, for example, a model of cultural *pedagogy* was powerfully transferred to national politics; white Australians began to be addressed not as competent oppressors but as young and ignorant people 'in need of teaching'.

More recently, Langton has used the model of 'a *theatre* of politics in which self-representation has become a sophisticated device' to describe Aboriginal media practices; and the notion of an '*actual dialogue*', in which all parties test and repeatedly adjust imagined models of each other ('be it at a supermarket check-out or in a film co-production'), to define a working form of intercultural exchange.[52] Another model is *diplomacy*, with the terms *negotiation* and *protocol* being used to enable an ethics of intercultural conduct as well as to assert Aboriginal rights in the political domain.[53] Pearson has argued publicly for a manipulation of middle-class cultural prejudices ('to capture the middle ground . . . you have to win them over by form'[54]), and a calculated orchestration of 'radical' and 'moderate' approaches, in order to *translate* 'a different culture, different language' and 'sometimes, pure emotion . . . anger and hurt and sometimes hatred about what has happened in the past' into 'action or results, something that people will listen to'.[55]

If these practical models exploit the performative dimension and participatory potentials of a mediated public sphere in ways that do translate between at least some of Australia's communities, they also extend to the daily news and to magazines the 'investigation of rhetorical tactics' that Curthoys and Muecke seek in a reconstructive movement *towards* 'nationhood'. However, they make the very idea of the nation provisional in ways that must complicate any contrast between the plurality of indigenous nations and a singular nationalism invested in a monolithic state, or between the divisive present and a more harmonious 'non-nationalist' future. On the one hand, Europeans have been told, pedagogically and dramatically, that our nation-building culture is the object of a reconstructive practice; old euphoric modes of national address are rendered unusable for state occasions, and the shift from a rhetoric of guilt to an ethos of responsibility requires us to participate in the reconstruction – a project which can carry its own euphoric charge. On the other hand, as the strength of the 1996 backlash against these changes suggests, actual dialogue and diplomacy demand a more strenuous and cautious response to the task of articulating what Tim Rowse calls 'the plurality of historical experience' in Australia, and the specificity of the narrative of nationhood as 'colonialist effusion',[56] than a happy-families version of diversity can provide.

In the immediate future, the Coalition government may take a more confrontational approach to Aboriginal communities and organisations. Even under Labor, however, it was clear that no singular model of citizenship can be extracted from 'Mabo' as a symbol of corporatist reconciliation. Australians are increasingly confronted with images of Aboriginal groups forming international alliances with other indigenous peoples, anti-colonial movements, and agencies such as the World Council of Churches and Amnesty International, to pressure or simply *bypass* Australian governments in order to secure basic rights for their communities. Moreover, the models of diplomacy and protocol are increasingly accepted by corporations seeking to negotiate amicable arrangements with the traditional owners of land, and by pastoral lease-holders anxious to avoid protracted legal proceedings under the Native Title Act; in early 1996, conservative politicians ebulliently testing their strength in Aboriginal affairs were asked to stop interfering by the mining executives and graziers who were once their natural allies.[57]

We are also confronted with Aboriginal regional self-government movements and distinctively urban voices challenging state-sanctioned Aboriginal organisations; and with a radically undiplomatic politics of critique and protest that continues to be necessary – not least in feminist contexts – to procure the kind of 'discursive power' for real people, not a floating cultural abstraction, that can translate as social and political empowerment. Discursive power does not mean that Aboriginal interests converge with 'the national interest' or coincide with the corporatist project. The same Noel Pearson who used an inclusionary national rhetoric to accuse the Liberal leader of 'urinating on a historic Australian achievement' when he threatened to repeal the Native Title Act, has said bluntly in another context, 'Mabo is extremely conservative. It is 90 to 95 per cent about protecting existing European interests.'[58] Insisting that Mabo is a beginning, not a culminating point, for Aboriginal politics, Pearson consistently derives his own discursive power from his community in Cape York.

It is often stressed in discussions of multiculturalism that the position of Aborigines is *particular*: the indigenous people cannot be subsumed by a 'national' policy that confirms their dispossession. The idea that an exemplary particularity can articulate something general has hovered on the fringes of theory for many years.[59] It is neglected, I think, because of the tenacity of a philosophical belief that 'the' particular (but exemplarists would speak of 'a' particular) can only *oppose* or *illustrate* 'the' general, resulting in bloody particularism on the one hand and typification, more benignly, on the other. Republican lunching plays on the second possibility. It uses the cultural resources of popular comic realism, casting 'the people' as a series of social types, to promote an additive, not a pluralist, model of multicultural nationality – in fact, a colonial 'logic of the collection' that, as Hage explains, exhibits the diversity of exotic ethnic life available in Australia.[60] The politics of Mabo have demonstrated the *general* inadequacy of this way of thinking, and they have also shown how challenges to it can work through national as well as local, regional and international frameworks.

Bruce Robbins has used the phrase 'comparative cosmopolitanism' to add to the inclusiveness and diversity of multiculturalism (in the US context) an edge of 'necessary but difficult normativeness' that 'makes room for moments of generalizing . . . without offering license for uninhibited universalizing'.[61] One generality useful to feminist critics that arises from the cosmopolitan example of Aboriginal media practices is that the possible nations we theorise can take shape in struggles to transform an actual nation; in this perspective on practice, the venerable *opposition* between identity politics, with their transversally local and transnational force, and a national politics thought only in terms of closure and containment, is itself of limited and local value. Mabo is not the only issue to have had a nationalising force while mobilising incommensurable interests in a transnational frame. The environment, massively, is another; so was an appeal by Tasmanian gay activists to the UN Human Rights Committee that forced the federal Labor government to introduce privacy legislation capable of overriding state laws which effectively prohibited all homosexual acts in Tasmania. These examples are not interchangeable. However, like the long-standing commitment of Australian feminists and multiculturalists to the 'regulatory practices and processes of social cohesion-building',[62] each has involved using the adversarial system to alter the contents and priorities of national politics.

To be involved is not the same as being subsumed by, limited to, or identified with a particular process. Something crucial about the abrasive flexibility of what I have loosely called identity politics is as easily ignored in a purist withdrawal from the contaminating space of the national as it is by lurid projections of the dangers of a republic. Such politics are not based on an ideal of the common good, and they do not derive their goals and values from a covertly sectarian abstraction of 'the' national interest.[63] For this very reason, they can construe both the state and the nation as practical sites of struggle and experiment. Moreover, social movements that collectively produce 'experience' are neither motivated nor organised to exclude what Rowse calls 'more troubling rhetorics'[64] from their own discursive spaces, let alone from the media or any other public sphere. Groups do try, of course; but it is much easier to eject an unwelcome guest from lunch than it is to purge identity politics of unnegotiably troublesome elements. To stress this is not to romanticise the ineffectual approach to politics that Beatrice Faust dismisses as 'expressive' ('happy to let off steam – especially if it can be done in front of a permissive and supportive audience').[65] It is rather to point to a real, even a pragmatic condition of the kind of democratic practice that Helen Irving envisages as 'a process of continuous debate, of continuous attempts to articulate new rights, new institutions and new models of representation'.[66]

None of this thinking is alien to feminism, and it puts us in a stronger position to deal in a positive way with republicanism in future. The media-centred logic of republican discourse is not just an anecdotal aspect of its social circulation, or a quirky by-product of 'Sydney' taste. One reason why our 'feminist critiques' of classical republicanism or of theories of civil society seemed so far removed from the *realpolitik* of Keating's republic is that the latter so baldly asserted the need for a national *marketing image*. It did not depend on restating the 'same old' nationalist mythology precisely because it was intended for economic and political conditions in which the borders of the nation, and the powers of the state to close them, can no longer be taken for granted. Keating's republic was about international trade, not civic humanism, and sales psychology, not democratic participation; 'becoming a republic' would make us feel better, which is good for the economy, and make Australia look better to its trading partners. With Keating's departure from the scene, there may be more space, not less, for feminist criticism in the media. In any case, what feminists need to do, in my view, is neither to accept nor to reject on principle the 'negotiation' process construed in general terms, but rather work out how to participate so as to further our particular agendas. This means thinking as constructively about the *realpolitik* of the present as we do about debates in cultural theory.

For example, the emergence of 'locality rights' as a basis for creating a regional, rather than a national, politics for indigenous peoples in Australia and countries in Asia should help to remind us that the marketeers' republic is not a product of European folkish nationalism, though it may arouse and manipulate nationalist feeling.[67] It is a product of a transnational economic and social order which savagely exploits women's labour and makes a mockery, in many places in our region and within Australia, of demagogic talk about citizenship. As trade unionist Pathma Tamby Dorai put it to a conference celebrating the centenary of women's suffrage in South Australia, 'fantastic economic growth is being projected for Asia as against Australia, but on whose backs?'[68] Dorai's question was not simply gestural: Australian feminists could, she suggested, pressure Australian companies to develop a formal code of conduct recognising the rights of workers in the Asian-Pacific countries in which they are investing – and her demand was itself an act of international pressure. A similar call has been made by a Bombay-based children's rights campaigner, Alpa Vora. Rejecting trade sanctions against third world goods made by children ('protectionism dressed up as social concern'[69]), she argues for the acceptance of ethical hiring and wage policies by Australian investors; recognition of the growing child labour problems in Australia's clothing industry; support for campaigns to provide schooling and health care to child workers in particular factories; and more co-operation between Australian aid agencies and anti-child-labour groups in Asian countries.

If we think 'regionally', in this way, of the republic as an occasion for an internationally oriented politics that uses the nation as open framework for action, then we are not back in the mythical world of the bushworkers and the lifesavers; it is crucial that these were not only white male but *protectionist* national icons. We are in a world being reshaped in many ways by the emergence of Asian capitalism and by the mythology of what we call, for convenience, economic rationalism.

This is not unknown territory for feminists. It is the very ground on which our practice of a conjunctive, not additive, pluralist politics – feminism *and* labour relations, feminism *and* immigration policy, feminism *and* human rights, feminism *and* environmentalism, even feminism *and* cultural theory – has been formulated and tested, often quite successfully, for many years. It is on this ground that we can work to make a difference between the monarchy and a republic. We may not succeed. But if we choose not to try, and in the end there is no difference, we will have no one to blame but ourselves.

Sydney, May 1996

NOTES

Acknowledgments: An earlier and shorter version of this essay was read at a seminar organised by the Research Centre in Intercommunal Studies, University of Western Sydney, Nepean, in November 1993; my thanks to Ghassan Hage and Lesley Johnson. My thanks also to David Bennett, Dipesh Chakrabarty, Kuan-Hsing Chen, Donald Horne and Ian Hunter for discussing particular points with me.

1 Helen Irving, 'Feminists to turn up heat on the republic', *Sydney Morning Herald*, 20 August 1993; Marilyn Lake, 'Sexing the Republic: what do women want?', *Age*, 2 December 1993.

2 On 'Asia-mindedness', see Tom O'Regan, 'Introducing Critical Multiculturalism', *Continuum*, vol. 8, no. 4, 1994, pp. 7–19.

3 Don Watson, 'Birth of a Post-modern Nation', *Weekend Australian*, 24–5 July 1993.

4 1993 AGB McNair Bulletin Poll, cited in Lake, 'Sexing the Republic'; 1995 Herald–AGB McNair poll cited in Milton Cockburn, 'Voter support strong, but only when they decide who leads', *Sydney Morning Herald*, 7 June 1995.

5 See Anne Phillips, *Democracy and Difference*, Cambridge, Polity Press, 1993, pp. 75–88.

6 David Burchell, 'The Virtuous Citizen and the Commercial Spirit: The Unhappy Prehistory of Citizenship and Modernity', *Communal/Plural*, no. 2, 1993, pp. 17–45.

7 Helen Irving, 'Republicanism, Royalty and Tales of Australian Manhood', *Communal/Plural*, no. 2, 1993, pp. 139–51.

8 Chilla Bulbeck, 'Republicanism and Post-Nationalism', in Wayne Hudson and David Carter (eds), *The Republicanism Debate*, Kensington, New South Wales University Press, 1993, p. 89.

9 See Desmond Ball, *A Suitable Piece of Real Estate: American Installations in Australia*, Sydney, Hale & Iremonger, 1980; Barrie Dyster and David Meredith, *Australia in the International Economy in the Twentieth Century*, Cambridge, Cambridge University Press, 1990.

10 See Henry Reynolds, *The Law of the Land*, Ringwood, NT, Penguin Books, 1987. The constitutional fiction that Australia was a land belonging to 'no one' ('*terra nullius*') at the time of British invasion in 1788 was overturned when the High Court recognised a form of native title in *Mabo* v. *Queensland* (1992).

11 Jürgen Habermas, *The New Conservatism*, Cambridge, Mass., MIT Press, 1989, p. 135.

12 Elaine Thompson, 'Giving Ourselves Better Government', in Donald Horne *et al.*, *The Coming Republic*, Sydney, Sun Australia, 1992, pp. 148–60.

13 Barry Hindess, 'The Very Idea of a Modern Republic', *Communal/Plural*, no. 2, 1993, pp. 1–15.

14 Warwick Brennan, 'ARM hails Libs' win', *Sunday Telegraph*, 10 March 1996. For confirmation of this view from a conservative republican, see Frank Devine, 'Yes to a president, but no to the rush', *Australian*, 7 March 1996.

15 Ann Curthoys and Stephen Muecke, 'Australia, for Example', in Hudson and Carter (eds), *The Republicanism Debate*, p. 181.

16 ibid., p. 179.

17 The strength with which racism persists in Australia was made clear by its electoral appeal in some parts of the country in 1996. During the federal election campaign, three conservative white candidates (two from Queensland, one from Western Australia) were rebuked by their parties for making remarks widely interpreted as racist; all received 'sympathy swings' in their favour at the election. One, Ms Pauline Hanson, was disendorsed by the Liberal Party for remarks about Aborigines. She stood as an Independent in a hitherto safe Labor seat, and won it with a 21 per cent swing.

18 Curthoys and Muecke base their notion of the 'exemplary' on Jacques Derrida, *The Other Heading: Reflections on Today's Europe*, trans. Pascale-Anne Brault and Michael B. Naas, Bloomington and Indianapolis, Indiana University Press, 1992. See also Wendy Brady, 'Republicanism: An Aboriginal View', in Hudson and Carter (eds), *The Republicanism Debate*, pp. 145–8.

19 'An Australian non-nationalism', *Sydney Morning Herald*, 12 February 1994; see also 'National independence a far cry from virulent nationalism', *Financial Review*, 14 June 1994.

20 Ann Curthoys, 'Single White Male', *Arena Magazine*, no. 8, 1993–4, p. 28 (my emphasis).

21 Peter Beilharz, 'Republicanism and Citizenship', in Hudson and Carter (eds), *The Republicanism Debate*, p. 115.

22 Kobena Mercer, '"1968": Periodizing Politics and Identity', in Lawrence Grossberg, Cary Nelson and Paula Treichler (eds), *Cultural Studies*, New York and London, Routledge, 1992, p. 425.

23 Horne *et al.*, *The Coming Republic*; Tom Keneally, *Our Republic*, Port Melbourne, William Heinemann Australia, 1993.

24 Ghassan Hage, 'Racism, Multiculturalism and the Gulf War', *Arena*, no. 96, 1991, pp. 8–13.

25 Michel de Certeau, *The Practice of Everyday Life*, trans. Steven F. Rendall, Berkeley, University of California Press, 1984, pp. 177–89.

26 The negotiations involved having the Act passed by the Senate before a deadline imposed by an impending legal challenge to Mabo by Western Australia.

27 On the difficulties of, for example, legislating to extinguish native title on pastoral leases (as some Coalition politicians wish to do), see Rick Farley, 'The Political Imperatives of Native Title', *Australian*, 15 May 1996.

28 Gary Shapiro, 'From the Sublime to the Political: Some Historical Notes', *New Literary History*, vol. 16, no. 2, 1985, pp. 213–35.

29 On this, see the special issue of *Australian Feminist Studies* on *Women and Citizenship*, no. 19, 1994.

30 There is a dissymmetry rather than a clear opposition between the Liberal and Labor parties on this point. While the Liberal Party's present leadership has shown a willingness to exploit racist and xenophobic feeling, and while it does express nostalgia for 'abstract' citizenship, its policy is not strictly anti-multicultural; much of today's policy framework was initiated by the Liberal Prime Minister Malcom Fraser (1975–83). Rather, the Liberals oppose the *regulation* of cultural relations, the *planning* of cultural futures, and the very idea of 'reconstructing' identity; they are much less likely to encourage new experiments in citizenship. So I have chosen to focus on the Labor version, as the more concrete and explicit of the two mainstream models.

31 Homi K. Bhabha (ed.), *Nation and Narration*, London, Routledge, 1990, p. 5.

32 Michael Kirby, 'Reflections on Constitutional Monarchy', in Hudson and Carter (eds), *The Republicanism Debate*, p. 74.

33 Hindess, 'The Very Idea of a Modern Republic', p. 15.

34 See Anna Haebich, *For Their Own Good: Aborigines and Government in the South West of Western Australia 1900–1940*, Nedlands, University of Western Australia Press, 1992.

35 Ghassan Hage, 'Republicanism, Multiculturalism, Zoology', *Communal/Plural*, no. 2, 1993, p. 117.

36 Michael B. Naas, 'Introduction: For Example', in Jacques Derrida, *The Other Heading*, p. xxii.

37 Donald Horne, *How To Be Australia*, Melbourne, Monash University, National Centre for Australian Studies, 1994.

38 Watson, 'Birth of a Post-Modern Nation'.

39 See, in this volume, Jon Stratton and Ien Ang, 'Multicultural Imagined Communities: Cultural Difference and National Identity in the USA and Australia'.

40 One factor distinguishing the history of the Australian Labor Party from that of the British Labour Party is the former's significant Catholic (and, until recently, usually Irish) constituency. See Ross McMullin, *The Light on the Hill: The Australian Labor Party 1891–1991*, Oxford, Oxford University Press, 1991. On the conflict over Communism, see Robert Murray, *The Split: Australian Labor in the Fifties*, Melbourne, Cheshire, 1970.

41 Bede Nairn, *Civilising Capitalism: The Beginnings of the Australian Labor Party*, Canberra, Australian National University Press, 1973.

42 Not unexpectedly, the Labor Party's practical efforts to move towards this goal have been unimpressive; one painful aspect of its defeat in 1996 was the unprecedentedly

high number of women elected for conservative parties from marginal seats, without recourse to a quota system. However, my interest is in the cultural shift entailed for Labor by the adoption of the 'goal' itself.

43 I argue elsewhere that corporatism as a political culture in Australia draws on Indonesian *exempla* and now looks ambivalently to Singapore as a model; '"Non-Nationalism" and "Post-Nationalism" in the Australian Republicanism Debate', *Trajectories II*, 1995 Proceedings, Institute for Cultural Studies, National Tsing-Hua University, Hsinchu, Taiwan.

44 Mary Kalantzis and Bill Cope, 'Republicanism and Cultural Diversity', in Hudson and Carter (eds), *The Republicanism Debate*, p. 143.

45 See Masao Miyoshi, 'A Borderless World? From Colonialism to Transnationalism and the Decline of the Nation-State', *Critical Inquiry*, vol. 19, no. 4, 1993, pp. 726–51.

46 Curthoys and Muecke, 'Australia, for Example', p. 190.

47 In most cases, at least two-thirds of all electors must vote 'yes' to secure this result. Votes cast in the Northern Territory and the Australian Capital Territory count only in the poll of electors.

48 Forty-two proposals to amend the constitution were put to the electorate between Federation in 1901 and 1993. All but eight were rejected, as were two further proposals for military conscription in World War I. See *Parliamentary Handbook of the Commonwealth of Australia*, 26th edition, 1993, p. 689.

49 Donald Horne, *The Public Culture: An Argument with the Future*, London, Pluto Press, 1994, pp. 40–57.

50 Marcia Langton, *'Well, I heard it on the radio and I saw it on the television . . .'*, North Sydney, Australian Film Commission, 1993, p. 84.

51 Langton, cited in David Leser's profile of Noel Pearson, 'The Cape Crusader', *HQ*, March/April 1994, p. 80.

52 Langton, *'Well, I heard it on the radio . . .'*, pp. 84 and 35 respectively.

53 See Catrina Felton and Liz Flanagan, 'Institutionalised Feminism: A Tidda's Perspective', *Lilith*, no. 8, 1993, p. 56; Langton, *'Well, I heard it on the radio . . .'*, pp. 91–2; Stephen Muecke, *Textual Spaces: Aboriginality and Cultural Studies*, Kensington, New South Wales University Press, 1992.

54 Cited in Leser, 'The Cape Crusader', p. 84; see also Sue Cant, 'Aborigines urged to target middle class', *Australian*, 6 June 1994.

55 Cited in Keith Scott, 'Last chance to translate grievance into change', *Canberra Times*, 14 October 1993.

56 Tim Rowse, 'Diversity in Indigenous Citizenship', *Communal/Plural*, no. 2, 1993, p. 49.

57 See Fiona Kennedy, 'Aboriginal consensus reached on Cape York', *Australian*, 6 February 1996; and Marcia Langton, 'No future in a return to racial paternalism', *Australian*, 18 April 1996.

58 Cited in Cameron Forbes, 'How green can a black afford to be?', *Australian*, 6 June 1994.

59 See Giorgio Agamben, *The Coming Community*, trans. Michael Hardt, Minneapolis, Minnesota University Press, 1993; and Gilles Deleuze and Félix Guattari, *A Thousand Plateaus: Capitalism and Schizophrenia*, trans. Brian Massumi, Minneapolis, Minnesota University Press, 1987.

60 Hage, 'Republicanism, Multiculturalism, Zoology', p. 132. Hage is glossing Susan Stewart, *On Longing: Narratives of the Miniature, the Gigantic, the Souvenir, the Collection*, Baltimore, MD and London, Johns Hopkins University Press, 1984.

61 Bruce Robbins, 'Comparative Cosmopolitanism', *Social Text*, no. 31/2, 1992, p. 183.

62 Kalantzis and Cope, 'Republicanism and Cultural Diversity', p. 143.

63 See Graeme Turner, *Making It National: Nationalism and Australian Popular Culture*, Sydney, Allen & Unwin, 1994.

64 Rowse, 'Diversity in Indigenous Citizenship', p. 52.
65 Beatrice Faust, 'Cultural clash of women in motion', *Weekend Australian*, 15–16 October 1994.
66 Helen Irving, 'Swissterhood', *Arena Magazine*, no. 11, 1994, p. 15.
67 See Terry Widders and Greg Noble, 'On the Dreaming Track to the Republic: Indigenous People and the Ambivalence of Citizenship', *Communal/Plural*, no. 2, 1993, pp. 95–112.
68 Cited in Catherine Armitage, 'Companies urged to halt Asian exploitation', *Australian*, 11 October 1994.
69 Cited in Adele Horin, 'Plea for businesses to combat child labour', *Sydney Morning Herald*, 6 March 1996.

16

RIDING MULTICULTURALISM

Gargi Bhattacharyya

I have been sitting in Britain, where I live, trying to think about multiculturalism. What does it mean now? To me in this place? This 1990s Britain seems very distant from any idea of the multicultural. I look at some other places – other sites of white anxiety – and I see that multiculturalism can be a key term of debate. In the United States the term seems to be clung to as the mantra which will somehow dispel the constant threat of violence.[1] In Australia multiculturalism seems to be regarded as heralding a cutting of ties with old dead Europe in favour of the new (economic) vibrancy of the Southern hemisphere.[2]

In Britain, however, the term seems to have faded from view. Just a talisman of some bad old time when dangerous extremists still roamed the corridors of local authorities or when people were innocent or hopeful enough to believe that racism could be cured through goodwill. No one seems to use the term 'multiculturalism' about anything happening today.

Instead, I think, some versions of multicultural thinking have sifted into various areas of life, while the term itself seems discredited and out of time. 'Multiculturalism' does not seem to be a key term in thinking around moves against racism any more – in 1990s Britain racism appears too violent a force for culture to fix.[3] However, even though far less is said about the necessity of recognising and representing cultural diversity (because we hope this recognition will improve everyone's quality of living and make for a more peaceable society), in some arenas multicultural thinking has seeped in as common sense. However bad things are in the era of backlash, they are not the same – things may not be any better, but they have changed. One change that I want to look at here is a shift in the status of 'multiculturalism' as a way of thinking.

MULTICULTURALISM IN BRITAIN AS A DEBATE ABOUT EDUCATION

In Britain, unlike some other places, multiculturalism has tended to refer to debates about schooling and education. 'Multiculturalism' means 'broaden the curriculum' – schools, and particularly the arenas of cultural education (literature, art, music, religion), have been designated as the places where demographic change can be represented as cultural diversity. This is the space in which the most public discussions of multicultural issues have taken place.

The Swann Report, *Education for All*,[4] is infamously the official version of multiculturalism in Britain – the declaration made by emissaries of the state, the promise made by government. Of course, this was all a long time ago. Swann is one of those early 1980s events which belongs more to the elongated decade of the 1970s in Britain. In the period from 1960s boom-time through IMF intervention to permanent large-scale unemployment, black people in Britain stopped being primarily 'immigrants' in the eyes of the state, and became 'communities'.[5] Swann is a recognition of this, that Britain is a changing place.

The best way to cope with all this unexpected (and unwanted) change is to embrace a new model of living called 'pluralism' – a doctrine which has had very particular meanings in Britain. The report outlined a vision of this pluralist future.

> It is important to emphasise here free choice for individuals, so that all may move and develop as they wish within the structure of pluralist society. We would thus regard a democratic pluralist society as seeking to achieve a balance between, on the one hand, the maintenance and active support of the essential elements of the cultures and lifestyles of all the ethnic groups within it, and, on the other, the acceptance by all groups of a set of shared values distinctive of the society as a whole. This then is our view of a genuinely pluralist society, as both socially cohesive and culturally diverse.[6]

Pluralism is a method of keeping the peace. Everyone makes small-scale compromises in the interests of the greater good. Individuals may follow their own paths, subgroups in society may live in all sorts of ways; the important thing is that we all agree about the important things. Social participation rests on the acceptance of certain overarching values – difference is acceptable as long as these are not disturbed. Distinct ethnic identities are to be protected, and even encouraged, but only within this framework of 'a set of shared values'. Difference is therefore acceptable as long as it does not lead to dissent, or the contestation of 'majority' values.

> It is essential, we feel, to acknowledge the reality of the multiracial context in which we all now live, to recognise the positive benefits and opportunities which this offers all of us and to seek to build together a society which both values the diversity within it, whilst united by the cohesive force of the common aims, attributes and values which we all share.[7]

At the time of publication, Swann was greeted with large-scale criticism from many quarters – its hopeful yet half-hearted appeals for pluralism seemed to gain little favour.[8] Now, in the mid- to late-1990s, 'pluralism' seems like a concept out of time, yesterday's slogan in all kinds of ways. However, whatever its considerable shortcomings, the recommendations of the report did represent a significant shift in official pronouncements about 'race' in Britain. There was an acknowledgment that the population of the country is diverse, that 'British' could mean a number of ethnicities, and that this was the way things were going to be from now on.

Since then many things have changed. Fewer people are optimistic about the chances of us all rubbing along together in cheerful diversity. In the aftermath of the *Satanic Verses* controversy and the war in the Gulf, Muslims in particular have been vilified as monsters who can never enter the contract of shared values. This shift in opinion has knock-on effects for other racialised groups. The spaces in which 'multiculturalism' might be imagined as a positive goal no longer seem available. The 1990s in Britain sadly seem more about frightening racist attacks and violent deportations than battles around cultural representation. Given this widely perceived shift, I want to think here about where those multicultural logics, with both their flaws and achievements, might have gone.

WHERE I LIVE

Birmingham is infamously the city with no centre. Like the rest of no-longer-industrial Britain, the place can seem tired even in its city centre. The quest to regenerate British localities has taken a variety of forms, including more recently the bypassing of dreams of a return to large-scale industry in favour of encouraging the development of the increasingly diverse service sector. Birmingham is no different in this case – the national trend towards viewing tourism and leisure as the most likely economic motivators in city development is evident here too. Perhaps what is particular to Birmingham is a damaging mythology which says that the second city has no defining characteristics, no attractions, nothing memorable, no culture that can be experienced as satisfying lifestyle. However unfair and unfounded these views may be, much of the promotion of Birmingham anticipates these criticisms in order to dispel them. The promotion of 'multiculture' – high, low and middling cultural forms, with obvious markers of being ethnically diverse – becomes part of heritage technique in Birmingham.[9]

AUTHENTIC ETHNICITIES IN HYPERREAL SPACES

The Arcadian Centre will be the first truly mixed development which addresses the problems of Inner City Regeneration. It will attempt to create a new heart for leisure and recreation which will encourage a flow of people across the inner ring road to revitalise a rundown area. The confidence this creates should encourage the upgrading of the adjacent sites.[10]

Billed as 'Birmingham's Covent Garden',[11] the Arcadian Centre is an example of the kind of heritage event I am thinking about. This complex highlights a number of the multicultural logics which I have been trying to identify. It is a mixed centre which has a large cinema and a variety of shopping facilities, located in a conspicuously 'dead' part of the city centre, full of boarded-over shopfronts and no-longer-operative restaurant signs (although this is changing now) – a prime site for attempted redevelopment.

The Arcadian tries to build on what this part of the city *has* represented – in order to highlight the positive assets which this hidden history could bring to the new tourism for which Birmingham hopes. To this end, part of the centre has been designated 'the Chinese Street' . The area of the redevelopment is close to what has been known as Birmingham's Chinese quarter – this is not a residential area but certain kinds of business and service outlets directed towards the Chinese community in Birmingham have been centred in this location. The Arcadian Centre feeds upon this existing ethnicised space in order to rebuild Birmingham's multicultural heritage as Britain's answer to Disneyworld, a pure hit of ethnic experience as you walk down the street.

When I first moved here I thought that this was an instance of the everyday postmodern. The look is sino-camp – obviously staged markers of ethnicity for even the least appreciative eyes to recognise and enjoy. The Ansells pub across the road aspires to pagoda-status and is called the Marco Polo. As Eco says: 'Disneyland tells us that technology can give us more reality than nature can.'[12]

In the Arcadian, the obviously fabricated symbols of Chineseness are more central to our recognition of ethnicities than any lived culture – to this extent, the 'technologised' appears more 'real' than the 'natural'. Either that, or the authenticity of everyday ethnicities can only be made visible to a general (intolerant?) audience through the use of heritage techniques which learn both from fun-parks and from Swann-style pluralism.

The business which is being promoted is very much the business of leisure, virtually the only business which seems viable in any British cities these days. The centre is in fact designed as a walkway – by various routes out and across from a central performance space, the pedestrian is invited to carry the feel-good of this shiny building out into the surrounding, more rundown areas.

As part of this, 'Chineseness' is redeveloped as one of the enticing and feel-good spectacles which walkers through this potentially threatening city space can enjoy and take away with them. Displaying Chineseness as a suitably entertaining spectacle is one of the things which will help to link different parts of a very fragmented city centre. In much the same way as multicultural logics within education, in this city redevelopment representing 'other' cultures, in however bizarre and toytown a fashion, is the process by which everyone learns to lose their fear and to rub along and move between spaces.

ATMOSPHERE

> There should be an atmosphere to the centre which should prevail at all
> times of day and in all sorts of weather. It should produce a place where
> people want to be. It will be created by many things . . .
>
> – the smells of Chinese cooking, coffee brewing, bread baking
> – the colours of flags and banners
> – the sounds of music and people
>
> A lot of these things which add to atmosphere are intangible and rely on
> people to make them happen. The Arcadian Centre should encourage the
> people to make them happen.[13]

The kinds of social changes which are implied here are in the manner of the ther-
apeutic – everyone will feel better if we just live this way. The development
brochure talks of atmosphere, of what people will *want*, but really what is
described are the factors which will create and maintain the optimum amount of
feel-good. The largest factor in this is the public display of varying ethnicities. The
development leaflet reads like a holiday brochure – the colours of flags and ban-
ners, the sounds of music and people – what is described is a way in which
everyday attributes, the ordinary cultures of daily living, can be seen through the
new eyes of the tourist. We will all be entertained into the right kind of atmosphere and then life will be good. Birmingham will be prosperous and peaceful.

Some of this peace and prosperity can be augmented by buildings, through city
sponsorship, by policy statements, but ultimately this whole way of thinking relies
upon ethnicised populations as assets, as the people who will make these things
occur. The redevelopment of the Arcadian Centre uses a kind of Disney
Chineseness to add flavour to its various entertainment projects. But in the end,
for this to be a truly entertaining spectacle, it also relies upon what the Chinese
community itself brings.

> Black B: This area is designated as Chinatown and the entrance off
> Pershore Street will be framed with a large Chinese gate. The choice of
> colours and materials together with the external lighting and the detail-
> ing of the gallery will add a Chinese feel to the area but it is the
> strength and vitality of the Chinese community itself that will create the
> right atmosphere.[14]

I think that this participation (both imagined and actual) from the Chinese community in Birmingham should warn us against too easy a slide into
postmodernising generalities. In some ways the Arcadian does feel iconic, artificial, displaced and unrooted in the manner of all sorts of late twentieth-century
experiences. But in other ways, this is a very local and specific story, reliant on
old histories of the people who have claimed this city. The display of heritage as

multicultural takes place in this interplay between architectural caricature and actual population. This could not be just anywhere.[15]

MORE CIVIC PRIDE

In 1993 Birmingham City Council sponsored an event called 'Together in Birmingham'. In some ways this was an echo of a 1980s local authority venture – the council sponsored a variety of groups, each of whom would put on a self-run event in its own community. The event promised to celebrate the cultural diversity of the city's population. Different groups would get the chance to represent themselves, with the aid of the non-directive patronage of the council.

The festival promised 'Strength through racial diversity' – a strangely aggressive slogan. The strength which is championed is both a version of the cohesive force cementing society (as outlined in Swann) and, more particularly, a pep-talk for Birmingham as a team. The publicity material opens with a rousing statement from the leader of the City Council:

> Over the years, Birmingham has witnessed the growth and change in its population. During the Industrial Revolution, the Welsh, Irish and Scottish communities joined us to uplift the City and more recently, communities from India, the Caribbean, Pakistan, Bangladesh, Greece, mainland Europe, Africa, China, the Middle East, Vietnam and others, have continued to invest in our City. Today, we are all Brummies working together for a brighter, richer future. (Sir Richard Knowles)

This is a civic echo of Swann's pluralist nation. There are many origins – but all the journeys have ended here. 'Brummie' is the umbrella identity which is strengthened by the variety of the embarkation points. Unlike Swann, there is no invocation here of some British way of life which is above cultural difference (justice and fair play as opposed to samosas and steel bands?), but instead these varied populations all have an interest in Birmingham the product. We are linked by our investment in a richer future. This is the work which joins people across their differences.

I think this a potentially slick move on the part of those whose job it is to promote Birmingham as an economically viable location. The publicity material trades in the usual damning mythologies of migration in Britain – the idea that these people come here and steal our jobs and/or scrounge off the state, that they ruin neighbourhoods and make streets unsafe – and substitutes a more upbeat take on what happens when people move around the globe. Instead of 'immigrant' in the bad British sense, we are offered something like 'pioneer'. In this myth, migrancy makes you enterprising and hard-working, willing to sacrifice for better futures. Birmingham, the place where many scattered populations meet, is fortunately reaping the benefits of this feisty stock. Britain's second city cottons on that its mixed bag of people might be an asset rather than an embarrassment and pretends to be New York.

Of course this is partly about tourism and civic pride, an attempt to increase the feel-good factor all round. This is the kind of thing I mean when I talk about multicultural common sense informing policies which make no mention of multiculturalism in its previous guises. The appeal is to the glamour of the cosmopolitan and the pay-offs of this glitz, but for this multiple difference to feel exciting rather than threatening, racism must be combated also. However we may feel about the practicality of this project, one version of the translation of multiculturalism into 1990s Britain is the assertion that feeling good about your city is about feeling comfortable with different people. Unlike some other calls to rally around your location, here racism cannot be part of the deal.[16] It might be no more than a paper pledge, but in this story anti-racist sentiment is good for city business.

> The City of Birmingham has a population derived from many races and cultures and as such must be seen to be at the forefront of initiatives to promote racial equality and the benefits of cultural diversity in British and European cities in the 1990s.[17]

Moving populations become tied to innovation and forward-looking thinking – the look of the future rather than the past, or the future and the past. There are two things going on here. On one hand, racial equality must be promoted, so we acknowledge that there might be a problem, that a population of many races and cultures does not necessarily lead directly to the joys of multicultural idyll. On the other, cultural diversity is a benefit, part of the European 1990s, especially for forward-looking British cities. 'Together in Birmingham' sells the population of Birmingham this image of itself – diverse in ways which are excitingly continental (as opposed to violently British). But to reap the benefits of cosmopolitan glamour you have to give up the truculence of racist fear. The publicity document describes the aims of the festival:

- to restate the City Council's implacable opposition to racism and all forms of racial discrimination
- to reaffirm the importance and the value of the contribution made to the City of Birmingham by all its many racially and ethnically diverse communities and their cultures
- to take pride in the cultural and artistic achievements of all the different communities that together make up contemporary Birmingham.

This agenda places the festival somewhere between campaigning and entertainment, somehow contributing to change in the future by enhancing everyday pleasures in the present. This kind of move has been typical of British take-ups of multiculturalism. There is an acknowledgment of the painful and damaging presence of racism in many facets of our lives. This is a result of too many people taking difference to be antagonism, a source of conflict. British attempts at multicultural practice have tried instead to promote a non-antagonistic idea of difference. Instead of difference being seen as different and competing interests, the plan has been to defuse the threat of diversity among the population by presenting this diversity as a life-enhancing thing for everyone. People come to be regarded as embodiments of their 'ethnic' culture, a constant display and entertainment for others. This is the latent possibility of diverse populations: in the multicultural city everyone becomes a perpetual tourist and everyday life becomes a constant, spectacle-filled holiday. This happy consequence is readily available if only we can all come to re-evaluate our perceptions and recognise the uncomfortable antagonisms of racism as the feel-good diversity of multiculturalism. The good life is here, and we have been living it all along, if only we could see it.

'Together in Birmingham' seems to be built around this logic – that we will all feel and act better when we realise just how much fun a varied population can be. What seems to be a slight shift from previous British multiculturalisms as promoted by local government is the joint stress on harmony within the city and the importance of this harmony for the public face of the city. The audience for this display is both 'Brummies' – who are all performing for each other all the time anyway – and 'outsiders', people for whom Birmingham must show its best side. Recognising our strength through diversity is an exercise in feeling good about ourselves and each other in order that the wider world can also feel good about us – pop-psych for a whole city.

RESPECTABLE DIVERSITIES

If the meanings of multiculturalism in Britain can be traced back to debates of the late 1970s and 1980s, the arena which enabled these debates to be influential was local government. A whole range of different types of people tried to re-imagine the role the state could play in creating a just society, their faith stemming from the belief that, in its local form, the state was an open and responsive entity. With the election of a Conservative government in 1979, the pursuit of any kind of progressive politics in a national parliamentary arena became increasingly difficult. For a period during the 1980s it seemed that local government could provide a place for a variety of political agendas that could not be encompassed by the national mainstream at that time. Jackie Stacey writes of this period:

> Many Labour councils were continuing to have substantial effects on the political and social life of people in Britain, particularly in major cities such as London, Manchester and Sheffield, despite the tightening grip of Thatcher's regime. Gender, sexual and anti-racist politics were a central part of the activities of the Greater London Council and other local

councils, before the central government stepped up their attacks on these bodies.[18]

It was in this period that the politics of identity meshed with a more established party politics in Britain. Multicultural initiatives at both a national and a local level stem from this time. However, whereas some form of multicultural logic seems to have entered other areas of decision-making (however unsatisfactory the outcomes may be), some of the other agendas sponsored by the former Labour-led Metropolitan councils are less evident in the day-to-day business of 1990s Britain. This is due, in part, to legislation passed by central government, most obviously in the prohibition of local attempts to develop more positive representations of lesbians and gay men. The infamous section 28 of the Local Government Bill of 1988 was a direct attempt by central government to curtail any gay-positive cultural initiatives by local authorities. This vindictive piece of legislation stated that:

(1) a local authority shall not:

(a) promote homosexuality or publish material for the promotion of homosexuality;

(b) promote the teaching in any maintained school of the acceptability of homosexuality as a pretended family relationship by the publication of such material or otherwise;

(c) give financial or other assistance to any person for either of the purposes referred to in paragraphs (a) and (b) above.

(2) Nothing in subsection (1) above shall be taken to prohibit the doing of anything for the purposes of treating or preventing the spread of disease.

What was being legislated against was any kind of 'multiculturalist' approach to sexual variation. The idea that the right kind of cultural intervention can improve the public profiles of lesbians and gay men is closely aligned to the thinking which says that affirming a variety of cultures will ease racism.[19] In both cases the assumption is that encountering positive and pleasurable representations of formerly despised groups will alter the perceptions of the viewer and that this new feel-good state will translate into more harmonious everyday living. Central government in Britain has actively legislated against this being possible in relation to varying sexualities. It has become hard to follow up initiatives concerning positive representations of lesbian and gay lifestyles in a climate where such initiatives cannot be funded legally by local government. While this law seems to have been rarely enforced, there are indications that fears of its enforcement have had an effect on funding and organising.[20]

Against this background I want to think about a very small-scale victory during the 'Together in Birmingham' festival. One group which gained a small grant under the auspices of the festival was the Birmingham Zami Network.[21] This is a local organisation for black lesbians in the old-style sense of an inclusive and spread-out kind of blackness.[22] The grant, despite its modest proportions, enabled an event with speakers and entertainment. It didn't change the world, but it did happen. I have been wondering about this event in relation to other lessons that I thought I had learnt.

> In making the local state the main vehicle for advancing anti-racist pol-
> itics they [proponents of anti-racism] have actively confused and
> confounded the black community's capacity for autonomous self-organ-
> isation. Here, we must make an assessment of the politics of funding
> community organisations and the dependency which that creates.[23]

This argument has become the common sense of a range of emancipatory struggles in Britain. How can groups maintain their own agendas when they are dependent on bodies which may sometimes become adversaries? Yet, for a variety of reasons, some kinds of group cannot maintain activity without some sponsorship from the local state, at however low a level. This would seem particularly true of groups which suffer prejudice from the larger black community as well as from white society. This may well mean that the group has an insufficient capacity for self-organisation, that the group's agenda and sense of itself is shaped by this relation of dependency, but I want to suggest that even in this compromised situation, useful things might get done.

Local authorities are no longer able to support positive representations of alternative sexualities. Gay groups are faced with a situation in whjch they have to think about how they reach their audience. For the multiple-minority combination of blackness and gayness (not to mention femaleness) you have to think realistically about who might give you your support. One of the reasons for the existence of a group like this is the (at least imagined) fear that the black communities in this country are not particularly hospitable towards varying sexualities amongst their own. The notions of having caught gayness off a white partner, of homosexuality as a Western disease, are still around.[24] The role of a black gay group is to create some kind of space in which to mark the double needs of this particular constituency. In the current climate in which sexual variation is actively stomped upon by central government, the dilemma is how to gain some kind of minimal funding from bodies which are not able to provide any active patronage of gay organising. This is not easy. Instead, what does become possible is that in a situation where multicultural logics have become mainstream – so that cultural diversity in some unspecified way is good for the local state to promote and sponsor – sexual variance can sneak in, semi-hidden, under that kind of agenda. Black gay groups can get some minimal funding under the ticket of diversity within blackness, rather than any more explicit discussion of different sexualities. Sexual identity becomes another exotic cultural attribute within broader categories of difference.

Admittedly, this reliance on what is acceptable in the eyes of the state in contemporary Britain limits or defines what a group of this kind can be or do. As Paul
Gilroy points out, there is a certain cost to dependency. Even if it is not total
dependency, the wish to be sponsorable has an effect on the activities and profile
of any organisation. However, I am loath to suggest that it would be better to
forgo this minimal sponsorship in the interests of some more authentic politics.
What would we be waiting for? And how would we ever get to that point of self-
organisation without these initial moves? So this is a half-way house, a kind of
semi-embarrassed, rather than out and proud, way of organising, but at least it is
some kind of organising on tickets which are too often not spoken for at all in
this country.

In the logic of multiculturalism, if you show a lot of different types of people
as manifestations of their culture, the world will be a better, fuller, more exciting and vibrant place. The opening for negotiation within this way of thinking
might be in the definitions of what counts as diversity and difference. How do
you mark a people's culture? Who are these groups of people anyway? As long as
diversity is the catchphrase, there can be many different kinds of organisings
which, as long as they highlight ethnicity as their defining feature, can still be
staged under the umbrella-term of multiculturalism and diverse cultural representation.

Sexuality is not the same as ethnicity in any of the usual ways in which we
might think about identity-formation. You do not necessarily grow up with it as
your home culture – with sexual identity you learn how to behave as you go
along. The notion of choosing what your cultural attributes are is more apparent in relation to sexual identity, where communities must form themselves after
everyone is pretty much fully grown. There is no sense of natural background to
fall back on.[25] However, under the banner of multiculturalism these differences
within categories of cultural identity can be evaded or glossed over. Instead, all
the various differences between people in their ethnic backgrounds and cultural
practices can be expanded to include variation in sexual practice. Zamis become
people who are as much in need of positive representation as any other racialised
group. The cost here is that sexual identity is subsumed under racial identity
because ethnicity is the agenda which has mainstream sponsorship, which can
somehow be made respectable. The benefit is that there is a space for black lesbians to receive minimal recognition from official bodies and, through this, to
run events and meet each other and others. In a situation in which the populations of various British cities are being reworked into positive assets, into the
heritage of those cities, it seems of potential benefit to sexual minorities that they
should also form part of this human capital which can bring pride to a city
because of its difference, rather than shame because of its perversity. In the current climate of attitudes toward same-sex relationships in Britain, it is very hard
to promote gayness as a positive choice, to suggest that that kind of diversity is
in itself an asset to the community, an enrichment of the wider society. By
hiding under the banner of 1990s multiculturalism, we can take advantage of

this small possibility. Suddenly, different ways of having sex are also part of what makes life enriching and vibrant. It may be that no one much believes this, including the people who are indulging in these different lifestyles, but it is still of some benefit to open the space in which these kinds of things can be suggested. I want to think of this as the process of riding multiculturalism for people who have very few other options right now.

My overarching argument is that multiculturalism has been transformed in 1990s Britain into part of a more liberal version of the heritage industry. Britain is largely considered, not least by its inhabitants, to be pretty much on its last legs. There has been a lot of work done on the violences which arise when people realise that imperial dreams are no longer viable.[26] Many of the attempts to give Britain a resurgence of hope and economic activity, or a sense of pride or positive vibe, have been tied up around the notion of heritage. The idea is that some places are receptacles of histories of past conquests and that this can be capitalised upon in the present when there are all too few battles that can be won. This way, we can all stop being losers because there has been a time when this was the home of winners on a global level. This version of heritage in Britain has tended to be conservative and regressive – it has been tied up with nostalgias for white nations that have colonised and even civilised other parts of the world. The dream is that there was a time when capitalism was broad and expansive and could grant people endless gifts and benefits, unlike the unhappy present in which there seems to be no economic future for any of the current generations. British versions of heritage have been concerned to efface this disappointing present in favour of reclaiming a far more valiant and gratifying past.

But this is not the only way in which British versions of heritage can work. I want to suggest that in some of Birmingham's representations of itself as the most multicultural of places, a more liberal version of the heritage industry is discernible.

This more liberal version of the heritage industry that I am trying to identify takes the diversity of Birmingham's population as one of the things which it is selling as a positive life experience and spectacle, both to outsiders, visitors to Birmingham, and to the people who live here themselves. Now the multicultural becomes part of the vibrant history of this city. As highlighted in the publicity for 'Together in Birmingham', there is a way of telling the stories of migrancy as heroic, as pathbreaking, as pioneering. By reclaiming this history of movement, of moving populations, as part of Birmingham's heritage, the city rebuilds itself as a tourist attraction by placing certain values upon these diverse communities. Instead of effacing the racialised from Britain's heritage and saying that the good times were before, when the nation was white and winning, now we can talk about the ways in which these waves of settlers are also part of the positive histories that people might want to come and look at. Of course, this relies upon certain exotic tendencies. The ways in which we look at the racialised (including ourselves?) seem inevitably tied up with the exoticising gaze.[27] But at least other kinds of people are allowed into the model, and civic histories make some attempt to acknowledge the different kinds of inputs communities might have had.

Of course, none of this takes away from the ongoing and seemingly escalating violence of racism in Britain. Wearing a dark skin and/or anything but North European features has always been dangerous in Britain's streets (and schools and police stations and homes, including your own) – even the white-dominated media now acknowledge this. Just because a version of multiculturalism has become commercial does not mean that it is working in any readily apparent way. Rather, multiculturalism enters mainstream logics in ways that might not touch racism at all, but which still shape everyday narratives of ethnicity. In tired old Britain this might mean that we all become part of the side-show, but at least in the new circus there are more types of freak to be.

CODA

Since this essay was written, Britain has gained a New Labour government which appears to have no more commitment to social justice than the bad Old Tories, and Birmingham City Council has amalgamated its Race, Women's and Disability Units into a new entity, the Equalities Division. One outcome of this process is that Birmingham has at last given up on the endless round of festivals for freedom – hopefully in the recognition that those kinds of local-authority jamborees can never touch people's everyday lives. We are all waiting to see what comes in their place. Birmingham now has a black gay group, Spyce, who receive funding from a local health authority in order to deliver community-based sexual health information. Multiculturalism continues to be evoked in all kinds of ideas about the excitement of urban living, but neither policy nor politics gives any clues about how we might begin to live together.

NOTES

I would like to thank the Management Suite of the Arcadian Centre, the Race Relations Unit of Birmingham City Council, Birmingham Zami Network and my ever helpful colleagues, John Gabriel and David Parker, for extra information when writing this. Of course, the end product is entirely my own fault.

1 For examples from the United States, see collections such as J. D. Buenker and L. A. Ratner (eds), *Multiculturalism in the United States: A Comparative Guide to Acculturation and Ethnicity*, New York, Westport, London, Greenwood Press, 1992; and perhaps more tellingly, counselling books such as D. C. Locke, *Increasing Multicultural Understanding: A Comprehensive Model*, Newbury Park, London, New Delhi, Sage, 1992.

2 For a piece about Australia which tangentially addresses the multicultural, among many other helpful issues for my purposes, see T. Bennett, 'The Shape of the Past', in G. Turner (ed.), *Nation, Culture, Text: Australian Cultural and Media Studies*, London and New York, Routledge, 1993, pp. 72–90.

3 There has been some national media coverage of the escalating problem of racist

violence in Britain; see, for example, 'An everyday story of racial hatred', *Guardian*, 6 July 1994, pp. 10–11.

4 *Education for All: The Report of the Committee of Inquiry into the Education of Children from Ethnic Minority Groups*, chaired by Lord Swann, London, HMSO, 1985.

5 For an analysis which represents intervention by the International Monetary Fund as a pivotal moment in recent British history, see K. Burk and A. Cairncross, *'Goodbye, Great Britain': The 1976 IMF Crisis*, New Haven, CT and London, Yale University Press, 1992.

6 *Education for All*, p. 6.

7 ibid., p. 7.

8 For an indication of the range of debates around educational multiculturalism in Britain, see M. Halstead, *Education, Justice and Cultural Diversity: An Examination of the Honeyford Affair. 1984–5*. Lewes, Sx, Falmer Press, 1988.

9 Richard Prentice uses the phrase 'heritage technique' in his book *Tourism and Heritage Attractions*, London and New York, Routledge, 1993. I take this to mean the process by which places and things, and possibly even people, become recognised as tourist attractions and spectacles of a supposedly still visible past and, sometimes, present. See Prentice's second chapter, 'The Heterogeneity of the Heritage Product'.

10 From building proposals for the Centre, courtesy of the Arcadian, Avatar and Faulkner Browns.

11 In publicity material from Grimley J R Eve and James & Lister Lea.

12 U. Eco, *Travels in Hyperreality*, London, Picador, 1986, p. 44.

13 Again, from proposals for the Centre.

14 ibid.

15 To find out more about everyday experiences of Chinese identity in Britain, everyone should read the work of my hugely talented colleague, D. Parker, *Through Different Eyes: The Cultural Identities of Young Chinese People in Britain*, Aldershot, Hants, Avebury, Ashgate Publishing Group, 1994.

16 In the 1990s, Britain has seen a resurgence of an organised far right which often uses rhetorics of place to mobilise racist feeling and action. The infamous election of a British Nationalist Party candidate as councillor in East London in 1993 provoked many debates around these issues. Old arguments about roots and family histories, home and enlightenment, re-emerged as both legitimation and explanation of white resentment and a turn to the racist right. In many ways, the anxiety has been about the failure to distinguish this from more liberal notions of heritage. The rhetorics of the two forms seem to flow together, however different the intentions.

17 Publicity for 'Together in Birmingham'.

18 J. Stacey, 'Promoting Normality: Section 28 and the Regulation of Sexuality', in S. Franklin, C. Lury, J. Stacey (eds), *Off-Centre: Feminism and Cultural Studies*, London and New York, HarperCollins, 1991, p. 285.

19 For more about this agenda and this period, and cleverness that I cannot match, see S. Watney, 'School's Out', in D. Fuss (ed.), *Inside/Out: Lesbian Theories, Gay Theories*, New York and London, Routledge, 1991, pp. 387–401. See also D. Cooper, 'Positive Images in Haringey', in C. Jones and P. Mahony (eds), *Learning Our Lines*, London, Women's Press, pp. 46–78.

20 For some indications of why this might be the case, see S. Sanders and G. Spraggs, 'Section 28 and Education', in Jones and Mahony (eds), *Learning Our Lines*, pp. 79–128.

21 The name is taken from A. Lorde, *Zami, a New Spelling of My Name*, London, Sheba, 1984, an autobiographical prose-poem about black women, sex and love in America.

22 The group takes its definition of blackness from the London Black Lesbian and Gay Centre. It includes those descended from Africa, Asia and the Middle East, China, the Pacific nations and Latin America, and descendants of the original inhabitants of Australasia, North America and the islands of the Atlantic and Indian oceans.

23 P. Gilroy, 'The End of Anti-Racism', *New Community*, vol. 17, 1990, p. 82.

24 I would like, however, to distance myself from the increasingly common argument that black people are the most hopelessly homophobic sections of humanity, and that this is an indication of their barbaric cultures. In the fraught interactions between black and gay communities in contemporary Britain, many false friendships are formed.

25 For some narratives of lesbian and gay identity-formations, see J. D'Emilio, *Sexual Politics, Sexual Communities: The Making of a Homosexual Minority in the United States*, Chicago and London, University of Chicago Press, 1983; and L. Faderman, *Odd Girls and Twilight Lovers: A History of Lesbian Life in Twentieth-Century America*, Harmondsworth, Mx, Penguin, 1992.

26 In relation to this, see P. Wright, *On Living in an Old Country*, London, Verso, 1985.

27 For an interesting (if speculative) exploration of these issues, see C. A. Lutz and J. L. Collins, *Reading National Geographic*, Chicago and London, University of Chicago Press, 1993.

RE:LOCATIONS – RETHINKING BRITAIN FROM ACCRA, NEW YORK, AND THE MAP ROOM OF THE BRITISH MUSEUM

Abena P. A. Busia

ON LOCATIONS: A LETTER TO MY FATHER

Dear Father,

Your life has left its mark on me. That is not unusual, all fathers leave some mark on their children. What I mean is, your so very public life has left all of us without the freedom to be private people, at least, at home.[1] Wherever we go, we are your children; forgive me, but this can be hard. It is not hard to have been your daughter, but the intimacy of what that means to me is in no way accommodated by the public nature of your name.

This comes to me with such force now because I'm trying to write an article for a collection on multicultural states. The trouble is, such reflections always assume so much: that we know who 'we' and 'us' and 'they' and 'them' are; that we know where and what 'home' is; that we have a sure sense of 'margins' and 'centres' to help us articulate the manifold implications of the movements of history that have brought into being these multicultural states in which we all live. Yet, as I sit down to write, I must begin with the fragments, the bewildering geography of my life that is a part of your legacy to me.

I made my first notes in the sixth-floor apartment on the edge of Harlem in New York City that has been my home these last few years. It's still strange to me that I have had homes you have not broken bread in. You don't know the homes of my adult life, the ones I created myself. This last apartment overlooked the Hudson River. It is a long way from the Windrush, and even longer from Ayaasu,[2] the last river we crossed when we returned you into the arms of your brother to take you home to rest with your ancestors. From one window I could see New Jersey and the George Washington Bridge, from the other, the 125th Street subway station and the towers of City College. Equidistant from the Barnard Book Forum and the Studio Museum, it suited my sense of myself as a person of multiple and contradictory worlds. I loved it there and wanted to buy it.

Forty-eight hours before the closing date, the deal fell through. At present, all my belongings are in storage. So I continued the notes in Standlake. I never did ask you why you built a house in a small village rather than buying one actually in Oxford. Anyway, I still consider it our family home though none of us has lived there permanently since you were carried out of it sixteen years ago. Do I hold on to it for your sake, or for mine? In our lives, thirty years is a long time to have had a place of legitimate address, even if we are never there. Thanks to you, we do own it, freehold, mortgage-free, even when empty.

Now I am here at 'Blue House', trying to finish, and being here seems to have made things worse. This bungalow at 'Zongo Junction' is no longer on the out-skirts of town. It is now a major crossroads on the edge of old Accra, separating Kaneshie market from the newer suburbs of Odorkor and Dansoman. Odorkor is unrecognisable now. I can't find my way to our confiscated home.[3] And this single-storey 'boys' quarters' seems as marginal now as it must have been to you and Mother some forty years ago. You didn't choose this place of refuge: the need for it was forced upon you by the quixotic history of our politics. In the hurried six weeks you had to put it up to house us before Sister was born, what were you thinking? Why didn't the University stand up for its rights in 1956 when Nkrumah insisted you be thrown off the campus at Legon?

Anyway, here we are again, at this sudden place of refuge whose location was determined by the fact that it was a vacant lot owned by Mother's father. And it feels as if we are still squatting, though we own this too, just about. It has the dubious distinction of being the only thing in this, our 'home' country, that you owned and that has never been confiscated by any of the governments since yours was overthrown. Still, our hold on this, the oldest home I have known, seems ten-uous.

After an entire lifetime (35 of my 41 years) spent in and out of exile because I was your child and thus the child of a *persona non* (or only partially) *grata*, noth-ing seems certain or secure. Mother and I are no longer sure in whose name the deeds to this land are registered – did Grandfather donate the land to her, or to both of you? Both you and Grandfather are gone now, so we can't ask, and for some reason the registered documents can't be found. A few weeks ago Mother and I found the papers for the original thirty-year mortgage on the house, but a few months after the first payments we had to leave so suddenly. Now, forty years later, there are no records of the subsequent payments. So we can't prove clear title even to the house we 'own'. Yet here I am, finding words, finding ground, in a home I discover I never left.

Yet, shuttling between all these tenuous homes, thinking about the politics of location in multicultural societies, I'm not even sure which 'location' I'm speak-ing from. In the United States I'm seen as so English; in England I'm an African; and here, in Ghana, I feel so keenly my African-American sensibilities.

'Home', in the most daily sense of the word, has for fifteen years been the small strip of the eastern USA between the Hudson and Raritan rivers linked by the NJ Turnpike between the George Washington Bridge and Route 18 – the road that takes me from Riverside Drive and 125th Street in Manhattan to Murray Hall at Rutgers University in New Brunswick. The other day, a colleague and I travelled that road north to Newark Airport. We had a witty, yet disturbing conversation about the question of exile and the choice of alternate homes. She is Indian, and her parents also had chosen Britain as their site of refuge. And, like you, they had been involved in the struggle for Independence and knew quite clearly, therefore, the intransigent imperial mind they had struggled against. Why, then, the choice of London as the place to flee to? 'What could they have possibly been thinking of, our parents, when they made such choices?' Her question hit me with full force. What indeed were you, all of you as a generation, thinking when, in flight from the places you called home, you brought your children to the very places that had stolen your homelands from you?

Her question came out of our reminiscences about the things that marked us as 'English'; we were speaking out of our consciousness that in the USA this is not expected of people of colour. We have lived in so many places where our blackness mattered. In Mexico City it signified 'USA', and it bewildered people when they found we were not in fact 'yankees'. In The Hague it signified 'colonial', and people were equally puzzled when our tongues tripped over the Dutch phrases we had memorised to explain that we were not from Surinam. But the meaning of that blackness was shaped centrally in Britain and the USA.

It has been a hard lesson, because in Ghana nobody notices. In a land where we are all 'black', that blackness is not significant to a child's mind. Years later, of course, I recognise that commonplace factor as very significant, for it gave us our strength. But we acquired something else we must face.

When we arrived in Holland, I was 6. My sister and brothers and I could sing the verses of the Ghana National Anthem as well as God Save the Queen. We did both with ease. But remember how, that year, the British International School was full and we were admitted into the American School? Each morning started with the Pledge of Allegiance. I remember my bewilderment that first morning when everyone else knew that this was to be said. No one had warned me of this strange ritual. And then everyone also knew it, so not even the teacher ever bothered to ask me if I did. It was assumed that everyone knew it, and would say it. I didn't know it, and couldn't say it. Today I realise it is quite short and simple, but I still don't know the words in order. I have to ask myself if, all those years ago, I couldn't or wouldn't say it. I don't recall what in the world gave me this prejudice against being American, for prejudice it was, but I do recall being initially quite bewildered, and then nauseated, by the jingoistic nationalism (I didn't name it as such then) that possessed my fellow classmates, a large percentage of whom were US military children, when the Americans launched their first rocket to the moon. The scene lives in my memory like a photograph. Even then I was unsettled by the aggressive virulence of the boys, cock-walking around the room. Yuri Gagarin was quite forgotten. That display of male cock-sureness still seems to me an inappropriate (and over-sexed) response to achievement and a mystifying, though apparently intrinsically human, response of one-upmanship that always elides history. Fifteen years in the USA have taught me that it can be called a national disease that sweeps across the natives in epidemic proportions at times such as the invasion of small Caribbean islands, the bombing of third world nations, or even a hockey match against the Russians. What amazes me now, on reflection, is how young we all were when these nationalistic expressions were already so much in evidence.

And I saw no irony in my affiliation to a Britain I had never seen. Where did it come from, this sense of alternate belonging? Listening to the BBC World Service?

But, travelling up the Turnpike, it later struck me and my colleague that our question was very much a second- or third-generation query? What choices did you have? And what was wrong with the ones you made? We have to be grateful for your motivations; what drove you all, as a generation, was a sense of excellence, a sense of donating something to your children to make us familiar with a world that had been introduced to you as strange. And you went to the places you could, wanting the best you could dream for us, no matter what the cost. For you personally it was not a matter of choice, but you are only an extreme case of a general generational dilemma, as I am of mine.

So if, in the end, my generation is marching through the streets of London reminding the Brits 'we are here because you were there', does that mean your dreams have failed? In a sense, your generation was dispossessed by the 'mother-land' of home, 'rootless on [your] own earth, chafing at its beaches'.[4] As a result, whether 'here' or 'there', my generation has been dispossessed in a motherland which is home.

On that ride to the airport, it seemed to both of us that in many respects to try to understand the history of the Empire and its dispersal is to try to understand and make sense of our own lives. To understand better how we as teachers construct that history is to find a way of interpreting our own experiences. And to comprehend how our orders of knowledge and affiliation uphold or trouble these seemingly monolithic imperial cultural centres is to comprehend our own troubled/disturbing and shifting relationships with them.

So Britain remains central to us, though in ways about which we are increasingly ambivalent. That the most solid 'home' − solid in the sense of size and of ownership − at the middle of these deliberations is in England seems to me appropriate. A house to which I am fiercely attached, it has the authority of longevity and a permanence that no other home in my life has challenged. Yet it is an empty house, seldom visited, vacant. If I am honest, it is also my 'home' because I spent my formative years there. Somehow the years between 9 and 19 seem longer than any other decade of my life. For both my colleague and myself, our English childhoods represent a kind of safety, at least from the dangers of what it has meant to be adult women of colour in the streets of New York and San Francisco. I, at least, started to work out my ideas of myself there, and more especially I started to learn my sense of the political world here (do you remember me asking you what a 'call girl' was in the middle of the Profumo affair?). All the questions of exile and identity, race and class which bedevil me now were medi-ated by a childhood and youth spent in the Cotswolds, in an England of the Swinging Sixties and Seventies.

That youth ended late, with your passing, and everything surrounding your leaving has left keloids around my heart.

ON TWILIGHTS

The condition of exile both invites and precludes nostalgia. The homeland, which increasingly in the mind of a child becomes an imagined homeland, is a place, not to which one *will* not return but to which one *cannot* return. It evokes nostal-gia as an originary, fixed place of perpetual longing and belonging. But the realities of having left, the reasons for leaving – political threat or persecution, economic deprivation or war – preclude sentimental fixations.

Then, having left the *adopted* homeland, in my case the Britain of my childhood, for yet another alien place, and claiming the idea of that adopted land as the nos-talgic homeland, itself becomes fraught with ironies and contradictions. Looked at from anywhere other than a perilously racialised USA, Britain of the 1980s was not a place a Black child would voluntarily go. The virulence of the aggression turned against all outsiders, in particular those associated with a faded, once impe-rial past, reminds one more of the USA in the 1970s than the England of my childhood. I grew up in a pre-Handsworth, pre-St Paul, country village.[5]

With time, distances contract, and – cities of contradiction – London seems no longer so very different from New York or Los Angeles. With its now large and very visible, vocal, minority population, and an increasingly palpable minority culture, Britain's youth is far more radically politicised than it was three decades ago. New York's yesterday has become London's tomorrow.

In the later sections of that monumental and troubling essay, 'What the Twilight Says', Derek Walcott addresses that 'cursed, colonial hunger for the metropolis' and the danger of its seductive betrayals. Yet in the end, caught in these metropolitan centres, we refuse to bow down before their simplistic con-cept of what we are. It is the process of reclamation which is hard. There is a sense in which all of us involved in colonial discourse are street walkers with Walcott through those twilights of memory, and dwellers with Reece Auguiste in Twilight Cities.

'Dear Mother, It is strange how a simple letter can change your life.' These words, the opening statement of the narrative that frames Reece Auguiste's film *Twilight City*,[6] changed mine. They are written by a daughter to her mother, in response to a letter from the mother in Grenada, to which she has returned 'home' after thirty years in London, only to find herself missing London and wanting to return 'home'. But 'the London you left behind is disappearing', says the daughter, as she begins to tell the story of what had happened in the decade (1979–89) since the mother left. I left London for New York in 1980.

Auguiste's film records the tension between London's seductions and its betrayals. It marks for me a watershed in my thinking about re-thinking Britain, negotiating, as it does, both the brutal realities of London in the years during which I was *absent*, and the nostalgia for an 'other' Britain that may or may not have been real but which exists in my memory, and in the memory of the mother being chastised. That film serves as my bridge. I have a kind of double vision. Of the generation of the letter-writing daughter, I am nevertheless in the place, and have the sensibilities, of the mother. I, like the mother, remember a Britain frozen in time before the 1980s. The daughter has lived through that decade and records the spiralling processes of dispossession for all minority groups, which I experienced not in London but in New York. For all of us, Auguiste, his fictional narrators and myself, London becomes a site of memory and contested histories; a site of history and contested memories.

The most striking visual image at the start of the film is that of the hand of the daughter, holding a pen, inscribing the words we are hearing onto a clean sheet of paper – writing the Nation. We can call it this, because what the letter becomes is a meditation on the meaning of home and belonging, which is in the end a meditation on the meaning of Britain as a nation. In Homi Bhabha's words, 'The nation fills the void left in the uprooting of communities and kin, and turns that loss into the language of metaphor'.[7] Auguiste's film, as a narrative of exiles and migrations, alienation and tenuous homecomings, makes that translation manifest. Bhabha's proposal that the cultural construction of nationness is a form of social and textual affiliation seems wonderfully evoked, spelled out, as it were, by this film. We witness the writing of cultures articulated in difference.

In responding to her mother's letter, the narrator tells a different story of London, or a story of a different London, by including different London stories. The mother's story, which we know only through the words of the daughter, becomes intertwined with the stories of other peoples – ethnic minorities, including Indian and Chinese migrants, and marginal groups like the homeless, and homosexuals. In the intermingling of her story with her mother's and with all the others' that she unravels, her historical narrative becomes also a contemporary meditation on the impact of Thatcherism on minority groups in London. The film takes us on a journey through the times and spaces of twentieth-century London, shifting from the contemporary 'driver's eye' view of the opening sequences to historical photographs of unknown Lascar seamen, and from archival footage of Nehru and Nkrumah to movies of newly arrived Caribbean immigrants, intercut with interviews and anecdotes of a range of London city-dwellers from all parts of the colonies who make up her population.

What Auguiste's film interrogates is a sense of national identity, which in the mythologies of most nations is known, collective and fixed. The articulation of difference from within the boundaries of the nation highlights the disjunction between mythic, uni-cultural worlds, which have never existed, and uni-cultural nationalist mythologies, which continue to be very strong. It is against these mythologies that the film writes itself. If 'the very condition of cultural knowledge is the alienation of the subject',[8] then the ambivalence and equivocation revealed not only by the fictional narrator and the histories she recounts, but also by the various cultural critics interviewed in the film, dramatise the contention that at the margins of a nation accrue multiple stories which implicitly challenge that nation's idea or knowledge of itself. 'From the margins of modernity, at the insurmountable extremes of storytelling, we encounter the question of cultural difference as the perplexity of living, and writing, the nation'.[9]

There are so many of us perplexed, always standing in between-places.

ON PEDAGOGIES

I re-think Britain from the ruptured and rupturing space of a different, embattled, racially stained and sign-posted, and aggressive society: the United States.

Staying home for the forty days of my father's funeral made me one week late for the start of graduate studies at Oxford. Two years later found me teaching in the USA, on a fifteen-month visit which, as I write, is now beginning its fifteenth year. What I wish to stress is the clear demarcation of the rupture. My entire adult, professional life has been shaped not by my father's life, but in his absence, continents away from both the 'homes' he gave me.

I have been socialised into racialised thinking as a teacher in the intellectually stimulating academies of the USA of the 1980s. It was there that I learnt to appreciate that my first birthright as a Ghanaian is a certain confidence. It guided me through a childhood in England, but I did not fully appreciate its power until as an academic I had to think about the implications of not having to deal, in my formative years, on a visceral and daily basis, with a dominant culture that dispossesses you of your being with every glance, denies you any history at all, in a way that makes the denigration of your history (as happens in Europe's imperial centres) seem almost a privilege in comparison. Ghana gave me, most significantly, no conscious need to defend my existence, something which every black child in the USA needs to learn to do with a life-long, life-sustaining vehemence if they are not to meet physical, and almost certain spiritual, annihilation. When you are born in a land where everyone seems made in your likeness, you do not, as a group, have to learn strategies of self-affirmation and self-love to counter the opposing, culturally dominant force of mirrors in which you don't figure, have no reflection, or are given images of yourself which do not in any way reflect the selves you see inside.

A few weeks after the publication of my poetry book, Testimonies of Exile,[10] a friend, another black woman poet, from New Orleans, threw a party for me. It was the end of a fellowship year we had both spent at UCLA, and we were surrounded by friends wishing us farewell. I was happy, and all dressed up for the occasion. Having dropped my family at my friend's apartment, I was cruising through Westwood trying to park, with not a care other than that of finding a parking space. Suddenly, seemingly out of nowhere, a white convertible VW pulled up beside me, and the driver, a fresh-faced youth with glowing cheeks and muscular physique, turned his California sun-bleached, tousled-haired head toward me, and with slow deliberation projected at me the words, 'Nigger bitch!' I looked at his eyes, expecting them to register something, anger, hatred even, some kind of passion I could hold on to, to explain the venom in his voice at my presence there, minding my business behind the wheel of a grey Honda Civic. But there was nothing. His eyes were dull, quite ordinary, everyday dull, as if shouting obscenities at black women in the streets, at me in particular on this occasion, was a quite unexceptional, only-to-be-expected kind of activity on a Friday evening in Westwood. I wondered what I had done to deserve that – what except, perhaps, just being. There was not the comfort of rage for me, only the dead commonplace of my invisible personhood rubbed out by his vision of my blackness and femaleness.

I had felt so beautiful that day.

I have told this story often. It becomes more chilling with each re-telling when there are black women in the room: they always know what's coming before I finish the story.

As an African child passing through Britain to the USA, you never forget the distorting mirror of 'race'. Fifteen years in the USA has inescapably and radically altered the ways in which I deal with this category, and thus the way it shapes my negotiations. Whatever 'race' means, however many ways we find to deny or contest the idea and wherever it may 'float' as a signifier, it always ends up lying on my skin, signifying, in those lands in which I've lived outside the continent of my birth, a great deal. When 'away' I am always Black, and African.

I have said frequently, and in many places, that I have known I was an African all my life. I did not know I was 'Black' until I started living in the United States.

A point of clarification. My claim is not that Britain is not race-conscious. Such a claim would be patently absurd. My claim is simply that the ways that race-consciousness, and racism, play themselves out there are radically different, or at least seemed different in the consciousness of a Black middle-class child in Oxford in the 1960s, as distinct from a Black academic thirty years later in the United States, where (unlike class-stratified Britain) everybody claims to be middle-class. Furthermore, that consciousness is markedly different not only from the world of a child in Britain thirty years later, but the world of a similar child almost anywhere in the United States even in the early 1960s. That is, both the shift in time and the shift in continental location are significant. I could not have been me in Britain today, or in the United States thirty years ago. Class mattered more in Britain then than it seems to do today, and it has, so far as I can witness, almost never mattered in the United States when it comes into contention with race.

The point of these life stories is the way in which they focus us, on a commonplace yet visceral level, on the living contradictions. I have been wrestling with these contradictions, as a teacher, and a teacher of teachers, for a long time. What is at stake for the student or the teacher in the classroom, in a shifting educational world besieged by the opposing armies of the 'multicultural' wars?

These questions are asked from a context in which ethnic minorities are articulating the desire to have our voices heard, a desire to celebrate our own signs of difference and validate our stories. We need to bear in mind constantly that on this issue we are battling from the 'margins' those very uni-culturalist mythologies on which the nations in which we live and work, at least in the western world, are founded.

In the USA, for example, it does not, institutionally and in the popular imagination of its birth as a nation, 'matter' about the decimated Native populations. Neither does it 'matter' about the Middle Passage. We all came over on the *Mayflower*, and have lived in a world of Boston Tea Parties with the self-evident truth of equality of manhood guiding our Manifest Destinies ever since. The attempt to bring the myth up to the level of reality can't be achieved, therefore, without institutional takeover, without revolutionising the very concepts on which national and state educational policies are structured. Nor can it be achieved without revolutionising our own approaches to what we say and do in our classrooms.

Rather than offering a blueprint for an unavoidable revolution, I want to speak of small examples faced by anyone standing up to teach anything about 'Africa'. Let us begin with language – and be warned, I'm going to speak in and of the banal, about commonplaces and clichés. For example, didn't we all learn in elementary geography that a continent is a large land mass surrounded by water? Where is the water that divides Europe from Asia, and where is the water that divides Egypt from the rest of the African continent? We know politics is geographical, but we also need to grasp that geography is political.

How many times have we heard friends say, 'Finally, I'm going to get to Africa'? They very rarely say, 'I'm going to Kenya or Tanzania or Egypt'. They're going to 'Africa' in a way that people rarely say they are 'going to Europe' unless they mean they will be visiting three or four places on the continent. Otherwise, they say specifically, 'I'm going to Sweden', 'I'm going to Germany'. Why this difference? We speak about Africa as if we could take a stroll from Marrakesh to Mombasa. Again, in the classroom it's hard to convince students, even with superimposed maps, that the continental United States is smaller than the Sahara Desert. And the continental United States is not growing, the Sahara Desert is.

And once we arrive on the continent, the 'natives' don't live exclusively in mud huts thrown up in jungles. A jungle is a tropical rain forest, and such forests cover less than 10 per cent of the entire continent. And I have yet to find anyone who can tell me the difference between an 'adobe ranch house' and a 'mud hut', except that when a single-storey structure made of building blocks fabricated from sand is found in New Mexico it is called the former, and when found in Mali it is called the latter. It is depressing to be still having to begin at ground zero, even in university classrooms, but such is the tenacity of pernicious stereotypes.

The point about beginning with such commonplaces of language is that it is in these commonplaces that the most intransigent assumptions reside. For example, there is a long and pernicious history behind the separation of Africa into 'North' (where there are ancient, proud civilisations with a material culture

275

Europe can venerate) and 'darkest' (where we have built nothing material that lasts – the ruins of Zimbabwe having been built by aliens from outer space – and therefore can have no sacred systems of thought or forms of social order that could have contributed anything for the benefit of mankind).

Clearly, we shape or alter human history in our allocation or re-allocations of agency, for to deny any peoples agency is to keep them perpetually in the status of dependants. Can this be our investment in teaching that for every Abraham Lincoln there was a Frederick Douglass, or for every John F. Kennedy a Martin Luther King? Further, can this be why it matters to me that my students know that the words 'if you educate a man you educate a person, if you educate a woman you educate a nation' were said not by Malcolm X, as is believed all over the United States, but by Aggrey, the Ghanaian educator and founder of Achimota College? Simple though these teachings seem, can we, through their means, create a cultural democracy in the classroom in defiance of culturally supremacist world-views?

In the USA, as in most of Western Europe, the last fifteen years have forced those of us in the academy to re-think our various (subject) positions on the many ways 'different' cultures become institutionalised. At the heart of the multicultural project, however defined, is an assumption of a pluralistic world in which many peoples can live together in harmony if we but learn to respect, and learn about, one another. Embedded in that assumption is another, namely, that cultures can be known, quantified and somehow acquired, and that each cultural component of that pluralistic whole is in itself unified and representable. Even if the first assumption be true, the second must surely be questioned.

Also vital to the politics of the debate is the contention by those of us who are 'hyphenated' others in the modern nation-state that our cultures and/or histories – and we often elide the distinctions – have been in some way marginalised, under- or mis-represented in the institutions of the states in which we live. This is as true of Blacks in Britain as of African and Native Americans in the United States. Thus the project of multicultural education assumes, or perhaps implies, a re-dress of history. In the United States, this is the implicit assumption underlying, for instance, the institutionalisation of 'Women's History Month' and 'Black History Month'. Both these celebrations work off the construction of gender as history or, central to our purposes, race as history. Furthermore, they promote the assumption that reversing the annihilation of racial history can somehow reverse the history of racial annihilations. While I am and will continue to be an ardent advocate of Black and Women's History months, to walk into the classroom with such an assumption would be an act of bad faith. We cannot believe that what we are undertaking now can either erase or rectify the histories that have led to the necessity of our actions. What concerns me is that unless we bear inside us all the time, in particular as we navigate our classrooms, a recognition that the long-range objective of all these exercises must be a re-negotiation of power, a shattering of the institutional structures that make learning about 'others' an exotic privilege rather than a strategy for the necessary transformation of how we face history, we will in the end betray ourselves again.

'AND NOW FOR COMMODITIES. FIRST, SOFTS . . .'[11]

I am concerned about the culture wars both inside and outside the classroom. I end with a meditation triggered by seemingly unconnected, trivial events of one week in the summer of 1993. At the beginning of the week I was shopping in an arcade on 125th Street, inundated by 'kente' cloth artifacts, from top-hats to candle-sticks, and, as an Asante, feeling myself very much 'on sale' as a cultural object. At the end of that same week I was in the Map Room at the British Museum, poring over eighteenth-century plans and inventories of the Slave Castles along the Guinea Gulf, and seeing myself listed amongst the commodities. I wonder about the connections . . .

It was the first time I had ever been to the Map Room and, for a bibliophile and lover of ancient things, such as myself, it was almost a place of enchantment. I did not find what I was looking for, but I found more than I had bargained for. Among the treasures secreted there was a series of drawings of the forts along the West Coast of Africa, including detailed plans of almost every fort and castle on Ghana's short but densely castled coastline. What struck me was the care, the meticulous care with which these plans had been drawn, the detail with which all manner of things had been itemised: numbers of gun carriages, numbers of European and Native soldiers, numbers of muskets, pounds of provisions and, of course, numbers of slaves. There we were, itemised, among the goods, chattels and property. It was a salutary reminder, if one were needed, that this is what we have always been, to them. It is this element of property that begins to nag at me: our eternal marketability. The influence of the marketplace makes me wonder nervously if the success we have had in our multicultural wars, within existing institutions, might not in the end result in a pyrrhic victory.

Over the last few years, the markets of the major cities of the USA have been flooded with African artifacts. For instance, you can get anything you want in simulated kente cloth. Yet few people, including few of the vendors themselves, know what kente cloth really is, know that the real fabric is woven on narrow looms to make strips which are then painstakingly sewn together – an ancient craft, remote from the fabrics and paper now commercially produced in imitative design and sold under the same name. The distinction is as important as the difference between silk and rayon, or real pearls and costume jewellery. Yet, getting this point across can be a losing battle. Why strive to appreciate authenticity when we can get by just validating the imitation? It is as if, having acknowledged that there is something to celebrate, out of Africa, we do not need to acknowledge anything else, but what has been claimed can be marketed for consumption. Everything we are or can produce remains a commodity, fetishised perhaps, but a commodity none the less. At a great jamboree we are selling ourselves again, maybe not for trinkets, but as trinkets.

My concern is not to decry the work we have done and the progress we have made, but to pause and raise the question about how much institutional change we have really wrought. For example, with the explosion in the number of books by and about black people in the USA, how many of our English majors across the country are required to take even one course in the history and development of African-American literature to graduate as well-educated American citizens? For the most part, they can still get through college without having to do so, regardless of the major impact black life and letters have had on the art and imagination of the literary landscape of the USA. We can sell a course on Toni Morrison, or one that includes her writings, but it is still possible to do this without having to make our students learn to take as legitimate the well-springs of that cultural existence which are the well-springs of her art. Why strive for understanding when we can get away with simulating knowledge?

In the eighteenth and nineteenth centuries, the map-makers brought treasures from Africa to Europe, and venerated the gold of Asante and the bronzes of Benin. A century later these same artifacts can be displayed to sell-out crowds in the museums of London and New York. What troubles me is how little recognition is given, in marketing these wonderful exhibitions, to the fact that, at the same time as these artifacts were being made, the artists who made them were being sent to Europe in ship-loads as slaves. Furthermore, just as the people were being massacred when those gold and bronze artifacts were being plundered, so countless numbers of our Black youth are now dying on the streets of London and New York, because they are Black. Meanwhile, the exhibitions flourish and the institutions simply count the dead. Floundering between High Art and degradation, we are trying to teach a new generation respect for things when we have proved incapable of teaching them respect for the peoples who produced those things.

Multicultural educational projects, if pursued with integrity, become radical, if not revolutionary projects. I used to believe it a simple goal to begin by teaching us all to admit that all of us are part of the same part-glorious, part-fallible, part-angel, part-beast, human race. Fifteen years later I still keep the faith but, a little wiser perhaps, I no longer believe it to be a simple task.

ON TIED TONGUES AND TRANSLATIONS

Wherever it is I live, I still feel an outsider. During my childhood in England I was a colonial, whereas in the USA it is my English childhood that makes me different. And yet I live with the awkwardness of knowing that once I return 'home', as now, to Ghana, that place of origin that has given me a sense of identity, a sense of belonging, even if shaped as the place I was away from, I am still a stranger on returning here. I am fiercely claimed not so much for myself as for my ancestry. I can't yet walk the streets of Accra with the assurance with which I negotiate the streets of New York, nor talk to vendors with the ease of a common language as I could in the markets of Oxford. There I spoke with the fluency of 'their' tongues, here I stumble over words of languages which are supposed to be my own. That discrepancy makes me tongue-tied with embarrassment in situations in which, in other places, I would be articulate. I have remained so firmly grounded in the language of England that sometimes I feel all England has done is to have taken away my language and replaced it with one that made me unfit both for where I was going and for where I came from and have now returned to.

I have grown nervous of writing. Years of transatlantic existence, negotiating two realms where spelling and punctuation are the same, but not quite, has made me wary of spelling or writing anything. All sentences, vowels and word-endings threaten to become wrong, and I live in terror of losing my words altogether. Forgetting how to spell is only the beginning of a form of insurgent terror through which my memory will exact an incomprehensible revenge, for a fault I can no longer recall. Yet, at other times, I speak – and walk the streets – with boldness, unselfconscious about the multiple identities I claim. They are seldom in contention. We co-exist, so to speak, for I can have no idea of who I would have become if I were not the woman who was once a little girl in Holland learning to skip (as they say in England) or jump rope (as they say in the USA), or with her brothers and sisters sneaking into a German newsagent's in Mexico City to read American comic books. Truly multi-lingual people think in their multiple tongues, and make translations as necessary.

For those of us exiles, migrants, immigrants and refugees who have turned the world into multicultural states, such 'translations' are our state of being. When not tongue-tied by a multiplicity of half-known languages, our fluencies are displayed not simply through languages, but by what we do with our adopted tongues to transform them into our own. And furthermore, our fluencies manifest themselves most crucially in our most commonplace 'cultural translations' – like those of Ghanaian women, such as my mother, who in the absence of yam, cassava and plantain and their mortars and pestles, learn to make fufu on electric and gas cookers using potatoes and potato starch, or who in the absence of cassava leaves make palaver sauce with cabbage, spinach, or kale. I have written elsewhere of how my mother taught me to track down corduroys and lightweight wools whose colours and lines most closely approximated the aesthetics of traditional cotton prints, so that I could wear ntama in mid-winter without either violating the elegance of their lines by wearing bulky woollen polo-necks underneath or, alternatively, freezing in cotton for the sake of 'cultural purity' in the snows of Europe.[12]

Translation is thus a commonplace in the lives of exiles and migrants, a means of making the strange familiar, or making the familiar out of the strange: we adapt. Such adaptations over decades and centuries can turn fontonform into the steel drum and the Kpanlogo into the Harlem Shuffle. And translations begin with the commonplace, with specific adaptations for the purposes of recreation, keeping, at least initially, recognisable signs of the original. We translate to keep ourselves familiar with ourselves, against all the odds.

Among the maps I discovered last summer were two sets, drawn in the eighteenth century, approximately half a century apart, of those Ghanaian coastal slave forts. The first set was drawn by the English, the second by the Dutch. I came upon the English maps first, and saw that on the map of Dixcove Castle, in what is now the Western Region of Ghana, outside the fortified walls of the fort, the British map-makers had written the words 'Negro Town'. On the Dutch map, drawn half a century earlier, with, naturally, most of the legends in Dutch, in the same place the map-makers had written the word '*cromme*'. The Dutch had recorded the native Akan word for 'town'. At the time, I was just excited that, unlike the British, all of whose maps record the slow decimation of our people-hood, this one map represented, in that soul-ravaging afternoon, a small glimmer of recognition of our being: a language of our own.

Afterwards, I had another revelation: my personal history has replicated the history of my nation; Akan, Dutch, English – I had access to all three languages. It is precisely that peculiar geography of my life that enables me to recognise and make translations.

NOTES

1 The aspects of my father's life that are relevant for an understanding of this letter are that, as a public figure in our native Ghana, he was, at the time of Independence, Leader of the Opposition against Nkrumah. For most of my childhood and youth, however, he spent two periods abroad, 1959–66 and 1972–78, as a university pro-fessor and Leader of the Opposition in exile. In between, he was, in Ghana, director of the Centre for Civic Education, and chairman of the Constituent Assembly before becoming the first (and only) Prime Minister of the Second Republic. His government was overthrown in January 1972, and he died, at our home in Oxford in August 1978, without ever returning to Ghana alive. Ghana is now in her Fourth Republic.

2 The Windrush valley lies south-east of the Vale of Evesham and north-west of the Thames Valley, in the countryside west of Oxford; the river, which runs through such historic towns as Burford and Witney, meets the Thames one mile east of Standlake, the village in which I grew up. The Ayaasu runs through Brong-Ahafo, the region in the centre of Ghana which lies between Ashanti Region and Côte d'Ivoire. It marks one boundary of the Wenchi Traditional Area, of which my father's family are the tradi-tional rulers. His final homecoming required that he return across that river to be received by his family for the last time at that border crossing.

3 One of the first acts of the military junta which overthrew my father's government in 1972 was to confiscate his properties and assets and those of most of his ministers. In the nearly twenty-five years since, almost all properties and assets have been restored to those individuals or their heirs, but not ours. Despite the fact that my father had been working for over thirty years before he became Prime Minister, and despite the fact that his assets had been acquired, and declared, before taking office, a committee chaired by Justice Taylor ruled (against all logic, common sense, and evidence to the contrary) that all those assets had been unlawfully acquired and paid for by public funds. Since then, none of the many governments of Ghana, either civilian or military, has had the political courage to reverse this decision. My father's properties remain confiscated and all his assets in Ghana remain frozen almost two decades after his death.

4 D. Walcott, 'What the Twilight Says: An Overture', in *Dream on Monkey Mountain and Other Plays*, New York, Farrar, Strauss & Giroux, 1990, p. 21.

5 There were several uprisings of Black youth in Britain in the 1980s in resistance to the

growing racism manifest throughout the country. Outside of London, perhaps the two most prominent were those in the Handsworth district of Birmingham and the St Paul's district of Bristol.

6 *Twilight City*, dir. Reece Auguiste, London, Black Audio Film Collective, 1989.
7 H. K. Bhabha, 'DissemiNation: Time, Narrative, and the Margins of the Modern Nation', in H. K. Bhabha (ed.), *Nation and Narration*, London, Routledge, 1990, p. 291.
8 ibid., p. 301.
9 ibid., p. 311.
10 Abena P. A. Busia, *Testimonies of Exile*, Trenton, NJ, Africa World Press, 1993.
11 Since childhood I have listened to the BBC World Service financial news, for the price of cocoa, Ghana's main financial staple in the world economy. Commodity prices were always given after currencies, and always introduced with the words, 'And now for commodities. First, softs: the London Daily Price for raw sugar . . .'; then would follow coffee futures, then cocoa. During the last decade, the formula has changed: the reports have begun with oil.
12 Abena P. A. Busia, 'Performance, Transcription and the Languages of Self', in Stanlie M. James and Abena P. A. Busia (eds), *Theorizing Black Feminisms*, London and New York, Routledge, 1993.

18

COUNTERPOINTS

Nationalism, colonialism, multiculturalism, etc. in personal perspective

Ihab Hassan

> It is necessary to uproot oneself. Cut down the tree and make a cross and carry it forever after.
>
> Simone Weil, *Waiting for God*[1]

The perspective of this essay is personal, a record of passages and crossings – not left, not right – of lived and meditated experience. Call it autobiography, a way to enter the subject, a way to question theory, ideology, the pride of mind. But autobiography deceives. And in a bullying age, it often serves as self-empowerment: 'I was there, I suffered, *hear me!*'

The autobiographical passages counterpointing this essay insinuate, I hope, a different query: 'I was born in Egypt, I have crossed, so what?' I regard my birth in Cairo as fortuitous, an accident, not a destiny. It is an accident, of course, full of resonances, gravid with memories. But do these suffice to sustain the pathos of exile, mummeries of alienation, horrors of revanchism and irredentism?

True, I have lucked out. Unlike Bosnian or Palestinian, Haitian or Vietnamese, Cuban or Ulsterman, fortune has granted me a place. This is humbling. But destiny dispenses with gratitude as it does with cant. It needs only lives.

Autobiography simulates the past in *the present*. It feigns recollection. But it cannot escape the pressures of its moment, the prejudices of its author. Why not admit, then, these pressures, these prejudices, from the start?

I confess a certain antipathy toward the intellectual tone, not the moral ideals, of current postcolonial and multicultural studies. Exceptions, of course, abound: for instance, some essays in Barbara Johnson's collection, *Freedom and Interpretation*, or in Tom O'Regan's *Critical Multiculturalism*. Still, the tone, in America at least, repels thought. Consider a gross instance. The Nigerian Nobelist, Wole Soyinka, reports that after a lecture in New York on African history and literature, a young, black American woman stood up angrily to ask him: 'What about the role of the Jews in enslaving Africans? Why did you leave that out?' Soyinka replied that he had done much research and had found evidence of English and Dutch, French and Arab forts, used in the slave trade, but no evidence of Jewish forts. The woman shot back: 'Facts don't matter.' Before outraged, no, outrageous desire, what can avail? Auschwitz did not happen, nor Hiroshima, nor Gulag, nor the Middle Passage with its ten or twenty million slave victims.

'Facts don't matter'? They matter enough when they serve grievance. In any case, I live in another climate of assumptions, another ambience of discourse. I share other dispositions. First among these I count a pragmatic distaste for 'strong' explanations, purporting to call the turbulence of history to order. (Have we something to learn here from chaos and complexity theories?) Such explanations often disregard error, misprision, sheer contingency in understanding other peoples, other times and other places, and they often are self-serving. I count, too, a growing allergy to politics, always the same gauche politics in academe, politics as the ultimate horizon to which all our ideas, passions, words must tend. Is not culture, is not morality itself, the expression of our resistance to power, raw politics? Like others, I have wearied also of the 'culture of complaint' (Robert Hughes), the 'routinized production of righteous indignation' (Henry Louis Gates). It is one thing to write as Frantz Fanon did in On National Culture, drawing deeply on the experience of colonial humiliation; it is quite another to rant by rote. Nor do I believe that everything is 'socially produced'; such a view blurs the infinite variations within biosocial space, within the same family even. Nor do I subscribe to the so-called 'materialist' view of existence; in the language animal, 'mind' and 'matter' interact enigmatically. 'What is matter?' William James asked. 'Never mind. What is mind? No matter.' Nor do I concede in every case 'cultural relativism' – in slavery, torture, suttee, cannibalism, female mutilation, castration to make singers or guard harems . . . Above all, a loner, I reject 'identity politics', forced filiations of an exclusive sort – that is why I came to America in the first place. No doubt, the mackerel, the starling, and the warrior ant adheres each to its own kind with primal ferocity. But in human beings, solidarity by blood, tribe, nation, class, gender, colour, caste? Is this the final fruit of five billion years of evolution?

Here we need to ponder George Steiner when he overstates: 'The polis is that structure designed to execute Socrates. Nationalism has "the necessary murder" and warfare as its direct sequel.' We need to ponder him when he avers that no community, 'no nation, no city, is not worth leaving on grounds of injustice, corruption, philistinism'.[2] For behind these statements also lies Bergson's persuasive argument, in The Two Sources of Morality and Religion, that the morality of 'aspiration' merits a larger role in human affairs than the morality of 'pressure' or obligation. Granted the two moralities join:

> That which is aspiration tends to materialize by assuming the form of strict obligation. That which is strict obligation tends to expand and to broaden out by absorbing aspiration. Pressure and aspiration agree to meet for this purpose in that region of the mind where concepts are formed.[3]

That region of the mind, alas, has not taken charge of our geopolitics. Instead, the 'mass-soul in ourselves' seems to rule; it 'foams', Elias Canetti says in *Auto-da-fé*, like 'a huge, wild, full-blooded, warm animal in all of us, very deep, far deeper than the maternal' – a theme he elaborates majestically in *Crowds and Power*.[4]

Valéry considered every theory a fragment of autobiography. In the present instance, autobiography has led us only to a fragment of theory: 'the mass-soul in ourselves' as agent in history. Nationalism, colonialism, multiculturalism, I would here submit, draw their immane energy from the adhesive instinct, 'the warm animal in all of us'. That is only the beginning, the beginning and perhaps even the end – alpha and omega – but still not the middle. I mean history, how the 'mass-soul' assumes all the forms we know, how it specifically inhabits the various 'isms' of the age.

Let me address nationalism, therefore, before turning to its autobiographical expressions, nationalism as synecdoche of certain geopolitical forces shaping our lives. A single word, nationalism is yet myriad, myriad and sometimes muck, as Donald Barthelme says about 'the human nation-state – which is itself the creation of that muck of mucks, human consciousness'.[5]

Muck may be right: the origins of nationalism recede into prehistory, into fogs and bogs and hominid instincts, back to a sociobiological imperative, pitting Us implacably, invariably, against Them. The Pharaohs of Egypt and Satraps of Persia, the Myrmidons of Thessaly and zealots of Massada, knew the power of those instincts. So did, of course, the people of Han or Yamato. For nationalism, in my sense, precedes nations, and ethnic or bonding passions can make and unmake empires. Barbarians – fierce in their tribal, not civic, sentiments – toppled proud Rome. Mongol hordes felled the Middle Kingdom from its high complacency. We know what ethnic nationalism has wreaked on the Soviet behemoth. Some wonder: can old Uncle Sam survive the fury of separatism?

In the broadest sense, nationalism may rest on biological, ethnic, religious, cultural, linguistic, political, or geographic premises. These have never coincided in recorded history, though modern nations, notably Japan, may boast of their insular 'purity' – call it 'homogeneity', for tact – or indulge in 'ethnic cleansing'. Indeed, as we shall see, nationalism creates, then thrives on, a myth of unity. Yet nationalism itself remains a plural phenomenon, no less various than the group behaviour of humankind.

Interestingly, modern *state* nationalism began to wane in industrial societies after the Great War, except in defeated nations like Germany, and in others playing catch-up like Russia and Japan. Nationalism of a particularly fiery temper, however, began to wax elsewhere: in former colonies (of both the first and second worlds), in developing nations, in suppressed ethnic or religious communities of various sorts. Thus, liberal democracy, still favoured by rich industrial societies, now confronts nationalist conflagrations around the earth.

The anguish fanning these fires is real. It is the anguish of social injustice, recollected outrage, persistent deprivation, technological change, shifting values, collapsing empires, desperate human migrations. Yet anguish and violence do not guarantee liberation. Racism, reaction, xenophobia, the lethal 'narcissism of minor differences' as Michael Ignatieff calls it in *Blood and Belonging*, ride the hot winds of planetary change, even if they can find no final sustenance in the scorched earth they waste. Thus anti-Semitism may still burn in Germany or Poland, with scarcely any Jews around, and ethnic or religious hatreds may flash wherever human beings feel dislocated, deprived, confused. Indeed, the more a society fails, the more it seems to find current solace and future redemption in nationalism. But for how long can the promise last, without bread, lies, or iron curtains?

Beyond the 'mass-soul', nationalism, we can agree, is complex, compound, the word finally misleading. But so are its submanifestations: terrorism, tribalism, separatism, fundamentalism, multiculturalism. What do the sentiments of the Chiapas Zapatista in Mexico, the Muslim fundamentalists in Egypt, the Azerbaijani, Kazhak, or Armenians in the Caucausus, the Afro-Americans, Hispanics, or Native Americans in the United States, the Basque, Palestinian, Tamil, or IRA terrorists, the Neo-Nazis of eastern Germany or extreme Rightists of Japan, the Zulus of South Africa and Lapps of Sweden, the Fijians, Okinawans, or . . . – this list is endless – what, I repeat, do their sentiments share, beyond hope and rage?

And is nationalism always rightist, as some believe, or can it also be leftist, centrist, or indeed nearly apolitical? What are its gradations, internal conflicts, hidden tergiversations? What obligation, for instance, does a Harvard-educated Iranian woman, wearing the *chador*, feel foremost: toward her occidental ideals, her family, her gender, her religion, or her country? And would a Somali rather starve than see a US Marine strutting around his village? In other words, what is the hierarchy of loyalties, values, and commitments within a society, let alone in the gallimaufry of the world?

The times, always out of joint, require from us now a cunning commensurate with the patchwork fantasies – not just hope and rage – of a technological age. Such fantasies can be retrospective; once empowered, they invent 'traditions', as Eric Hobsbawm has shown.[6] But nationalist fantasies can be prospective too – 'The Thousand Year Reich' – or prospective and retrospective at the same time, as in some Islamic movements, which recover the Middle Ages to instore the Millennium of the Faithful. Indeed, how can one know to which group, to which nation one is supposed to belong, except by fiat or fantasy? Colour of skin? There are so many shades. Circumcision? In Arabs and Jews. The long slender fingers that a Serbian woman believes distinguish 'true Serbs' from Bosnians and Croats? We do not all carry calipers in our pockets. A language? Some, like myself, speak all languages with a foreign accent. A community of suffering? Perhaps, but what of those who have suffered little or who can transcend their pain?

Still, the arbitrariness of belonging, the contingency of nomination, will not deter the nationalist sentiment, potentially exclusive, however temporarily liberating. I do not underestimate the power of that sentiment, not in myself, not in others. Nor are all those sentiments baneful; some may be quixotic, others enabling, even glory-sped. On some days, though I count myself unhyphenated

American, I take a certain pride in the ragged, invincible cavalry of desert Arabs who swept across the world on the edge of their scimitars and inexorable faith. On other days, I recall the cruel splendour of Rameses II and Thutmose III. Such distant pride becomes tenuous, though, weary with time. And why did the British invade Egypt instead of the Egyptians invading Britain in the first place?

The question returns me contrapuntally to autobiography, scenes recorded variously in Out of Egypt, passages and crossings in my life.[7]

I was born in a country belatedly feudal and still colonial in my youth. Once Mameluks skewered 'insolent' fellahs on great, iron spikes. A century after, in the bougainvillea-draped villas of La Compagnie Universelle du Canal Maritime de Suez, foreigners plundered the wealth of Egypt and flouted its laws. My childhood, I came slowly to realise, lay in an imperceptible force-field: colonialism.

As child and boy, though, I had no aversion to the French or English languages; Arabic was the only subject I failed in school. True, the phrase El Ingileez would sometimes catch my ear, carrying some hint of menace or obloquy. True also, before my birth, the British had detained my father three days for some unacknowledged political act; that single feat provided my family with its myth of heroic resistance for years. But the sting of colonialism remains often invisible; its ravages lie within. The British rumoured themselves civilised colonials, and so they were, compared to the Spanish or Portuguese. Subtle, distant, and discreet, the British divided to conquer, and acted ruthlessly in whatever touched their needs. How else could they have ruled Egypt for seventy-five years?

Like every schoolboy, I grew up with fantasies of liberating Egypt, which remained for Nasser's Free Officers Movement to accomplish in 1954, with a little help from history. But, like most schoolboys too, I had never directly experienced the 'oppression' of the British. Once during the war, when the Afrika Korps threatened Alexandria, I saw a red-nosed 'Tommy', taunted beyond endurance by two students, knock one of them down. That, and a few tanks rumbling on the way somewhere, was all I saw of British power in Egypt. Even their large barracks at Kasr El Nil, displaced now by the Nile Hilton, might have blended easily into Cairo's cluttered landscape except for the high-flying Union Jack. Urchins on the street would sometimes look up and, seeing a British soldier lean casually across his window bar, make some wildly funny face or obscene gesture which the man above invariably ignored.

The British, I repeat, divided to conquer: in this, the squabbling political parties of Egypt seemed eager to oblige. Ultimately, Britain ruled through a decadent royal house, a corrupt Egyptian bureaucracy, and a landed oligarchy, inept, venal and vain. After the revolution of 1952, after the confiscation of royal properties in 1953, schools and hospitals rose rapidly everywhere, more in that year, Sadat claimed, than in the preceding twenty. Still, I wonder: had Britain brought illiteracy and disease to Egypt in the first place? Did it impose poverty on the fellah for the millennia? Who makes imperialism possible? And how healthy, free, or affluent are Egyptians four decades after their liberation?

Like some invisible worm, the colonial experience feeds on all those seeking redress for old wrongs and lacks. Self-hatred and self-doubt twist in their bowels, and envy curls there with false pride. 'Baladi, baladi', Egyptians cried to dismiss someone uncouth or vulgar, forgetting that the word means countrified or native. But Egyptians also feigned scorn for Europeans whom they strove to emulate. Was European skin a little fairer? 'Allah, what difference can it possibly make? My cousin is fair.' Was European literacy, or power, or technology, pre-eminent? 'Mallesh, never mind. Those frangi perform no ablutions and eat pork. How foul!' Thus the tacit principle of the colonial complex: to extol only such differences as serve oneself, other differences to depreciate or ignore. Thus, too, the colonial complex both constitutes and institutes its necessary bad faith: necessary for resistance, self-respect, sheer survival, yet shady, shifty, abject none the less.

Long ago, in Cairo, beggars sometimes addressed me as khawaga (foreigner), presumably because my appearance diverged from their idea of an Egyptian. And what idea could that have been? The French and British, after all, had invaded Egypt only after Hyksos, Lydians, Medes, Greeks, Romans, Arabs, Mameluks, Turks, and Albanians had cleared the way for them. As for myself, out of pride or pain, pain at seeing the legacy of colonialism maim so many, I resolved, early, never to give that legacy a place in myself.

We all know the horrors of colonialism, though I suspect few of us have ever crawled in atonement on a jungle floor. It is enough to read a casebook on *Heart of Darkness* to recognise the abominations of Belgium in the Congo. It is enough to read Robert Hughes's shattering work, *The Fatal Shore*, to realise the ultimate degradations of Anglo-Celtic convicts in Australia. (Nota bene: the first gulags in history were perpetrated by an enlightened colonial power against its own English and Irish poor, white on white, you might say.) Colonialism, in any colour, is blight.

Where's the surprise? I have never regarded Europe with untrammelled esteem, nor regarded Europeans as paragons of the human race. Cultured, creative, even genial, they are murderous still. Think for a moment about their 'civilised' nations: within living memory alone, they have filled trenches with the blood of a generation while the century was young, decimated Spain, bred the unsurpassed malignancies of Fascism, Nazism, Communism, gassed, bombed, and tortured their way through Ethiopia and Algeria, and continue their 'ethnic cleansing' to this very day. Can Asia or America – despite its mushroom terrors – begin to match this record? I understand well Fanon when he cries: 'Leave this Europe where they are never done talking of Man, yet murder men everywhere they find them, at the corner of every one of their own streets, in all the corners of the globe.'[8]

Yes, colonialism is blight; yes, Fanon here, if not always, is right. And yes, Camus has a point when he mordantly remarks on the disease of Europe, which is to believe in nothing while claiming to know everything. But let us be lucid. After decolonisation, what? In Africa, Bokhasa, Idi Amin, the Somali lords of death, the genocides of Rwanda; Ghaddafi and Saddam among the Arabs,

Khomeini alive still in a version of Islam; Pol Pot in Cambodia; in China, the Cultural Revolution, the Gang of Four, Tiananmen Square; religious wars in India, Bangladesh, Pakistan; the Shining Path in Peru and revolutions perpetual in Latin America. And for the rest? Poverty, illiteracy, famine, torture, plagues, tyrants, sects, castes, and tribes all running amok. Are all these cancers, ravaging the world south of the Tropic of Cancer, simply a metropolitan disease?

I find something abject, ignominious, in the eagerness of so many people nowadays to claim the status of victims. In the case of colonialism, I find continual self-exculpations craven. These narratives of self-absolution debase the colonised even more than the coloniser. Ironically, just as the discourse of 'orientalists' once embalmed natives in derogatory images, so does a certain emancipatory discourse embalm them in images more disparaging still. I recognise myself in none of these images. If this is what psychoanalysts call 'resistance' on my part, it has not proved acutely disabling.

But the issues, again, are not wholly personal. They concern ideological discourse, concern its *nuances*: that is, *the form truth takes in a pragmatic* (non-transcendental) *age*. They concern, more pointedly, some third-world writers who sometimes betray a kind of self-colonisation, a surrender to idioms generated in Paris, London, Frankfurt, Moscow, and New Haven. Invoking all the idols of the hour, such writers hope to turn the metropolitan idiom against itself. This impulse may or may not avail. It reminds us, at any rate, that the critiques of Western hegemony most often derive from Western thought itself.

We can ignore such prevarications; they may be intrinsic to the project of self-liberation itself. But what of the penchant for hyperbole, self-excited exaggeration? It is not confined to America. In the last decades, for instance, some Australian academics seem intent on deprecating Anglo-Celtic lineages, as an expression of tolerance for newer immigrants, and in expiation of the massacres of Aborigines in the past. This intention leads to statements, in a textbook called *Constructing Culture* (what else?), dismissing the last two centuries of colonial rule as a 'brief, nasty interlude'. Does Aboriginal dignity or restitution really require such condescending claptrap?

In America, of course, many critics consider the voyages – I dare not say discoveries – of Columbus as unmitigated disaster. And so they were for certain populations of the Americas. But unmitigated, really? Many revision American history, from Plymouth to Port Huron – I have in mind the radical Port Huron Statement of 1962 – in the light of elisions and suppressions in former narratives. And indeed, elisions and suppressions abound in conventional American histories. Yet, in exposing a portion of that history, should we not guard against propounding counter-myths? How easy is it for liberal critics who claim the 'end of American literature' to find themselves companions in absurdity to conservatives who claim the 'end of history'?

Serious criticism comes naturally to serious writers in every epoch. Consider Herman Melville. Even young, he showed in all his white-man wanderings a critical attitude toward imperialism. In *Typee*, for instance, he shadowed his

Marquesan exoticism with ambivalences. The narrative questions Church and State, Nature and Civilisation, Cannibals and Christians, questions its own motives and veracity. The anti-heroic voice already carries darker resonances. Sometimes the voice angrily cries against the 'fatal embrace' of the imperialist, against his destructiveness toward himself, thus proving 'the white civilized man as the most ferocious animal on the face of the earth'. Sometimes the voice cries against 'the fickle passions which sway the bosom of a savage' – no academic tenure for that author![9] Nearly always, the voice probes, qualifies, hesitates between the ambiguities of its own subject, the ironies of its own echo. Melville, writers as diverse as C. L. R. James and Martin Green have noted, ended by offering us a de-energising myth of empire, a myth of metaphysical shades and political nuance. We call it self-criticism.

Self-criticism? This recalls me to autobiography again. Egypt was not addicted to it, nor to cultural introspection. But that is not why, on a burning August afternoon in 1946, I boarded a Liberty Ship called the *Abraham Lincoln* in Port Said, bound for New York. That is not why, gliding past the great bronze statue of Ferdinand de Lesseps, who rose from the barnacled jetty above breaker and spume, one hand pointing imperiously east, I could only think: 'I did it! I am leaving Egypt!' Nor is that why I never returned to my native land.

Why, then, was I so eager to cross? Once again, I must decline powerful explanations. (How, in any case, explain a preference for the fluency of water over the clotting blood?) Let me offer instead shards of recollection: images, as I now see it, of boyish aspiration, openings on a larger life. Or are they only fictions of self-recreation?

School days were not happy. The government schools, primary and secondary, that I attended proved intellectually demanding, socially bruising, physically dismal. Once inside the lead-hued gates, privileged and unprivileged children alike abandoned all hope. They jostled, relying on their wits, fists, and unbreakable skulls – a quick, sharp blow with the head to the enemy's nosebridge – to absolve themselves of cowardice, effeminacy, class. Though I belonged to no racial or religious minority in Egypt, I was tormented more than if I had been a freak. Perhaps I was: an only child, tutored first at home, I was shy, solitary, a little perverse. I liked to go against the grain. And I liked literature, especially English and American literature.

Most pupils perceived only the ludicrous quirks of their teachers. One, dubbed 'The Klaxon', kept tapping his hip pocket during class to check on his wallet; another, called 'The Clutch', reached for his crotch and glared to stress a point in the lesson; a third, nicknamed 'The Bullet', fired chalk pieces with the accuracy of a high-powered rifle at nodding or chattering boys. Other teachers, however, evoke images of richer hue.

I recall Mr Miller who taught us the King's English, and conveyed a certain hurt radiance even to the rowdiest spirit. His pale, pinched face and distant, sunken eyes rendered all the horrors of W. W. Jacobs's 'The Monkey's Paw', and his flashes of mock braggadocio infused *King Solomon's Mines*, *The White Company*, *Montezuma's Daughter*, *The Coral Island*, *Kidnapped*, and *The Prisoner of Zenda* with a delightful irony without impairing their romance. He had a taste for things Gothic, a gentle way of shaming obscenity into silence. He may have also inspired me to work for the first prize I ever won at school: a handsome combination desk calendar and writing pad, inscribed, 'For Excellence in English'.

Mr Miller had reached the dreamer in us, awakened in some a long desire to travel. 'There is no frigate like a book / To take us lands away', Emily Dickinson knew, and I found in the attic of our dilapidated country estate many galleons and frigates. In some unfurnished rooms, I found books piled there on books and across buckling shelves; magazines rose in teetering columns from the floor; and the scent of thick, musty paper greeted my nose in closed, high-ceilinged rooms, a call to faraway times and places.

Pell-mell, I found French novels, classical Arabic poetry, English detective stories, German technical manuals, medical books in sundry languages. I found old wrinkled maps of the earth, glimmering celestial charts, inscrutable surveying deeds, spectral anatomy drawings, still-lifes in ornate, gilded frames, and sepia photographs of mustachioed men and crinolined women, some with *yashmak* (veils), whose names I never came to know. Rows upon yellow rows of the *National Geographic* magazine took me around the world in an hour; and huge folios of the *London Illustrated Gazette* unfolded before me the Great War, Ypres, Châlons, Amiens, Verdun, the Marne, mud and blood filling the trenches of battles that rumbled still in my family's talk.

Strange country pleasures these, which, enchant though they may, also swathe a boy in unreality. Unreality? No, I believe these were my first encounters with *other* people – call it multiculturalism as romance. I could not resist these invitations to voyage, and promised myself secretly, desperately, to leave some day on an endless journey, and see all the sights and strangers in the world.

A few years later, the strangers came, Yanks. Like many Egyptian students, more frantic than informed in their idealism, I saw Rommel in 1942 as a liberator. Surely, we thought, the enemy of our enemy must be a friend. Yet when the Allies defeated the Desert Fox at El Alamein, the same students, changing allegiance, found in Americans, if not liberators, new models for their aspiration. We consumed Coca-Cola, devoured the *Reader's Digest*, affected Ray-Ban aviator glasses, and gawked at all those gangling, loping, gum-chewing, foot-propping GIs who began to appear in Cairo, their drawl so different from any sound we had ever heard. Hollywood seemed almost within reach. But the Yanks, some of them, also brought books, fragments of the American dream. America began to seem then, in F. Scott Fitzgerald's phrase, 'a willingness of the heart'. Half a century later, I would wonder if it had become a tyranny of resentments, an imperium of degradations.

The day came: the Egyptian Government sent me on a generous Mission Fellowship to study in America for a PhD in electrical engineering and return to help build the Aswan High Dam. I studied for a PhD in English instead, and stayed. I have never felt exile.

My sense of multiculturalism certainly emerges from the labyrinths of a personal past. But multiculturalism, now *international* in scope, also engages the geopolitical realities of our moment. That is why I began by addressing nationalism and colonialism. Nationalism insists on the identity, cohesion, often exclusiveness, and finally force of a group. It can lead to imperialism, since as Nietzsche knew, the will to power is a will not only to be but also to be *more*. When empires break or recede, however, when superpowers crumble, the colonies, the tribes, the sects, find their freedom again. But this is a most equivocal freedom. The axis of violence is no longer vertical only (oppressor and oppressed) but residually vertical (colonisation by other means) and also horizontal, as all the fragments collide. Think of Africa, Asia, Europe, the Middle East. These collisions, these ethnic confrontations, less military than cultural, religious, and economic, breed multiculturalism in its postmodern guise. Thus the legacy of European or Ottoman imperialism can haunt multiculturalism across oceans; thus separatism in far places cracks windows next door.

Multiculturalism may be the child of decolonisation from within (African-Americans) or from without (African-Nigerians), but revolutions have been known to eat their children. Put more equably, it is a 'complex fate' – the phrase, interestingly enough, is Henry James's about Americans in the last century – to live multiculturally and still maintain personal, moral, and intellectual poise, all the more so when personhood, personality, even a personal name, are all challenged in favour of some human abstract called 'gender', 'class', 'race', or most frequently, 'cultural identity'.

Paradoxically, I have said, multiculturalism *can* tend to separatism. As Georg Simmel perceived long ago: 'Groups, and especially minorities, which live in conflict . . . often reject approaches or tolerance from the other side. The closed nature of their opposition, without which they cannot fight on, would be blurred.'[10] Thus, seeking wider recognition, the group enforces its isolation, very much like artistic vanguards that thrive only on shock, agonism, antagonism, even as they yearn, deeper still, for acceptance.

The situation of the individual from an impoverished migrant group is no less paradoxical, no less complex. The more 'developing' his or her country of origin, the more he or she will tend to bristle in his or her 'developed', adopted land. Where hunger and deprivation menace existence, the economic motive will, of course, prevail; beyond that point, dignity, self-esteem, the need for transcendence – yes, immaterial motives all – will capture the affective life. Thus the immigrant cries: 'I may come from a backward country, but I have my culture, I have my honour. Don't look down on me!' Yet he or she knows in the bone that the very fact of their displacement implies a judgement on their origins. Thus self-worth struggles with self-contempt, and the guilt of desertion wrestles with pride in both the abandoned and acquired land. How more admirable and rare to look at the world with level gaze, eschewing the colonial complex, with all its insidious feelings of inferiority and superiority, resentment and defiance.

Intellectuals in exile or self-exile may experience these ambiguities even more keenly. They live in the West, earn generous Western wages, marry Western women or men, carry Western passports, speak, read, write Western languages, and, as we have seen, assume Western critical values by which they criticise the West. What identity can they claim? What authority? What mediating role? The complexity remains even when the intellectual is, like Agnes Heller, a European. Born in Hungary, she emigrated first to Australia, then America, and now reflects on the concept of home at the end of the century. What can substitute for 'the binding sense' in exiles, in migrants, in nomads, in intellectual errants, she wonders? 'They are searching for an identity to replace the home, but this can ultimately lead to an obsession with gender, racial and ethnic differences', she remarks.[11]

Is multiculturalism, then, simply an ideological substitute for roots, for homes? The answer cannot be single; for multiculturalism reflects all the geopolitical havocs of our time and reflects as well the need to surmount, transcend them. Still, one may inquire: how far can multiculturalism go without rending societies? Can the limits of tolerance, in Britain or Germany, in Canada or Australia, in the United States particularly – with its enormous African, Asian, Hispanic populations, with its drugs, guns, poverty, plagues, illiteracy, its fantasmic violence and broken families – can the limits of tolerance stretch to permit a genuine multiculturalism, with commitments to margin and centre at the same time, if not quite E Pluribus Unum? Or do we face, nearby as in far places, the 'blood-dimmed tide'?

Again, the alternatives here may not be quite so stark. Certainly, societies have been multicultural from the dawn of history. But this does not always mean they have been multiculturalist. Certainly, multiculturalism pervades the experience of our daily lives, nearly everywhere in the world. But this does not mean that it coincides with the claims that ideologues make for it, left and right. Nor is multiculturalism itself uniform: it takes different forms in Australia, America, Singapore, Lebanon. Nor is the 'West' any less various than 'Africa' or 'Asia', though the internal diversity of the West hardly precludes shared values and interests that may justify its name, and so may feed the oppugnancy toward it in the 'southern tier'.

These are but small nuances in a field that begs for, and begs, nuances. Someday, we may hope for an aesthetics of multiculturalism to match its ethics and politics. Why not read, for instance, read tactfully, works like Sally Morgan's *My Place* and David Malouf's *12 Edmondstone Street*, about Australian multiculturalism, instead of textbooks like *Constructing Culture*? Someday, history and morality may coincide, not simply converge, as so many theorists of the subject constantly seem to presume. And someday, a society may emerge, wholly innocent of dominant and subordinate cultures, and immaculate of power relations. Meanwhile, we might hope, with Sara Suleri, for a multiculturalism that knows how to locate its holes and lacunae, and to undo temporarily the distinction, say, between mosque and temple. Such a multiculturalism would also know how to reach beyond itself. That way tough pluralism lies, the pluralism of William James at his best, the pluralism of Isaiah Berlin or Henry Louis Gates when he revisions Berlin.

For the last time, I turn to autobiography, from which we can never wholly depart. Valéry we have encountered; Emerson saw temperament as 'the iron wire' on which our opinions are strung; Wittgenstein gave the idea a further postmodern turn. 'It is sometimes said that a man's philosophy is a matter of temperament, and there is something in this', he wrote. 'A preference for certain similes could be called a matter of temperament and it underlies far more disagreements than you might think.'[12] My own metaphors, I admit, tend to motion, an independent stance.

Multiculturalism simulates diversity, multeity, but its primal instinct, in most cases, is rootedness – the power of the term resides in '-culturalism', the care and cultivation of roots. I find my diversity elsewhere, and prefer other similes: wind, water, fire, errancy, dispossession. In *The Need for Roots*, Simone Weil argued that money (fluidity) and the state (totality) have uprooted us all. Multiculturalism, then, may embody not only the 'mass-soul' in us but also our revenge on money and on the state, ubiquitous agents of our time. Still, I like other tropes: literature itself. Harold Bloom remarks: 'Literature is not merely language; it is also the will to figuration, the motive for metaphor that Nietzsche once defined as the desire to be different, the desire to be elsewhere.'[13] That will to figuration, that desire for empathic difference, difference not from other groups but within one's own group, may serve as breakthrough for a new kind of multiculturalism, a sensation of one's own being as sensuous and sharp as water traced on Helen Keller's palm.

As an immigrant, an Egyptian of mixed Arab blood, Turkic and Albanian – and what else? – extraction, I have never experienced prejudice in America, nor would I have recognised it necessarily had it come my way. Once, when I had completed my doctorate at the University of Pennsylvania, I went to see the chairman of the English Department about an instructorship. He leaned back in his chair and said benignly: 'We have given you scholarships and we have given you fellowships, but an instructorship is another matter. There are still non-standard elements in your spoken English.' Those 'non-standard elements' persist in my speech, but they have not crucially affected my academic life in America.

Men and women have flocked to Australia, Canada, America, fleeing or seeking, driven by the most diverse motives. But psychological exiles stand apart, their case shadier, thicker with complicity and silent intrigue. Who are these beings, full of dark conceits, rushing to meet the future while part of them still stumbles about, like a blind speleologist, in caverns of the past? What urgency speaks through their self-banishment?

All leaving is loss, every departure a small death – yes, journeys secretly know their end. Yet self-exile may also conceal, in counterpoint, a deeper exigency. It is not an exigency that multiculturalism can meet. Yet few, very few, can, like Simone Weil, so deeply intimate with affliction, uproot themselves and carry their tree perpetually as a cross.

NOTES

1 S. Weil, *Waiting for God*, New York, Harper, 1973, p. 7.
2 N. Scott, Jr and R. Sharp (eds), *Reading George Steiner*, Baltimore, MD, Johns Hopkins University Press, 1994, p. 227.
3 H. Bergson, *The Two Sources of Morality and Religion*, Garden City, NY, Doubleday, 1954, p. 256.
4 E. Canetti, *Auto-da-fé*, New York, Seabury, 1979, p. 411; and *Crowds and Power*, New York, Seabury, 1978.
5 D. Barthelme, *City Life*, New York, Bantam Books, 1971, p. 179.
6 E. Hobsbawm and T. Ranger (eds), *The Invention of Tradition*, Cambridge, Cambridge University Press, 1992.
7 I. Hassan, *Out of Egypt: Scenes and Arguments of an Autobiography*, Carbondale, IL, Southern Illinois University Press, 1986.
8 F. Fanon, *The Wretched of the Earth*, New York, Grove Press, 1968, p. 311.
9 H. Melville, *Typee: A Peep at Polynesian Life*, Harmondsworth, Mx, Penguin, 1972 [1846], pp. 63 f., 123, 180.
10 Quoted in E. Hobsbawm, *Nations and Nationalism since 1780*, Cambridge, Cambridge University Press, 1990, p. 175.
11 Lecture at the Ashworth Center for Social Theory, University of Melbourne, reported by C. Jones, 'Philosopher of Nomadic Necessity', *Australian*, 10 August 1994.
12 L. Wittgenstein, *Culture and Value*, Chicago, University of Chicago Press, 1980, p. 20.
13 H. Bloom, *The Western Canon*, New York, Harcourt Brace, 1994, p. 12.

INDEX

295